The Model Country

Batlle and wife in Paris.

MILTON I. VANGER

The Model Country

JOSÉ BATLLE Y ORDOÑEZ OF URUGUAY
1907-1915

PUBLISHED FOR BRANDEIS UNIVERSITY PRESS
BY UNIVERSITY PRESS OF NEW ENGLAND
HANOVER, NEW HAMPSHIRE AND LONDON, ENGLAND
1980

The University Press of New England

Brandeis University
Clark University
Dartmouth College
University of New Hampshire
University of Rhode Island
Tufts University
University of Vermont

Copyright © 1980 by Trustees of Brandeis University
All rights reserved
Library of Congress Catalog Card Number 80-50489
International Standard Book Number 0-87451-184-4
Printed in the United States of America

LIBRARY OF CONGRESS CATALOGING IN PUBLICATION DATA

Vanger, Milton I
    The model country.

    Includes index.
    1. Uruguay—Politics and government—1904-1973.
2. Batlle y Ordóñez, José, Pres. Uruguay, 1856-1929.
I. Title.
F2728.V27   989.5'061'0924   80-50489
ISBN 0-87451-184-4

To Elsa

PREFACE

Uruguay, considered until recently Latin America's premier democratic welfare state, is not a model country today. It has endured over twenty years of economic stagnation. It incubated the Tupamaro urban guerrillas; its government is now dominated by the military. In the good democratic time of "Uruguay feliz" (happy Uruguay), the years immediately after World War II, explanations of Uruguay's success centered on José Batlle y Ordoñez,[1] whose second presidency from 1911 to 1915 was credited with making it possible. As Uruguay's situation worsened, interpretations of that presidency changed. Batlle was blamed for Uruguayans' preference for the "easy life," and now we are beginning to see arguments that Batlle couldn't have accomplished much then if the country today is in such a disastrous condition. The presentism behind such explanations is compounded by a lack of knowledge of what actually happened during that presidency, which was historic for Uruguay and of great interpretive significance in the understanding of twentieth-century Latin America.

From Paris in 1908, Batlle wrote to his closest political aides in Montevideo, "I here think of what we could do to make Uruguay a small model country." This book, based on Batlle's private papers, which I am the first to use, as well as other private papers, the archive of the opposition National Party, telegrams and letters from the British Foreign Office, interviews, newspapers of the period, Uruguayan parliamentary debates and government documents, and a wide variety of published primary and secondary sources, focuses on Batlle's reelection and second presidency in the context of his own times. It is an interpretative narrative divided into three parts, each followed by an "Appraisals" section which makes explicit my analytical position and confronts alternative outlooks. The interpretations

1. In Uruguay, Batlle is pronounced Bah-jay, with the "j" sounded like the first letter of the French name Jean. Batlle himself did not accent the second "o" in Ordoñez when signing his name, even though the accent appears on official documents. This book will not use the accent.

advanced here should be of interest well beyond Uruguay. In particular they should be of importance comparatively in understanding the emergence in the Southern Cone (Argentina, Uruguay, and Chile) of popular politics during the first three decades of the twentieth century. In the spirit of Batlle I have been careful not to use obscure language that would make the book difficult for the general reader. This should be no real burden on social scientists who want to use the book's evidence and interpretations. One warning is necessary: readers should not be surprised that a book on a lifetime and fulltime politician has a lot of politics in it.

With a good deal of sadness at the death of many who helped me during the years since 1950 when I did research and wrote, I want to acknowledge assistance from César Batlle Pacheco, Rafael Batlle Pacheco, Dionisio Trillo Pays, Nicolás Fusco Sansone, Juan E. Pivel Devoto, Juan C. Gómez Alzola, and the staff of the Biblioteca Nacional. I particularly want to acknowledge the friendship of Anita Chervière de Batlle Pacheco.

Grants from the Doherty Foundation and the American Philosophical Society and leaves from Brandeis University permitted me to do research in Uruguay and complete the book. The Ruth Newton Fund of Brandeis University aided the book's publication, and I greatly appreciate this spontaneous contribution by Chancellor Abram L. Sachar. My old friend Joseph T. Criscenti read the entire manuscript and made suggestions for improvement. The book also has benefited from the corrections and interpretative challenges of my wife, Elsa M. Oribe de Vanger, to whom it is dedicated.

Milton I. Vanger

Cambridge, Massachusetts
June 1979

CONTENTS

ILLUSTRATIONS

Unless otherwise identified in the legends, all illustrations are reproduced by courtesy of the Batlle Pacheco family, Montevideo. Illustration 3, a map of Uruguay, is applicable to the entire book, not merely to the chapter in which it appears.

PART I *Civic Dreams*

CHAPTER 1 *To Paris*

"I can still hear the ovation and the music Montevideo saw me off with. I have left power with the popular support I sometimes dreamed about in my civic dreams. It is very sweet to be the object of so much affection." On March 24, 1907, Don Pepe Batlle—José Batlle y Ordoñez—one day out of Montevideo, heading for Cherbourg on the British liner *Araguayana*, was beginning a journal. He had just turned the presidency of Uruguay over to his personally chosen successor, Claudio Williman, and was on the way to Paris with his family. There he expected to wait out three years and return to Uruguay to be reelected president. The crowd that saw him off, 20 to 25,000 on the pier, another 10,000 in small boats which followed the *Araguayana* out to sea, was the greatest ever in Montevideo.

It is true that I have always had a deep interest in the people and that the reason I dedicated myself to politics, from which my intense inclination to the study of philosophy and science kept me when I was young, was that I was dragged into it by the indignation I felt over the maltreatment and crimes which victimized the disinherited classes of my country. Love of truth first brought me to study, love of justice then dragged me into the struggle. No material interest of any sort determined these two orientations of my life.

If I had been born the son of a free and established country I would be a completely different man from what I am. My life would have been completely peaceful and obscure and my great and constant pleasure would have been the most advanced scientific concepts of which I perhaps would have been an active, but tranquil and serene propagandist. Instead the storms have carried me along and I have tried to resist and conquer them.

Though there was a certain wistfulness that politics not scholarship had become his life's career, Don Pepe was satisfied, even smug. And he had cause to be. His presidency had been a watershed. He had led his party, the governing Colorados, to decisive victory over the traditional Blanco opponents in the War of 1904. Stable peace after the war opened the way to an economic boom. Peace, prosperity, and undisputed Colorado control of government permitted the emergence of a distinctive Batllista program: moral legislation (divorce and the end of the death penalty), state enterprises (strengthening of the State-owned Bank of the Republic and Montevideo Electric Power System), support of labor (police neutrality in strikes and Batlle's not yet enacted bill for an eight-hour day), public works, school-building—all this was capped with a budget surplus and Batlle, the Colorado hero since the 1904 war victory over the Blancos, had excellent prospects to be elected President of the Republic again in 1911—the Constitution did not allow immediate reelection.

This was his second trip to Europe. In 1880, as a 24-year-old philosophy student and son of ex-President Lorenzo Batlle, he had enjoyed a year in Paris, sitting in on classes, reading at the Bibliothèque Nationale, going to gym, sightseeing. Lorenzo Batlle, in his presidential travails—his presidency, which ended in 1872, brought on the era of military government from 1875 to 1866—had neglected his family flour mill and left office a poor man. He could not long finance Pepe's European stay, and the young man had returned to Montevideo in steerage. Now Don Pepe, prominent citizen, fifty-one years old, a huge man six foot four in height, weighing over 220 pounds, an athlete gone to fat, was going to Europe in first class, accompanied by his wife, four children, two servants, Colonel Bernassa y Jérez in charge of security, and young Pedro Manini y Ríos, Batlle's political protégé, who had arranged his honeymoon so that he could help his mentor install himself in Paris.

When the *Araguayana* stopped at Santos, Brazil, the Uruguayan consul took the party on a beach tour; in Rio, Brazilian Foreign

1. Crowd in front of Batlle's Montevideo house before his departure to Europe, 1907. By permission of the Museo Histórico Nacional, Montevideo.

Minister Baron Rio Branco gave them lunch at the Ministry Palace. Don Pepe's first sight of Santos through a telescope—astronomy was one of his youthful interests—was a church with a huge cross, which he was told was dedicated to the Virgin of Montserrat, "a super-miraculous virgin." The sight aroused Batlle's determined anti-Catholicism, which had so scandalized Uruguayan society during his presidency. He wrote in his journal: "Wouldn't it have been better to have constructed a good astronomical observatory on that spot? Wouldn't human thought have been elevated much higher? Why should mystification and error always occupy the place of truth?"

Batlle continued his journal through the long transatlantic crossing. At Madeira, a British lord, "the first I have seen in my life," came aboard and had his bed made up in the reading room, though this violated the ship's rules. At 8 A.M. passengers "could enjoy the spectacle of the lord sleeping deeply between the sheets." Don Pepe was not one who believed in aristocratic privileges. The lord's behavior "was a somewhat depressing irregularity towards other passengers, especially those traveling with wives and daughters . . ." and Batlle suggested a "collective protest" to Colonel Bernassa y Jérez. Bernassa immediately sent a personal protest to the ship's captain. Don Pepe, gruff-voiced and huge, was ill at ease with strangers, and noted that Bernassa y Jérez had "done what I should have done."

> If, even in trivial matters like this one, everyone was not too timid to accept the responsibility that justice prevail, things would go better in the world and respect for rights would be much more widespread even in important matters.

The ship's captain assured Bernassa y Jérez that the abuse had occurred without his knowledge and would not be repeated. Don Pepe, as was his way, meditated further on the matter and prepared for future action.

> It doubtless was a mortification for the lord who appears to be quite arrogant.

> I should note here that the lord's conduct did not really wound me personally because neither Matilde [his wife] nor Ana [his daughter] come up to the reading room early. Nevertheless, I will take it as my own affair if the lord decides to express his anger.[1]

II

The *Araguayana* was boarded at Cherbourg by a group of Uruguayans led by the Uruguayan Minister to France, who accompanied Don Pepe's party on the railroad trip to Paris. Don Pepe stopped keeping his journal. He had never been able to do routine things for long. As a student he had difficulty attending classes and had never received his law degree, although he was only four courses short. He had surprised those who knew him by his care as an administrator during his presidency—he had disciplined himself to do this—and now he was preoccupied with settling into expensive Paris.

Batlle, while in the best economic shape of his life, was not a rich man. He had earned 136,000 pesos (the peso's exchange value was 96.6 United States cents) in his four years as president; had used part of it to buy a house and land in Piedras Blancas in the country outside Montevideo, where he could be free from public scrutiny; and had taken several thousand pesos with him to Europe. His newspaper, *El Día*, would send him funds regularly, assuming that its circulation kept up now that it no longer was the presidential newspaper. In charge of *El Día* was Batlle's confidant, the remarkable Domingo Arena. The self-made Arena, born in Italy, had been brought to Uruguay as a six-year-old by his cobbler father, had graduated in pharmacy and law, was a bohemian intellectual, everyone's friend, and when he spoke on politics, it was with Don Pepe's authority.

To Arena, Batlle confided early in May that settling into Paris had kept him "constantly preoccupied." The elegant Hotel Mercedes where the family had stayed first charged the equivalent of 2,300 pesos a month. They had moved to less costly quarters, where expenses for food and lodging would be 700 pesos: "passable but . . . by no means definitive." Batlle was reading *El Día* avidly. The government's decision to use one million pesos of the budget surplus to increase the capital of the state-owned Bank of the Republic, which issued Uruguay's banknotes and provided credit to businessmen and ranchers, drew an enthusiastic response from Don Pepe, proponent of state enterprises. If, from now on, the Bank's annual profits were used to expand its capital and not turned over to the treasury, the Bank would become a "colossus." "I tell this to you and you alone because I do not want to appear to be intervening in the issues that are being decided over there."[2]

These European years were going to be trying for Batlle. If rumors got started that Batlle was governing from Paris, his successor Williman would assert himself and endanger Batlle's 1911 reelection. So when Uruguayans in Paris came to visit Don Pepe, and they made it a point to, he preferred to talk French politics. Returning travelers reported in Montevideo that ". . . señor Batlle is little interested in Uruguayan matters."[3] In fact, Batlle's interest in France was almost entirely what he could find for use in Uruguay. Paris, he advised Arena, got much income from foreign tourists.

I cannot but think frequently of the enormous profits we could make if every year we could attract a great mass of Argentines to our beaches. The outlay Montevideo would make to beautify itself and to offer attractions during the beach season would be excellent business, even if it seemed to be luxury.[4]

Batlle was impressed with Paris, especially with the crowds. (Montevideo's population had just reached 300,000; Paris' was nearing 2,000,000.) He confessed that it took him an hour to catch a carriage. Typically, he had a solution; he was buying an automobile. But in Don Pepe's eyes Montevideo did not come out second to Paris.

For example, our public lighting is equal to or better than Paris'; electricity in the home is cheaper there than here in Paris and will be enormously cheaper when the expansion of the Montevideo power plant is completed. Our electric trolleys are superior. The general appearance of Montevideo's population is not inferior to the population of this city.

If we have honest governments for the next twenty years, which I think likely and not too much to ask, and we are a little careful about giving money away to businesses that have their headquarters abroad, I believe we can accomplish miracles.[5]

CHAPTER 2 *The Williman Years*

The Williman years, 1907 to 1911, were very prosperous, even more prosperous than the last two years of Batlle's administration. Uruguay's economy was export oriented. The export of wool, meat, and hides provided income for ranchers, transporters and processors, and paid for the imports of goods for consumption and raw materials for economic development. No figures for Gross National Product existed; but using imports, whose rise and fall determined the level of Uruguayan economic activity, as a rule-of-thumb substitute indicator of economic growth, for the Williman years there was a very healthy 5 percent annual rate of growth.[1]

Other indicators were equally encouraging. Rural land values rose 80 percent from 1906 to 1910. Montevideo businesses, land values, construction—all followed the same satisfying pattern. By 1911 a reliable estimate put the total value of the Uruguayan economy at the mouth-filling figure of one billion, nine hundred million pesos.[2]

At the base of prosperity were the flourishing ranches. Uruguay had been ranching country from the beginning of colonial occupation. Modernization, begun in the 1870's and 1880's with wire fencing and the import of pedigreed bulls and rams, by now was yielding excellent results. The 1908 census, the best ever run, concluded that 91 percent of the sheep and 63 percent of the cattle were of the new, improved, heavier crossbreeds. And even if these percentages reflected the ranchers' exaggeration about how far their crossbreeding had proceeded, there was no doubt that livestock were both improved and continuously improving. Not only were they improved, their numbers were up. The 1908 census counted 8,192,602 head of cattle (a 20 percent increase since 1900) and 26,286,602 sheep (up 42.5 percent). The delighted census takers acknowledged that "the livestock riches of our country are much greater than we believed."[3]

Prosperity increased government revenues—import duties were the principal source of revenue—and surpluses in the national budget, begun under Batlle, now became annual affairs. For the Williman years the total budget surplus was 8.1 million pesos, equal to half the national budget in 1903, Batlle's first year. The surplus, used to build schools and public works and increase the capital of the Bank of the Republic, extended prosperity. Budget surpluses also made it easier to sell Uruguayan bonds in Europe by reassuring investors that the country could pay interest and redeem bonds on schedule. Uruguay had a substantial government debt, the result of its tragic history of civil war and government deficits, but in this new era of budget surpluses, bonds no longer went to pay war costs and routine government expenses. Now they financed productive undertakings too big to be paid for out of current revenue, like the new port of Montevideo. In 1909 Williman's government floated six million pesos of 5 percent Public Works Bonds in Europe at 91.5, the best terms the nation had ever received.[4]

The veteran Professor of Political Economy, Carlos María de Pena, who had lived through the devastation of civil wars and the economic depression of 1890, gave his annual opening lecture at the University of Montevideo on April 2, 1910. "The economic potential of the nation is really astonishing. . . . And the fact that we began as a nation with very modest and limited resources and that in spite of all kinds of subsequent difficulties we have acquired admirable economic power which places us in the position of a consolidated nation augurs for a great national future."[5] A later generation economist would have said that Uruguay had reached the level of self-sustaining economic growth.

II

Batlle had been pushing all kinds of programs, including ending the death penalty and an eight-hour day, even the use of government-owned lands to settle landless rural poor, a veritable rain of radical projects which frightened the self-identified "conservative classes" —the local and foreign business and professional community. Williman, a lawyer and educator, himself a member of the conservative classes, governed quietly. During his presidency he continued to give his physics classes at the Military Academy and to appear Sunday morning for coffee with longtime acquaintances at his regular table at the Confitería del Telégrafo.[6] As president, Williman concentrated on road and railroad building—in 1907 there was a respectable 2,004 kilometers of railroad in Uruguay, with 500 more in operation by 1911; there were new water and sewage systems in the interior towns, noncontroversial projects that were everywhere welcomed.

Williman was an administrator rather than a politician. His first bill established two new ministries, Education and Public Works. Throughout his administration he reorganized government offices and kept public employees on the job. The first complete census in Uruguay's history was carried out in 1908. His greatest success was in expanding primary education. Uruguay long since had adopted free public education patterned after the American system, in the hope that it would transform *criollos* into hardworking Yankees. Money had always been the problem, and enough schools could never be built. A dramatic moment of Batlle's administration had been the one-million-peso appropriation for schools. Williman went far beyond this, doubled the school budget, and oversaw the staffing and building of new schools. The school situation had been disheartening—the 1908 census listed a national illiteracy rate of 49.4 percent—but by the end of Williman's administration there were 82,852 children in 931 public schools compared with 57,638 children in 619 schools in 1906, and the flourishing public schools were taking over elementary education from private and religious schools.[7] By 1911 it was apparent that if subsequent governments routinely continued Williman's primary school program, illiteracy as a national problem would be eliminated in Uruguay.

III

Amidst the optimism over accomplishments, there was one great disappointment. The 1908 census revealed a population of 1,024,636, almost 200,000 fewer than had been supposed. Uruguay was the smallest country in South America, but it was twice the size of

Portugal, whose population was 5.5 million. Montevideo, the capital, fed by three railroad lines, processed the nation's exports and imports, contained workshops and factories, and was growing; its population was 291,467, close to one third the nation's total. The underpopulated ranching departments of the interior, varying from 2.2 to 4.2 persons per kilometer, could support only small regional urban centers. The river towns of Paysandú and Salto, the second and third largest cities, each had populations of around 20,000.[8]

Ranching since the fencing in of range lands in the 1870's and 1880's, required few hands. Even while the gauchos were being expelled from the fenced ranches, a commentator in 1880 predicted, "Fencing should bring as a logical consequence artificial [sown] pastures and the cultivation of forage suitable to feed the new kinds of livestock . . .," which would require more and more technically able ranch hands.[9] Similarly, the railroads, built and run by English companies under profit guarantees paid for by the Uruguayan government, were supposed to break up ranches into farms, as they had done across the river in Argentina. But so far, cereal agriculture was limited to marginal farming to supply Montevideo, there was no artificial pasture or forage agriculture, and the sons of the gauchos were now the permanent rural poor, who got a few days work each year at sheep-shearing time. A 1910 survey described them:

> they live in what have come to be called rat towns [pueblos de ratas] . . . miserable groups of huts made of sticks, hides, tin cans, branches, and other rubbish. In general, the huts do not even have mud walls, because their inhabitants are not sure how long they can live in them, since they install themselves on sites that belong to someone who lives far away, or on government land, or land whose ownership is unknown, or else the owner has given them temporary permission to put up their huts, either out of compassion or in exchange for guarding a pasture.

The survey was sponsored by the rancher-oriented Rural Congress, and its compiler, reluctant to expose the full size of the problem, estimated the minimum number of permanent rural poor at 35,000.[10]

Ninety percent of Uruguay's land area was unimproved natural pasture owned by relatively few. The 1908 census indicated that 7295 ranches (properties of 500 hectares, approximately 1235 acres, a

2. Claudio Williman. By permission of the División Fotocinematográfica, Ministerio de Instrucción Pública, Montevideo.

moderate-sized ranch, or more) controlled about three quarters of Uruguay's land area. Within this small group, 1391 large and very large ranches occupied about half the country's land area. And since some ranchers operated more than one ranch, actual land concentration was even higher. As the Director of the government's Property Evaluation Office concluded, "there are regions where the number of proprietors is so reduced that some zones are owned by two or three landowners."[11]

Current ranching operations required only a handful of peons, who earned only five to ten pesos a month plus keep and were forbidden to have families on the ranch with them, to look after thousands of cattle and sheep grazing on unimproved pasture. Artificial pasture and forage agriculture would double livestock production. Cereal agriculture would diversify and expand Uruguay's exports. Farms and modernized ranches would provide employment—Canelones, the agricultural department next to Montevideo, had a population density three to nine times that of the ranching departments—would reduce emigration (an estimated 100,000 Uruguayans were living in Argentina); and, by populating the interior with settled families instead of footloose men who had nothing to lose, cut off the manpower recruitable for a possible civil war.[12] There was a constant campaign by publicists to convince ranchers to subdivide. The ranchers were not moved. The way to make money was to ranch more land, not subdivide. Artificial pasture involved substantial capital expenditure and risk; Uruguayan farming had always been unprofitable.

Williman considered "the development of agriculture, which brings with it the increase of population and production . . . the greatest problem of national economic life," and on December 11, 1909, he sent a bill to the legislature doubling the land tax on any property over 300 hectares which did not devote at least 5 percent of its land area to agriculture.[13]

Ranchers had ignored such proposals when advanced in the press, but now that the government proposed to penalize them monetarily, they came together. Their voice, the powerful Rural Association formally petitioned the legislature to reject the bill as a denial of property rights. When agriculture became more profitable than the present kind of ranching, the petition maintained, "evolution will come automatically." The denizens of the *pueblos de ratas* were completely useless individuals; to think that giving them a piece of land would make them farmers was a "dismal error."[14]

Ranchers were strong, prosperous, and organized and Williman did not propose to fight them. Faced with the Rural Association's opposition, Williman contented himself with noting, "Whatever the outcome of discussion this Government will always have the satisfaction of having valiantly pointed out the evil and having proposed an energetic remedy to combat it." The bill never came out of committee.[15]

IV

Across the river in Buenos Aires, government crackdowns on Anarchists led to general strikes, the assassination of the police chief, and the attempted assassination of the President of Argentina. Using its famous residence law, Argentina expelled Anarchist labor leaders. Montevideo, only an overnight trip by ferry, was the obvious stopping place for them. Uruguay had no law forbidding the entry of Anarchists, and Batlle had gone so far in his legalism as to wire passage money to an expelled Buenos Aires Anarchist to whom the Montevideo police had refused entry. Williman and his police chief, Colonel West, shared the apprehensions of their Buenos Aires counterparts. Expelled Anarchists were refused entry, even one born in Montevideo.[16]

Williman's hostility to Anarchists carried over to Uruguayan unions, which, following Spain and Italy, were Anarchist led. Montevideo's public men argued that Uruguayan workers were better off than European workers, but this was largely a consoling fiction. Most Uruguayan workers were unskilled. The most common job category in the 1908 census was "day laborer." Many were immigrants, who were easy to replace. Although the percentage of immigrants was declining, 30 percent of the Montevideo population was still foreign born (compared with 48 percent in 1889). There was little large-scale industry; the average employer had four workers.[17] Unskilled, easy to replace, these workers earned low wages. A carpenter earned 1.85 pesos a day, a laborer 1.20 pesos or less.[18]

Their weakness made Uruguayan workers hard to organize into unions. They were afraid to lose their jobs by striking. A lost strike meant the end of a union, and even after a victory by strikers employers would not rehire strike leaders or sign contracts with the unions. Batlle had ended the existing government policy of using the police as strikebreakers, made the police chief a mediator, and during a big port strike had Arena publish a series of editorials defending union leaders against the charges of being foreign-born agitators. But Batlle's policy of benevolent neutrality did not change the power relationships between employers and strikers.

Williman, the administrator, established the labor office, which kept strike statistics. In 1908–10 there were 31 strikes against private industry. Only eight strikes involving 850 strikers were classed as successful, and 23 involving 4,243 strikers were unsuccessful. Among the unsuccessful were the 3,500 workers who took part in the railroad strike of 1908, the major labor crisis of the Williman administration.[19]

The railroads were Uruguay's largest employers and railroad workers had the country's best organized union. Under Batlle the railroads, anxious to get government approval of railroad extension contracts, had quietly settled a strike on terms favorable to the strikers. Although they did not go so far as to recognize the union, they had put the strike settlement terms in written form to continue until June 1909. But Batlle was gone and Williman, who had been a railroad attorney, was in power.

In February 1908 workers on the Midland line struck over the dismissal of four workers. Workers on the connecting and major Central line to Montevideo refused to handle Midland cars. The Central brought railroad men from Buenos Aires, and at its request received 2,500 Uruguayan soldiers to guard the trains. Strikers attempted to stop the trains by weakening rails and putting oil and soap in locomotive boilers. Williman responded by closing down union halls, prohibiting strike meetings, and forbidding strikers from going near the railroad.[20]

The strike lasted forty-one days before collapsing. The Central took back only those it did not consider union activists, and previous concessions were revoked. From now on, working conditions would be set exclusively by management. The Central's manager and its attorney visited Williman "not only to advise him of the end of the strike but also to express the company's gratitude for the measures adopted by the government during the emergency." The Unión Ferrocarrilera, the railroad union, dissolved.[21]

V

Years later Williman, who respected ranchers and businessmen and distrusted unions, wrote an Argentine historian "in the area of economic, social, and labor reforms, my government differed so fundamentally from that of señor Batlle y Ordoñez, that my government was considered, not entirely justly, conservative."[22]

One reason why Williman could feel it was not entirely just to call his government conservative was his support of the state-owned Bank of the Republic and the Montevideo Electric Power System, both of which expanded under his administration. Williman even advanced a proposal to nationalize the telephone system, though like most potentially controversial measures nothing came of it. Another reason was that two of Batlle's moral legislation bills, the one establishing divorce and the other ending the death penalty, became law during Williman's first year, and Williman rejected Catholic appeals to veto or delay divorce.

Williman in his youth had been, together with Batlle, one of the anti-Catholic students of philosophy in the group of moralists headed by Prudencio Vázquez y Vega, and during most of his administration his policy was not to interfere with the anti-Catholic campaign being pushed by Batlle's appointees. Under the Uruguayan Constitution, which would soon be reformed, the Catholic Church was the state church. The Colorado liberals in the legislature wanted to terminate the Church's remaining advantages under the Constitution, even before reform. Religious instruction in the public schools, already reduced to the reciting of prayers at the end of the school day, was ended; the law was signed by Williman. A companion law forbade military units to dip the flag or show any other sign of respect for the Church. Williman vetoed this last law as unconstitutional.[23] The archbishop had died and Williman wanted to exercise the government's rights under the Constitution to propose candidates to fill the episcopal vacancy. He named a prominent Uruguayan Catholic as his envoy to the Vatican.

This desire to be a religious liberal yet also to have a voice in the naming of the archbishop was typical of Williman. It was not just Williman—the political elite wanted to be progressive. When Clemenceau visited Uruguay in 1910, the young senators elected under Batlle's influence boasted that on moral issues Uruguay had gone further than France itself in carrying out the aims of the French Revolution.[24] But the political elite did not want to be too progressive. Batlle had begun to restrict foreign capital, vetoing tax reduction for the famous British-owned Liebig's meat extract company and requiring new railroads, also British owned, to be built through less populated zones. Williman quietly withdrew Batlle's Liebig veto and renegotiated railroad contracts to meet the English companies' preferences, and the new railroad contracts received legislative approval. Foreign investment in Uruguay, estimated at 600 million pesos, with British investment in the lead, was worth fifteen times all the gold in Uruguay (the best estimate was that banks held 25 million in gold and there was 15 million in private hands). If foreign investors and businesses, dissatisfied with the treatment they were receiving, began to withdraw capital, the gold drain could break down Uruguay's monetary system and shatter prosperity. Besides, the elite believed that foreign investment had helped build the country, was still helping to build it, and deserved favorable treatment.[25]

Under Williman, a measure for progressive inheritance taxes, encouraged by Batlle, became law. However, the bill was so amended that in its first year the progressive tax yielded only 29,278 pesos more than the previous inheritance tax had.[26] Batlle's eight-hour-day bill was transformed in committee to what amounted to an eleven-hour day. Batlle, from Europe, advised Arena to keep the bill from being debated until he could return and get a real eight-hour day enacted.

CHAPTER 3 *Politics during the Williman Years*

Lord Bryce, whose book *The American Commonwealth*, was one of the most influential analyses of political power in the United States, passed through Uruguay in 1910. Bryce concluded that the Uruguayan political parties "have become largely hereditary; a child is born a little Blanco or a little Colorado, and rarely deserts his colour."[1] Bryce, invoking Gilbert and Sullivan's catching assertion that every English boy and girl was born either a little Liberal or a little Conservative, was responding to the obvious intensity of Uruguayan party feeling—feeling so strong that party members referred to one another as "coreligionaries."

The parties dated back to Independence but it was during the Great War when the Blancos, supported by the Argentine dictator Rosas, besieged the Colorados, aided first by the French and English then by the Brazilians, inside Montevideo—Alexander Dumas called it the New Troy. Those nine years from 1843 to 1851 seared party loyalties into permanence. The parents of middle-aged Uruguayans had lived through that period, and there had been so many revolutions and party fights since then that every generation had its own reasons to consider each member of the other party as basically a different kind of person from themselves.

Don Pepe Batlle's decisive victory in the War of 1904 over the Blancos—their modern name was the National Party—followed after the war by a decisive Colorado victory in the first contested elections in memory, had achieved what Colorados had been dreaming of since the Great War: full control of the country and an honest election victory. Batlle was now the Colorado hero and did what his father, General Lorenzo Batlle, Minister of War inside Montevideo during part of the Great War, had tried and failed to do during his disastrous presidency in the 1860's. Don Pepe instituted one-party Colorado government and ended coparticipation, a kind of consensus government where Blancos were part of the administration. All important government positions and patronage went to the triumphant, satisfied Colorados; Nationalists were read sermons urging them to repent of their atavistic revolutionary ways. (Uruguay's one-party government [gobierno de partido] presumed the functioning of opposition parties, a very different political system from later one-party states elsewhere, where opposition is outlawed.)

The prospect of Batlle's reelection in 1911 inspired Colorados and appalled Nationalists. The Nationalists, though, were divided on how to stop Batlle. Nationalist Conservatives, as they called themselves, strong among the party's legislators, eminent lawyers, professionals, and businessmen, did not approve of revolution. Revolution would hurt the economy; ranchers, who made up the bulk of the Nationalist officer corps, would not go to war and would not let their peons go to war because ranches and livestock, now so valuable, were too vulnerable to destruction; the government's army was too powerful. The result of revolution would be another, perhaps fatal defeat for the party. The best Nationalist tactic was to conciliate Williman, whose general views of government were unobjectionable, move him away from Batlle's intransigence and ultimately from Batlle's candidacy. Nationalist Radicals, who dominated the Directorio, the party's board of directors, doubted that Williman, who had been Batlle's Minister of Government during the War of 1904, would stop his reelection. The argument that ranch modernization had made revolution impossible because ranchers would no longer go to war had been disproven by the late Nationalist caudillo Aparicio Saravia's revolutions in 1897 and only three years ago. The National Party should oppose the government, not be conciliatory. Outright opposition would excite the party mass and push the Nationalist

military, now despondent on their ranches, into resisting Batlle's
return by civil war.

The first test of Williman and of Nationalist strength came early,
the legislative elections of 1907. The Nationalists, divided and disheartened by defeat in the War of 1904, had done badly in the 1905
elections, and held only 21 seats in the Chamber of Deputies, to the
Colorados' 54. They attributed their low legislative representation to
changes in the electoral law Batlle had put through, increasing the
size of the Chamber of Deputies. Uruguay, on the French pattern,
was divided into nineteen departments. Batlle's reform required that
the minority win one third of a department's vote in order to win the
minority one third of the department's seats in the Chamber of
Deputies.[2]

Nationalists charged that Batlle had undercut the minority representation that their caudillo, Aparicio Saravia, killed in the War of
1904, had won for them in the Revolution of 1897. Since only a
plurality was sufficient to win two thirds of a department's seats, it
was discriminatory to raise the minority quotient from one quarter
to one third, especially since Nationalists operated under enormous
electoral handicaps.[3] Voting was public. The voter put his ballot in
an envelope and signed it. Government employees were expected to
vote Colorado; rural police chiefs knew which residents, government
employees or not, dared to vote Nationalist. And Batlle, rather than
calling for neutrality, had invoked the doctrine of moral influence,
the right of government officials, from the president on down, to
express political preferences.

The Nationalists, divided now more deeply than in 1905, were
likely to do even worse in this election and they announced that they
would abstain unless the minimum vote quota was reduced back to
one quarter. Abstention was a prerevolutionary stance; it would cast
shadows on the government's legality and frighten businessmen and
investors. Williman, who as Batlle's Minister of Government had
countersigned the 1905 electoral law, proposed a compromise. The
two thirds–one third seat formula would be retained in some departments and replaced by a three quarter–one quarter formula in
others, where only one quarter of the votes cast would be sufficient
to win one quarter (not one third) of the department's seats. What

Williman had done, in fact, was to abandon Batlle's equal representation by population criteria, go over the 1905 election results, and
work out a patchwork solution that would give the Nationalists one
third of the seats in the next Chamber of Deputies.

Nationalist leaders wanted more. At this, Williman allowed himself to be interviewed by the influential Buenos Aires newspaper
La Prensa:

> . . . at worst, the Nationalists will be able to win *twenty-seven* of a
> total of *eighty-six* seats.
>
> I could not and would not do more. To exceed that limit right
> now would be knowingly to denaturalize the mission of the minor-
> ity. Under my proposal the minority would enjoy a position
> which any minority in any political arena should welcome. Be-
> sides, I believe that when a minority gets large enough to prevent
> the formation of a quorum in parliament, it becomes dangerous.[4]

Williman was warning the Nationalists that he was prepared to
accept their electoral abstention, which would push him towards the
ultra-Colorados, and this brought the Nationalist leadership around.
In exchange for the prospect of one more seat, they agreed not to
debate Williman's patchwork electoral reform on the legislative
floor.[5]

Nationalist Conservatives, hopeful that Williman would now
leash the Colorado organization so that they would win all the seats
the law permitted, appeared at a government ceremony at the Salto
cattle fair. Young Nationalist deputy Luis Alberto de Herrera
spoke, and acknowledged that he was not accustomed to praise the
government, "but in these happy hours of new hope, he was pleased
to toast Dr. Williman, President of the Republic, and he wished for
Dr. Williman's government the wisdom and noble tact that all
Uruguayans were waiting and hoping for."[6]

Herrera's speech caused a sensation, and *El Día*, Batlle's newspaper, knowing that Herrera's call for tact really was a call to
Williman to preserve peace by dropping Batlle, proclaimed, "Batlle
is the leading Willimanista in the country and Williman is the leading
Batllista."[7]

Radical Nationalists, anxious to wake the party mass, were indig-
nant at Conservative subservience to Williman. The Radical-con-

trolled Directorio, the party's executive, required all candidates for the legislature to sign a secret pledge promising "constant and energetic opposition" to the government.[8] Conservatives considered the pledge repugnant, refused to sign and, even worse, decided to run rival tickets to the Directorio in Montevideo and five other departments.

The Colorado campaign was simple. All authority was given to the National Executive Committee, composed of Batlle's supporters, which arranged, through the departmental organizations, to have most of the present Colorado deputies, originally elected under Batlle, renominated. Williman intervened to assure places for several of his bright ex-students, but beyond that, *El Día* was delighted to note, "the President of the Republic is limiting himself to giving friendly advice so that the whole Colorado Party will march as one man in the November elections."[9]

The elections themselves resembled the one Batlle had run in 1905. There was no violence, votes were counted honestly, and "moral influence" (Colorado voting of government employees) flourished. The Colorado vote went up slightly from 1905, the Nationalist vote dropped 15 percent, and Nationalist ticket-splitting between Directorio and Conservative slates cost additional seats. Instead of the 28 Chamber seats Williman had worked out for them, the Nationalists won only 14 (9 Directorio, 5 Conservative), to 73 Colorado. Of the approximately 170,000 men eligible to vote, 44,693 or 30 percent actually voted—a long way from the kind of mass political participation Batlle and his young Colorados wanted for Uruguay's future.[10]

Nationalists and the conservative classes, the foreign and local business community which abhorred political disruption, criticized Williman for not holding down the Colorado vote. Nationalist failure to win more than minimal representation was bound to build up Radical Nationalist abstentionism. This criticism, excoriated by *El Día* as undemocratic, was not entirely justified. In Montevideo the Nationalists failed to win any seats. Williman, it was rumored, had tried late in the afternoon to have Montevideo Colorados stop voting so that the Nationalist vote would be sufficient to reach one quarter of the total, a rumor given indirect confirmation by Williman himself in his annual presidential message when he said "Colorado party authorities did not throw all their forces into the electoral struggle."[11]

II

At the same time that the election was demonstrating the pro-Batlle Colorado organization's hold on the country, Uruguay's relations with Argentina were ominously worsening. Argentina, growing in wealth and self-confidence, saw Brazil building up its navy. Argentina must emulate the great powers of Europe, build its own navy, and establish supremacy over Brazil in Southern South America. Historically, troubles between Argentina and Brazil were fought out in Uruguay and, once more, Uruguay was in the middle.

In 1906 Argentine President Figueroa Alcorta had convoked a Junta of Notables to advise him on strengthening the navy. At the Junta, Estanislao Zeballos warned that if Brazil dominated Uruguay and the jurisdiction of the Río de la Plata (the River Plate) which opened on the Atlantic and was the border between Uruguay and Argentina was still unsettled, grave dangers to Argentine defense would result. Plata jurisdiction had little practical significance, since the river was open to the shipping of all nations. Because the ship channel to Buenos Aires lay close to the Uruguayan shore, the Argentine government had been reluctant to accept the Uruguayan position that midstream should be the boundary, and the matter had been left open. In 1906 Zeballos heated up the issue. The colonial province of the Banda Oriental del Uruguay, the East Bank of the Uruguay River, had become the Uruguayan nation. Therefore, as Zeballos interpreted the 1828 treaty between Argentina and Brazil which recognized Uruguayan independence, the boundary of Uruguay ended on the bank of the Plata, and the river itself was Argentine.[12] Zeballos was now Argentina's Foreign Minister.

Zeballos created an incident in August 1907 when an Argentine naval launch refused to allow an Uruguayan salvage ship to remove the crew from an Uruguayan shipwreck about 2.5 kilometers off the Uruguayan port of Colonia. When Uruguay protested, Zeballos responded that there was no cause for protest, since the Argentine authorities "have exercised the right of river police which belongs to them."[13] Uruguay's young Foreign Minister Varela Acevedo, who had been Batlle's private secretary, wanted to break relations with

3. This map of Uruguay, 1907–1915, shows places pertinent to events described throughout the book.

Argentina. Williman refused. Varela Acevedo, to the cheers of university students and Colorado clubs, resigned as Foreign Minister.

To replace him Williman chose Antonio Bachini. The choice worried Batlle's intimates, for Williman had brought back into the center of Uruguayan politics a well-known, intelligent, and ambitious Colorado, who if events went his way might become an alternative presidential candidate to Batlle. Bachini had once been on *El Día*, yet had close ties with the pre-'97 Colorado leaders who had sat out the 1904 War and been discredited when Batlle won. Bachini had fought in 1904, but his relations with Batlle had cooled thereafter over Don Pepe's intransigence toward the old-line Colorado leaders. In years past Bachini had edited a Buenos Aires newspaper, and Batlle had named him Consul General in Buenos Aires, in part to use his Argentine connections to ferret out Nationalist plots, in part to get him out of the way.

Williman was not concerned about Bachini's political future. Bachini would be especially valuable as Foreign Minister, because when he had edited *El Diario* in Buenos Aires he had carried on furious polemics with his rival, Zeballos, editor of *La Prensa*. This rivalry was an advantage, for Williman intended to play a classic diplomatic gambit. As Bachini explained later, "in the mind of our government it was inalterable policy to avoid all conflicts [with Argentina], in the belief that Doctor Zeballos' theories were repudiated by responsible Argentines."[14] Identifying the Plata jurisdiction dispute as Zeballos' personal aberration and not Argentine government policy would keep open alternate channels toward settlement. Of course, Zeballos' views were known to the Argentine president before he became Foreign Minister, and the distinction the Uruguayan government was attempting to establish between Zeballos' views and Argentina's might be illusory.

To give Uruguay more visibility on the Plata, Williman began to expand the Uruguayan navy, composed of a few launches and gunboats. The newly established Naval Academy was given funds for a building. In December the over-aged Italian cruiser *Dogali* was purchased. It was not a great warship, but it could show the Uruguayan flag.

Williman also skillfully exploited Argentine hostility toward Brazil, to Uruguay's advantage. In 1851, as its price for intervening to break the Great Siege of Montevideo, Brazil had secured from Uruguay all navigation and jurisdiction rights on the Laguna Merín and the Yaguarón River, the Uruguayan borders with Brazil. Now Williman sent a delegation to Rio de Janeiro and got from Foreign Minister Baron Rio Branco the assurance that, once the warships it was having built in Europe were ready, Brazil would spontaneously grant Uruguay equal rights of navigation on the Merín and Yaguarón, a historic victory for Uruguay.[15]

Brazil's cooperative attitude toward Uruguay convinced Zeballos that Brazil, supported by Uruguay, planned to attack Argentina. On March 15, 1908, England protested to Uruguay its seizure the previous year of an English ship for allegedly hunting sea lions off Punta del Este. Britain took the position that the Río de la Plata was a bay (Argentines and Uruguayans consider it a river; geologically, it is a gulf). The nations bordering it had jurisdiction extending three miles from shore, the rest being "open sea." It was traditional English policy to deny rights asserted by other powers which might restrict British maritime interests. In the immediate context, however, England was attempting to defuse the Argentine-Uruguayan dispute by arguing that the Plata was open sea. Simultaneously, Baron Rio Branco suggested to the Argentine Minister in Brazil that Argentina settle its jurisdictional dispute with Uruguay amicably. For Zeballos, this confirmed the existence of a European-South American alliance to force Argentina to arbitrate on the Plata.

Argentina reacted. On the night of April 15, 1908, the Argentine navy without previous notice staged maneuvers off the Isla de Flores, Montevideo's quarantine station, from 9 to 11 P.M. and again from 1:30 to 2:15 A.M. Cannon fire and signal lights wakened Montevideo sleepers. The exercises were repeated the next night, then the squadron steamed away South East. Immediately, Uruguayan Foreign Minister Bachini ordered the Uruguayan Chargé d'Affaires in Buenos Aires to inform Zeballos that Uruguay was disturbed by the maneuvers "in waters of our exclusive jurisdiction."

Zeballos promised to consult President Figueroa Alcorta, and within a week, on April 30, the Argentine Government replied. There really was no substance to the Uruguayan complaint. The maneuvers had occurred between seven and nine miles from the

Uruguayan coast "in waters open to free navigation, which in any case are not subject to the exclusive jurisdiction of Uruguay, since the defense of the entrance to the Río de la Plata is precisely one of the principal causes for the existence of the war fleet of this Republic." There followed a further exchange of notes, ending on May 17, with both sides holding to their positions but calling the incident closed.[16]

On June 12 Zeballos warned the German Minister in Buenos Aires that "Brazil is provoking Uruguay" in the conflict on the Río de la Plata.[17] Alarming rumors of Argentina's next step caused Williman on June 13 to convoke a Junta of Notables to convene on June 20 and advise him on "international matters." There were thirty-two notables, mostly ex-Foreign Ministers, but political leaders were also included. No more than ten were strongly pro-Batlle, seven were Nationalists, a few were pre-1897 Colorados, and most were distinguished lawyers, members of the conservative classes.[18] Sooner or later in their deliberations the notables would advise Williman that the international crisis required national unity. The prospect of Batlle's reelection was blocking national unity. The notables, if the Plata crisis had made Williman receptive, would then suggest a decorous formula to remove the block by replacing Batlle with a unity candidate.

On June 14, the day after Williman's invitations went out, Zeballos resigned as Argentine Foreign Minister. Zeballos, using reports by the Argentine War and Navy Ministers that Brazil was defenseless, had proposed to mobilize 50,000 additional men and hand an ultimatum to Brazil. It must, within eight days, cancel the purchase of the warships being built for it in Europe. The Zeballos proposals upset the Argentine Senate, which opposed war with Brazil over manufactured grievances. There were public alarms in Buenos Aires, and President Figueroa Alcorta had been obliged to ask for Zeballos' resignation. His letter of resignation contained a paragraph on Uruguay which indicated the potential for Argentine involvement in an overthrow of the Uruguayan government had the Argentine government continued Zeballos' policies: "As for Uruguay, it is notorious that the powerful Nationalist party and a notable nucleus of independent Colorado statesmen do not participate in the groundless agitation against our country."[19]

The Plata crisis eased off. In Montevideo the Junta of Notables met only once and decided that each member would send a written opinion to Williman. In July the Argentine Senate interpellated the new Foreign Minister on government policy toward Uruguay and Brazil. Early in August, Williman named Gonzalo Ramírez Minister to Argentina. Ramírez, who had successfully negotiated the 1899 Arbitration Treaty with Argentina, carried instructions to negotiate a settlement on the Río de la Plata.

Brazil kept its promises. That same August of 1908 the President of Brazil announced that his country was prepared to grant Uruguay jurisdiction to the approximate midpoint and joint navigation on the Laguna Merín and Yaguarón river. By mid-1909 the treaty was ready and shortly afterward ratified.[20] The policy toward Brazil that resulted in this tremendous coup had been directed by Williman, but Bachini got most of the public credit.

The crisis with Argentina, which could have seriously complicated Batlle's reelection chances, was over, but Antonio Bachini who, in Uruguayan eyes, had made Argentina back down and convinced Brazil to cede rights Uruguay had wanted for almost sixty years now had presidential hopes of his own.

CHAPTER 4 *Batlle in Europe*

Batlle had brought a number-letter code with him to Europe, to decipher coded cables from Montevideo.[1] Such cables were reserved for only the most urgent matters and were to enable him to keep abreast of these matters. Don Pepe had to wait weeks for letters and newspapers. An opportunity to do more than wait, yet not be openly involved in Uruguayan politics, presented itself shortly after he settled his family in Paris.

The South American nations were invited to the Second Hague Peace Conference of 1907—for the First in 1899 they had been considered insufficiently civilized—and Williman appointed Batlle to head the Uruguayan delegation.[2] Don Pepe soon regretted that he had accepted the mission. Uruguay, seated by alphabet, was at the back of the hall where they were rarely able to hear what was going on. Diplomatic life "mortified" him:

the banquets which I had to attend, almost always seated next to people I didn't know, the necessity to keep up with invitations, to answer them and keep dates and hours in mind in order to be punctual, put me beside myself. Was it for this that I came to Europe?[3]

The source of Don Pepe's discontent lay deeper. Uruguay's role at the conference was, he wrote to his Foreign Minister, "insignificant."[4]

During the entire four-months meeting the Uruguayan delegation was permitted only two speeches. Batlle wanted more for Uruguay:

I had an obsession to do something to create a promising situation for our delegation, but I could not find the means. Every day some new idea occurred to me, one which I had to abandon for one reason or another the next day. I was even unable to sleep, I who have always slept so well![5]

Then an idea jelled. On July 5, 1907 the delegation of Uruguay presented a proposal for an alliance for obligatory arbitration. Once ten nations, five of which had populations of at least 25,000,000, had agreed to submit disputes between them for arbitration, "they shall have the right to form an alliance for the purpose of examining the disagreements and disputes which may arise among other countries and to intervene when they may deem it advantageous to secure the most just solution." All nations which accepted obligatory arbitration could join "the alliance intended to abolish the evils of war."[6]

Anglo-German rivalry prevented approval of far milder proposals than Batlle's plan, which authorized military intervention by the alliance anywhere to prevent war. The Uruguayan proposal was referred to committee, was the last item on the agenda for one meeting, was not discussed then, and was dropped from the agenda. Don Pepe was advocating collective security, and when first the League of Nations and then the United Nations were formed Uruguayans wanted the world to remember that in 1907 at The Hague it was an Uruguayan who called the nations to organize force for peace. The actual reception the call received in 1907, though, produced "really black days" for Don Pepe:

what most mortified and preoccupied me was that our motion, which was almost totally my work, could have made us appear a little ingenuous. The day after presenting it I was already upset and I remained that way all the time I was at The Hague.[7]

It appeared that Batlle would not even get a chance to speak on his motion. He had taken advantage of a lull in the meetings to go to Paris and to bring his wife Matilde and two youngest children to the seashore near The Hague when a plenary session on arbitration was

4. Hague Peace Conference. On the right, Uruguayan delegation seated after the Turkish delegation (wearing fezes). Batlle is the first delegate on the right.

announced and the other Uruguayan delegate, Juan Pedro Castro, the Uruguayan Minister to France, inscribed himself to speak. Don Pepe returned before the Uruguayan turn came, but not wanting to deprive Castro of the opportunity, contented himself with adding a few paragraphs on his proposal to Castro's remarks. To counteract aspersions of ingenuousness, the paragraphs' tone was realistic. The Uruguayan delegation did not insist that its motion be discussed, knowing that because it was advanced by a "young and sparsely settled" country, there was no chance for its approval, "but if such a plan were supported by one of the great nations that cherish advanced ideas, human aspiration toward peace would perhaps have found a concrete form around which would be grouped all its friends, individuals, and peoples."[8]

The failure of a proposal by the United States for a permanent fifteen-judge Court of Arbitration, a proposal Batlle considered unworkable, decided him to speak out, just before the end of the Conference.[9] It was a mistake, Batlle insisted, to identify *international* jurisprudence where only a few nations with divergent interests and legal systems existed, with *national* jurisprudence, where millions of individuals living under the same law were involved. Judicial impartiality, no great problem in internal justice, had proved beyond the Conference's ability to assure when setting up the Permanent Court. Even if this problem were surmounted, the attempt to create uniform jurisprudence would result in the refusal by nations whose claims would not be supported by the Court to take controversies to the Court. The American proposal already exempted controversies "in which the honor and essential interests" of nations were involved. "Even today, war might threaten to break out at any minute," Batlle prophesied, "and in the regulations presented one could not find a single paragraph by which it could be prevented."

Don Pepe reminded the Conference of the Uruguayan proposal to combine material and moral force, using a sentence that would ever after be identified with him. "Since so many alliances have been concluded to impose that which is arbitrary, it might be well to conclude another alliance by means of which justice might be imposed."

If the rest of the world was not ready for these ideas, America was:

and if two or three of the most powerful republics of that continent were to agree to constitute an alliance which, by greater right than any other might be called holy, the object of which would be to examine the causes of armed conflicts that might arise between the American peoples, and to offer an effective aid to the one that had been unjustly incited to war, there is no doubt that other American nations would group around this alliance, and that the international peace of the continent would no more be disturbed by discussions between the countries forming such an alliance.[10]

Don Pepe's confidence that America was ready for collective security was not limited to rhetoric. He reported to Varela Acevedo, then Uruguayan Foreign Minister:

> In these last days I believed I had accomplished a triumph for our country: I had enthusiastic opinions in favor of a project creating an arbitration tribunal, which I was confident would be established in Montevideo, from the Argentines, the Bolivians, the Chileans, and even from Ruy Barbosa [of Brazil], when Ruy Barbosa stopped my enthusiasm by advising me that Brazil did not want to add to the grief given to the North Americans these days, lest the North Americans might believe that Brazil wants to establish a separate tribunal for our countries. And to convince me that he had done all he could for the project, he showed me the cables he exchanged with Rio, which confirmed the truth of what he said.[11]

In his archive, in Don Pepe's handwriting, is a draft of a letter evidently prepared for the Uruguayan minister in Washington on the occasion of the Anglo–North American Treaty (August 1911). The minister is to urge the government of the United States to sign an alliance with one or two of the principal South American nations, Brazil, Argentina, or Chile, "whose object would be to make arbitration prevail in all the differences that develop between the American nations." Once the great powers sign, all the others will and "the nation which may have been refused arbitration and upon which another nation may wish to impose its will by force will have the protection of the league." The draft reiterates Western Hemisphere readiness for this advance and paraphrases Batlle's Hague speech,

"So many alliances have been made to impose violence that nobody can object when one is made to make justice prevail."

At The Hague, Batlle spoke immediately after Ruy Barbosa, the dominant Latin American at the Conference, who received prolonged applause. No applause followed Don Pepe's speech. His speech, Batlle acknowledged to his confidante Arena, was "diametrically opposed to everything accepted as unquestionable truth in the course of Conference discussion," but he was satisfied with it:

> How the members of the Conference judged it, I do not know. I was always rather unsociable towards them, first because so many of them evidenced low opinions of the countries of America and second because the idea that they might have a low opinion of me involuntarily kept me away from them. Only a Mr. Max Huber, delegate from Switzerland and Professor of Law at the University of Zurich, congratulated me, telling me that my ideas seemed entirely correct to him . . . and that he had announced his favorable opinion of my speech in various conversations with delegates.[12]

Max Huber's congratulations, Don Pepe's "only personal satisfaction" at The Hague, would have been even sweeter had Don Pepe known of Huber's fame in international law.

Batlle's actions at The Hague had been revealing. He must do something for his country; Uruguay must not be overlooked. His proposal was dismissed as visionary; he tried to mount a Latin American version of his plan, and when that did not work, he kept the idea ready for an opportune time. Collective security, dismissed as visionary at The Hague, became reasonable twelve years later at Versailles, when Woodrow Wilson, President of the United States, advocated it. So it was not necessarily the wisdom of a plan which determined its acceptability; it could be the power of its advocates. At The Hague, Batlle was obscure; in Uruguay he would not be. And he had great plans for Uruguay.

Don Pepe had had all he wanted of being a diplomat. Juan Pedro Castro was going back to Montevideo, and during the conference Don Pepe was offered the post as Uruguayan Minister to France. He declined immediately. Batlle's final report to the Foreign Minister, Varela Acevedo, concluded: "I have left The Hague, not satisfied,

5. Auto trip in Europe. From left to right: Batlle, chauffeur, eldest son César, daughter Ana Amalia, and wife Matilde.

but relatively tranquil." To Arena, Don Pepe was more explicit. "I find myself, at last, free of the Conference."[13]

II

Batlle had bought the automobile and hired a chauffeur. Free of the Conference, he took his family on a leisurely October motor trip back to Paris by way of Holland, Belgium, and northern France. Colonel Bernassa y Jérez, in charge of Batlle's security on the trip to Europe, returned to Montevideo. Young Manini, Batlle's protégé, also returned to look after Don Pepe's political interests. In keeping with Batlle's scrupulousness with official funds, Manini, who had been secretary of The Hague Delegation, refunded 500 pesos of the Delegation's unspent expense money to the government.[14] Adolfo, Don Pepe's servant, whose family missed him, went back too, "because he and I agree that his services are no longer indispensable to me."[15] Misia Matilde, Batlle's wife, and his older sons, twenty-two and nineteen, were homesick and wanted to be in Montevideo, but Don Pepe was determined to stay away from Uruguay to avoid political complications.

The Colorado victory in the November 1907 elections demonstrated that everything was under control and no change in Batlle's plans was needed. Don Pepe was delighted with the outcome. "It was necessary that a party which commits offenses like the insurrection of 1904 suffer the consequences of its conduct in as acute a way as the Nationalist party just has. Otherwise the worst crimes would remain unpunished." Europe obviously had not made Batlle more politically conciliatory, as many in Uruguay hoped. His newspaper, El Día, he advised his editors, should resist any proposal to appease Nationalist revolutionaries by changing the electoral laws to give them more seats. Instead, El Día should play up Nationalist defeat.

> because it is in the country's interest that they become convinced that their party is destined to disappear, so that they look for other combinations and other means of acting in public life. I, for my part, am convinced that they are heading for complete dissolution or at least complete impotence, unless the Colorados work to give them life and vigor.[16]

El Día was not being edited and printed to Batlle's satisfaction.

Now back in Paris, he read it avidly, sending daily letters of criticism and enclosing fiction and stories clipped from Parisian newspapers, even some he thought "a little daring," for publication in *El Día*. He decided that new presses must be bought, offered to mortgage his house if necessary, got prices from French manufacturers, and when *El Día*'s business manager remonstrated at the expense, he underlined "*I order*" the purchase of two new presses.[17] An *El Día* article critical of foreign insurance companies pleased him:

> We must stop letting them take money from us as though we are fools. And I don't refer only to insurance but to all companies whose capitalists live outside the country. As for insurance, why shouldn't the State create an Insurance Bank? Doesn't the Bank of the Republic give excellent results?[18]

Manini and Arena, both deputies, should file a bill setting up a State insurance company. No capital would be needed, the State's guarantee would suffice. Money which now went to North America would go to the State. "The insured would be much better served and the nation would save many hundreds of thousands of pesos, amounts which go on increasing in the future." If Uruguay kept its gold instead of letting it be drained away, immigrants would flock in like flies to sugar. "Gold represents all the material goods and most of the moral ones." Also, "the real property of all those residing abroad should pay a special tax."

"Many of our businesses produce 15, 20, and 25 percent profits. Why should we leave them in the hands of people who live abroad, when we can obtain capital at 5 and 6 percent?" "The modern tendency is for the State to undertake all great public services."

> It is necessary to react against the ideas reigning in Montevideo. The thinking and calculating elements of our city, those who up to now have made public opinion in money matters, the only matters which really interested them, have been the merchants, and they represent the interests of the European houses whose products they sell to us. The newspapers have depended upon them and in large part they still sustain them with subscriptions and advertisements. The lawyers, to whom they give their legal affairs, have also lived off them.[19]

These were old ideas of Don Pepe's, first published after the 1890 economic crash, restated toward the end of his Presidency, and now being reemphasized programatically. To develop economically, Uruguay must stop the gold drain, must control foreign capital, must set up state enterprises, even a novel one like an insurance bank. Nothing was holding Uruguay's economic emancipation back more than the proforeign attitudes of Montevideo's "thinking and calculating elements"—the merchants, newspapermen, and lawyers. Another generation would call them the opinion-making elite.

Montevideo was on Batlle's mind. Luis, his only brother, was suffering from kidney trouble. "If a trip to Europe could help him, we will have to bring him."[20] The chacra [Batlle's home in Piedras Blancas] on the outskirts of Montevideo, could be mortgaged. Luis was not well enough to come to Europe; he wrote that his doctor advised a year of rest and special diet in Uruguay. Luis added news "that is not going to please you at all. The idea of getting permission to hold bullfights is being talked up and I am told that things are well along."[21] Bullfights had long since been outlawed, and Don Pepe was one of their principal enemies. Recently, though, simulated bullfights had been permitted. On February 7, 1908, the same day Don Pepe received Luis' letter, he wrote Arena and Manini: "Is it true?" Would Williman, who, he knew, was against them, veto a law authorizing bullfights? "Would his opposition be as heated as mine?" "Bullfights, in my estimation, would be a step backwards towards barbarism, since the pleasure experienced in seeing a man's life in danger and the spilling of blood, even if not always human blood, can be nothing else."

I here think of what we could do to make Uruguay a small model country in which education is enormously extended, in which the arts and sciences are cultivated with honor, in which people's customs are refined. I take pleasure in imagining that we could create universities in all the departments and great scientific and artistic institutes in Montevideo, develop the theater and literature, organize olympic games, build up the national wealth by preventing foreign elements from taking it out of the country, provide for the well being of the poor classes, etc. etc. And meanwhile over there they come out with plans for entertainments that are the negation of good sense and all healthy tendencies!

Frankly, there are very few notices from my country which could produce so disagreeable an effect on me as the rehabilitation of bullfights. I assure you that my discouragement would be great and my stay in these parts would be much longer than I had thought up to now.

This is a matter on which I stake my political future. [Es un asunto en que hago cuestión de cartera.]

Try to prevent this step backwards towards barbarism from happening.[22]

Don Pepe's letter had the desired effect. Arena came to reassure Luis, who, alarmed at what he considered his brother's overreaction and fearful that Pepe really would stay away, went to see Williman. Williman assured Luis that he had already been approached and had advised the interested parties that he would veto any law permitting bullfights.[23]

III

Before he could make Uruguay the model country, Batlle would first have to be reelected. Don Pepe was equally an idealist and a political tactician. He had threatened not to return if bullfights were permitted, knowing full well that the threat would be sufficient to forestall them. But there were other matters he could not so easily influence. The dispute over the Río de la Plata with Argentina, whose ultimate ramifications could be disastrous, was one. Batlle had trouble with Argentina in 1904 and had an anti-Argentine reputation, but the last thing he wanted was war with Argentina. He warned Arena, "Even supposing that, with the support of Brazil and even Chile, we chop Argentina into pieces, we would gain nothing except to destroy the international equilibrium that is the guarantee of our existence. We would find ourselves face to face and without aid, with another great power, Brazil." Uruguay had defended its rights; "having done this we should proceed with great prudence to solve things peacefully, which is what is best for us and for everyone."[24]

Don Pepe, anxious to head off bellicosity, broke his policy of not openly commenting on Uruguayan politics. Varela Acevedo, Batlle's former secretary, had resigned as foreign minister when Williman refused to break relations with Argentina. Concerned that Varela Acevedo's attitude would be interpreted as reflecting his own, Batlle cautioned the young man: "things should not go further than they have." And Don Pepe sent letters to others endorsing Williman's Argentine policy. As Batlle had intended, the recipients let others know what Batlle had written; the news soon appeared in the press.[25]

Williman was the key to Batlle's reelection. As President he had control of the army and of patronage, and had great influence with the Colorado Party. Williman's hostility would endanger, conceivably even destroy, Batlle's candidacy. To avoid antagonizing Williman, Batlle had gone to Europe, but from Europe, Don Pepe reminded Arena and Manini not to let Williman be split away. His instructions that *El Día* must resist any proposal to propitiate the Nationalists—a much more vital issue than bullfights—had contained a proviso, "unless it comes from Williman."[26]

Williman's appointment of a potential presidential rival for Batlle as foreign minister presented a new concern. From Paris, Don Pepe wrote Manini and Arena "for you alone."

I believe that Bachini could do good in the Ministry of Foreign Relations if he decides to settle things with the Argentines. In another ministry perhaps he would not be so useful.

Where he surely would be worst would be in the Senate, since he would not be satisfied with a seat there, but would immediately aspire to the presidency of that body. Given the restless and complicated spirit of our friend, he could not fill the post of Senate President as he should, if only because of the doubts he would raise in some and the illusions in others.

The Senate President served as President of the Republic in the absence or death of the elected President and after the expiration of the President's term when the legislature was unable to elect a successor. The Senate President was the focus of plots, and Bachini, with his ties to the pre-'97 Colorados and the old Colorado military, could be troublesome. "But he will not be able to do anything if he is not put into a favorable situation," Batlle cautioned.[27]

Batlle, after waiting about a year, was sufficiently concerned to write his first letter to Williman, twelve pages long. He endorsed Williman's policies on the Río de la Plata, and without overtly advising him not to sponsor electoral legislation favorable to the Nationalists, he dismissed the danger of a Blanco revolution:

> Nothing remains for them except the cuckoo of civil war the menace of which they constantly raise. Civil war is easy against governments like Idiarte Borda [in 1897] or when controlling a third of the Republic [the six Nationalist run departments from 1897 to 1904] and after having freely made all kinds of military preparation; but not when combating a government supported by public opinion and without other aid than their own demoralization.
>
> We have nothing to preoccupy ourselves except to continue to progress . . . [Batlle's ellipsis dots] and to avoid international complications. In all the people I talk to who come from home, I note great satisfaction with your government. They believe that we are going in the right direction and they have faith in you. —Forward![28]

Don Pepe knew his old friend very well, and there was nothing in the letter about keeping foreign companies from draining Uruguay's wealth.

Williman, in turn, had enormous respect for Batlle's abilities. In March, Williman asked Bachini to write Batlle, asking him to find an expert to study the fortifications of Montevideo. Don Pepe didn't like the mission, though he would do it if Williman really wanted him to. For one thing, "this armament apparatus" would do no good if something serious was up, "since they wouldn't give us time to fortify ourselves, and if there isn't anything serious perhaps we could postpone it to avoid heightening international tension by new suspicions of hidden and crafty plans." Batlle kept the letter to Arena for a week and then completed his thoughts. In addition to his reservations about the mission's advisability, "it will oblige me to put myself in relations with presidents and ministers, whom I have avoided seeing up to now. That was why I did not accept the Uruguayan Ministry to France." In France they were not sure where Uruguay was; a request from an Uruguayan ex-President for an appointment would be honored, out of courtesy, but likely to be considered a sign of South American exhibitionism. He had received an invitation to use the Presidential Box at the Opera and had been prepared to thank the President of France personally, then desisted when he discovered that Herosa, the Uruguayan Chargé d'Affaires, had arranged it. On Batlle's instructions, Herosa had done the thanking. Batlle rationalized his timidity with high placed Europeans: "my character resists soliciting considerations that are not offered me spontaneously." Arena was to go to Williman and see if Herosa could replace him in the fortification mission.[29]

For Uruguayan sophisticates living in Paris, Batlle was a bitter disappointment. Years later one recalled that Batlle's suits were not pressed, his tie was badly knotted, and he refused contact with the right people. "He made errors in speaking French, he lacked the literary and artistic facility indispensable for sociability in societies of inherited culture."[30] Don Pepe, however, was enjoying the freedom of Paris. He and his wife were able to go to the theater without causing excitement, something impossible in Montevideo. In his letter to Williman, Batlle was enthusiastic about the Parisian theater, its naturalness, the splendor of its staging, its variety, and the elegance of its audiences: "frequently one does not know if the ladies sitting in front or at one's side are cocottes or princesses."

IV

Pleasant though it was, life in Europe for Batlle was self-imposed exile. Events that could alter Uruguay's future and prevent his own reelection were taking place over there, and he could only write letters. When the Río de la Plata jurisdiction crisis finally climaxed in April 1908 with the Argentine naval maneuvers and cannon firing off Montevideo (above, Chapter 3), Batlle warned Arena that *El Día* must exercise "extreme prudence." War with Argentina would threaten Uruguayan autonomy even if the Brazilian-led coalition won. The Nationalists would use war to revolt or to obtain outside intervention. They would not settle for concessions "because they want power." Fortunately, Zeballos' resignation ended the threat of war; and after Williman named an envoy to negotiate a Plata settlement with Argentina, Don Pepe wrote Williman congratulating him on "the turn our relations with Argentina have taken due principally to your firm and circumspect conduct."[31]

Batlle's cardinal rule was to avoid antagonizing Williman. When Williman broke the railroad strike of 1908, the major labor event of his administration, pro-labor Arena wanted to challenge the government in parliament. Batlle restrained his disciple. He shared Arena's feeling, "especially since it involves a struggle between Uruguayan workers who are their families' support and a resident company that extracts plentiful profits from the country. The less Montevideo workers have, the more London gentlemen will have." But Don Pepe, the political tactician, realized that Williman, the key to his reelection, must not be provoked. A parliamentary challenge would split the Colorados and accomplish nothing for the workers. "Ideas for protection of the working classes are far from generalized among us. Besides, the power of the President is almost unquestionable." And "even if it wasn't," Williman was so satisfactory in other matters that it would be unwise to break with him over the first disagreement.[32]

Batlle wrote the letter, marked "private," in April; a month later, in the same letter in which he had recommended "extreme prudence" with Argentina, he brought the labor issue up again.

> If Williman is against it you can do nothing. On the one hand, the questions involved do not excite anybody in the country except you, me, and a handful of others. On the other hand, you know how hard it is to do something against the wishes of the president in our legislative assemblies. . . . It will be necessary to furl the banner along almost all the line. But that will be a small loss, in the face of long term interests, if after a few years we can wave it again with new enthusiasm and great prospects of success.[33]

Unions were weak: "only you, me, and a handful of others" were excited about helping the working class. To appeal for labor support would endanger rather than further Batlle's reelection. Nor could Batlle rely on the "thinking and calculating elements of Montevideo." Don Pepe was relying on the Colorados, on continuing control of the Colorado organization, and on Williman.

6. The Batlle family in France.

7. The Batlle family in Paris.

8. The Batlle family in their Paris apartment, 1908. From left to right: Matilde, Ana Amalia, Batlle, and sons César, Lorenzo, and Rafael.

V

Winter was over and Batlle planned a family trip. Then his brother Luis worsened. Batlle had arranged that Dr. Ricaldoni, Uruguay's leading physician, examine Luis, who was operated on. Luis, after a seeming postoperative recovery, relapsed and died on June 29, 1908. For Batlle his family was inseparable from himself. His wife, Matilde, had been married to his first cousin, Ruperto Michaelsson, who had left Matilde with five children, the youngest about three years old. Pepe, then a young philosopher moralist, had set up a household with Matilde. Because there was no divorce legislation, the couple had to wait some ten years until Michaelsson died and they were legally able to marry and bring together Matilde's children by her first husband and Pepe. Now Pepe was also looking after his brother Luis' children, and was bringing two of Luis' boys to Europe for study. In addition to his house at Piedras Blancas, Batlle owned a piece of land that could be sold to pay their way. He wrote Arena:

I have abandoned the plan I had to go sightseeing through the North of France and Belgium and then spend a few days in London. At the end of this month I will go to Switzerland to spend some time in some chalet on some mountain. Up to now Europe has not been a rest for me. My nerves have been in constant tension, first with The Hague conference, then with the news of Luis and the international conflict with Argentina. Perhaps I would not have suffered so much had I stayed home. I thought I could forget about you people for two or three years. Hard experience has showed me how absurd that was.[34]

A postscript added "I am alarmed at *El Día*'s drop in sales." Before leaving for Switzerland, Batlle made clear what was on his mind. "If things begin to go bad with *El Día*, I will return immediately to Montevideo, and so carry out an idea that has begun to germinate in the family with the death of Luis."[35]

Arena hastened to dissuade Batlle. *El Día*'s sales were holding, even though down slightly from their historic peak (during the railroad strike) of 19,000 copies daily. When the new presses Batlle had ordered in Paris arrived, circulation would exceed 20,000 copies and Batlle's old dream, "something that several years ago seemed to me a delirium of yours, that *El Día* would produce a monthly profit of five thousand pesos," would come true. Until then, Arena would take a salary cut, if necessary, to provide Batlle with funds to stay in Europe.

> Upon reading this far you must have read a predominating theme between the lines: my holy terror, our holy terror at your return ahead of time.—Exactly, Pedro [Manini, Batlle's political agent] Feliciano [Viera, President of the Senate and Williman's campaign manager] Blengio [Colorado Party leader], all completely dedicated friends of yours, all of us are convinced that your remaining in Europe is a necessity required by the political well being of the nation.

To clinch the argument Arena wrote that even Luis had realized this, which explained why he had not wanted to alarm Pepe about his health.

Williman's character required that Batlle stay away. "When the newspapers begin again to say that he doesn't govern, that the Batllistas dominate him, etc., he limits himself to saying that those who think such tactics are going to influence him don't know him." But "more careful observation reveals that the President has his weaknesses, weaknesses of the most dangerous character . . . fear of what people will say." Williman had vetoed Viera for a ministry and now Arena himself for the Senate because they were too Batllista and he wanted to keep up appearances.

> How many disagreeable surprises could be presented us when your being present began to give verisimilitude to the intrigues of your enemies?
>
> You must sacrifice yourself, if staying in Europe begins to be a sacrifice. You must sacrifice not so much for our personal interests nor even for our group, but for the interests of the nation. . . . And you no longer have the right to say that you are unwilling to make further concessions to your political ambitions, because now it is no longer your ambition which enters into play, but the legitimate ambition of three quarters of a country that has its hopes fixed on you,—and if you should disappear would be completely disoriented.[36]

From Switzerland, where the family was installed, Don Pepe did the closest thing he could to returning: "I have decided to contribute to

El Día from here." The new presses could print 50,000 copies an hour. *El Día* must use better paper, the best, like *Le Figaro*. Batlle had discovered that to save money *El Día*'s administrator bought cheap ink; from now on, only first quality ink. Don Pepe sent Arena a copy of Naquet's book *L'Union Libre*, which advocated men and women living together without legal marriage and separating, again with no legal complications, when living together ceased being attractive. *El Día* should not endorse all of the book, although "it appears very reasonable to me" because it "can be badly interpreted at first" but could print excerpts as an exposition of the most advanced French ideas on the subject. Don Pepe remembered a book of his youth, *The Woman*, by Concepción Arenal. *El Día* could stir up reader interest with Concepción Arenal's arguments for political rights for women.

Carlos Michaelsson, one of Matilde's sons by her first marriage, needed medical treatment. Don Pepe, who had brought two of Luis' sons to Europe, as noted, was also bringing Carlos. Don Pepe, restrained from coming home, was gathering his close ones closer to him. "You will say I am bringing half of Montevideo."[37]

CHAPTER 5 *Timing the Return*

In Uruguay it was feared that the Radical Nationalists were preparing a revolution. There were meetings in ex-Foreign Minister Zeballos' Buenos Aires office, meetings across the border in Brazil. Arena, on October 20, 1908, reported to Batlle that Williman had put the army on alert and "the curious thing, a most curious thing, is that these alarmist rumors swept over us just when insinuations reached me from various sources that it was necessary to do something to soften up the Blancos and see if it was possible to make them accept your return to the presidency with resignation. . . . I should confess to you, hastening to beg your pardon just in case, that those voices of quasi-concord began to influence me."[1]

> The only thing that tempts me is the desire to see you return to the government and carry out some of the ideals that you are caressing in those old worlds, instead of coming to kill people even if in the name of justice and good principles. Since concessions within the law could not be transformed into subversion, with you holding the reins it might be wise to loosen up a little so as to be in condition to do good for everyone.[2]

Don Pepe set Arena straight. He was not interested in becoming president for his personal interest, only to do good, and "for that very reason I will not enter into transactions of any type or make concessions of any sort, except those that I am disposed to make because of my own ideas and for which I have no need to make deals with my adversaries."[3]

II

Batlle was so confident that everything in Uruguay was under control that in February, 1909 he advised Arena that he, Matilde, his daughter Ana, his twelve-year-old son Lorenzo, and Rosa the maid, "my caravana" were going off on a long trip to Italy, Egypt, Greece, perhaps Palestine and beyond. The older boys, his, Luis', and his stepsons, would remain, some in Paris, some in school in Switzerland. Don Pepe's expenses would be up but *El Día*, with new presses, new paper, new ink, and the editorial improvement about which he had been badgering Arena, "will be a great newspaper and I will not have to worry much over spending a few francs more or less."[4]

In Cairo a letter Arena had sent in January finally caught up with Batlle in April. Arena analyzed the Nationalist struggle between "warriors and evolutionists." "With simple good treatment" by the Colorados, Arena hoped the evolutionists would win out over the war faction, "because I feel that it would be a great relief to be able to continue our politics in peace."[5]

Don Pepe once more demanded the hard line.

What can we offer the Nationalists? I believe that no party in the world can offer a better *realizable program* than ours. We can offer everything worthwhile in the way of reforms, inspired in full justice, in sincere love of liberty, and in the well being of all the inhabitants of the country. What more can they ask of us: Deals for political patronage, etc. We should not relapse into those mistakes which caused the country so many misfortunes.

The comments were merely postscripts to Batlle's description of Egypt. Egypt was crowded: "ten million people in a territory that doesn't reach one-third our size." The steamship trip down the Nile stopped at temples everyday. "On visiting them one feels antiquity taking charge."

The boat touches shore and immediately the muleteers with their donkeys appear together with the vendors of curiosities of the country. The employees of the ship manage them with whip blows.

9. In front of the Sphynx. Batlle and son Lorenzo on camels, Matilde and Ana Amalia in sulky.

There was scarcely a stop where blows were not abundantly bestowed for trivial reasons, like too many people conglomerating on the landing or because a burro was placed in an awkward spot. The Egyptians, accustomed to unbroken foreign domination since the time of Cambyses, support this treatment without being much upset.[6]

From Egypt the family went to Palestine—"Jerusalem, where they don't do anything but beg and pray"[7]—Syria, and Greece. From Athens, in May, he wrote Arena that he was heading for Italy: "it is three months since I have seen a person I knew, except my family." He had not seen *El Día* either. "I enclose some fiction material." "I acknowledge that I have neglected the section, but I supppose you must have looked after it."[8]

In Rome the Brazilian Minister invited him to dine, and Don Pepe was going to see Roque Sáenz Peña (the official candidate and assured next president of Argentina) to find out what Sáenz Peña "thinks about our international question with Argentina." Batlle authorized Arena to speak with Williman about expanding the plans for the new Uruguayan Legislative Palace, which must be "a building for several centuries."[9] "I have entertained myself here, in the presence of monuments, parks, and gardens, ruminating about what we could do at home."[10]

III

The family was back in Paris, where Manini was waiting. Batlle rented an apartment on the Avenida Marceau and was again criticizing *El Día*, which he wanted expanded to ten full pages, to maintain itself as the biggest newspaper in Montevideo.[11] He also wanted the "chacra" at Piedras Blancas remodeled so that the family could live there when they returned. It was July 1909 and "my trip is going to end in a few months. You know that I came for three years."[12]

Once again, Arena had to dissuade Don Pepe from coming home. He had consulted Batlle's associates. Viera, president of the Senate, believed Batlle should not come back until August 1910, thirteen months off. Senator Pérez Olave thought Batlle should delay returning until after the elections of November 1910 for legislators who would in March 1911 elect the next president. Batlle's presence would "inflame Blanco passions," involve him in political disputes, produce grudges:

> I know that by now your ostracism must be beyond endurance for you and especially for Misia Matilde and the girl; but I believe that sacrifices cannot be made by halves and that if another little excursion up the Nile really becomes advisable for the cause, you will have to make it even if it has to be on a camel. [13]

Manini, who had summered in Switzerland, returned to Paris in September, where he planned to stay until the end of the year before returning to supervise Batlle's presidential campaign. Four years later, Manini recalled a talk with Batlle "one afternoon in Paris, around October or November, 1909." He remembered Batlle telling him:

> After the end of the next presidency I will retire from politics and move to Europe permanently; but I will not influence the election of my successor. I want him to be chosen with complete liberty. Whichever of my friends has the most support and the greatest prestige will be President through his own efforts. [14]

For Manini, just turned 30, it was an unforgettable conversation. Don Pepe was close to a father. Manini's own father, an Italian immigrant, had died when he was four. Manini had come into *El Día* in his teens—and he signed himself Manini y Ríos, like Batlle y Ordoñez, whom he so admired, instead of the modern Manini Ríos.

Manini had ambitions to be president himself some day. During this conversation, Don Pepe had prefaced his announcement that he would not intervene in the choice of his successor with an assurance that Manini's concern that his youth hurt him politically was unwarranted. Don Pepe was placing in Manini's mind the prospect that he would be president much sooner than even he hoped. Manini would do his utmost to elect Batlle president in any event. But when Manini returned home and told others of Batlle's friends, men who had their own future presidential hopes, that Don Pepe had no successor in mind and intended an open succession, proof that Uruguay had reached full democracy, their ambition would reinforce their efforts to elect Batlle in 1911.

IV

Batlle did not reject the advice that he delay his return to Uruguay but he did "reserve the right to embark when the desire becomes strong"[15] and after a month and a half visit in England ("the English race appears to be very vigorous, perhaps because of their dedication to sports—much more vigorous than we consider it from the examples we know"),[16] he sought advice from a source that might give him an answer he preferred. In December 1909 he wrote José Serrato, his ex-Minister of Finance and Williman's 1906 rival for the presidency, and asked whether he should come home to direct his presidential campaign. Batlle had wanted Serrato, whose election to the Senate he had arranged, elected Senate President, but Williman disliked him. Serrato, with no ties to Williman, could give a judgment independent of Williman's preferences. Don Pepe sent the Serrato letter for Arena to deliver, along with a reminder to Arena that he would need to pay for eight first-class and four second-class tickets on the trip back.[17]

Don Pepe, who had refused to talk Uruguayan politics with visiting Uruguayans, now began to. Ex-Nationalist Senator Rodolfo Vellozo, who had been helpful to Batlle after 1904, after seeing Batlle in Paris reported in Montevideo that Batlle was confident of reelection. Batlle wanted this corrected. He wrote Arena:

> I have never said such a thing to anyone, not even to the closest members of my family, nor even to my own self because, in fact, I have never been so certain. I remember that once Vellozo asked me if I thought I would be elected president. Speaking with all sincerity as he had asked me to, I answered that if things continue to go as they have up to now, I thought my candidacy would have great probability of success.[18]

Vellozo came away from his talks with Batlle believing that Batlle had authorized him to tell Nationalists that he would use them in his government.[19] Juan Cat, manager of the English-owned trolley, asked Batlle about his "state of mind" towards the Nationalists:

> and I could tell him, without being untruthful, that I hated no one and that if I aspire again to the presidency of the Republic, it is to put all my ideas and efforts at the service of the well being of the

Republic, which is the well being of all. I also told him that in politics I do not have friends except for those who believe in the same ideas I do, nor adversaries except for those who combat those ideas. In synthesis, that I could not but look more kindly than before on Drs. Lamas and Rodríguez Larreta [Nationalist moderate leaders] and in general on all those who follow their policies now that they have adopted a policy of peace, that is, of action within legal institutions.

What he had not done was promise the Nationalists proportional representation. He had explained to Cat that he favored proportional representation if the constitution was reformed and "the presidential election was turned over to a special college . . ." but not now.[20]

That same day Manini gave the same explanation in a letter to Williman's confidante Amézaga, and in passing remarked that "Batlle expected, from the very beginning, that certain Nationalist politicians with whom Cat would speak would be advised of his way of thinking."[21]

"I would like you to make all the public rectifications this information requires," Batlle wrote Arena. But Manini put it this way: "Batlle would have no objection to these declarations being made public in *El Día*, as long as Williman and our friends consider them opportune." Don Pepe, the political tactician, was preparing his presidential campaign. To his intimates, he offered the prospect that any one of them might be his successor. He let Nationalists think he would return forgetting the past and prepared to welcome them into his government, while simultaneously telling his intimates that the Nationalists should get no concessions. Batlle, the principled man, was prepared to have the Nationalists disabused of their illusions about what they could expect from him. However, he left it up to Williman to decide whether to make a public rectification, and Williman, anxious to avoid Nationalist revolution, was unlikely to disabuse them.

CHAPTER 6

Presidential Nomination

The Conservative Nationalists, convinced that revolution to prevent Batlle's election was foredoomed and could destroy the party, mounted a successful effort in December 1909 to control the party organization.[1] There were rumors of revolution, rumors dismissed by Radical leaders as "preposterous."[2] On December 21, Williman ordered all Jefes Políticos— political heads of each department, appointed by the President—to arrest and send to Montevideo, "a small group of hot heads belonging to the Nationalist party . . . who have been propagandizing for a revolution which was to break out very shortly."[3]

By Christmas Day—the rumored date of revolution—all was quiet. The government announced that the emergency was over and began releasing the remaining prisoners. That day the Nationalist Electoral Congress convoked to elect a new Directorio which would decide whether the Nationalists participated in the 1910 elections began its sessions. Those advocating a coalition with the Radicals were easily defeated. Alfredo Vásquez Acevedo, another of the small group of cautious, business-oriented Nationalists who had been running the party since the caudillo Saravia's death in the War of 1904, accepted the Directorio presidency. Vásquez Acevedo, a distinguished educator and jurist who was lawyer for the Uruguay Central Railroad, recorded for his personal archive that he had accepted reluctantly, "to stop revolutionary tendencies."[4] On New Year's Eve the new Directorio issued its first manifesto: "The National Party in the present circumstances is pacifist and oppositionist. It finds unacceptable the government's policy denying coparticipation to our community, which represents half the voters of the Republic."[5]

II

The event of the New Year was the arrival in Montevideo of Dr. Roque Sáenz Peña, the next President of Argentina, sent by Argentine President Figueroa Alcorta to conclude a protocol settling the Río de la Plata jurisdiction controversy. On January 10, 1910, the document was signed with full diplomatic pomp. The incidents that had caused the trouble were "insubsistentes"—groundless. Any future differences would be resolved "with the same spirit of cordiality and harmony that have always existed between both countries." The basic issue of where the boundary line lay between the two nations was left open, but that Argentina was formally ending the controversy and that the next president of Argentina had been entrusted to negotiate the settlement made for a tremendous feeling of triumph in Montevideo.[6]

It was public knowledge that Ex-Foreign Minister Zeballos of Argentina had been meeting with Radical Nationalist leaders in Buenos Aires; and the Sáenz Peña mission seemed to be Argentine President Figueroa Alcorta's signal that his government was disavowing Zeballos.

The Radicals refused to submit. In mid-January a sensational rumor spread through Montevideo that 4,000 or 5,000 Argentine troops would attack the capital in combination with a Nationalist uprising in the interior.[7] In the department of Treinta y Tres, Nationalists were in arms. Williman mobilized the army. The Directorio urged its supporters to remain calm. The single rebel band in operation was captured without bloodshed on January 18, but alarms did not end.[8]

The Radical Nationalists set up a War Directorio in Buenos Aires and several men of substance were in it. Even more important, an Argentine tender, the *Piaggio*, had left Buenos Aires loaded with arms for Nationalist groups waiting in the Argentine littoral to invade Uruguay. When Uruguayan navy ships attempted to intercept the *Piaggio*, two Argentine warships interceded. Their captains insisted that the *Piaggio* was an Argentine ship that had left one Argentine port and was heading for another. Montevideo insiders were sure the Argentine cabinet Ministers of Army and Navy, still sympathetic with Zeballos' program of confrontation with Brazil, were cooperating with Radical plans. Finally, the *Piaggio*, escorted by the Argentine warships and followed by the Uruguayans, docked at the Argentine river port of Concepción del Uruguay, almost in sight of Paysandú, the Uruguayan city across the river. Waiting in Concepción del Uruguay for the arms was Carmelo Cabrera, one of Saravia's closest lieutenants, leading a group of Uruguayan and Argentine recruits.

Cabrera, realizing that he would not get the arms peacefully, attacked the garrison at Concepción del Uruguay, seized two Argentine vessels, but could not reach the *Piaggio*. There were dead and wounded. Williman, leaving diplomatic formalities aside, telegraphed President Figueroa Alcorta directly, complained of complicity by Argentine officials, and asked him to intervene. Figueroa Alcorta answered that he had already sent reinforcements to Concepción del Uruguay. The revolutionaries fled the city and started to disband. Cabrera, disheartened, was reported to have said he had been betrayed by the Argentines, that he "never would have gathered all these forces if the Argentine government had not planned to overthrow Dr. Williman, influenced as he is by the government of Brazil, in order to put my party, which is free of such ties, into power."[9]

Williman explained, in a triumphant letter to Batlle, "if those imbeciles had dared to move out of Concepción they would all have ended at the bottom of the river. Their plan was preposterous and so absurd that at one time I intended to appear to leave the way open for them, but I realized it would result in a hecatomb. Undoubtedly it would have been an action that would have settled with them for some years, but I felt it was too great an atrocity. As you can imagine, I don't expect thanks from them." Williman sent a special envoy to Argentina, who got complete cooperation on his requests to snuff out the remaining revolutionary organization. On February 11 the Radical War Directorio announced its dissolution, for reasons it felt inopportune to discuss.[10]

III

Don Pepe's reaction on reading in Paris newspapers of the *Piaggio*'s movements was to leave for Uruguay immediately and by himself.[11]

10. Batlle reading newspapers, Paris, 1910.

Then a reassuring coded cablegram from Viera, which had been agreed upon for such situations, arrived, and Don Pepe decided that his departure was not necessary. Arena and Manini—Manini had just returned from Europe—doubtless fearing that Batlle would take it upon himself to return, simply refrained from writing until everything was over; and Don Pepe, hungry for information, had to rely on the slowly arriving Montevideo newspapers. His evaluation was entirely positive. The government's measures had all been well taken. Beyond that:

> I believe that what has happened will have very beneficial projections. It will force everyone, even the most obstinate, to recognize that half a dozen men, men without ideas, completely ignorant of the aspirations and necessities of the nation, cannot pick up rifles because they want to break the peace. For the nation's peace to be broken either great causes and deep reasons are necessary, none of which exist, or a state of national disorganization which happily no longer exists.[12]

IV

Batlle had been out of the country for three years; those in Montevideo still expected more revolutions. In February 1910 an anonymous manifesto directed at "banking, industry and commerce," started circulating. The way to prevent revolution and avoid devastating the economy was to assure potential revolutionaries that the next president of the Republic would be "a pledge of concord." The citizen, name unmentioned, whose candidacy was "the banner of war," must give up his candidacy, voluntarily or "compulsorily." Williman must intervene "legally" against this candidate. The public and the legislators who would vote the next president of the Republic must support "a statesman who is sufficiently talented to reconcile the Uruguayan family, who is capable of glorifying the name of our country, who is capable of making it strong and respected beyond our frontiers."[13]

This statesman was, of course, Foreign Minister Bachini. His public prestige had peaked with the signing of the Plata settlement. Indeed, he claimed later that Sáenz Peña, after signing for Argentina, visited him at his home, told him that he, Sáenz Peña, was convinced public opinion was in favor of Bachini's candidacy for President of the

Republic, and asked Bachini's permission to talk with Williman about it.[14] It was time for Bachini to make a long-postponed visit to Europe to talk with his old friend Don Pepe Batlle. He took leave of absence from his post, was given an honorific diplomatic mission by Williman to justify the trip, and departed on February 13 with the enthusiastic blessing of the Directorio newspaper, which described his ministry as "full of patriotic inspiration."[15]

Manini now broke the silence he had maintained during the January revolution and wrote Don Pepe a long letter, his first since returning from Europe. Relations between Williman and Bachini had cooled because Bachini had put himself at the center during the ceremonies marking settlement of the Río de la Plata jurisdiction of the waters controversy and because Bachini had attempted to act as intermediary with the War Directorio during the January revolution. Williman's confidante Amézaga, invoking Williman's name, had asked Manini to write Batlle "and warn you—given Bachini's custom of disfiguring the truth—not to believe that Williman is involved in any way in the political combinations Bachini may propose to you . . . that he [Williman] has discussed nothing and wants to discuss nothing about internal politics with Bachini."[16]

Manini was not worried about Bachini any more, but he had hit hard at the anti-Batlle manifesto circulating among business groups. *El Día* attacked it for advancing the fraudulent doctrine that a popular candidate should resign if he was opposed by even "the most infinitesimal of minorities," and it then set the Batllista campaign line. For a candidate to give up because of the "menace of subversion,"

> would be something more than civic cowardice, much more than a personal sacrifice. It would be abandoning the cause of institutional government, it would be treason to the well being of public safety. It would be a shameful precedent of political subversion which would forever in the future allow brazen violence to supplant the peaceful and constitutional transfer of the power of the Presidency.[17]

V

Serrato, Batlle's ex-Finance Minister and Williman's bête noir, responded to Batlle's December letter asking when he should return with the answer Batlle wanted. In a carefully reasoned response, Serrato, who expected a Nationalist revolution to prevent the November elections from taking place, advised: "You should be in the country a month or two before the [November] general elections unless unexpected events make you speed up your return."[18] Don Pepe twice wrote Arena asking for funds for the return trip. "I want to be ready to leave in July on the day which seems best to me."[19]

The Batlle family spent March and April 1910 touring Spain. There were Uruguayan consulates in Spain, and direct contact with home should the situation suddenly worsen. Madrid was a beautiful city, but "it is hard to explain how the wealthy can promenade in their shining carriages in the midst of so much misery." In Seville, "I watched a bullfight which made me even more of an enemy of bullfights than before, if that is possible." Generally, "the opinion I had of Spain has improved. I now believe it capable of returning to a major place in Europe. But first of all its politics will have to be completely revolutionized."[20]

In May, near Sitges, from which his grandfather had left for the Banda Oriental in 1800, Don Pepe received a letter from Williman recounting the events of January. Batlle answered immediately, congratulating him on his handling of the revolution, saying "not a single measure was badly taken." Williman's desire to avoid bloodshed was "as it should be." "Our adversaries are lucky to find themselves facing men who don't become blinded by passion and want to save their adversaries' blood as well as the blood of their own followers." Don Pepe himself had done the same thing at the end of the War of 1904.

"I believe this will be the last alteration of order for many years." Don Pepe left implicit the conclusion he hoped Williman would draw: there must be no concessions to Nationalists. Instead he promised to give Williman, who was planning a European trip at the end of his administration, advice on how to avoid unnecessary expenses and on what to see in Europe, "from which we still have so much to take, and which, if we work with ardor and faith some day we will, perhaps, surpass in many things, since it is easier to straighten out a young and tender tree than an old and stiff one."[21]

Williman, by now, was clearly supporting Batlle's reelection. He admired Batlle, was grateful to Batlle for making him President; besides, to oppose Batlle, whose reelection was so popular with Colorados, would produce an enormous crisis during which Williman would likely be on the losing side. He wrote Batlle that "everything will come out as we want it to."[22] But Williman was still adamant that Batlle stay in Europe and that the official opening of Batlle's Presidential campaign be delayed. That way he could govern in peace as long as possible and could, as he explained to Manini, repeating the phrase several times, "prepare himself to be able, well armed and well organized, to resist the worst of eventualities."[23]

VI

To ensure that revolution would be quickly put down, Williman further strengthened the army, adding artillery units and increasing the size of the infantry regiments. But Williman wanted to avoid revolution and was assisting the campaign against revolution undertaken by *El Siglo*, the newspaper which appealed to businessmen and was the official organ of a rancher's organization. A revolutionary army would be officered in considerable part by Nationalist ranchers who would bring their men with them.[24] The editor of *El Siglo*, Juan Andrés Ramírez, a member of the distinguished Ramírez family whose head, José Pedro Ramírez, Batlle blamed for the War of 1904, realized that there was no real alternative to Batlle for 1911 and told first Manini, then Williman, that it would strengthen the *El Siglo* peace campaign if Batlle would commit himself, either publicly or privately, on several points. Williman suggested that Ramírez prepare a memorandum which Williman would forward to Batlle. Ramírez then presented an eight-point, ten-clause program for Batlle's endorsement. Some points were ones Manini had told Ramírez that Batlle favored: proportional representation; constitutional reform, taking the election of President of the Republic from the legislature; no extension of the presidential term or reelection; strengthening of the legislature and of cabinet ministers. Others were Ramírez' own; delay of Church-State separation and labor legislation, except on hours and working conditions, until after the 1914 legislature was elected by proportional representation, and a declaration that the government would use competent men regardless of party.[25]

Williman called together Manini, Arena, Viera, and Williman's confidante Amézaga. Arena reconstructed Williman's conversation for Don Pepe.

> For some time I have been working on Ramírez to win him for our cause. . . . It appears to me that now we have him. . . .
> . . . What seems to me undeniable is that it would be convenient if Batlle could satisfy the greater part of Ramírez' pretensions, because the opinion of *El Siglo* can considerably influence conservative opinion and the interior of the country—where, in parenthesis, I am told that the newspaper's articles against war are making a deep impact.[26]

Arena was entrusted to send the memorandum, forgot to enclose it in his covering letter to Batlle, and had to send a second letter. Arena's oversight quite likely had a psychological explanation, since he knew how Don Pepe felt about the Ramírez family. Nevertheless, Arena endorsed the idea, even though he was sure Batlle would disagree with the religious and labor points, because Ramírez' support was extremely valuable. His articles against subversion "I believe, as do many others, are producing a sensation."

VII

Simultaneously, under Directorio auspices, a special Nationalist Civic Propaganda Committee made up of some able young party activists organized a campaign to get Nationalists to register to vote during the March–April 1910 registration period. To excite the party mass, the Committee protested "against anti-democratic dogmas launched by the circle which wants to impose the candidacy of señor Batlle y Ordoñez, as a challenge to the peace of the nation."[27] In spite of the committee, in spite of assurances that even if they registered they could later decide not to vote, very few new Nationalist voters bothered to register.

Nationalist voters were apathetic, and Nationalist military officers once more were meeting in Buenos Aires. Stories circulated of a new revolution scheduled to begin shortly before the November elections, to force their cancellation and prevent Batlle's election. From Buenos Aires, Basilio Muñoz, Radical military chief, insisted that "our attitude will be one of waiting. The forthcoming change of governments and many other circumstances force us to do this."[28] The Directorio acceded to new attempts at reconciliation with the Radicals, while *El Siglo* complained that the Nationalist leadership was attempting to make the party swallow the pill of Batlle's election by coating it with furious attacks on him. Instead this tactic was exciting the party mass to war.[29]

To counteract the danger of war, distinguished members of the conservative classes met on April 20, 1910, at *El Siglo*'s offices, organized the Peace League, and issued an inaugural statement:

> The undersigned, believing that peace is the supreme good of the nation, concerned that patriotism demands subordination of any other consideration of subaltern nature to the maintenance of peace resolve:
>
> To found the Peace League as a permanent organization with the aim of indicating the conviction among governing and governed that the perfection of republican institutions, the aspirations of all Uruguayans, must be entrusted to peaceful and orderly evolution.[30]

All who cared to add their names to those of the signers—Eduardo Acevedo, ex-Rector of the University, José Pedro Ramírez, dean of the conservative classes, José Irureta Goyena, principal rancher's spokesman, and others—could find lists for their signatures at the offices of *El Siglo*, the Stock Exchange, the Chamber of Commerce, the Manufacturers Association, the Asociación Rural, and the Center of Retail Storekeepers.[31]

The Directorio contributed to the peace movement on April 24, when a great barbecue was held on the modern ranch of Nationalist Alejandro Gallinal. Two trains brought a thousand Nationalists from Montevideo and San José; a column of some 2,000 horsemen rode in from Flores to enjoy the barbecue and hear Martín C. Martínez, once Batlle's Finance Minister, now a Nationalist leader, speak for the Directorio. He pleaded with Nationalists to vote. Nationalist legislators would be the only brake on the "personal domination" being forced upon Uruguay by the "oligarchic tutelage" presently controlling the nation. Revolution now would be premature "in a country so scourged by fratricidal war and at a moment in which prosperity, in spite of everything, smiles on it, the 'last resort' should only be considered if aggressive and humiliating intolerance begins to assume intolerable character." Martín C. Martínez concluded:

> It would not be the first time in our history that evils which the evolution of the country probably would have surmounted, or which it would have been possible to combat successfully at the moment when they reached their peak, have been worsened and prolonged by generous but thoughtless rashness. . . .
>
> The time has come to have some confidence in the power of economic interests, whose calming influence can be seen in neighboring and friendly countries. This basic desire for peace, which the whole nation feels, will in the end outweigh narrow and reactionary solutions.[32]

The Peace League spoke for the major economic interest groups in Uruguay—the ranchers, merchants, stock exchange, manufacturers, and shopkeepers. Batlle's candidacy was not their candidacy, but Batlle supported by the Colorado organization and the President of the Republic was not going to be replaced, so between Batlle and war they preferred Batlle. Nationalist revolutionaries were being put on notice: they would not get economic support or political backing. The Directorio's representative, Martín C. Martínez, using socioeconomic analysis—prosperity was too precious to be spoiled by war, economic evolution would eventually sweep away Batlle's kind of intransigent politics—was giving a slightly different version of the Peace League's message: Nationalists, let us hold off revolution until we see whether Batlle's government forces it on us.

VIII

Manini, Arena, Viera, and a few others were meeting regularly with Sursum Corda ("Lift Up Your Hearts" in Catholic liturgy), Manini's nickname for Williman. Batlle had written Senate President Viera, who had been Williman's campaign manager and was the Batllista closest to the President, to clear the presidential campaign's opening date with Williman. The campaign would be organized the way Don Pepe wanted it. Williman, however, did not want it to build up too fast nor seem to be run by Batlle's intimates; a new newspaper, not *El Día*, would be the official campaign organ. Williman was particularly anxious that twelve or fifteen important businessmen be on the committee that would direct the campaign, "because"—Manini explained to Don Pepe—"he wants in this way to destroy the canard that the conservative classes are opposed to your candidacy."[33] But Manini and Viera, worried about whether they could gather a distinguished group of businessmen or what kind of campaign such men would demand, convinced Williman to leave the directing of the campaign to the politicians and have separate committees of commerce and industry, Colorado youth, university students, and the like form in support of Batlle.[34] Williman, now that the Directorio was resigned to seeing Batlle's reelection, finally consented that the campaign could begin.

On May 23, 1910, two days after Batlle's fifty-fourth birthday, the Colorado Senators whose terms were not expiring—and who would therefore vote on March 1, 1911, when the Senators and Deputies meeting in General Assembly would elect the next President of the Republic—called a meeting of the Party's National Commission and Montevideo Commission. After amicable discussion, the participants agreed to organize "a great movement of public opinion in which members of all political parties and all social classes would participate." Those present formed themselves, under Viera's presidency, into "a Committee of Initiatives" and voted to ask the Colorado Executive Committee, in accord with the party charter, to convoke the Colorado Convention to endorse Batlle's presidential candidacy.[35]

The Colorado Executive Committee convoked the Convention to meet in July. Colorado youth quickly organized and proclaimed their "resolute adherence to this already distinguished figure."[36] *El Día* published enthusiastic endorsements by young Colorados, such as Héctor Miranda's:

> Colorado youth can not remain indifferent to the candidacy of Batlle, man-guide and man-symbol. Batlle synthetizes our program, because he is animated by the spirit of youth.
> Batlle is good and he is strong, therefore he is necessary.[37]

The campaign newspaper, *El País*, got all the funds needed to begin publication within a week.[38] *El País* directed itself to the responsible elements in society. Its first issue published a pro-Batlle letter from Uruguay's best-known intellectual, José Enrique Rodó.

His adherence now was significant, and his message was that a mature Batlle would return from Europe cleansed of his political intransigence. "Absence and time have interposed their regenerative influences." Rodó urged Nationalists not to repeat the mistake they had made in 1903 when they refused to vote for Batlle even after his candidacy was assured. As Martín C. Martínez speaking for the Directorio had done, he asked them

> simply to maintain themselves in an attitude of waiting and reserve that has been the concession made so many times to personalities infinitely inferior to his, and in the face of perspectives much more naked of hope.[39]

Lasso de la Vega, a bohemian intellectual and an *El Día* writer whose abilities Batlle greatly admired, had recently urged the formation of a Labor Party to support Batlle. Workers did not recognize "the unbeatable force" they could exert on Uruguay's fragile political machinery if only they would vote. There were 80,000 workers in Montevideo, the total number of registered voters was less than 25,000. Labor leaders, though beaten down by Williman and looking forward to Batlle's return, would not as Anarchists respond. The Centro Internacional de Estudios Sociales, the radical locale closed down by Williman during the railroad strike, resolutely rejected the idea of supporting Batlle. "The workers will not vote. They will not go to the ballot box and leave there their limited independence of the present, their anxiously awaited future liberty. . . . We do not combat a specific person or government, we will always be against The Government, whatever its political color!!"[40]

Labor's response did not trouble the campaign leaders. They already had the votes to elect Batlle. They had won the 1905 and 1907 elections on the platform that the Colorados had defeated the Blancos in war and must defeat them in peace.[41] There was no doubt that they would win in 1910 on the platform "Batlle symbolizes our program." Their problem was to convince the Nationalists to accept his return. Their solution was to set up the "mature Batlle" image; if the Nationalists accepted Batlle's inevitable victory, they would discover that Batlle's political intransigence had been mellowed by Europe into cooperativeness. An Anarchist labor-backed Batlle could backfire politically. Ranchers and business preferred a "mature Batlle" to war; they might feel otherwise about a "radical Batlle."[42]

IX

Don Pepe and his whole family wanted to come home. Williman remained adamant. He called Manini, Arena, Viera, and Amézaga together on May 22, the day before the campaign officially opened, and asked them to write Batlle "in his name":

> I believe decidedly that Batlle should not come back now. Even further: that he should not come back until after the [legislative] elections. Let him stay quietly in the Old World, and let all the enmities that are likely to emerge when men are excluded as candidates for the new Legislature fall on me.

Manini explained Batlle's desire to come before the elections, and his assurances, previously communicated to Williman through Viera, that he would not make any difficulties for Williman over the selection of candidates. Williman had responded that he had no doubts on that score; even so it was to Batlle's "political advantage" to stay away:

> I am absolutely certain that Batlle will be president, he added. All [Colorados] will vote for him. . . . But if Batlle is here for the elections all the aspirants [for legislative seats] will assault him, and he will be blamed for all the aspirants who fail. Others, whom we might oppose, if they are elected will be cool towards him, if they do not openly declare themselves his enemies. To avoid this I prefer to carry all the enmities and angry feelings on my shoulders. On the other hand, if Batlle remains in Europe, everyone will be satisfied with him.[43]

It was left for Viera, the campaign manager—for Batlle now as he had been five years earlier for Williman—to inform Don Pepe of Williman's unstated reasons:

> It is absolutely certain that with you being here, everyone would congregate around you and would naturally leave a vacuum around our friend while he was still President. I can see him in his house almost abandoned, reflecting with bitterness on just what

his lack of strength in the party means.—That would be deeply mortifying—and it would have to be so, because Williman does not have, not by a great deal, the prestige in the party that you do, and by then he will not even retain the prestige of power which will be escaping him. Now, my dear friend, it is in your hands to save Williman, who has behaved so well and who is so obviously with us, from these mortifications. These things must not escape Williman himself, because without mentioning them, he has indicated to me his express desire that you do not return until January.

Viera promised Don Pepe he would send a coded telegram should the slightest danger to his candidacy arise. "If you decide to accommodate Williman and stay in Europe until January, we will circulate the rumor of your imminent return, to throw those who might try an attempt on your life off the track and to calm impatient friends."[44]

For some months now Batlle's intimates, including Williman, had been concerned about assassination—there had been an attempt on his life in 1904. In March, Manini warned that Nationalists or Catholics, more likely the latter, "are capable of ordering you to be sacrificed, using any of the European mafia." In June he began what would be a continuous series of alerts. "Be careful, be very careful . . . things are going so well here that we live trembling thinking that just because no war or political upheaval can stop the triumphal march of your candidacy—implacable enemies desperate in the face of inevitable defeat will turn to a mercenary to eliminate you, first to satisfy their personal hatreds and second to throw us into such confusion that could bring us to a situation analogous to the 21 days [at the end of Herrera y Obes' presidency in 1894, when the legislature was unable to achieve a majority and elect a new President]."[45]

Williman, as Batlle had feared, sponsored a new electoral law reform to give the Nationalists more seats in the Chamber of Deputies and so reinforce the Directorio's willingness to contest the November elections. And, as Batlle had instructed, his followers did not oppose the changes. Williman proposed a sliding scale of vote requirements—in Montevideo the Nationalists could elect deputies if they got one twelfth of the vote—and assurance of seats in the smallest departments. Under Williman's proposal the Nationalists would have got 21 instead of 14 seats in 1907; and now if they overcame their dissensions, they could get as many as 27 of the 89 seats in the Chamber of Deputies.[46]

Rodríguez Larreta, the Directorio's leader in the Chamber, was not satisfied that the reform would give the Nationalists the number of seats Williman predicted. With the present party apathy, if the Radicals ran rival tickets to the Directorio, the Radicals might so split the Nationalist vote that the Directorio's candidates would not even reach the minimum number of votes required to win minority seats in many departments. Williman acknowledged that this was a real problem, but his Minister of Interior, José Espalter, had a favorite solution. For years Espalter had been advocating the adoption of the double simultaneous vote, a system devised by the Belgian constitutionalist Borelly.[47] The double simultaneous vote, cumbersome to describe but simple to operate, would permit the votes for rival Nationalist tickets to be pooled to determine whether the minimum number of votes necessary to elect minority deputies had been reached and then award the seats to the Nationalist ticket which had more votes than the other.[48]

Though for the record he called for proportional representation, Directorio leader Rodríguez Larreta acknowledged on the Chamber floor that the Nationalists had got the best deal possible. Colorado legislators boasted that Uruguay's electoral legislation would now become the most advanced in America and, from some points of view, the world. Manini reminded his listeners that the Colorados were making concessions not to the Nationalists but to the nation— for peace. The handful of Radical Nationalist deputies reserved judgment, and within a week the bill was passed and sent to the Senate; it became law on July 4, 1910.[49]

Assurance that the new law would largely nullify anti-Directorio Nationalist tickets made the Directorio decide to break off negotiations with the Radicals. On June 27 it met, ratified the break, and, even though the November elections were still some months off, voted that the party would contest them.

> We are aware that because of the decided governmental support for the candidacy of señor Batlle y Ordoñez, a candidacy the National Party rejects for multiple and powerful reasons, the enthusiasm of our coreligionaries is going to be limited by their

conviction that their efforts are not likely to contribute to the triumph of a different presidential candidacy, which might assure the advent of a tranquil and encouraging situation.

Even so, the party mass must vote. "In this way we will clearly demonstrate how great is our desire not to be an obstacle to the nation's progress and our desire not to have to go to the extreme and saddening measures which the obstinacy and injustice of our adversary has forced more than once on us."[50]

This tough language, the overt hostility to Batlle, the dangling of "extreme measures" (civil war) in front of the Nationalist party mass provoked the Batllistas. But the Nationalist situation required tough language.[51] Otherwise, the Radicals, with their separate organization intact, might win over the party mass and be the beneficiaries of the new double simultaneous vote. Or they might win the party mass for abstention and negate the lowered requirements to win legislative seats. Or the Radicals might win adherents for war.

XI

The Colorados had been busy screening delegates and preparing the Colorado convention that would nominate Batlle. The abortive January Radical Nationalist revolution had prepared a manifesto that included the charge, "the regime in power oppresses our ranching industry, grinds it down with oppressive taxes, and menaces it with laws of a Socialist cast to take real property out of private hands." Convention organizers, who knew that they had failed to get enough business support to organize the planned pro-Batlle committee of businessmen, made a special effort to name Colorado ranchers as Convention delegates. On the eve of the Convention, *El Día*, as it had done before the last convention in 1907, noted that among the delegates there were "a great number of ranchers, who by themselves are enough to demonstrate the sympathies and prestige with which the name of the candidate is surrounded."[52]

On July 3, the Salon of the Sociedad Francesa was decked with Colorado banners. Each delegate received a portrait of Batlle done by the *El Día* cartoonist. Ricardo Areco, editor of the campaign newspaper, moved that the Convention approve Batlle's candidacy by a standing vote. Amidst great applause, every single delegate arose. Then the previously designated orators spoke. Baltasar Brum, a young man who was making a name for himself in Viera's department of Salto, representing Colorado youth, was especially successful. "Batlle is the living program of the Colorado Party. His name is simultaneously symbol and banner. Let us adopt that symbol and wave that banner!" A committee made up of the presidents of all the Colorado departmental organizations was formed to visit Williman "in homage" of his successful administration. To Batlle, the Convention dispatched this cable: "The National Convention of the Colorado Party, in solemn session, proclaimed you candidate for the future presidency of the Republic."[53] Viera sent Don Pepe a private, one-word cable: "Abrázolo" ("I embrace you").[54]

All through June, returning to Paris from Spain by way of Italy, Batlle had expected to leave for Montevideo immediately after arriving in Paris. He had told his wife and children. His nephews, at school in Switzerland, were packed. But in Paris were the letters advising him that Williman wanted him to stay away, and instead of going home, he installed his family on the Champs Élysées.

Bachini was waiting in Paris. He had warned the new Uruguayan Minister to France, Rafael Di Miero—Don Pepe's friend who could be expected to relay any conversations—that the only way to head off "a formidable revolution" was to eliminate Batlle's candidacy.[55] Bachini had a plan which required Batlle to make major concessions to the Nationalists as the condition for peaceful reelection.[56] Bachini, however, was no longer a serious threat, and Batlle, already nominated by the Colorado Party, simply refused to be drawn in. When Bachini, a famous conversationalist, finally was invited to lunch, Don Pepe said he was looking forward to a delightful afternoon but imposed one condition: "We cannot talk any politics."[57]

The memorandum from Juan Andrés Ramírez, editor of El Siglo, was a much more serious matter. Matilde had written their sons that Pepe had been bothered all the way back from Spain by the "conditions from the Buenos Aires pipsqueak" (Ramírez had been born in Buenos Aires). Ramírez had an emissary in Paris, to receive Batlle's reply.[58] The memorandum was virtually endorsed by Williman. Manini and Arena wanted Batlle to accept. Manini had just written, "Ramírez is panting to declare himself an overt Batllista. He only awaits your declarations, which will serve him as a pretext more than a reason."[59] *El Siglo*'s propaganda against war, its assurance that a wiser Batlle would return from Europe, that "Batlle will speak" to Uruguay from Europe and demonstrate new statesmanship—all would continue to be enormously useful in cutting off support for any Radical Nationalist attempt at war.

Don Pepe didn't see it that way. He didn't trust *El Siglo*, he didn't trust the whole Ramírez family—a distrust which dated from the days José Pedro Ramírez had helped ruin his father Lorenzo Batlle's presidency. What Juan Andrés Ramírez wanted was not Batlle but "the ideal candidate," an "obsession" of Ramírez' "family fanaticism" which had caused much blood to flow in Uruguay already. Instead of talking about revolution, revolution should be dismissed as impossible. Furthermore, the Peace League, which spoke for ranchers and businessmen, was dangerous. To assure peace, it would demand concessions from Batlle, as similar organizations did before and during the War of 1904:

> *El Día* and *El Siglo* have demonstrated that I should not give up my candidacy because of the menace of war. All right, should I give up my ideas because of this menace? But are not my ideas my candidacy? . . .
>
> Do you think, my dear friends Arena and Manini, that for the pleasure of strutting as President I am going to forget the sorrows the country suffered during the last war, or forget those who fell forever in defense of a cause I deem to be of the highest good and destroy the program that was consecrated with so much blood?[60]

When the Ramírez memorandum reached him at the end of May in Marseilles, Don Pepe decided to write directly to Williman. He began a long letter, then decided to hold it and speak to Williman when he returned to Montevideo. Williman's request that he stay in Europe required that Don Pepe send the letter. Dated July 6, 1910, Batlle told Williman in it that as a result of Williman's request, he was going "to reside here several more months and wait here while the events preparatory to the presidential election are completed." But Batlle refused to cooperate with Ramírez. Rather than have misinterpretations result through use of intermediaries, he was telling Williman directly of the "reasons which decide me not to contract any agreement at all, however vague, with that citizen."

Don Pepe went through Ramírez' memorandum point by point. Batlle favored constitutional reform and proportional representation, but not proportional representation for a constitutional convention as Ramírez did. Batlle also could not accept Ramírez' desire that he bring the Nationalists into his government, or the Ramírez request that Batlle's government postpone passage of labor and social legislation until its last year, when it would be too late for enactment. Batlle, in turn, did not believe Ramírez would back him if an alternative emerged.

> But even supposing that his disposition was the very best . . . it would be extremely disagreeable and troublesome for me to be tied to Ramírez by a kind of political pact which I had accepted in the interest of having his propaganda favor me.
>
> Whatever my answer would be it would mean a solemn obligation on my part to do or not to do certain things, and I would be obligated not to the country, not to my party, not even to an opposition party, but to Ramírez for its strict compliance.

Batlle insisted on full freedom of action for himself: "I understand that the clearest bases of my program as candidate are those that can be deduced from my previous government. Therefore, I could only answer this way: my future conduct will be determined by my past conduct." This was far from the "mature Batlle" image which the official Batlle for President campaign was projecting in Uruguay.

Having cleared the board of Ramírez, Don Pepe went on to the subject of how he was going to be elected, "now that I am not going to have any intervention in it." Batlle, who was more experienced in politics than Williman or any of his own confidantes, was reluctant to accept their certainty of his presidential victory. Some months earlier, Batlle's old friend Eduardo Iglesias wrote that he feared Williman would want all current Colorado deputies reelected. This would mean some twenty hostile Colorados in addition to perhaps thirty Nationalist legislators. Iglesias warned that "by neglect" a victory might be put into the opposition's hands.[61] Without telling Williman whom to elect deputy, Batlle warned him that the dangerous time would come after the legislative election, "when everyone will be able to show his true face without danger of being excluded from candidacy." Then the Nationalists might pull off "a new chirinada [guerrilla attack], not in the expectation of winning or even lasting more than a week," but to justify the splitting away of anti-Batlle Colorado legislators:

I consider that if my candidacy is not proclaimed by an absolute majority of electors [legislators] in the four or five days following the general elections [of November 1910], the environment will become heated, all means of combat, legitimate and illegitimate, will be used against my candidacy, and it will be extremely difficult or impossible to proclaim it later. . . .

Do not look at these appraisals as the daughters of fear of losing something that I greatly desire. I make them with complete calm as far as I am personally concerned, without any alarm of a personal character, with my sights fixed on the interests of the country, interests which concern me just as much today as they did in the days when my person was far from having any important political role. [Williman had been with Batlle in those days.] I think that our group, our political outlook, so closely tied to the good cause, runs the risk, though not imminently, of suffering a profound reversal, which in all probability would modify the orientation of national politics, and I can do no less than communicate my alarm to you, since you can powerfully influence the ending or reducing of this danger.[62]

Ramírez' emissary, Serapio del Castillo, had visited Batlle the day before to get his response to Ramírez' memorandum. Don Pepe reported to Williman: "I told him that I do not consider it opportune to make declarations, and I have limited myself to talking with him in generalities." But Serapio del Castillo did not come away from his meeting with Batlle empty handed. On July 31, 1910, *El Siglo*, under the headline "Batlle and His Ideas," printed an interview with Batlle signed "The Correspondent." "The Correspondent," *El Siglo* explained, was an Uruguayan living in Paris who had been asked to interview Batlle, and this was the first interview Batlle had granted a Montevideo newspaper. "The Correspondent" reported that, contrary to some Montevideo rumors, Batlle was in excellent health, though somewhat older in appearance.

Batlle's views, as relayed by "The Correspondent," were not direct quotes. Batlle wanted "to widen the basis of politics," and through constitutional reform "extend the influence of the Legislature and invigorate the ministerial institution." The President should not be elected by the legislature, and the legislature to be elected in 1913 should be elected by proportional representation. Answering the rumors that Batlle planned a violent campaign against large landowners, "The Correspondent" reported that "Batlle does not recognize the existence of an agrarian problem which calls urgently for government attention." Even on labor, where Batlle favored legislation, "he recognized nevertheless that the labor problem in our country does not have the same character or the same gravity it has in European countries." "The Correspondent" concluded with his hope that this sampling of Batlle's views—Batlle was working on the platform he would submit to the Colorado convention—"will be favorably received by public opinion, will contribute to moderating passions and weakening hatreds, and will facilitate the effort towards peace in which *El Siglo* is involved."[63]

El Siglo, though it felt obliged to await Batlle's manifesto to the Colorado convention, judged the interview "highly promising for patriotism."[64] And well it might. Much of the interview coincided with the Ramírez memorandum; nothing opposed it. On land and labor Batlle sounded like a ranching and business spokesman. Of course the only direct quote was not very revealing: "'I was in Switzerland for three months,' Batlle says, 'and I found many people there who do not know the name of the President of the Confederation.'"[65] Still, *El Siglo* readers and its editor could assume that the promised "mature Batlle" would return from Europe.

Nationalists were being told that a conciliatory Batlle was coming; business and ranchers were being told that Batlle's radicalism had been calmed by Europe. Don Pepe himself, though, was refusing to make any concessions whatever on his freedom of action as President. He would pick up in 1911 where he had left off in 1907; he would make Uruguay a model country. He was privately telling this to people who, he believed, should know it. But he was also allowing the public "mature Batlle" campaign to go on. Indeed, by letting "The Correspondent" publish "generalities" as an interview which came out the way *El Siglo* wanted it to, Don Pepe was consciously contributing to the "mature Batlle" image.

CHAPTER 7

Revolutionary Reaction

Batlle's nomination, expected though it was, coated with the "mature Batlle" image though it was, strengthened prowar Radical Nationalist sentiments. To prevent themselves from being outflanked, the Nationalist leadership, the Directorio, which had ordered the party to contest the November elections, heated up its own response to events. The Directorio newspaper published stories that Batlle was dying, was coming home immediately because his campaign was in trouble, or—even though professing disdain for the idea—was dangerously close to assassination. For the first time there was overt Nationalist hostility to Williman, "a mediocrity" whose refusal to stop Batlle was comparable to Pontius Pilate's refusal to save Christ.[1] Even Williman's July circular to all departmental *Jefes Políticos*, barring them and all subordinate policemen from joining political clubs or taking any part in party politics, in direct opposition to Batlle's "moral influence" doctrine, was dismissed as merely a paper restriction on Colorado police activities.[2] For the first time, the Nationalists proposed their own presidential solution: not Batlle, but a Batllista—the still absent Foreign Minister Bachini?—since without Batlle the officialist machine would soon break down into less objectionable components.[3]

To sound out the effect of Batlle's nomination, the Directorio sent on July 15, 1910, a confidential questionnaire on their electoral situation to the departmental organizations.[4] The responses were discouraging. For example, Eduardo Moreno, the Colonia leader, was horrified at Batlle's return: "apart from the danger entailed by the socialist and revolutionary ideas of which he boasts, we can not forget his angry and vengeful conduct towards us after his accidental victory [in 1904]: he stripped us of everything, he humiliated us . . . to go to the polls, disunited and with the prospect of Sr. Batlle and his band of ragamuffins in the government, exposes us to total defeat."[5]

On July 30, three weeks after Batlle's nomination, the Directorio resigned. A new Directorio of conciliation, containing four Radicals, was elected; the Directorio newspaper proclaimed the Conservative/Radical split ended, but the separate Radical organization continued. The new Directorio, early in September, reaffirmed the decision that the party would contest the elections: "The sensible and prudent conduct of the National Party must bear fruit; and if, unfortunately, it does not, nobody will be able to blame the National Party for the evils which then take over the Republic."[6] This message by newly reelected Directorio President Vásquez Acevedo was aimed at Batlle. Nationalists did not want to vote, knowing Batlle would be the victor, but their leaders were requiring them to. Unless Batlle, once in office, allowed Nationalist pride to be restored by bringing Nationalists to the government, Nationalists would repudiate these leaders and Uruguay once again would be convulsed by civil war.

II

With the Directorio prepared to accept Batlle's reelection and await its consequences, the prospect that some frustrated group would try to prevent his return by assassinating him had reached the stage of public speculation in the newspapers. Don Pepe, though, considered himself safe, at least for as long as he remained in Europe. "For some time now my return has been announced as imminent and it is easier for them to await my return."[7]

The Champs Élysées in the summer was not a place for macabre thoughts. Don Pepe was enjoying Paris and was busy with plans for renovating his house and land at Piedras Blancas outside Montevideo, where the family would live. He was a little apologetic about the grandiosity of the plans for the main part of the house. He told Arena on August 10: "The only inconvenience I see is that if they are attributed to improvements to be made for the presidency, I will look a little ridiculous if someone else emerges as President. For that reason, I am in no hurry for this part of the work to begin."[8]

Don Pepe simply was not convinced by Montevideo's confidence. He instructed Viera to contest every election with the Nationalists, to win both majority and minority seats in every department, even in Saravia's Cerro Largo. He wrote Williman, the final arbiter of candidacies, and this time listed the names of present Colorado deputies whose allegiance he distrusted. Manini, in turn, was still worried about assassination. "The way things are going, the only way of avoiding your presidency is to eliminate you."[9]

Williman, by now Batlle's unofficial campaign manager, reassured Don Pepe: "in this struggle more than a man, a whole system, is at stake, and any other candidate besides you would be a disaster for the country." Batlle's concern that there would be twenty potentially hostile Colorado votes could be put to rest. His concern that the Nationalists would elect thirty deputies was unfounded. In their present divided state, with strong abstentionist currents, Williman believed the Nationalists would win only twenty to twenty-five seats. Even so, Batlle's plan to have the Colorado deputies pledge to vote him president immediately after the elections would be carried out.

In a postscript Williman informed Batlle that he would be taking over the government with a budget surplus even larger than the one he had bequeathed to Williman in 1907. The surplus was a great temptation to the legislators who wanted to spend it. "I believe it necessary that you indicate to your friends the necessity that they accompany me."[10] This last was Williman's acknowledgment of why he had wanted Don Pepe to stay away so long.

III

Bachini, who had absented himself all through the Colorado nominating procedures, was back in Uruguay. Before leaving Europe he had been careful to bid Batlle a friendly goodby. On returning to Montevideo he insisted, publicly and privately, that talk of his candidacy was "pure fantasy"; he supported Batlle.[11] Manini, who had visited him on arrival, also reported that Bachini was saying that Batlle had told him he was returning immediately. Manini felt this piece of false information very helpful, since it would confuse the timing of assassination plots.[12]

The formal election campaign continued. Posters with Batlle's picture—Don Pepe's sense of propriety had prevented him from responding to a request for a new photo—were all over Montevideo. A new Hymn to Batlle, with the chant BAH-JE, BAH-JE, BAH-JE, now opened party meetings. On September 27, Batlle's presidential program was published. He had completed and dated it on August 10, the same day he wrote Arena he did not want the improvements on the main part of the house at Piedras Blancas begun too soon.

Batlle had been reluctant to send a program, which had been requested by the campaign committee. He had complained to Manini, "my state of mind does not permit me, except with great effort, to think here in an environment so different from our own about things I will have to repeat over there about my way of thinking in politics." This complaint was strange, since Don Pepe had been thinking about these things from the day he left and had just written Williman a long letter on Uruguayan politics. Don Pepe advanced a more convincing objection. He was sure Manini was behind the request and suggested it was designed to satisfy Juan Andrés Ramírez of *El Siglo* (Williman was in the process of writing Batlle "As you must have expected, I have not thought of showing your letter to Juan Andrés Ramírez, who is still waiting for your declarations"). "It is necessary that you know that I consider him an adversary and that he surely will be because I will give him motives if necessary."[13] Nevertheless, since a formal request had been made, Batlle had written his program, taking the best part of a month to compose it. And when it was finished, he was sufficiently satisfied with it to arrange for excerpts to be published in French and English newspapers.[14] On Williman's instructions, Batlle's program was published simultaneously as an extra in *El Siglo* and the official campaign newspaper, *El País*, on September 27. *El Día* was not allowed to print his program until the next day.

The program was Batlle's first campaign statement, and he faced the problem of reconciling his refusal to make any political concessions with the "mature Batlle" campaign being carried out on his behalf.

I believe that since I have already exercised the Presidency of the Republic during a recent period of government, the National Colorado Convention by again proclaiming my candidacy has tacitly approved my conduct in government, and I promise that if elected again I will continue to act along the same principal lines, since the ideas and aspirations which then inspired my conduct constitute the general program of government which I now present.

He was making public what he had been saying privately, that he would pick up in 1911 where he had left off in 1907, something totally at variance with his campaign image. He quickly followed this declaration, though, "with some ratifications and amplifications." While he considered "the theory of coparticipation,[15] according to which the cabinet should be made up in part of men whose opinions and political tendencies are contrary to those of the Executive Power" to be "erroneous" because policymakers had to have common views, "nevertheless, below the level of policymakers there are many areas untouched by the disagreements and opposition of political life in which the assistance of all can be asked for and offered with great advantage to the nation." So Nationalists would go to the government, though not as policymakers.

Coparticipation was a mistaken medicine for Uruguay's real political disease, "the excessive influence which the Executive Power exercises in every administration without violating the law."

The remedy consists in strengthening the Legislative Power by opening it to all the ideas which have any prestige in the country, through the means of proportional representation. To do this it will be necessary to increase considerably the number of legislators and to perfect the operation of the Public Powers, better determining their relations and accentuating the control that the Legislative Power should exercise in respect to the Executive—this last task would correspond to the Assembly which reforms the Constitution. Under these conditions the leader of a parliamentary group would have much greater importance, backed by his party and depending only on it, even though he was in the minority, than he could by being elevated to a cabinet ministry by the decision of a head of government designated by the opposition, before whose will he would have to bend in order to keep his position. Parliamentary debates would then have great resonance.

Proportional representation was a traditional Nationalist aspiration. And though Batlle was careful to note that proportional representation could not come until constitutional reform, which was to take place during his government, provided for "the direct election of President of the Republic," this vision of an Uruguayan parliament with party blocks and floor leaders would mean a greater influence for the political opposition; it also suggested that Batlle had indeed undergone some European mellowing:

> Along with revindications of the political parties, I will have to consider those, no less just or respectable, of the working classes. They demand the right to life, to health, to liberty, rights frequently wounded and destroyed by the system of production, and which have to constitute the elementary rights of a civilized society. They ask only a little more rest from their arduous labors and some greater participation in the enjoyment of the wealth they produce, using as their only weapon abstention from work, at the expense of their own misery, when they have lost all hope of improvement.

Batlle noted that he was reproducing the arguments he had advanced in his eight-hour day bill. "I will insist that the bill be approved and I will propose others on working conditions, protection of children, help for invalids, retirement of the aged."

Don Pepe's labor program was stronger than anything that might be anticipated from "The Correspondent's" *El Siglo* interview, but he gave only a glimmering of his plans to control foreign capital. The state should form a merchant marine that would stop the drain of funds to foreign shipping companies and open a new source of national income.[16] Further, Uruguay had reached the stage where the government could undertake "great public works" by itself, instead of hiring "exotic companies." There was much emphasis in the program on education and culture,[17] though critics felt it was largely padding. To ranching and farming, "the principal source of our production," Batlle promised "all my interest." Consistent with his longtime views he promised continued protection of industry, especially industries which used Uruguayan raw materials.[18]

Ramírez of *El Siglo* liked Batlle's program. *El Siglo*, with its influence on the conservative classes and ranchers, using Batlle's language of diseases and remedies, concluded that "Señor Batlle y Ordoñez' program mixes into a medicine bottle labeled 'one party government' and still containing a few drops of it, a strong dosage of coparticipation." Proportional representation would revolutionize Uruguayan politics, bringing in new groups and weakening the Executive by forcing it to seek parliamentary support. Capital need not fear Batlle or his labor program, which though its details were yet to be made known, fit the general lines of Williman's.[19]

Even Arena considered the program conciliatory. "The political part in which you have had the enormous skill not to weaken your theories of government a millimeter and still open new horizons of hope to the opposition is impeccable." Arena, in the midst of supervising the improvements at Piedras Blancas, reported that the program's reception was a "complete success."[20]

III

Whatever *El Siglo* said, Batlle's program distressed the Nationalists. It rejected coparticipation, the sharing of government between Colorados and Blancos; it made Batlle's first administration, when Blancos were treated as outcasts, the standard for his second. On September 30, 1910 the Directorio met, had a long discussion about "the terrible impression" Batlle's program had produced, and decided again to poll the departmental organizations of the interior on their electoral prospects.[21] The eighteen answers came back quickly. Seven departments were absolutely hopeless. Nationalists would not vote; the party would not be able even to win the minority seats. In Treinta y Tres, Nationalists were talking of emigrating if Batlle returned. In Río Negro the situation was so disheartening that the President of the Departmental Commission ended his report with his resignation. In Canelones, Batlle's program, "which does not have a word of forgetfulness or concord," had removed what little Nationalist enthusiasm still existed, and the party would be lucky to win one seat. Six departments had some chance of reaching the votes necessary to win minority seats, and only in Saravia's Cerro Largo was there real confidence: "the triumph of the party is assured."[22]

On October 10, the Directorio met to consider the reports. Two Radical members had not waited and had already resigned. The Directorio nevertheless ratified the decision that the party would go to the polls. Martín C. Martínez wrote the explanatory manifesto, which pointed out a disagreeable truth to Radicals who advocated Nationalist abstention from the elections:

> Unless extraordinary developments occur, and nothing indicates that they will for some time, whenever the National Party decides to get out of the quicksand into which you want to condemn it, it would have to accept the role of minority in Parliament.[23]

Two days later the last two Radicals resigned from the Directorio.

IV

The Directorio continued its electoral preparations. On October 21 Manini wrote Batlle: "There is almost no political news. . . . The Nationalists will go to elections shattered." Three days later Manini sent Batlle a succinct cable: "TAKE CARE."[24]

That same day, October 24, Williman mobilized the army, intervened telephones and the telegraph lines, prevented Uruguayans from leaving the country without permission, decreed war censorship, and announced to the legislature that "a faction of the Nationalist Party" was trying to destroy "public peace."[25] Radical Nationalist leaders were arrested. Some sought asylum in foreign embassies. The Directorio newspaper proclaimed:

> The hour . . . of high decision has sounded. . . . The name of señor Batlle is on every lip. He is the only cause of the present upheavals. . . . Will señor Batlle and his system return once more to spill the blood of brothers for the third time? Will civil war exhaust us once more?
>
> These questions do not have answers today because events are not yet defined in a way that can be understood in all their ramifications. We await tomorrow.[26]

On October 25 Mariano Saravia, brother of Aparicio, the

Nationalist Caudillo killed in the War of 1904, made his long-attempted move. Mariano, who had been preparing in Brazil since 1904, crossed the border to join with Nepomuceno Saravia, Aparicio's oldest son, at the home ranch in Cerro Largo. In the South, at San Ramón in Canelones, Basilio Muñoz, military commander of the Radicals, and his followers started North along the railroad line to meet the Saravias.[27] Other Nationalist groups were reported forming and cutting telegraph lines.

Army units were sent after the revolutionaries; Williman invoked the interdiction law—which the Ramírez memorandum had proposed that Batlle abrogate— freezing the assets of known revolutionaries.[28] President Sáenz Peña of Argentina was advised of an arms shipment headed for the revolution and quickly seized it.[29] Brazil assured Uruguay it would seal off the border. The government press promised that peace would be restored within a few days.

The Directorio met on October 26, and resigned, convinced that "its policies had completely failed." Its resignation message concluded that it "prayed that a solution of national confraternity could be found, something that all men with any heart must deeply desire in these anguished moments."[30]

That same day, Williman asked Bachini to resign as Foreign Minister because Bachini had sent the Foreign Ministry's Chief of Protocol to visit an imprisoned Radical Nationalist leader. Williman feared the visit would be interpreted as a signal that his government was involved in the anti-Batlle plot. Bachini dismissed the visit as a courtesy to an old friend and insisted that there were more basic reasons for his separation from the cabinet. He released a letter of resignation to Williman in which he asserted that more than two years ago he and Williman had worked out an agreement on ways of preventing "this sad and tragic end of the government of Your Excellency" of which "plan" Bachini had "advised my friend Don José Batlle y Ordoñez in Paris, in our last patriotic conversations."[31]

Bachini and the Directorio were using similar phrases: "patriotic conversations," "solutions of confraternity," "the hour of high decisions." It was common knowledge that the Radical Nationalists expected their revolt to be the pretext for an anti-Batlle army revolt. On October 27, in cooperation with Colonel Guillermo West, anti-Batllista Police Chief of Montevideo, the military, supported by

Colorados opposed to Batlle, would overthrow the government and, alleging the need for peace, set up a Junta to preside over elections, which would result in the emergence of a Colorado president who would give the Nationalists coparticipation in the government.[32] The Directorio's resignation statement was its endorsement of such a solution, and Bachini's resignation letter was his announcement that he was available for the presidency.

The Nationalist military, which had given up revolutionary plans even after Batlle's program had been published, were told in October by Radical politicians or, as the revolution's manifesto put it, "respectable persons of their party," that the two principal government generals, Galarza and Escobar, would revolt "to make the presidential election of señor Batlle impossible, if the National Party would second that initiative with a mere show of force." Nepomuceno Saravia confessed that the plan "seduced me."[33] Yet who could believe that Colorado officers who had fought for Batlle in 1904 and could expect continuing favorable treatment when he resumed the presidency, would revolt against him? Even the Melo lawyer, Arturo Olave, who had brought the plot to Nepomuceno Saravia, was unable to get his own followers to join, and could not participate.

Still, the Saravias came down from Cerro Largo, and Basilio Muñoz came up from Canelones. Both groups escaped pursuers and united at Mansavillagra, scene of a 1904 battle. They had about 4,500 men, only half of whom were armed, and because of Argentine and Brazilian governmental hostility, they were unable to get more arms. Generals Galarza and Escobar, who were supposed to lead the revolt, were, instead, pursuing the revolutionaries. Williman put 30,000 men into the field.

The revolutionaries, nevertheless, felt they must make their show of force, so that the Colorado military would be able, finally, to revolt. They attacked the town of Nico Pérez, scene of the Peace of 1903. Nico Pérez (renamed Batlle y Ordoñez in 1907) was defended by a garrison of 150 men who resisted the attack all day but surrendered the next morning to the revolutionaries, who headed North. There had been heavy casualties on both sides—all told, about 250 killed and wounded.[34]

Viera's coded cables from Montevideo on the revolution did not satisfy Batlle. He booked passage for himself, Matilde, his daughter,

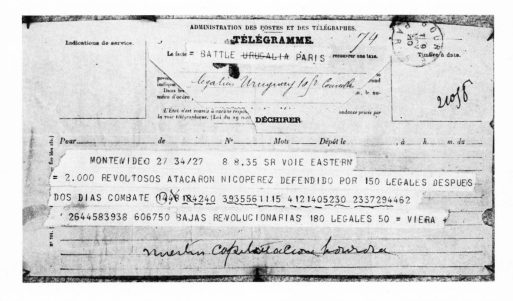

11. Coded telegrams from Viera, October 1910 Revolution. The bottom telegram reads: "2,000 revolutionaries attacked Nico Pérez defended by 150 soldiers. After two days combat our capitulation honorable. Revolutionary casualties 180 soldiers 50—Viera."

and his youngest son on a ship leaving immediately, with the rest of the family to follow. "I was dominated by a great anxiety to know what was going on. I believed, besides, that it was my duty to be there, in case I could be useful in something."[35]

V

The battle of Nico Pérez produced no Colorado revolt, and the Saravias and Basilio Muñoz finally admitted there would be none. They insisted not that they had revolted without confirming the promises made to them, but that the government military participants in on the plot had "defected."[36] Their goal now was to get across the Brazilian border, but between them and the border were two government armies.

Even before Nico Pérez, Montevideo Nationalists had recognized that continuing the revolution would only mean more men killed. Manuel Quintela, who had served as intermediary in the abortive January revolt, offered himself as mediator to Williman. On November 4 Williman agreed to give Quintela, Nationalist Alfonso Lamas, and José Irureta Goyena, attorney for the Asociación Rural whose brother was one of the revolution's officers, safe-conduct passes to the revolutionary army to arrange for them to submit.[37] Viera cabled Batlle: "Do not take rumors of rebels importance seriously. . . . Doctor Quintela asked authorization to see revolutionaries so that they would submit . . . Talking with President I said probably they will call for elimination of your candidacy. He answered me that would be a subversion."[38] Don Pepe concluded that it would be all over before he could get back and stopped packing.

The Asociación Rural and the newer Federación Rural met together with ranchers and decided to wait for the peacemaker's return. If war continued, they would call an open meeting to decide on further steps.[39] El Día did not print this news, for the further step could still be a call for Batlle's replacement. Nor did the Montevideo labor unions rally to assure Batlle's return. At a meeting of all the Montevideo unions, the Workers Federation, in spite of a speech by libertarian poet Ángel Falco that "we revolutionary ideologists" could not turn their backs on Batlle, voted the traditional labor stand in Uruguayan civil wars—workers should stay out. Only the tailors' union disagreed.[40]

Colorados took decisive action. On November 8 the Batlle campaign committee issued a statement that Batlle's candidacy "will never be retired under pressure of irregular armed movements." The statement was accompanied by a pledge signed by seventy-two Colorados, candidates for the legislature and present Senators: "the nominated candidates announce that in the event they are elected they will vote for señor Batlle y Ordoñez for President of the Republic."[41]

This was far more than the number of votes required to elect Batlle president and was designed to show that there were no Colorados involved in plots, that Batlle would, in fact, be President. Batlle's plan to have his candidacy formally voted immediately after the legislative election had been speeded up. Such a pledge by candidates before their election to the legislature was unprecedented—it would normally have been criticized as the equivalent of selling their vote as the price of their election. El Siglo, which could be expected to make just this criticism, did not; instead El Siglo judged the pledge "worthy of applause."[42]

On November 14 the mediators, who had caught up with the revolutionary army attempting to reach Brazil, had a telegraphic conversation with Williman. The revolutionaries were willing to submit and be disarmed, but wanted the usual amnesty and the lifting of property interdictions. Williman agreed to do this after submission, not as a formal condition of submission.

Messengers were sent to the government armies, which were hot after the revolutionaries. Both sides suffered casualties on the fourteenth and fifteenth; the sixteenth was calm; on the seventeenth, disarmament formally began. The Nationalists hid as many arms as possible, and Nepomuceno Saravia shipped rifles over the border to Brazil, where they would be ready for the next revolution.[43]

From Paris, Batlle cabled Williman: "Receive felicitations for ability and firmness with which you have ended era of fratricidal wars."[44]

VI

Williman's message, on November 21, 1910, formally announcing the end of hostilities and providing for amnesty, was angry. Because the plot they had relied upon had not materialized, the revolutionaries dared to call themselves victims. Victims they were, but of their own "dangerous passions," from which the Republic must be protected. The legislature must enact the law first proposed by Batlle, making it a crime to address non-members of the army with military titles. (Nationalists were called Colonel, Major, etc., in accord with their own rank in the revolutionary armies.) Williman also wanted legislation to punish political crimes more seriously. In addition, the army would be strengthened even further. The legislature quickly added 4,176 men, and plans called for the government army to be expanded to 80,000 in time of war.[45] Williman, using a phrase from Don Pepe's private cable received the day before, concluded: "Let us by our decisiveness declare the cycle of revolutions closed."[46]

During the revolution, Batlle's intimates had been desperately worried that it would drag on so long that elections could not be held before Williman's term expired.[47] Now, with the revolution over, Williman, at the same time he sent the bill on military titles, sent another bill, which was quickly passed without debate, postponing the elections scheduled for November 27, one week off, until December 18, to give the nation, and in particular those "who have just finished tearing the nation apart," time to complete electoral preparations.[48]

Elections made no sense now to the Nationalists. The revolution's failure had demonstrated that the Conservative warning in quieter times was correct—that revolution to stop Batlle was foredoomed. The Radicals were discredited but Nationalists, already doubtful about voting before the revolution, had no desire whatever to vote now and legitimize Batlle's return. The issue that had divided Conservatives and Radicals, namely how to confront Batlle's reelection, had been decided. Both Radicals and Conservatives had lost. There was no reason to continue their split, which had been greatly narrowed by the Directorio's standing aside at the beginning of the October revolution to allow the hoped-for army plot to materialize.

On December 5 a genuine unity Directorio, with Alfonso Lamas, who had mediated the end of this revolution as he had mediated for Saravia in 1903 and was acceptable to all, was elected President, and Carlos A. Berro, chief Radical leader and First Vice President, was installed. Nationalists presently serving resigned from the legislature on December 6. The new Directorio announced its abstention in the upcoming elections. Nationalist participation would be "complicity" in the preestablished agreement between Batlle, his circle, and Williman, which dated from Williman's election. The Directorio called for Nationalist "stoicism" to preserve "the permanent interests of the nation."[49]

Nationalist abstention was a disappointment to Williman, Batlle's intimates, and the conservative classes. While the strengthened army should be able to restrain or quickly snuff out any repetition of the October revolution, Williman wanted to minimize the negative effects of Nationalist abstention, because abstention would give Batlle's election an air of spurious legality and hurt national credit, since foreign lenders could think Uruguay's government was *de facto*.

Williman proposed a solution; Batlle's intimates, except for Viera, agreed; and on November 29 the Colorado Executive Committee issued a manifesto. In the "permanent interests of the national representative system," it was asking the departmental Colorado commissions, where they had not yet proclaimed complete slates of candidates, to include as candidates "respectable citizens of different political affiliation than ours or without fixed affiliation." They could serve as a minority to oversee the acts of the Colorado majority. Especially because the next legislature would arrange the procedures for constitutional reform, "our party will need and will call for the enlightened dispassionate collaboration of all representative elements."[50]

The Colorado Executive Committee had already offered places to eleven distinguished citizens, and a total of twenty chamber and Senate seats was envisaged. At 10:30 A.M. on December 2, seven of the eleven met in the law offices of José Pedro Ramírez, dean of the conservative classes, who was detested by Batlle. Three, after satisfying themselves that it was impossible to get the Nationalists to go to the polls, were willing to accept seats if the other notables would too. Four, including the host, were not. The result was that all eleven—the final count was four in favor, seven against—declined the offer. Once more, the notables were showing that they wanted to keep their distance from Batlle. Several of those opposed to accepting explained that their presence in the legislature could not prevent civil war. José Irureta Goyena, lawyer for the Asociación Rural, was blunt: the only way to prevent Nationalist civil war was to withdraw Batlle's candidacy.[51]

The notables' refusal opened a career in parliament to a number of Colorados. Departmental organizations were busy working out the bottom names on their tickets, positions which this time were certain of election. Nationalist abstention also encouraged the newly founded Catholic Party to present candidates, since if they received at least one twelfth of the vote in Montevideo—something under 1,000 votes—they would elect two deputies. The Nationalists caustically referred to them as Catholics for Batlle, but the Batllistas, for whom anti-Catholicism was a fundamental ideological position, planned to block Catholic entry into the legislature by sponsoring a rival Socialist-Religious Liberal ticket to contest the minority seats.[52]

Emilio Frugoni, against Anarchist opposition, had been trying to organize a Socialist Party since 1904. The Karl Marx Center, "the organ and seed ground of a party in formation" as it called itself, so far had only 300 members, and as the left-wing young Colorado intellectual Alberto Zum Felde somewhat regretfully observed, only a minority were workers.[53] Frugoni himself, a friend of Manini's, had fought for the government in the War of 1904, and wrote literary criticism in *El Día*. The Socialist manifesto, written by Frugoni, announced the entry of the working class party into the Uruguayan political arena against the landowners, against the military, against the October revolution.[54]

> The cause of this revolt,—which was intended to prevent the coming to power of a man representative of democratic and liberal principles, a man in whom the people have put their hopes of seeing some important reforms carried out and who is, in the present circumstances and within the relativity of things under bourgeois institutions and bourgeois governments, the only candidate who can be considered a sure pledge of a government respectful of the rights and demands of the working class—was not only the cause of the Nationalist opposition, but also the cause of the church, of unscrupulous politics, and of intransigent conservatism.[55]

Bachini, Colorado candidate for Senator in Paysandú, resigned his candidacy, complaining that police spies were following him "as they do professional conspirators." His resignation statement seemed to justify the police attitude: "in my judgment, the political state of the nation has reached such a point of confusion and anarchy, that patriotism advises those who cannot exercise influence to resolve or avoid the crisis not to involve themselves uselessly in it."[56] The pre-'97 Colorados displaced by Batlle in 1904 took a similar position. They met (only twenty or thirty came to the meeting) and announced that they, the Traditional Colorado Party, would not contest the elections because of government fraud in registering voters on Batlle's behalf.[57] The dissident Colorados, like José Pedro Ramírez, dean of the conservative classes, were letting it be known without saying so explicitly that in spite of the October Nationalist fiasco, they expected a violent upheaval to wipe out the present political situation, and that when it came they would be available. Bachini went so far as to tell the German Minister that after Batlle became President, there would be more Nationalist revolutions and, this time, an army revolt.[58]

The Nationalists encouraged this expectation. The Directorio newspaper insisted that Batlle was gravely ill in Paris, that suspicious shifts of army commanders were afoot, and even published rumors that Williman had been poisoned. Starting three days before the elections, it daily published a "permanent" editorial: "The electoral force which Batllismo is preparing for Sunday, with the cooperation of official Power fully dispensed to it by a citizen [Williman] without will power or character, is a bloody mockery of popular sovereignty." There followed eight charges that the country was still under war mobilization, with armed Colorados and the police terrorizing citizens. "Therefore the Sunday elections, openly violative of the Constitution, are null and void."[59]

The Montevideo Colorado ticket was headed by Batlle for Senator—a strategy decided long before so that he could be elected Senate President should anything then happen to prevent the presidential election. Batlle's first substitute, and very proud of it, was Arena, who would become Senator when Batlle became president. The Colorado campaign was simple. There was no desire to discuss issues. "Batlle symbolizes our program" was the Colorado message. As a Colorado Club proclaimed:

And the Colorado Party cannot, without treason to its past, forget or disavow the man who has ended its long humiliation and restored it to its place in the nation. José Batlle y Ordoñez, in his own right, through the force of evolution of events, and by the will and love of his coreligionaries, is the unquestioned and unquestionable chief of the Colorado Party.[60]

Election day, December 18, 1910, after two months of revolution and postrevolutionary maneuvers, was quiet. In Montevideo, carriages flying Colorado banners brought voters to the polls. In most of the interior the day was uneventful. In four interior departments, local Colorado splits, encouraged by the chance of winning deputyships because of Nationalist abstention, resulted in two rival tickets, both pledged to vote for Batlle. In those departments all the usual, and some new, troubles occurred: caudillos marched their men to vote; polling places were opened early to let friendly voters in and closed early before hostile ones could vote; police, constitutionally forbidden from voting, were given one-day discharges. Police chiefs, in spite of Williman's decree, made their preferences known.[61]

From the Colorado standpoint the election results were very good. The final count gave the official Colorado tickets 28,386 votes, compared with 27,351 in 1907, and 26,705 in 1905. The anti-organization Colorado tickets polled 1,329 votes. The Montevideo Colorado vote, 7,782, was about 500 less than in 1907, partly because the police were not given one-day discharges to vote, partly because, in *El Día's* phrase, "numerous Colorado elements" were instructed by Manini to vote for the Socialist-Religious Liberal coalition, which polled 902 votes, enough to outvote 350 Catholics and elect Socialist Frugoni and religious Liberal Pedro Díaz deputies.[62]

VII

On January 14, 1911, Batlle wrote Arena that he was in Berlin "which is very inferior to Paris." This would be his last letter, and Arena could let the word out that Batlle was in Berlin. (It would throw off assassination attempts, since by the time Arena spread the news, Batlle would be elsewhere. The revolution had confirmed for Batlle's intimates that his life was in serious danger. He should not return in Spanish or German ships because they were Jesuit owned. He should come unannounced, incognito, alone, with his family traveling on a different ship.[63] Though Don Pepe, on the verge of embarking, did not follow this advice to the letter, he was cooperating: "Viera will receive a telegram announcing my arrival, or, to be precise, the name of the ship on which I am sailing." Not even Batlle's intimates would know his return arrangements until after his ship had departed. He still had not received full information about the election results but "What I do know is that the Blancos have committed another blunder and that if I do become President I will be able to carry out my program with much less difficulty than I would have had with a parliamentary minority in systematic opposition."[64]

Batlle's supporters, nevertheless, renewed the "mature Batlle" image, which had been so effective in keeping support from the revolution. After all, Nepomuceno Savaria still had rifles hidden in Brazil waiting for the next revolution; Bachini was predicting that next time the government army would join in; the notables were keeping their distance from Batlle so that they could mediate his overthrow if the time came. In a series of newspaper articles, Don Pepe's friend Pedro Figari, later to become famous as a painter, revealed that the telegram announcing Saravia's death in 1904 had brought tears to Batlle's eyes. Figari told the Nationalists that if they revolted, they would again fail, but if they came out of abstention and joined in constitutional reform to reduce the power of the presidency, they would be on the way toward achieving the rotation of parties in power.[65]

El Siglo, so influential with ranchers, continued to preach that a mellowed Batlle was returning. And Don Pepe, for all his distrust of *El Siglo* editor Juan Andrés Ramírez, once more cooperated. On January 5, *El Siglo* published another interview with Batlle, from Paris, this time by "a progressive and wealthy rancher." Recent events had not made Batlle "rancorous"; "through good means" he planned "to win the sympathies of his enemies." In Europe, Batlle had devoted "the greater part of his time" to exploring markets for Uruguay's products and gathering data on ranching and especially on the formation of *granjas* (vegetable, fruit, swine, and poultry farms).

> Señor Batlle's ideas on the development of our rural wealth are wide-ranging, and I dare to assert that without violence they will produce a real revolution in our country: but one of those peaceful and economically fruitful revolutions, which is what we need, since it will solve, in part, the problem of the subdivision of land and of employment.[66]

Nationalists gave no signs of welcoming Batlle, but their press attacks were directed less at him than at Williman, "a real political mummy," whose only accomplishment as president was to increase his private fortune.[67] And though Nationalists complained that the country was an armed dictatorship, and rumors of a Nationalist revolution combined with an army uprising still circulated, Nationalists who had fled to Brazil and Argentina in October were returning. By mid-January 1911 Uruguay had calmed down and was awaiting Batlle's second inaugural.

APPRAISALS: I

Explanation of Batlle's reelection as the victory of an urban middle class–working class coalition led by the middle class has become standard. In 1958 John J. Johnson's seminal work, *Political Change in Latin America: The Emergence of the Middle Sectors*, argued for the emergence of "the new amalgams" of middle and working class from Latin America's late nineteenth-century economic transformation. For Johnson, Batlle was Latin America's first successful middle-class political leader. Johnson's expectations of a democratic Latin America have been tarnished by time, but analysts have held on to the middle class. Germán W. Rama, the Uruguayan sociologist who has written most on the rise of its middle class, concluded that Batlle was "the leader of an unequivocal middle classes movement in 1911" and that "we must explain his action as leader in the identification of the middle classes with the proletariat in a common program." A recent article by Peter Winn, "British Informal Empire in Uruguay in the Nineteenth Century," comes to similar conclusions. The "emergence in the nation's capital of a white-collar middle class, politically aware and distribution oriented" and the "emergence of a militant organized working class" formed "the mass base for Batlle and his politics of social reform and economic nationalism."[1]

Yet when one actually looks at Batlle's reelection campaign, one finds no contemporary mention of the middle classes whatever. The dynamic group postulated by historians and social scientists simply did not exist. In 1876 the historian Francisco Bauzá had called for the formation of a middle class in Uruguay, "since there is no middle class." By 1960 a survey of Montevideo heads of households discovered that 69 to 75 percent of them defined themselves as middle class.[2] During the years of Batlle's presidencies, public men occasionally referred to the middle class. In 1905 Serrato, then Batlle's Finance Minister, talked of the economic pressures on "middle class" "among us," "which will provide the governing classes of the future";[3] but about the same time, Serrato divided up Uruguayans into the "privileged" and the "popular classes,"[4] a reference which contemporaries doubtless found more familiar. In 1914 nine years later, toward the end of Batlle's second presidency, Gabriel Terra, then a Deputy, spoke about "the middle class of my country, made up largely of public employees," a highly restrictive definition.[5] Other references to the middle classes obviously can be found, but they were sporadic and contradictory. Had a survey like that of 1960 been taken in 1910, household heads, except for public employees, would have been puzzled by the question and at a loss how to answer. Between the 1960 survey and Serrato's and Terra's observations there is a big gap, and what recent analysts have done is to postulate a dynamic 1910 middle class on the basis of the Uruguayan social structure they saw after World War II.[6]

The other half of the supposed middle class–working class coalition for Batlle in 1911, the urban working class, presents fewer analytical dilemmas. There indeed was an "organized working class" led by militants, but (1) unions were much weaker than has been realized, as shown by the disappearance of the strongest Uruguayan union, the railroad workers, when their strike was broken in 1908; and (2) workers did not vote massively for Batlle, because they were not citizens, were not motivated, feared that they would get into trouble with their employers or others if they voted wrong (voting was public by signed ballot), or followed the advice of their Anarchist leaders: "The worker will not vote." Nor did workers fight for Batlle, as witnessed by the rejection by all the Montevideo unions except one of a plea to back Batlle during the October 1910 revolution.

Those who explain Batlle's reelection as the result of a middle class–working class coalition have confused *the* social base of politics with *a* social base. They assume that a government like Batlle's must have had a middle class–working class base and rather than actually looking at the relationship between politics and social structure, they have postulated a relationship. Batlle himself relied on no such analysis. I have found no reference at all in his correspondence from Europe and during the presidential campaign to an Uruguayan middle class, either as an existing group or as one whose formation he wanted to encourage (compare this with the statement in a new book, *The Batllista Era*, "It appears evident that Batlle's intention was to create a middle class country").[7] Batlle did favor labor but was under no illusions about its political strength. Remember his letters to Arena, "ideas for the protection of the working classes are far from generalized among us" "except for you, me, and a handful of others." And he later stated publicly that "labor's revindications exercised no influence at all" on "the success of his candidacy."[8] So neither subjectively in the calculations of the candidate, Batlle, described by John J. Johnson in 1958 as the "catalyst" of the middle sector-worker coalition,[9] nor objectively in the campaign itself did any middle class–working class coalition exist.

Those organized interest groups that did take part in the campaign were fearful of or hostile to Batlle. Much of the campaign was a successful effort to prevent their fears from being translated into support for revolution. Ranchers were prosperous, strong, and organized. They were calmed with the reminder that Batlle was better than war; they were reassured by "The Correspondent" that "Batlle does not recognize the existence of an agrarian problem which calls urgently for government attention." Nationalist ranchers were assured that a "mature" Batlle, mellowed away from political intransigence, was returning. Colorado ranchers were welcomed as delegates to the nominating convention. The conservative classes (the phrase was still widely used—remember Williman's desire to have businessmen on the campaign committee because "he wants in this way to destroy the canard that the conservative classes are opposed to your candidacy"—though its use probably was declining),[10] the conservative classes (that is, the local and foreign business community) feared Batlle, and they were asked, do you prefer war to Batlle? Their answer, together with ranchers, was to form the Peace League.

Batlle relied basically on a group with tremendous self-identification—the Colorados. They were bringing back their hero—Don Pepe Batlle and for them the campaign was simple. There was no need to expound on issues: "Batlle symbolizes the Colorado program." When Batlle, still in Europe, learned that there would be no Nationalists in the legislature when he took office, he wrote back: "I will be able to carry out my program with much less difficulty." Yet there was a problem here. Had there been a real middle class–lower class coalition behind Batlle, he could have relied on their support to carry out his program. The political elite's progressivism, I have argued when describing the Williman years, was superficial. Only with the enthusiastic backing of the Colorado Party could Batlle achieve what he wanted. From Europe he had written his confidantes that he intended to make Uruguay a model country, to transform and expand its economy, reduce foreign control of the national wealth; he wanted to redeem the "disinherited classes." But he did not run on this program. What would happen when the Colorados, who had elected him out of party enthusiasm, were asked to support an advanced program about which they were only dimly aware? Batlle had spent some time in Europe thinking about just this question. He had an answer that he had kept to himself and his family. Only a clairvoyant could have grasped it from the one direct quote in "The Correspondent's" interview: " 'I was in Switzerland for three months,' Batlle says, 'and I found many people there who did not know the name of the President of the Confederation.' "

Batlle had been in Europe for almost four years, far longer than he had wanted. Uruguayans were being told that he was returning "mature," without political intransigence. Actually, he had arrived in Europe mature, in the sense that he had already thought through what he wanted for Uruguay. Benjamín Nahum states: "It appears obvious that the spectacle of a Europe that was transforming itself socially and economically exercised a powerful influence in the receptive spirit of Batlle y Ordoñez." Nahum points to the separation of Church and State and labor strife in France as things that must have influenced Batlle's thinking.[11] But Batlle's ideas on such questions were formed well before his second trip to Europe. In 1906, shortly before leaving Uruguay, he had sent his eight-hour day message to the legislature.[12] Batlle stated then: "our condition as a new people permits us to put into effect ideals of government and social organization which could not be made effective in other countries without overcoming enormous and tenacious resistance." In 1910, from Barcelona, Batlle commented to Williman about Europe: "from which we still have so much to take, and which, if we work with ardor and faith, some day we will surpass, since it is easier to straighten out a young and tender tree than an old and stiff one." For Batlle, Uruguay remained the place where it would be easier to bring "ideals of government and social organization" into being than Europe itself. His use of the phrase "we still have so much to take" is revealing. What Batlle had been looking for in Europe were not ideals; he already had them. He wanted to take back with him practical ways of implementing his plans: building techniques, vegetable and poultry farming, parks, tourism, enterprises the state could operate effectively.

From Europe, Batlle was insisting that the era of Uruguayan revolutions was over. In Uruguay those on the scene expected that new revolutions were coming. Was this an indication that Batlle, away so long, had lost touch with Uruguayan reality?

PART II *Rain of Projects*

CHAPTER 8

Second Inaugural

Don Pepe and his whole family—in this he disregarded his confidantes' instructions—were coming on the ship *Re-Vittorio*, which had left from Barcelona, a secondary port, and stopped only in Dakar, Africa, before arriving in Montevideo. By avoiding Rio de Janeiro, the usual stop on the Europe–Montevideo–Buenos Aires route, where the news would surely leak, the moment of Batlle's return could be kept from those preparing assassination in Montevideo. While press reports had him on the high seas, while Colorados were preparing a great reception, with Batlle medallions and even Batlle cigarettes on sale, and while the Directorio newspaper was denying that it was inciting his assassination, on February 12, 1911, the word spread that Batlle was entering the Montevideo harbor.

His friends had not learned of his arrival until the night before. Led by War Minister General Vázquez, they immediately took the Uruguayan navy cruiser *18 de Julio* to meet the *Re-Vittorio* at quarantine. At 7 A.M. the *18 de Julio* docked, but Batlle was not on it. To avoid potential assassins, he had been taken by launch to a different pier, where an automobile spirited him off to a house in the center of Montevideo, rented and furnished with Don Pepe's old furniture in accord with his recent instructions to Arena. The family would use it until the remodeling of Piedras Blancas was completed and then keep it as a city house.

All day visitors came to greet Don Pepe. At 5 P.M., in the company of two friends, he left his house for the seashore neighborhood of

12. Shipboard, returning 1911. Batlle is seated, wearing a white cap. By permission of the Museo Histórico Nacional, Montevideo.

13. Crowd on Montevideo pier expects Batlle's return. By permission of the Museo Histórico Nacional, Montevideo.

Pocitos, to pay his respects to Williman. After that, he took a short walk on the beach Rambla—his first in four years. At 6 P.M. he returned home and found it hard to get through the crowd around the house. There was an improvised demonstration; Batlle was saluted with a speech, and the young poet Ovidio Fernández Ríos recited his "Hymn to Batlle." Batlle responded and, using the word coreligionaries as a sign of intense party loyalty, emphasized his Colorado ties:

> What you are acclaiming . . . is not my triumph, but an impersonal victory that is due entirely to the country. . . . You have spoken of my goodness. . . . If goodness means carrying out the obligations each of us sets for himself, he accepted the title gladly, but first he must say that his coreligionaries, who gave him so many honors, were better. [1]

Everyone who saw Batlle was astonished at the physical changes. He was almost 55 years old and still a huge man, but he had been dieting to get himself in shape for what he was planning as president, and he was much thinner. His hair was gray and his moustache absolutely white. *but look at photo !*

In *El Siglo* Juan Andrés Ramírez hoped that Batlle would "by a word, a gesture, an act, which would have little importance coming from another citizen, morally pacify the Republic." Batlle answered with his first editorial in *El Día*. A newspaper had reported him as saying: "If I am able to govern in peace for a few months, just long enough to demonstrate my aims, civil war will be over in our country, perhaps forever."

El Día replied:

> Señor Batlle y Ordoñez has not said that, nor does he believe it.
>
> The reason is very simple: he governed in peace for ten months at the beginning of his first administration, but all his good intentions did not keep revolution from breaking out.
>
> Why should the good intentions he might now announce, should he be elected President of the Republic, be more successful than the ones he announced then?
>
> Nevertheless, señor Batlle y Ordoñez is certain that peace cannot be seriously disturbed.
>
> But for an entirely different reason.

14. Pre-inaugural political demonstration, Montevideo, 1911, two views.

15. The same pre-inaugural demonstration. Batlle, standing, and Arena, with hands on ledge, are on the center balcony. Manini, with arms crossed, is in the center of the right balcony. Ana Amalia and other family members are on the left balcony.

The Government now has superabundant means available immediately to repress any attempt at disturbance.

That's all.[2]

Don Pepe, not yet inaugurated, back only four days, had just destroyed the "mature Batlle" image.

II

The morning before inauguration, the government received information that there would be an attempt on Batlle's life during the ceremony. As a diversion, Nationalist-dissident Colorado revolution would break out on the streets of Montevideo. Police spies followed the likely leaders of such an undertaking, and when that night Carlos A. Berro, principal Radical Nationalist leader and now First Vice-president of the Directorio, and Valentín Aznarez, Radical and Directorio member, "secretly" attempted to board separate steamships for Buenos Aires, where they could organize a War Directorio, they were arrested. The next morning two more Nationalists and an army colonel on inactive service were also arrested.[3]

On the afternoon of March 1, 1911, police, firemen, the ceremonial army corps of Blandengues, and the Third Infantry kept crowds back from the Cabildo in which the election would be held. Crowds were also kept from the Plaza de Independencia, where inside Government House Batlle would receive the Presidential sash from Williman. Batlle himself arrived almost surreptitiously in an automobile accompanied only by the director of police security. In the crowds being held back by police, fervent Colorados loudly vowed that Nationalist blood would flow if anything happened to Don Pepe.[4]

Inside in the large salon of the Cabildo, a colonial building too small for current needs, the tiny gallery was absolutely packed with invited guests (all men—women were not yet involved in active politics). Promptly at 3:40 P.M., Ricardo Areco, Senate First Vice President (Senate President Viera, who would be Acting President if Batlle were assassinated, stayed away from the inauguration lest he, too, be killed and complete chaos result) called the session to order. The legislators entered, and when Batlle, now Senator from Montevideo, took his seat, the gallery cheered.

Each legislator signed a ballot indicating his presidential candidate.

16. Government House (the presidential office), Plaza Independencia.

17. Montevideo, 1911. Plaza Constitución. On the right is the colonial Cabildo, the building used by the Chamber of Deputies and the Senate for their debates. Batlle's inauguration took place in the Cabildo. Source: Reginald Lloyd and others, editors, *Impresiones de la República del Uruguay en el Siglo Veinte*, London (Lloyds Greater Britain Publishing Co.), 1912.

Ushers gathered the ballots, the Secretary read off each one. Batlle had voted for Areco, everyone else, the 96 legislators present, including Socialist Frugoni specially authorized by his party, voted for Batlle. The legislators applauded and applauded, while the gallery shouted Bravos and Vivas.

Don Pepe stepped forward and to the right of the Chair took the oath of office.

I, José Batlle y Ordoñez, swear by God Our Lord and by these Holy Scriptures that I will faithfully carry out the office of President which is being conferred on me, that I will protect the State Religion, that I will preserve the integrity and independence of the Republic, that I will faithfully observe and require the faithful observation of the Constitution.

Don Pepe, the anti-Catholic, had a surprise prepared. He continued to speak:

Permit me, now that I have fulfilled the constitutionally required oath which has no meaning for me, to express in another form the solemn promise I contract at this moment. I swear by my honor as a man and as a citizen that justice, progress and the welfare of the Republic, under strict compliance with the law, will be my greatest and constant concern as President.

He then asked the legislators "united by ideals and effort" to cooperate with his government. Areco, speaking for the General Assembly, interrupted by applause and shouts of agreement, assured Batlle that the legislature would accompany him in carrying out "in all its parts, your wonderful Government program."[5]

The newly elected President—the only man in Uruguay's history to be twice elected President of the Republic—and his electors then adjourned to the antechambers for the traditional buffet, champagne, and exchange of toasts. Chamber President Antonio María Rodríguez gave Batlle a flattering welcome, then concluded, unexpectedly, that Batlle did have one defect, "that of not forgetting." Don Pepe did not use the offered opportunity to say something that would please Nationalists:

If not forgetting means to harbor unjustified passions against one's

18. Batlle reading the inaugural oath, March 1, 1911. By permission of the Museo Histórico Nacional, Montevideo.

adversary, to persecute him illegitimately or meanly, to disregard his rights, I have forgotten.

But if forgetting means to disregard what one has learned through experience, to deprive oneself of the wealth of knowledge about human affairs that experience provides, to disqualify oneself from taking the past into account when judging the future, I have not forgotten.

Newspapermen were forbidden to leave the Cabildo during the entire ceremony. Batlle, surrounded by his electors, emerged, and some of the crowd broke through the police lines. Instead of going on foot to Government House, as was customary, Batlle, once more accompanied only by the head of police security, went by automobile.

In the Salon for Public Ceremonies, behind a table on which the Presidential Sash lay on a red cushion, stood Williman. Batlle entered and faced Williman and his ministers. The crowd of legislators and foreign diplomats watched the ceremony transmitting the presidency of the Republic. The outgoing President assured listeners that the nation and the Treasury were flourishing. His own administration had "continued the task of moral and material progress" begun by Batlle. Uruguay could have confidence in Batlle's sentiments of justice, respect for the rights of all, and "unbreakable energy for the maintenance of order. . . . I turn the government over to you."

Batlle, who had been given an advance copy of Williman's speech, then read his own. His praise of Williman was more measured than might have been expected. Batlle intended to continue Williman's political and administrative policies "in many of their aspects. . . . You, Mister President, on ending your government, can tell us and yourself that the welfare of the nation, as you conceived it, has always been the goal of your actions."[6] Williman put the presidential sash over Batlle's shoulders. Batlle gave Williman, who would shortly be leaving for Europe, "a strong handshake" and then accepted the congratulations of the foreign delegations.

The police were having great difficulty retaining the crowds. Batlle and Williman appeared on the balcony of Government House, and Don Pepe, now that his inauguration had been completed without any assassination attempt, gestured to the police to let the crowds come through. After a moment, Batlle and Williman left the balcony. The ex-president went to his home, Batlle to the familiar presidential office. At 6 P.M., again by automobile, Batlle went to Williman's home. At nightfall, accompanied by Manini and Colonel Laborde, he returned to the Montevideo house. He was recognized and amidst great excitement carried to the stairs by a great mass of men. A big crowd formed below. Batlle appeared on the balcony and told them: "I am counting on you!"

At 11 P.M., a semiorganized demonstration by the Colorados of the Seventh and Fifteenth Section of Montevideo appeared and received another welcome from Don Pepe. "I assure you that I will spare no effort to satisfy you, by carrying out my program, which is the reason, without any doubt, why you are so enthusiastic toward me."[7]

Long through the night Montevideo's Colorados celebrated—without Don Pepe, who disliked late hours and party-going. Bonfires were lit and firecrackers shot off. The Seventh Section contingent returned from Batlle's house to their torch-lit headquarters. They drank champagne, and their leader announced that the Committee pro-Batlle of the Seventh Section was dissolved—its mission accomplished.

Batlle was determined that his second presidency would be historic. His source of strength was the Colorado mass. Colorados, though, were organized around patronage and elections. The Colorado legislators had pledged only to vote Batlle president; they had no other obligation to him. This was why Batlle, in his inaugural, solicited Areco's response that the legislators would carry out Batlle's program "in all its parts" and why Batlle told the cheering Colorados of the Seventh and Fifteenth Sections that he intended to carry out his program, "which is the reason, without any doubt, that you are so enthusiastic toward me." Their response, though unintentional, was to dissolve their Committee pro-Batlle; Colorado Clubs did not function to carry out programs.

III

Don Pepe easily organized his cabinet. For the political ministry, Interior—to which had just been added responsibility for Church relations—Don Pepe named Manini, still only 32 years old. Interior was the ministry for future presidents, and *El Siglo*, delighted with this nomination, predicted that Manini was "surely destined to go very far." For Finance, Batlle again named Serrato, who had been so successful in his first presidency. General Bernassa y Jérez, who had accompanied Batlle to and from Europe, went to the War Ministry. Don Pepe had talked with him in Europe about "scientific" army reorganization and promised Bernassa he would be able to make major improvements in the army. The Ministry of Industries went to Eduardo Acevedo. Acevedo, son of a distinguished jurist and himself a lawyer, bank director, and ex-*El Siglo* editor, was a leading member of the conservative classes but one of those willing to accept Williman's offer of a deputyship. Acevedo, who was best man at Don Pepe's wedding, had been Rector of the University during Batlle's first administration, and like Batlle constantly wanted to do things for Uruguay. He and Don Pepe had a long talk and Acevedo accepted. For Public Works, a ministry Batlle expected to be very active, he chose Víctor Sudriers, reputed to be Uruguay's best engineer. A new ministry, Public Education, went to another of the bright young Colorados, Juan Blengio Rocca, head of the Montevideo party organization.

And as Foreign Minister, a post much sought after, Don Pepe picked his own former foreign minister, José Romeu. This was really a "I have not forgotten" appointment. Romeu was one of the Acevedo Díaz Nationalist minority who had voted for Batlle in 1903 and had been blamed by Nationalists for the Revolution of 1903 and its aftermath, the War of 1904. By 1911 the group had absolutely disappeared from Uruguayan politics. *El Siglo*, still trying not to break with Batlle, considered Romeu's appointment "one of the most unfortunate acts with which to begin his government." Romeu himself was surprised, and when asked about his plans for the ministry, he confessed that the appointment was so unexpected he had not yet thought about them.[8]

Batlle named Virgilio Sampognaro Secretary of the Presidency. He was an Uruguayan diplomat whom Batlle and Matilde had befriended in Europe. *El Día* defended another new member of Don Pepe's entourage from charges of being an Anarchist.

> Señor Batlle's chauffeur is simply an advanced Republican with Socialist ideas. . . . In his neighborhood in Paris he had considerable prestige, leading his comrades at elections. He is an

excellent chauffeur, practically a mechanic, and his fine character decided Señor Batlle to bring him here after having him at his side during the four years he was in Europe.[9]

IV

On March 8, with extremely simple ceremony, the ministers were sworn in. Finance Minister Serrato and Public Works Minister Sudriers had to give up their private businesses. Although when Batlle received the presidential sash, he had lauded Williman's personal honesty, some of the involvements of Williman's government were suspect, and Don Pepe, always a zealot on these matters, wanted to prevent any suspicions during his own government.

Within days that "rain" of projects which so disturbed conservative opinion during Batlle's first administration again began to fall. In Montevideo, the Intendent ordered the Health Department to inspect all *conventillos*—the slum tenements—two thirds of which a 1906 survey had concluded lacked adequate light, air, and space, and to close within a year all that had not been renovated. The Ministers of Finance and Public Works met with the Senate committee studying plans for the Port of Montevideo; the Executive wanted them expanded. The special labor division of the Montevideo police, set up under Williman, was abolished. And Don Pepe announced that he would reintroduce his bill for an eight-hour day.

The Chamber of Deputies approved a bill originally submitted by Sudriers to make the Río Negro navigable—a project begun by Batlle during his first administration.[10] In the Senate, Ricardo Areco was putting another of his moral legislation projects through, this one establishing inheritance rights for illegitimate children when they were accorded "tacit recognition" by being publicly treated as children of their fathers. During the debate, Areco announced that he and his new Senate colleague, Arena, who as Batlle's first alternate had become Senator from Montevideo when Don Pepe took the Presidential oath, had a bill prepared for forced recognition in cases where the father denied paternity.[11] Catholic opinion generally opposed legislation aiding illegitimate children in the belief that it would weaken family ties and encourage illicit sexual relations. In another anti-Catholic move, Batlle recalled the envoy Williman had sent to the Vatican to negotiate the naming of the new archbishop.

19. Ministers are sworn in, March 8, 1911. From left: Foreign Minister Romeu, Interior Minister Manini, and Batlle, wearing the Presidential sash. By permission of the Museo Histórico Nacional, Montevideo.

Williman's concession authorizing simulated bullfights in Colonia would not be renewed. "In this matter, the standards of the President of the Republic, who is opposed to bullfight spectacles, prevail."[12]

By the end of his first month in office, the campaign image of a mellowed Batlle had been completely dissipated. Ramírez, who had the right to feel deceived, complained ironically in *El Siglo*: "It is now clear: Batlle has not changed. Instead, he has perfected himself."[13]

It was equally clear—and in this Batlle had proven to understand Uruguayan reality better than those who had expected the worst unless Nationalists were taken into the government—that the danger of a Nationalist revolution, at least immediately, had also dissipated.[14] Batlle, though he was pushing for passage of the bill to forbid Nationalist non-army officers from using military titles, took action which showed that he, too, felt the danger of revolution, if not of assassination, was over. The last of the mobilization measures ordered by Williman during the October revolution was ended; war military commands were dissolved; Interior Minister Manini ordered the police to return the machine guns they had been issued when mobilized in October to the army.

CHAPTER 9 *General Strike*

With Batlle back, the obstacles Williman's government had confronted labor with were removed. Three weeks after Batlle's inauguration, some 10,000 workers marched in protest against the high cost of living. The police, as *El Día* put it, "shined by their absence," and the marchers cheered Batlle when they passed his house. *El Día* proposed that rent control be explored and that the Government and the Montevideo municipality build workers' housing. In April male nurses in the government's Hospital Maciel went on strike. Batlle received them, explained his opposition to strikes by public employees but promised that he would intercede with the Director of Public Assistance on their behalf once they returned to work. The next day they did.[1]

On May 2, 3, and 4, 1911 the Federación Obrera, the Labor Federation, held its Third Congress, attended by (depending on the sources) 26 to 40 unions claiming a total of 7,000 members.[2] The Congress, split between Anarchists believing in immediate improvements in workers' lives and those favoring revolutionary action, endorsed "Anarcho-Communism" as its final goal and proposed "boycotts, sabotage, partial and general strikes" as "revolutionary means of reaching the complete economic and social emancipation of the world proletariat," but it also advocated abolishing child labor, better shop conditions, a six-hour work day, the organization of new unions, and the resurrection of dormant unions.[3]

The railroad union, once Uruguay's strongest, had disappeared after the 1908 strike was broken, and railroad workers, still hurting, resisted unionization. Anarchist organizers instead got jobs as motormen and conductors on the Montevideo trolleys, and secretly began unionizing trolley workers.[4] The two electric trolley companies—the English-owned La Comercial employing 1,000 men and the German-owned La Transatlántica employing 800—were the country's largest employers except for the railroads; and when the company managers learned of the secret unionizing, they fired nine men who were active organizers.

On May 11, as soon as news of the firing spread, a meeting was called at Federación Obrera headquarters. Small groups of motormen and conductors started arriving as early as 1:30 P.M. A trolley workers' union was officially formed, and the union sent a note to the companies calling for the rehiring of the fired nine. The two company managers, both Uruguayans, jointly refused.[5] The union immediately responded by calling a strike.

The trolley strikers complained that not only was the work day 10 or 11 hours, but work runs were at least five hours long, "without time off for eating or attending to physiological necessities," and made sixteen demands, including a raise in the basic pay to 40 pesos a month from the present 35 pesos, a work day of 8 to 8½ hours, revision of work rules, rehiring of the fired nine, and a requirement that all trolley workers be union members.[6] Batlle's government announced that it would respect the right to strike but would protect operating trolleys from strikers' violence. If, even with protection, the trolley companies did not, as required by their concessions and municipal ordinances, run the scheduled trolleys, the municipality would fine them 3,000 pesos a day. Failure to pay would be a criminal act subjecting the managers to imprisonment. The Williman years were over!

Even with soldiers riding the trolleys, very few operated, and after 6 P.M. none of La Comercial's. Government inspectors ordered nonlicensed motormen off the cars. Aspirants for motorman had to pass a complete examination, including maintenance ability. Specially hired strikebreakers were not yet a factor, but strikers who could no longer hold out soon would be. Passions heated. Three strikers were arrested for advocating that cars be burned, fourteen for threatening working conductors with death, and one for beating a

20. Montevideo, 1911. Avenida Sarandí. Electric trolley en route to the Customs House. Source: Reginald Lloyd and others, *Impresiones*.

conductor. In a yard accident a foreman was killed. The Federación Obrera met secretly to decide whether to call a general strike in support of the trolley strikers.

The strike was now five days old and all attempts at mediation had failed. Manini entered as mediator and won two major concessions from the companies: the strikers' demand for a monthly basic pay of 40 pesos would be granted and the workday would be reduced to nine hours. But the companies would go no further. Arena had been anguished by the 1908 railroad strike and had been advised by Don Pepe to wait for better days, which now were here. He and the Socialist Frugoni counseled with the strikers. In "a beautiful gesture," the fired nine "voluntarily sacrificed themselves" and agreed to look for employment elsewhere. The strikers gave up their demand that all trolley workers be union members but insisted that striking mechanics and inspectors also get pay raises. Arena, Frugoni, and the two strike delegates brought these proposals to Manini, who then called the company managers to his office and argued with them for three hours. While the managers were willing to give a little, they would give no wage increases to striking mechanics and certainly not to striking inspectors. The strikers rejected the terms.[7]

The Federación Obrera completed plans for a general strike. Eight strike orators were arrested for "verbal excesses" and defended in court by Frugoni. Only 35 trolley cars were in service and the daily fines continued. The companies warned that negotiations must end, one way or another, because they "were preparing to reorganize service with new workers."[8]

Two days later the Newspaper Reporters Circle took over as mediators and obtained assurances from the strike committee that it would accept the companies' last offer if slightly improved. The managers agreed to raise inspectors' wages to 50 pesos a month and promised to raise mechanics' wages. The strikers voted acceptance, the managers acknowledged the concessions but told the press they had signed no agreements with the strikers; on the night of May 21, after ten strike days, the trolleys ran. *El Día* happily noted: "The triumph of the strike is unquestionable."[9]

Though the settlement called for rehiring all strikers except for the nine fired leaders, some men reporting back to work on La Comercial the next day were told that there was no work for them. The trolley workers, furious at being "betrayed by the companies," called on the Federación Obrera for support. Delegates of 35 unions unanimously voted to close down Montevideo with a general strike of indeterminate length as a protest "against the falsification of the terms by the managers."[10]

Around 11 P.M., after a mass meeting, about 1,000 demonstrators cheering "Viva the General Strike! Viva Batlle!" headed for Batlle's Montevideo house, broke through the police, and shouted for him to appear on the balcony. Don Pepe, accompanied by his sons and his Presidential aides, appeared and was greeted with a salvo of applause. Ángel Falco (high on Williman's police chief's list of dangerous radicals), the tall libertarian poet whose call to workers to vote for Batlle in 1910 had been rejected, climbed a tree to address the President of the Republic.

> Citizen Batlle y Ordoñez:
> Many demonstrations have filed past your house, but none like this one, none moved by the great burst of sincerity which guides the proletarians you see here united.
> The masses who know you expect that you will conduct yourself as always during this emergency, in the battle which is being waged between the strikers and the companies. You who have guided the nation on the path of liberty to reach its magnificent destiny in the conquest of universal rights, you cannot remain outside of this movement, in which there is now being debated not just the interests and aspirations of a class but the interest and security of all the nation.
> The Federación Obrera, the authentic representative of the workers of the Republic, has decreed a General Strike, not as in other countries against the Government, which has known how to maintain its neutrality, but against the companies who have not respected the conditions agreed upon with the workers. Thus this demonstration takes its leave of you in this crucial hour, shouting: Viva Batlle y Ordoñez.

The vivas rang out; the demonstrators called on Batlle to speak. He stepped to the front of the balcony, thought for a moment, and began:

The duties of my office which oblige me to maintain law and order do not permit me to take an active part in your struggle.

I am entrusted with keeping order and maintaining the rights of all the citizens of the Republic. Therefore, the Government will guarantee your rights so long as you remain on the terrain of legality.

Organize yourselves, unite, and try to achieve the improvement of your economic conditions. You can be sure that the Government will never be your enemy, so long as you respect law and order.[11]

Don Pepe's sentiments were not inflammatory, but the President of the Republic was blessing the crowd at the beginning of the first general strike in Uruguay's history, called by an organization which had dedicated itself this very month to the achievement of "Anarcho-Communism."

II

At 7 A.M. on May 23 red flags, the symbol of the general strike, went up. At 9 A.M., in the center of Montevideo, six stalled trolleys were stoned by 200 to 300 strikers. The soldiers on the cars had orders not to fire their mausers, but mounted police sabre-charged the strikers. Fortunately, Police Chief Colonel Pintos was on the scene and able to keep things from getting entirely out of hand. One policeman and one soldier were hurt, 19 strikers were arrested, and the trolleys were ruined.

Thereafter very little moved in Montevideo. Workers dressed in Sunday clothing took the day off. Newspapers weren't printed. The garbage collectors joined the strike. The Federación Obrera issued passes to doctors and authorized meat deliveries to hospitals.

By mid-afternoon it was becoming clear that the cause of the general strike had been something between a misunderstanding and an attempt by each side to upstage the other. Juan Cat of La Comercial had insisted on keeping 21 new men hired during the strike. There would be jobs for all because the reduced hours would require hiring an additional 120 men. The new hours, though, would not go into effect until June 1—nine days off—and until then 21 strikers would have to be on non-paid call. Cat explained this in a letter to Manini, while the Municipality attempted to mediate.

The Chamber of Deputies was in an uproar. Socialist Frugoni demanded that the government revoke the trolley concessions. Interior Minister Manini, interpellated in the Chamber and clearly angered by what he felt was the strikers' irresponsibility in still refusing to return to work, was pessimistic about when the strike would end. "To maintain order," the Executive, in a decree signed by Batlle and Manini, prohibited a street meeting called by the Federación Obrera.

May 25, fortunately, was a national holiday. Manini was again called to the Chamber of Deputies, accused by some deputies of letting the Federación Obrera run Montevideo and by Frugoni of supporting Cat. Manini's patience with the general strike had evaporated. He insisted that police and army units were in control of Montevideo. The street meeting had been forbidden because it "offered the most serious danger." Its sponsor, the Federación Obrera, "an entirely anarchist federation, as deputy Frugoni knows, is made up of revolutionary elements, sabotage, destruction, and violence." A general strike was "either a grave error or subversion." If the population should lack meat, bread, water, and light, even for twenty-four hours, "because of the strike . . . the Executive Power would use servants of the State [i.e. the army] to assure essential services."[12]

That evening the Municipality's mediation efforts succeeded. The trolley strikers agreed to return to work on the basis of Cat's letter of May 24 to Manini. The Federación Obrera voted, with six unions opposed, to end the general strike. Uruguay's general strike, which had lasted 48 hours, was over. *El Día* proudly noted that no one had been killed or even seriously wounded, and that was far better strike handling than Europe could claim.[13]

Not everyone was as satisfied. Anarchists and Marxists complained that Batlle's government had exposed its fundamentally bourgeois basis by forbidding public demonstrations and arresting 85 men during the strike. The Directorio newspaper, which had been sympathetic to the first trolley strike, blamed Batlle for the general strike. First he had tried to win "cheap popularity" with impossible promises to the strikers; then he had "fomented" the general strike with his balcony speech; finally, "the President of the Republic led it."[14]

El Siglo called Manini, whose hostility to the general strike was evident, "the man of the hour." Batlle refused to allow Manini to be separated from him. Manini's Chamber speech agreed with Batlle's views except in one particular: "although the President is aware that among the elements constituting the Federación Obrera there are those with revolutionary ideas, advocates of sabotage, destruction, and violence, he also believes that he does not have proof that the organization itself has that character." The Federación made Batlle's statement somewhat more plausible by issuing a manifesto saying there was room in it for all those, regardless of ideology, who wanted honorably to struggle against man's exploitation of man.[15] *El Día* had not published Don Pepe's balcony speech to the strikers—the speech might have angered the public—and *El Siglo* criticized him for the omission. Don Pepe now answered that he would make the same speech under the same circumstances.

> The labor element is an important part of the nation and the nation cannot be said to be really well off as long as the worker's economic situation is not good.
>
> This is not yet recognized because up to now our worker had suffered in silence. The day when he organizes politically, goes to elections, makes up a considerable part of the legislature and makes his voice heard on all public questions, it will no longer seem so strange that a President speaks to him and treats him with respect.[16]

His support of the strike had cost Batlle political support. The Nationalists were picturing him as the strike's leader; there were attempts to split away Manini and there were Colorados who felt Batlle had gone too far in backing a revolutionary strike. Batlle tried to downplay the revolutionary aspects; he had reminded the strikers to stay within the law; he refused to admit that the Federación Obrera was Anarchist. For the short term the political loss was not too serious; Don Pepe had just taken office and the legislature was virtually all-Colorado. And for the long term, when the worker "organizes politically, goes to elections, makes up a considerable part

SIGNO TERRIBLE

21. *El Siglo* cartoon during the general strike. The cartoon is entitled "Terrible Symptom." Manini: "But President, don't you see that the whole country is protesting?" Batlle: "Never mind. The country is crazy." *El Siglo* regularly drew Batlle as a huge man with a tiny head and carrying a *macana* (club, Río de la Plata symbol of blunder), to show that he was a big *macaneador* (blunderer). This cartoon implies that Batlle's condition was worsening, that he was going crazy. From *El Siglo*, June 1, 1911.

22. *El Día* cartoon during the general strike. Juan Andrés Ramírez, editor of *El Siglo* had written, "The Origin of the Strike is Disagreeable." Batlle asked *El Día* cartoonist Hermenegildo Sabat (Carolus) to draw Ramírez inside a cheese, a Río de la Plata symbol of living the good life. The cartoon is entitled "The Origin of the Strike is Disagreeable" and is captioned "When someone has more than he needs, that is, when someone is inside the cheese, it is easy for him to think that someone else who asks for a little more bread and a little less slavery is disagreeable." Ramírez, pictured in the cartoon with guns in hand and surrounded by strikers' corpses (labeled the people), had criticized Batlle's orders to soldiers not to fire their rifles. From *El Día*, May 29, 1911.

of the legislature," Batlle was moving to ensure worker support for the Colorados—support that would counteract defections that likely would result from his pushing Uruguay in the direction he intended it to go. Meanwhile, Batlle was well pleased with the strike's outcome.

> In addition to undeniable moral advantages, the trolley workers have obtained material improvements that can be easily translated into numbers. . . .
>
> Approximately 1,700 workers improved their situation; the average improvement is fifteen cents a day per man, a total of 255 pesos daily. Also, because of the reductions in hours, the companies need to employ 150 additional men, which at 1.35 each represents an expense of 202.50 pesos; total 457.50 per day.
>
> The strike has, therefore, obliged the companies to pay out 13,725 pesos monthly, which will be transformed into a little more bread and a little less fatigue. Besides, 150 new families have their poor existence assured.
>
> Without the strike . . . this money, which represents the appetizing sum of 167,000 pesos per year, would have continued to go to London and Berlin along with other fat profits, with the pleasant prospect of making the pockets of the British and German stockholders a little heavier. Now these 167,000 pesos will stay in the country and be spread—along with a little bit of happiness— among the poor people.[17]

The Montevideo Municipality failed to collect the fines levied on the companies during the strike. The judge ruled that the requested embargo and sale of the lines was not authorized by law. Don Pepe was not fazed. He had the Intendent draw up a new list of infringements and fines.[18]

III

Manini's appearances in the Chamber of Deputies during the general strike were exciting afternoons for the Deputies, who were now extremely busy. Batlle's projects were being rushed through committees and out to the floor, while the Executive constantly sent down new projects—expansion of the Bank of the Republic, authorization of state-run railroads, a tax on imported mange medicine for livestock (a protectionist measure which alarmed rural interests), a university for women.

A new law authorized the Montevideo Municipality to repave the entire city with asphalt and to require property owners who would benefit to pay two thirds of the cost. The Montevideo real estate tax law was revised to allow the government to expropriate property at appraised value plus a maximum of 40 percent. This would make expropriation cheaper and simpler and could increase tax collections; owners who felt their appraised value was too low could set their own higher property value for payment of real estate taxes. And Batlle pushed for quick completion of the Montevideo house-to-house property appraisal he and Serrato had begun in 1905.[19]

Batlle was taking advantage of prosperity to press projects that would change Uruguay and both strain and expand the economy. For economic expansion to continue, it was necessary that its ranching base grow. More intensive ranching would build up the interior, reduce its backwardness relative to Montevideo, provide employment for the rural poor, and substantially increase Uruguay's exports, something absolutely vital to pay for the constantly growing imports brought in by prosperity and Batlle's economic expansion program. Ranchers, however, opposed efforts to force growth on them. As Deputy Sánchez put it during debate, rural progress could not be forced: "it comes slowly and judiciously in the constant evolution of rural life."[20]

Ranchers had good reason to be satisfied with their rate of progress. The process of breed improvement begun in the South of Uruguay under the influence of the Argentine market and example in the 1870's when resident European ranchers in Uruguay imported pedigreed bulls and rams had moved North and East, encouraged by railroad building, and now covered the whole country providing heavier steers and sheep. Livestock numbers, shown by the 1908 census, were up. So were livestock prices: for the years 1905–11, the average price of a steer was 23.5 percent higher than in the previous decade; the price of wool was up 20.3 percent.[21]

Ranchers had been watching the declining market for *Tasajo* (salt beef), the traditional product made from lean, non-crossbred criollo cattle and exported to Brazil and Cuba as food for slaves. The single refrigerated packing plant in the country, the Frigorífico Uruguayo, which exported higher priced frozen meat to England, had commenced operations in 1905 and only slowly expanded slaughtering. In 1911 it was bought by an Anglo-Argentine meat packer. There was concern in Uruguay that their steers and sheep would be neglected in favor of Argentine livestock. The Uruguayan Minister in England worked out arrangements for a second refrigerated packing plant. A British firm would build and run the plant, the Uruguayan government would provide the majority of the capital, the British firm would buy the government out once the plant was operating successfully. This was not the kind of state enterprise Batlle preferred. Minister of Industries Acevedo, the principal architect of the proposal, referred to the proposed plant as "semi-official," and when Swift, anxious to break into the Río de la Plata to provide frozen meat for sale in England, announced that it was building a packing plant in Montevideo that could slaughter 1,000 steers and 3,000 sheep daily, the government shelved its project for a second *frigorífico* (refrigerated packing plant). To meet the new competition, the old Frigorífico Uruguayo was being expanded. Ranchers, though there now was concern that Uruguay was falling into the hands of the beef trust, now had an expanding market for their improved livestock.[22]

Uruguayan ranchers felt that they knew their business. The country's natural pasture was one of the world's finest grazing regions. Ranchers managed this range skillfully. Ranch productivity was maximized by grazing cattle and sheep together. Virtually unique to the world, Uruguay made no distinction between cattle ranchers and sheep raisers; all ranchers grazed both. Cattle ate the high grass, sheep the short grass. Over the years ranchers had learned the carrying capacity of their pastures, the sheep-cattle ratio most suitable to their region of the country. Grazing sheep and cattle together was also a pragmatic form of insurance against the country's climate. Because Uruguay is a border region where cold air masses coming up around the frigid Atlantic tip of South America run into tropical air from Brazil, its rainfall pattern is erratic. Some years bring drought; others bring excessive rainfall. Cattle die during drought, but sheep are hardier; rain-soaked pastures incubate parasites that kill sheep, while cattle thrive in wet years.[23]

But ranchers had also reached the limit of the carrying capacity of their natural pastures. In fact, there now were fewer cattle on the range than there had been when the 1908 census was taken, because of a serious drought in 1910–11. Ranchers did not irrigate; they did not seed land for artificial pasture; they did not use fertilizer; they did not feed cattle maize; they did very little in disease control—hoof and mouth disease was widespread. The result was that it took four to five years to prepare a steer for a refrigerated packing plant compared to two years in more advanced systems; wool yields and the percentage of lambs and calves born were well below those of Australia and New Zealand, and livestock mortality was higher. Going beyond natural pasture and into intensive ranching could quadruple production and assure the continuation of Uruguay's economic expansion.[24] Ranchers were obstinate, however. They remembered that the pioneers of the 1870's had lost money. They realized that intensive ranching required heavy new investment and additional labor and would bring on a whole new set of problems.

Ranchers were not a closed group. Land was the classic form of investment in Uruguay. In 1911 alone 471,960 hectares valued at 51 million pesos would be sold, and at this rate in 35 years land equal in area to the total rural property in private possession would change hands. Ranchers invested in land, but so did nonranchers. Nonranchers bought land, held it until it rose in value (for the five years from 1906 to 1910 land had gone up 80 percent) and meanwhile rented it out. Nonranching owners were content with low rent yields, just as investors elsewhere were willing to accept low dividends if their stocks rose. The result was that somewhere between a quarter and a half of all Uruguay's ranches were operated by renters. Leases were short, three to four years, to keep investments liquid; improvements accrued to the owner. This meant that renters did nothing to improve pastures, accentuating the bottleneck in moving from extensive to intensive ranching.[25]

Agronomists were urging ranchers to seed their lands with oats as artificial pasture (alfalfa did not do well in Uruguay). "At present a steer needs a hectare and a half of natural pasture during four years to reach 450 kilograms in weight, worth 20 pesos; by cultivating artificial pasture it is entirely possible to grow two steers on the same land, who will reach 500 kilograms in weight in three years, bringing a price of 25 pesos each," a profit of 100 percent on the additional investment. But

23. Uruguayan ranching, 1911. Source: Reginald Lloyd and others, *Impresiones*.

in all Uruguay, a country with a ground area of 18,700,000 hectares, only 34,000 hectares, an infinitesimal amount, were in oats.[26] To sow oats a rancher had to buy tractors, hire and train help—make a very substantial investment. Suppose his land was not suitable for oats? Suppose there was too much rain? The entire investment would be lost.

Ranching was profitable. Contemporaries put profits at above 12 percent annually; later analysts put it much higher. If a rancher wanted to expand production, the surest and most profitable way was to buy more land, or else rent it. If a rancher wanted to speculate for high-risk profits, he could become an *invernador* and buy cattle for fattening. All these solutions were economically rational; but none shifted Uruguay's ranching from extensive to intensive. Here was a classic example of the nonworking of Adam Smith's invisible hand; self-interest was not promoting the general interest.[27]

Batlle had a long-range program to force intensive use of land which would also result in more revenue for the government from landowners. But that would come when the political situation was assured for well beyond this presidential term. For now there were other methods of expanding rural production. The state railroads, which would charge low rates and by competition force the English-owned railroads to lower their rates, were designed to open new lands to agriculture. The 1908 Census listed only 870,000 hectares under cultivation, less than 5 percent of Uruguay's land area, and railroad costs were now considered too high to make farming expansion profitable at any distance from Montevideo. State railroads were one way to expand rural production; greater technical knowledge was another. On May 27, by decree, the Executive awarded scholarships to the first graduating class of agronomists for study trips to Europe, the United States, and Australia, to bring back techniques for use in Uruguay.[28]

Eduardo Acevedo, the new Minister of Industries, had long been concerned with modernizing rural production, and Batlle encouraged Acevedo to put his ideas into operation. Acevedo was studying the problem of short-term ranch rental contracts which prohibited any plowing of the land. He wanted to require minimal contracts of ten years, with the renter having the right to be recompensed for improvements made during the contract.[29] Acevedo had many other rural projects. On one day, June 6, the Chamber of Deputies took up three of them. One had come from Batlle's presidential program. It set up six agronomy stations in different parts of the country. They would be up to 1,000 hectares in size; each would be staffed by professionals—this would take care of the first class of agronomists— and "model worker families." The stations would act as instruction and demonstration centers in improved agricultural, dairying, poultry, ranching, and agro-ranching techniques.

Acevedo was confident that within forty years these stations would improve the knowledge level of the rural population, "so that the productive capacity of the country can be quadrupled using the same capital now in operation." Not all the deputies shared Acevedo's enthusiasm. Deputy Sánchez estimated the bill's cost at one million pesos plus an annual budget of 150,000, an excessively elaborate program for Uruguay. Acevedo defended his project. In order for demonstration farms to impress the rural population, large-size plots were necessary. Results obtained otherwise were considered artificial. The great problem of Uruguay was to improve the feeding of livestock by associating agriculture with ranching. Finally, Acevedo announced that foreign professors would be contracted to assist in the program. Some deputies wanted more time and more information, but this piece of legislation had been in Batlle's Presidential program, and Batlle wanted it passed now. The bill, exactly as it came from committee, was approved on June 24, 1911. The Senate quickly approved it with minor changes, and by September it was law.[30]

The second Acevedo bill provided for twenty annual prizes, totaling 200,000 pesos, to ranchers "who have most distinguished themselves in the agro-ranching colonization of their establishments." Acevedo explained that the Government intended to encourage ranchers to set up five or six small dairy, poultry, forage, or tree plots on their land. This bill angered Socialist Frugoni. The way to make latifundists useful was not to give them cash rewards but to institute a progressive land tax. Objections in the Chamber were strong enough to return the prize bill to Committee. In the interim, *El Día* chided the objectors. Those who called for taxation to aid agriculture had a point, but taxation was only one part of the "general plan" of agro-ranching transformation.[31] A compromise emerged. On January 1, 1915, there would be "a contest of ranchers, landowners, or renters of pasture land who had distinguished themselves in the partial agro-ranching colonization of their establishments" in every department. The total prizes were reduced to 180,000 pesos, and for proprietors of over 2,000 hectares the prize would be honorific.[32]

The third Acevedo bill proposed to raise the land tax 25 percent for every rancher who did not devote at least one percent of his lands to forage agriculture and also plant five trees for every hectare of land. Trees provided shade for livestock and, because they kept moisture in the ground, mitigated drought. The proposal was similar to Williman's but produced no comparable outcry. Acevedo insisted that even on poor land, ranchers could find some small area for forage. He promised that the government agricultural school would have one million trees available for distribution this year and eight million next year.

It was apparent that the bill was inadequately drafted. It would require ranchers to plant trees when trees were not yet available. In Uruguay, where natural conditions permitted tree growth mostly along river and stream beds, tree planting required more than digging holes: trees had to be watered and cared for until mature. But the bill simply called for planting. The deputies were not satisfied and sent it back to committee.[33]

The indefatigable Acevedo had other projects. The Chamber approved his bill to advance the cost of sea passage to immigrants. He proposed to set up a Fishing Institute that would consist of a director, subdirector, photographer, two foremen, and eight sailors. It would purchase a ship, fish, and investigate how to establish a modern fishing industry. This bill was also approved, after some protests at the size of the Director's salary.[34] The law of Defensa Agrícola, establishing a corps of inspectors and financed by an increase in the rural land tax of one half peso per thousand pesos of assessed land value, to take measures against locusts and other harmful insects, passed the Chamber. Deputies grumbled that nineteen inspectors could do nothing against a plague of locusts.[35]

IV

Batlle viewed this administration as the end of the beginning. It would establish the course Uruguay would take long into the future.

But he also viewed it as a great opportunity to make changes now. His handling of the general strike showed this; he was delighted at the gains it won for trolley workers and used it to begin a process of winning labor for the Colorado Party. Similarly, he was instituting parts of the rural program which he believed to be possible now— Acevedo talked of the forty-year effect of agronomy stations—while preparing the way for the later, more radical parts.

Toward the end of Batlle's first administration, Serrato had talked of economic development. Then, the words sounded strange. Eduardo Acevedo clearly was an early development economist. He recognized the needs and prospects of rural development. He realized that Uruguay, which virtually ignored fishing, had a potential for a great fishing industry. But Acevedo, because he recognized so many opportunities, preferred the pilot program approach. His projects, except for the agronomy stations, where Batlle's hand was involved, provided very small means to reach the desired ends. In a country with a negligible fishing tradition, what could thirteen men and a single fishing boat accomplish? If Batlle's long-term political solutions triumphed, the Fishing Institute would be expanded. The danger was that if Batlle, their protector, passed from the scene, pilot programs designed to meet ends that most Uruguayans were not excited about, would degenerate into bureaucratic offices that accomplished little.

CHAPTER 10

The Model Country

Minister of Finance Serrato, who was much closer to Batlle than was Acevedo, had a very different approach to economic development than Acevedo did. Serrato favored large, well-financed projects. The Board of Directors of the Bank of the Republic had proposed to Serrato in April that its authorized capital be raised and that its legal status conform to its real status, that it legally be state owned. The Bank of the Republic, together with the Montevideo elective power system, were the great successes of Uruguayan state enterprise. Their success demonstrated that the state was a productive and efficient manager in both credit and industry and served as justification for Batlle's program to establish many new enterprises. The Bank of the Republic itself, founded in 1896 after the failure of the privileged Banco Nacional in 1890, had at first been ultracautious. In recent years, however, the Bank had greatly contributed to prosperity by expanding money and credit. The Bank's total commercial credit outstanding went up from 6.3 million pesos on December 31, 1900, to 23 million at the end of 1910. It now monopolized banknotes in circulation, having replaced the paper currency issued by private banks with its own, and expanded the total circulating by over 30 percent in the five years ending in 1910. Private banks, especially branches of foreign banks, concentrated on financing foreign trade. The Bank of the Republic, which had branches in every department, financed business and ranches. The Bank had lowered its basic interest rate to 8 percent from 10 percent, driven the traditional usurers of the interior out of business, and became an influence to force lower interest rates on Montevideo private banks, which resented its competition.[1]

The Bank had originally been chartered as a joint public-private venture, but at that time private capital had not invested. Batlle, who had been one of the earliest advocates of a State Bank, had refused two offers to sell the Bank of the Republic during his first presidency.[2] He welcomed the Board's proposal to convert it officially to a State Bank. The Bank was well managed—too well managed for those who wanted its lending policy to emphasize the enterprise and character of borrowers rather than their financial worth. But the Bank's policy had enabled it to more than triple commercial credit in only ten years and still keep its loan default rate at only one third of one percent.[3] The Bank's paid-in capital, constantly increasing as the result of Williman's legislation allowing it to reinvest its profits, was getting close to its authorized capital of 8.2 million pesos, and the Board proposed to Serrato that the Bank's authorized capital be raised to 10 million pesos.

Batlle and Serrato saw the chance to speed up the process of making the Bank the colossus that Batlle, in Europe, had predicted it would become. Their bill revising the Bank's Charter to make it a State Bank increased its authorized capital to 20 million pesos and, of greater immediate impact, authorized it to raise its banknote issue to three times paid-in capital instead of the present double.[4] This meant that the Bank could immediately increase its lending capacity by close to 40 percent. To maintain confidence in the Bank—as the successor of the failed Banco Nacional, maintenance of public and business confidence in the Bank of the Republic was a constant preoccupation of the management and every government—the requirement that banknotes of 10 pesos and over in circulation plus sight deposits have at least a 40 percent gold backing was retained (currently, the Bank gold holdings were at 58 percent). And the Bank was authorized to rediscount private bank paper, the beginning of a central bank role.

The Executive's message to the legislature accompanying the new charter stated that now the Bank of the Republic would be "a great State Bank." The legislators were willing. The only point that concerned them was the interest rate on small loans to public employees—vital Colorado electoral elements—by the Bank's Caja de Ahorros (Savings Division). They wanted a maximum interest rate of 7 percent on these loans, which were repaid by payroll deductions. Serrato, who favored strong enterprises that would operate successfully and could expand operations from earnings not just through government subsidy, refused. To the surprise of some, Arena, who acknowledged that he had "borrowed money many times from the institution," supported Serrato. "Nobody should do business in which he must lose money." The legislators were adamant; Serrato compromised. The current rate was 9 percent; it would go down to 8. From legislative debate to enactment into law required only ten days. On July 13, 1911, the Bank of the Republic, under its new charter, was officially operating as a State Bank.[5]

II

There had been no significant opposition to formalizing the status of the Bank of the Republic, and the prospect of its immediate expansion and of increased lending to businessmen and ranchers was very welcome. Batlle and Serrato's project to establish a State insurance monopoly was an entirely different matter. No one was very interested in the State becoming an insurer. The bill Manini and Arena had filed in 1908 after Batlle urged them to from Europe was absolutely dormant.[6] The State as an insurer inspired few, but the State's monopolizing insurance without any previous experience as an insurer alarmed many. In May the legislature had received formal objections from twenty-six insurance companies and eighty-seven commercial firms. There were growing rumors that foreign governments would demand that compensation be paid to foreign private insurance companies, which would be forced out of business.

On August 17, 1911, the Chamber began debate on the bill. The Executive message written by Serrato[7] was short: "the permanent outflow of money is inconvenient." Foreign insurance companies received an average of 926,000 pesos annually in premiums; local companies received 381,000 pesos. The State insurance monopoly, if it kept the same premium structure, would earn substantial income; if it lowered premiums, it would popularize insurance, and either way it would stop "the annual exportation of large sums of money."

Article One of the bill stated: "Insurance contracts, covering fire, maritime, agricultural, ranching, life risks, and in general risks of all kinds, are declared a State monopoly." Until the Executive decided to monopolize a particular class of insurance, private companies could operate. Policies written by private companies before the state took over would continue until expiration. (This was the way to avoid paying compensation to the private insurance companies, who would ultimately be forced to close down. *El Día* had already explained: "No property is going to be taken from the companies, and obviously they cannot claim rights or ownership over future action, which would be the only apparent justification which could be invoked.")[8] The National Insurance Bank was established with a capital of two million pesos in 5 percent government bonds, which it could sell. The Bank's investments must be conservative—in government bonds, short-term commercial paper, real property, and mortgages. It was explicitly forbidden to buy stocks, speculate in real estate, or trade on the stock exchange. Profits, after debt service, would go to reserves until a special law made other provisions. If capital and reserves were inadequate, the State would guarantee payment of the Bank's obligations. The State Insurance Bank would be run by a president and six directors, with the same salaries as the Board of Directors of the Bank of the Republic.

Batlle's original idea, sent to Arena and Manini from Europe in 1908, was to establish a state insurance company. Now, after consulting with Serrato, who was disappointing conservative opinion by seconding Batlle, Don Pepe had gone further and was proposing that the State monopolize all insurance. Serrato had produced a plan for a solid institution that would meet Batlle's goal of stopping the outflow of gold and also, through the State Insurance Bank's investments, strengthen Uruguay's credit system.

The insurance companies' protest to the legislature warned that 180 million pesos in insurance was written in Uruguay. To protect itself against catastrophe and spread its risks, a State Bank would have to reinsure. Foreign companies, driven out of Uruguay, might be unwilling to do business with the State monopoly. If, in spite of everything, the State decided to monopolize insurance, the companies "should be indemnified for damages caused by stopping operations and the earning of legitimate profits, the fruit of long years of perseverance and constant advertising." Not only were the insurance companies and Uruguayan businessmen hostile, but the Chamber Committee studying the bill had to admit that while such proposals were discussed in Italy and France, in America "nobody of whom we are aware had awakened the interest of the public on this question." The committee's majority preferred that the State compete with private companies rather than monopolize insurance, and asked Serrato "to refute this opinion."

Uruguayan policy holders, Serrato answered, were now inadequately protected because the foreign companies had negligible assets in Uruguay. (Batlle's basic contention was that the companies paid all claims out of part of the premiums collected in Uruguay and sent the balance abroad as profits). The State Bank would reinsure major risks, estimated at 5 to 10 percent of the total, until its reserves were large enough to be its own reinsurer, in the same way that major fire insurance companies operated. The Bank's premiums would be lower because it would be exempt from premium taxes. Estimated annual profits, after reinsurance, would be at least 400,000 pesos. Uruguay now had 30 insurance agencies; if the state competed there would be 31. There was not enough insurance business in the country to justify this. On the other hand, a single insurer with substantial administrative savings resulting from 30 offices combined into one would be strong and profitable.[9]

While Serrato's well prepared presentation was being studied, Don Pepe made it known that this was a must bill. He kept a list on how legislators stood on the insurance bank, each name followed by A: Adverso (Opposed); F: Favorable; or V: Vacilante (Vacillating).[10] The Committee thought further, found compelling the Serrato argument that a non-monopolistic State Bank would be unsuccessful, and by a majority of 5 to 2 voted out favorably the Executive's project with some modifications. The monopoly would be limited to life insurance, fire insurance (which accounted for 121.5 million of the 180 million pesos of insurance written), and accident insurance. Maritime insurance, which was likely to be written abroad anyway, would not be monopolized. The Bank's capitalization was raised to 3 million pesos and its Board of Directors reduced to five members.

On the Chamber floor Deputy Zorrilla rose, announced that he wanted to propose a substitute bill limiting the monopoly to accident insurance, and asked for a delay in further debate until September. The Finance Committee chairman agreed to the delay.[11]

Something had happened. On July 29, the British Minister in Montevideo had cabled the British Foreign Office. On August 16, the day before debate in the Uruguayan Chamber of Deputies was to begin, a question was asked in the House of Commons: "whether it is proposed to take any, and if so what, steps to protect the interests of the British insurance companies transacting business in the Republic?" Mr. McKinnon Wood answered for the Government: "Yes Sir; and I am telegraphing to his Majesty's Minister to make representations to the Uruguay Government."[12] The next day the British Minister in Uruguay, Robert J. Kennedy, delivered this letter to Foreign Minister Romeu:

MONTE VIDEO
August 17th 1911.

PRIVATE

My dear Minister,

I hope you will allow me the privilege of an old friend of your country and of yourself to draw through you the attention of the Government of this Republic to the difficulties which in the opinion of His Majesty's Government will probably ensue if a State Insurance Monopoly be established in Uruguay. Those difficulties, as you of course are aware, are ably explained in the memorials signed by representatives of the Insurance Companies, and of the Principal Commercial Houses of this city which were presented to the Honourable Chamber in the month of May last. My Government has specially telegraphed desiring me to remind the Government of this Republic of the disadvantage which would accrue to the people of Uruguay if they are debarred from continuing to enjoy the maximum benefits and minimum rates ensured to them by the freedom of competition between Insurance Companies.

I am able to ask Your Excellency to bear in mind that in the event of British Companies and their Agents being precluded from continuing the Insurance business which they have honourably conducted for many years past under the protection of the constitution of this country, legal and Diplomatic claims will probably be preferred against the Uruguayan Government. Such an eventuality would be greatly deplored by His Majesty's Government. . . .

I am also to state that as the public credit of this country stands at the present time extremely high, Sir Edward Grey would much regret if the confidence of European Firms should in any way be shaken in its Commercial and Financial stability.[13]

England was taking this matter seriously. Far more than the small Uruguayan insurance operations were involved.[14] Italy was considering a life insurance monopoly, and other nations might follow. If the Uruguayan position won out—that no compensation need be paid because existing insurance policies were not being expropriated and because British insurance companies had no fixed assets in Uruguay—worldwide harm to British insurance, an influential industry contributing significantly to the British balance of payments, would result. England had a powerful weapon, suggested by the British Minister's sentence on Uruguay's extremely high public credit rating, to use in making Uruguay desist from monopolizing insurance. The Montevideo money market was too small to provide the funds needed for Batlle's projects. Batlle was using Uruguay's high credit rating, the result of balanced budgets and prompt debt payment, to float low interest Uruguayan government loans abroad. These loans would finance his economic development projects and, directly or indirectly, the replacement of foreign capital by government enterprises. Put oversimply, Batlle was using foreign capital (funds obtained at low interest and fixed terms abroad) to reduce the role of foreign capital (private enterprises making high profits) in Uruguay.[15] To indemnify the private insurance companies would produce a gold outflow; it would also burden the State Insurance Bank with the cost of financing the indemnification. Such a burden could make the new enterprise unprofitable when it was essential that the State Insurance Bank be successful if state enterprises were to secure the public approval necessary for them to spread into new operational areas. But if Batlle monopolized insurance without indemnifying the private companies, the British money market and the other foreign sources of loans so essential to the carrying out of

Batlle's economic development and state enterprise projects could be closed to Uruguay.[16]

The Directorio newspaper noted that receipt of the British Minister's letter had resulted in postponement of the debate and concluded: "We confess that in spite of the fact that we never had a very high opinion of the President's courage, we never believed he would break down so quickly and so completely." *El Siglo*, which had predicted the protest, called it a "hard lesson." The government, not the people, wanted an insurance monopoly. The companies should be compensated. A clause in the bill acknowledging the right of compensation, with the amount to be determined by the Uruguayan courts, would remove the grounds for foreign protest. (*El Siglo* had good sources in the insurance companies; and since the British government was acting for the companies, the suggested clause was likely the companies' terms for settlement.)[17] Batlle, using the pseudonym "Frutos"—the nickname of Fructuoso Rivera, founder of the Colorado Party (in times of trouble Batlle went back to the source of his strength, the Colorados), hit back:

> Why is the mere announcement of a diplomatic reclamation a hard lesson? . . . Is it a decision against our laws by an impartial judge? Not at all. It is an act saddening to our patriotism. It is nothing more than the fact that a world leader, a nation whose power is overwhelming for us, whose influence is as great as its power, declares that it will persist in continuing to enjoy what we consider to be ours and what we wish to apply to our own needs.[18]

III

Early in September Chamber debate on the State Insurance Bank resumed, and Serrato acknowledged that the British Minister had sent a letter to Foreign Minister Romeu. Since the letter was personal, it would not be made public. Basically, however, the British letter stated that "if the bill on monopoly is passed in its present form, this will probably give rise to legal and diplomatic reclamations." Serrato also announced that Romeu, again in a friendly letter, had answered: "Naturally, it [Romeu's letter] does not accept the doctrine that passage of the bill on monopoly can give cause for reclamations of any sort."

Pedro Cosio, Chairman of the Finance Committee and informing member on the bill, rose to make a point. "Mr. President, it is my position that no indemnification is applicable, and it is my position that no appeal to the courts to ask for indemnification will be applicable, once the law on insurance monopoly is passed." Having made the Committee's intent clear for judges later to see, Cosio sat down.

To educate public opinion, "generally conservative in our country," Serrato promised an extended defense of the bill. It was false to say that this project was the beginning of "communism or collectivism."

> If by socialism one means the improvement of the working class, the raising of their culture, their means of existence and their human dignity, if one also means a more rational distribution of wealth, if by socialism one means the defense and well being of that great economic factor called man—without which there can be no progress—then this project is clearly socialist; but if by socialism, or immediate socialist goals, one means the disappearance of private property, if by socialism one means the appropriation of all the means of production, I say that this bill is not based on the ideas of that school.

Obviously, Serrato was referring less to insurance than to the whole thrust of Batlle's economic policies. Insurance, in spite of all the talk about its complexity, was an "extraordinarily simple" business. Actuarial tables were readily available, premiums were really double what was mathematically required. The only difficult aspect was investment of the income from premiums. The Bank of the Republic's success demonstrated that the State would invest these funds "to the advantage of everyone, for the nation and for the insured."

Private companies selected their risks, especially in life insurance; currently, only the well-off were insured. Premiums left Uruguay, in the case of life insurance for up to 30 years before part returned, to contribute to the economic development of foreign countries. The bill had two aims, to keep capital from leaving the country and to cheapen insurance. Serrato envisaged eventually a "great mutual society administered by the State," which would provide all Uruguayans with life and fire insurance, but the immediate goal was premiums "reduced to the minimum necessary to guarantee the policies."[19]

On September 11, British Minister Kennedy delivered the English reply to Foreign Minister Romeu's note of September 5:

> Your Excellency will, I feel sure, excuse me from entering into official correspondence with regard to a Project of Law which is under the consideration of the Honourable Chambers but in order to prevent the possibility of some misunderstanding, I have the honour to say that the opinion expressed by Your Excellency in the Note which you have been so good as to address to me, so far as it denies the right of British Insurance Companies to compensation, is not shared by His Majesty's Government.

And on September 19, in London, the Foreign Office made its position public through the device of answering a letter of inquiry:

> I have the honour to inform you that His Majesty's Government takes exception to the measure on the general grounds that it involves the expropriation without compensation of the British Companies established in Uruguay for the transaction of Insurance business; that British Insurance Companies have spent large sums in creating and extending their business to the regulations imposed by Uruguayan law; that it is only by continuing to carry on this business that they can expect to recoup themselves for their large expenditure in the past; that under the proposed Law all the valuable assets of the Companies comprised in the term "good will" are to be annihilated; and that the measure proposed by the Uruguayan Government is consequently of a confiscatory character.[20]

On September 12, the day after the British Minister had delivered the note officially rejecting the Uruguayan position on compensation, Serrato, without mentioning the note, concluded his presentation. Monopoly was the only efficient solution but, if necessary, there was another way to achieve the twofold end of keeping gold from leaving Uruguay and reducing insurance premiums. To set up a State Bank, which would charge low premiums because it did not need to make profits, to compete with private companies, which would have to be required to keep substantial reserves in Uruguay to protect policyholders, "did not appear to us to be completely proper; nevertheless we will do it if we cannot set up the monopoly."[21]

IV

During these first six months of Batlle's government, the Nationalist Directorio—its old Conservative-Radical split healed—did very little. It was content to watch Batlle antagonize group after group: business, by his support of unions during the general strike and now with his insurance monopoly; ranchers, with the programs to encourage intensive land use; Catholics, with his recalling of Williman's envoy to the Vatican. And, as was by now common knowledge, Batlle had plans to use constitutional reform to abolish the Presidency of the Republic.[22] If Batlle actually persisted in this fantasy, he would split his base of support, the Colorados. Then the Nationalists—united with the dissident Colorados and with all the others horrified that instead of the promised "mature" Batlle, Uruguay now was being governed by a "radical" Batlle—would triumphantly come out of the electoral abstention they had imposed on themselves after the revolutionary fiasco of October 1910 and go to the polls.

Saravia's sons had other ideas. They were living across the border in Brazil, had bought a boatload of German arms, organized the Club Nacionalista—Uruguayo in Bagé on the Brazilian side of the Uruguayan border—and were bringing in men for the next revolution. They sent Abelardo Márquez, one of their late father's most trusted lieutenants, to the Directorio with the news.

The Directorio, whose predecessor had stepped aside at the beginning of October 1910 revolution so as not to complicate its prospects, had no hesitation in stopping revolution this time. Batlle was digging his own political grave, but Nationalist revolution would save him. The Colorados would forget their grievances, the conservative classes once again would prefer Batlle over war. The government army was more powerful than ever—it had just been on field maneuvers, an innovation in army training—and revolution now would be a worse disaster than in 1910. Abelardo Márquez was told that the Directorio would "disauthorize" the Saravias if they continued the wild idea of revolution.[23] And without mentioning names, on September 26 the Directorio publicly warned Nationalists that it had received inquiries from coreligionaries about imminent outbreaks of war.

> It is not necessary to analyze the causes of the anxieties which motivate this note, but the most important are the attitude of the man in government whose duty should be to insure peace and public tranquility. The movements of army units and the increase in army size, and the inflammatory press diatribes which the President of the Republic himself daily directs against the National Party [Don Pepe had started reprinting the 1903 "Nationalist Crimes in the Department of Rivera" in *El Día*], all these actions seem to be directed toward provoking Nationalists to an armed movement in which they would be at a notorious disadvantage, and which would constitute an exact repetition of the policy followed in 1903 by the same citizens who today direct the nation.[24]

Brazilian troops dispersed the group the Saravias had formed. The Saravias, realizing they had no support, vowed to live in Brazil as long as Batlle governed.[25] Batlle, who had seemed out of touch with Uruguayan reality when he insisted from Europe that the way to end Nationalist revolution was not to appease the Nationalists but to demonstrate that revolution had no chance of success, had once more shown that he understood Uruguayan politics very well indeed.

V

The Chamber of Deputies, meeting three times weekly on insurance, was reaching the end of the first phase of debate. Chairman Pedro Cosio of the Finance Committee explained that in London the little known Fire Office Committee, "a force which, as part of the powerful financial forces which operate in London, contributes as all the rest toward extending from England those multiple tentacles with which they absorb the economic lifeblood of many, many new countries, countries which over there they still confuse with colonial trading posts," set uniform premiums charged by all the companies. When they had to pay the business license tax based on invested capital, the companies had confessed to the tax director that they had no capital in Uruguay. Their only real assets were the buildings that some of them owned, which could be sold at a profit, and the government bonds they were obliged to deposit, which had increased in value since purchase. There was simply nothing to indemnify. Finally, at 9:27 P.M. on October 5, 1911 the Chamber took the first vote: Affirmative in general. The bill next had to be approved article by article.[26]

Simultaneously with insurance the Chamber was processing a whole series of Don Pepe's protectionist bills. Uruguay had a long way to go before it was industrialized. The Manufacturers Association, by including dentists, photographers and the like, had compiled a list of 4,540 industrial establishments in 1907, but when the Cámara Mercantil de Productos del País prepared a brochure for the 1910 Brussels Exposition, its list, industry by industry, barely reached 450, most of which were workshops, not factories.[27] Batlle intended, El Día explained, "intense stimulation to industry and production. The Executive Power has directed its attention to the creation of new activities and to the strengthening of old ones."[28]

The Fábrica Nacional de Sombreros was exporting hats to Paraguay and proposed to "conquer" the Chilean market; it got Executive endorsement of its request that it receive refunds of duties paid on the import of raw materials used in the manufacture of the hats it exported. Hat export was so minimal that it did not appear in export statistics—shoes valued at 1,577 pesos and cigarettes at 14,715 pesos officially made up Uruguay's manufactured exports. The Chamber broadened the refund to all manufactured exports. A bottle-making plant had been established on the sands of the dump at El Buceo and 150 glass workers had been brought from Europe. The company could not sell its bottles, suspended operations, and asked the Executive for additional tariff protection. A tariff of 25 percent of the price of imported bottles was approved.[29]

So far, objections to Batlle's heightened protectionism had not been serious, but when the Executive proposed in May an import duty of 10 cents a kilogram on sarnífugos (livestock mange curatives), resistance was intense. Mange damaged livestock hides and reduced wool yields. According to optimistic estimates, ranchers were bathing 70 percent of Uruguay's sheep annually in sarnífugos. To encourage the use of sarnífugo, rural leaders and wool exporters had asked that sarnífugos, which though imported duty free did pay internal sales taxes, be totally tax exempt. Don Pepe saw the problem differently; from 1904 to 1908 sarnífugos valued at 1,614,070 pesos had been imported, resulting in a substantial outflow of gold.[30] Manufacturing sarnífugos, Arena later explained to the Senate, was "an uncomplicated industry, which only requires a little assistance to come to life here. We should encourage it for national self confidence, if for no other reason, so that people no longer continue to believe that we have to depend totally on foreign suppliers for even the most elementary preparation of industrial antiseptics."[31]

On July 4 the Asociación Rural, "with all the prestige which this organization enjoys as the oldest representative of rural interests," forwarded to the Chamber of Deputies a memorandum opposing import duties on sarnífugos. Cheap sarnífugos were essential to expand wool production. The great wool nations, Australia, New Zealand, Argentina, even the protectionist United States, allowed sarnífugos free entry. The Executive's bill would raise imported sarnífugos prices 300,000 to 350,000 pesos a year. The one Uruguayan producer, the soap makers Strauch and Co., now supplied only one third of the market. "Is Uruguay at the first moment of its industrial debut able to produce a product that can compete with the English, American, and Austrian ones, which have behind them long years of experience, the patient observation of specialized technicians . . .?" Local manufacturers could be encouraged to develop their product by exempting raw materials from import duties.

The Chamber Committee, impressed, by a vote of 4 to 2 reported out a substitute bill continuing free entry and exempting raw materials. Chamber debate began on October 10. Minister of Industries Acevedo insisted on the Executive's bill as "a means of defending the gold holdings of the country against the drainage to which it is now condemned." Alfredo Vidal, speaking for the Committee, argued that the Executive's bill, ultimately, was a tax on wool exports and quoted from Acevedo's book—written before he became Batlle's Minister—against export taxes. When the vote came, the Chamber approved the Executive's bill, and the Directorio newspaper fumed: "We are living under complete absolutism."[32]

In the Senate, Arena, the bill's spokesman, insisted that, at most, the cost of bathing 1,000 sheep a year would go up 15 pesos, which would not have the slightest effect on the "succulent profits" of ranchers who, say what you will, were "right now" the least taxed group in the nation; "it is obvious that our existing taxes, even though they appear heavy to some, will have to be made heavier still in order to improve the lot of so many unfortunate people who deserve some help from the State." On November 13 the bill became law. On November 16 *El Día* printed a short announcement in a prominent place. Francisco Comas and Co. of Buenos Aires was starting up a sarnífugo factory in Montevideo.[33]

Batlle was encouraging what economists of a later generation would call import-substituting industrialization. He realized that protectionism would raise prices, but it would also provide employment and diversify the economy.[34] Protectionism dovetailed with state enterprises. Both kept gold from draining away. Batlle saw this as the base for a strong currency which permitted credit expansion and further economic growth. Later economists would emphasize the favorable effects on the balance of payments of holding down gold outflow, something that would counter the inflationary effects of credit expansion. And state enterprises, by reducing the cost of services, would counteract the high prices of protected Uruguayan manufactures. Uruguayans now had cheap electricity and they soon would have cheap insurance; as state enterprise spread, more and more cheaper services would become available. The result would be generalized enjoyment by all Uruguayans of a high standard of living.

VI

The sarnífugo bill and Arena's comments during debate that ranchers would have to contribute more to the State so that it could help the unfortunates were further indications, should any be needed, that ranchers were not going to be left alone. Potentially, the most troubling outstanding question to ranchers was over the disposition of *tierras fiscales*, government lands occupied by private individuals, who neither bought them nor paid taxes on them.

The problem dated back to the first apportionments of Crown lands during the colonial period and became scandalous during Uruguay's nineteenth century chaos. In 1893 Alberto Márquez estimated that at least 1,000 leagues of land of the 7,000 in Uruguay were privately occupied tierras fiscales. But nobody really knew. To find out, Batlle and Serrato had begun a national land survey during Batlle's first administration, and it was close to completion. Before presenting a plan to recover government rights in tierras fiscales—so volatile an issue that over the last thirty years nothing had ever come of the variety of proposals to settle it—outstanding *Títulos de Ubicar Tierras Fiscales* had to be liquidated.

Títulos de Ubicar Tierras Fiscales, rights granted creditors and servitors of the nation to locate and become owners of government lands, could not be used directly because the courts had ruled that occupants of tierras fiscales had quasi-legal rights and could not be displaced by third parties until legislation finally clarifying ownership of tierras fiscales was passed, but the Títulos could be used by the occupants to clear their title. Since much of the privately occupied tierra fiscal land was surrounded by lands the occupants owned legally, landowners planning to sell their ranches bought Títulos de Ubicar Tierras Fiscales to establish their title to the tierras fiscales within the boundaries of their property. This was necessary to meet the demand of would-be purchasers for clear title.[35] Márquez' estimates were therefore high; not until the land survey was completed would it be known just how much land was still tierra fiscal, neither owned by the occupants nor taxed by the government. Serrato advised Batlle that the best way to liquidate the outstanding Títulos de Ubicar Tierras Fiscales was to have them exchanged for government bonds. Títulos entitling holders to claim 182,097 hectares were outstanding, the Bank of the Republic owned rights to 65,506 hectares, and the rest were in private hands. To secure the consent of the holders, the Títulos, which sold at between 6 and 8 pesos a hectare, were redeemed at 8.50 pesos, and a two-year period for holders to exchange their Títulos (and occupiers of tierras fiscales to purchase Títulos from holders) was negotiated.

Batlle was moving slowly but inexorably to recover government rights on tierras fiscales. So far he had not spelled out whether he intended to require illegal occupiers to pay the State for the tierra fiscal land they occupied or keep recovered tierra fiscal land for the State, or sell it off to new owners. The Executive announced that "at an opportune time" it would present

> a solution which, while making land ownership secure, makes its real distribution known . . . cheapens its transfer and at the same time that it prevents tax evasion reconquers for the private pat-

rimony of the State at least a good part of its lands, so providing the basic element for an agrarian policy of positive benefit for the national economy.[36]

VII

On October 19, two weeks after it had approved the State Insurance Bank proposal in general, the Chamber began the required article-by-article approval of the bill. Don Pepe, in the interim, had used "personal intervention with his political friends,"[37] as Serrato later put it. The result was quiet, efficient debate and Chamber approval of the State Insurance Bank in five days. Serrato, treated with great deference by the deputies, proposed, and the Chamber approved, several modifications to his original bill. From the date the law went into effect, no new private fire, life, or accident insurance companies would be permitted to open. The Bank itself could begin functioning "before the date in which some insurance operations will be monopolized by decree."[38] Batlle, without publicizing it, was backing away from a confrontation with England. (Also, Argentina had just advised the Uruguayan foreign ministry that should the law go into effect, it would support any claims that Argentine insurance companies operating in Uruguay might make.)[39] The State Insurance Bank would be legally authorized to monopolize insurance, but the Executive would not, at least at the beginning, decree monopolization. For the immediate future, as some Deputies noted, there would be a monopoly shared by the bank and existing private firms. In September, after the British note had been received, Serrato had warned that for the State to be both regulator and competitor of private insurance companies was not "completely proper," but if forced to act this way, it would. Now it was going to do just that, and a confident Serrato predicted that the State Insurance Bank would be operated as a "great corporation."

VIII

Don Pepe's vision of a model country did not stop at a high standard of living which would result from increased rural production, industrialization, and state enterprises. In his letter to Arena and Manini he looked to a nation "in which education is enormously extended," with universities in each of Uruguay's nineteen departments. His presidential program, echoing ideas he had announced at the end of his first administration, had insisted that "we cannot be outstanding because of size, nor can we or do we want to distinguish ourselves by our armed force; but we can, if we will, do ourselves proud by the intensity and brilliance of our culture . . ." and promised to establish a public *liceo* (preparatory school) in every departmental capital.

At the end of his first administration, Batlle had plans prepared for departmental liceos. Williman, who had done so much for primary education, opposed State involvement in secondary education because he feared the emergence of an intellectual proletariat and kept Batlle's plan from going into operation. Back in office, Batlle got funds authorized to complete Williman's massive primary school building program, and asked the legislature to pass a special law authorizing the Executive to establish eighteen liceos, one in each departmental capital. Existing private liceos in the interior (in 1908 there were five with 770 students), while "meritorious," were not the equal of the public liceos of Montevideo. Parents had to send their children to Montevideo. They were reluctant to send sons away and very rarely sent daughters; besides, only the rich could afford it. Liceos in every department, "a powerful factor for the intellectual, moral, and social improvement" of the interior towns, would change all this and be the beginning of "university extension" throughout the Republic. At the outset the liceos would only provide a four-year secondary education. Students would still have to go to Montevideo for the two additional years of preparatory education required before admission to the University faculties.[40]

The interior was avid for liceos, and deputies who might have shared Williman's doubts did not make them public. Education Minister Blengio Rocca assured the deputies that the Executive would inaugurate liceos as soon as possible; existing private liceos were petitioning to become public, recognizing that State liceos would give "a better, more complete, and absolutely gratis education." On November 23 the Chamber approved the law and sent it to the Senate.[41]

Liceos for the departments pleased a substantial constituency. A companion measure, introduced and discussed simultaneously, "to create in the University a Section for Secondary and Preparatory education destined exclusively for the female sex," or more popularly, the Women's University, did not. Although there were individual feminists and a handful of women professionals in Uruguay, women's organizations were primarily connected with the Church. Batlle wanted to free women from Church influence and get them out of their homes and into the wider world. He had just sent a circular to all public offices ordering them to hire women where possible, and considered the establishment of the Women's University a high priority measure.[42]

Recognizing trouble, the Chamber passed the bill to the University of the Republic for its opinion. The University Secondary and Preparatory Council met and by majority vote came to a Solomonic decision. A four-year secondary school for women should be established but not, for now, the two additional years necessary for entry into the university faculties. While professional careers for women were "a noble theoretical idea . . . the best understood interests of our society . . . at least for the moment" would not be furthered by encouraging girls to go beyond secondary school. (Girls could enter both the University and its preparatory section, but parents considered such propinquity with males dangerous. In primary schools sexes were separated after the second grade, and though some 2,000 males, aged 12 to 19, attended the preparatory section, only 104 females did.) Unfortunately for the Chamber, Don Pepe did not agree with the University Council. A new message was sent the Chamber: "the Executive Power has the honor of again presenting for your respected consideration the Bill . . . by which a Section of Secondary and Preparatory Education for the Feminine Sex is to be established in the University of Montevideo."

If preparatory education was not now included, a new law would be required later. This was "generally a slow process." If, on the other hand, preparatory education was provided at the beginning, it would encourage girls to enter secondary education classes.

> There are no convincing reasons to limit women's education when the State invests considerable sums of money to expand male education. . . . The Executive Power, therefore, asks you to pass this bill which will be, as it sees it with no reservations at all, a decided conquest for the moral and material progress of the Republic.

The Chamber Committee got Don Pepe's message, prepared an erudite report, with citations from Europe and the United States, on separate university schooling for women—something in fact different from Batlle's aim of getting more women to go to the University—and unanimously advised acceptance of the Executive's project, with only the minor change that "proved pedagogical aptitude" be required of the professors.

The extended Chamber debate took the course that debates on women usually did. Deputy Melián Lafinur, blind historian, companion of Batlle's youth, previously named by Batlle Minister to the United States, worried that trained male professionals were leaving Uruguay now. Women professionals, "because of the inferiority of their brains," would expand the intellectual proletariat. Women would be better off as dressmakers. This process, Melián Lafinur and others were certain, would end with women voting and "women who go into politics dislocate their homes." Melián Lafinur concluded with the complaint about Batlle's projects, which by now had become familiar: "what a new country like ours needs . . . is not to advance too far in things which are still very much disputed even in old societies."[43]

IX

Debate on the Women's University had begun in November and was still going on in December 1911, but there was no reason to doubt that after the deputies had talked themselves out, Batlle had the votes to pass it. The legislature was all-Colorado, and as Serrato put it, Batlle was "the undisputed leader of the Colorado Party."[44] He was using this presidency to advance Uruguay toward the model country, from women's emancipation to recovery of government lands; but however great the impetus he was giving Uruguay, it would not necessarily carry over beyond his term of office. He could, of course, pick a successor—Serrato, who was seconding his programs so effectively, was the leading candidate. But after Serrato, what?

Batlle felt it was time to unveil the beginning of his solution to the problem of how to institutionalize reform. The mechanism was constitutional. Stories had been floating that Batlle intended to use constitutional reform—this legislature would determine reform procedures—to extend his term or have himself reelected, or through the establishment of a government junta which he would head, perpetuating himself in power.[45]

Don Pepe refused to take the bait and announce his personal plans. Instead, in December he wrote a series of editorials in *El Día* on constitutional reform. On December 18, 1911, under the title "El P.E. Colegiado" ("The Collegiate Executive"), he gave the first exposition of the new government he advocated.

> The Executive Power is conceived of as a warlike power. It is force, action, speed in attacks, far-seeing unity in defense. Whoever exercises it should forever be ready to leave his house at any hour, even during the middle of the night, to discharge a pistol shot at an adversary, order the deployment of guerrillas, or take command of an army. His voice should be resonant, his manner imposing, his gestures dry and menacing. If he goes out on foot he should walk with a military step, and if on horseback or in a coach, the shoes of his equine chargers are obliged to shoot sparks from the pavement. The person in charge of the Executive Power cannot be thought of in any other form.

There was historical justification for turning over "public power without limits . . . to men of action" but "there is no doubt that the most advanced peoples in every age recognized at some time the inconvenience of domination by a single man and attempted executive government by various men."

> The idea is on the march. In the Swiss federation the executive faculties are confided to a council of seven citizens, who are elected every three years and can be reelected. One of them carries the title of president, but his mandate does not last more than a year, and his attributes are extremely limited, because the real government is in the Council. No catastrophe has occurred in that country because of its institutions. Quite the contrary! There is not a happier nation in Europe; and not because of its size and power. Its territory is only a third of ours. Its population is scarcely three times ours. . . .
>
> In France, the Executive Power is exercised by a commission. The President of the Republic has only a decorative role . . . he does not govern. The council of ministers governs. It is a commis-

sion which in turn is responsible to a much larger commission, the Legislative Body. Under this type of government France has been reborn from its immense disaster of 1870.[46]

Now the statement "I was in Switzerland for three months and I found many people there who do not know the name of the President of the Confederation" in Batlle's 1910 interview with "The Correspondent" took on new meaning. No future President in Uruguay would be able to overturn the institutional advances paid for with so much blood in 1904 if there were no President. No future President could convert himself into dictator—and every Uruguayan over thirteen years old had lived under at least one dictator.

Of equal importance, the Colegiado, the plural executive, was the way to ensure that Batlle's presidency would only be the beginning of the transformation that would convert Uruguay into the model country. Now the President dominated the Colorado Party, but under the Colegiado the Party would dominate the government. Candidates would be nominated, some for the Colegiado, some for the Senate, some for the Chamber of Deputies. They would have to pledge to carry out the party program. Now the party was quiescent except during elections; once the Colegiado was in operation, the party organs would function continuously, to guide party members in the government.

Batlle saw two great tasks ahead. One was to shepherd the Colegiado through, the other was to supervise the reformation of the Colorado Party, to give it the program, organization, and continuous popular input it needed. Batlle, as Serrato put it, was "the undisputed head of the Colorado Party." Using his source of strength, the Party, Batlle would give the Colegiado enough momentum that it would soon operate without him. In Europe he had thought he would do all this during this presidency and then retire to Europe. Back in Uruguay, he realized that the tasks required more time. He would have to stay in Uruguay and guide the party.

His opponents saw the Colegiado as a machine to disguise Batlle's remaining in office, but Batlle didn't like public office—its compromises with the ideal, or the perennial seekers of government jobs. He intended the Colegiado to come into operation in 1914, cutting his presidency by a year.[47] To disarm opposition, Don Pepe would not serve on the Colegiado. He would say so publicly when he judged the time to be right. Batlle's place would be in the Colorado Party, which would oversee the Colegiado. And when the new system worked smoothly and he was no longer needed, then he would leave.

The idea had taken hold of Batlle in 1908 when the family went to Switzerland so that Don Pepe could recover from the effects of his brother Luis' death. He had proposed the Colegiado to his sons at the dinner table and told them that once he put it through, the family would retire to Europe. The boys didn't want to live in Europe and ridiculed the idea of the plural executive. Don Pepe began explaining the Colegiado's benefits, and his sons became his first converts. Absolutely no one else was told, not Arena, who later claimed otherwise, and not Manini, whom Batlle instead told that he would allow a free choice of presidential successors and would then retire to Europe, for the idea was so removed from Uruguay's experience that to announce it could have derailed Batlle's candidacy.[48]

There was nothing in the Colorado tradition upon which to base a Colegiado. The obvious argument against government by committee—that it would be ineffective—could be countered with variations on the proverb that two heads are better than one. But Batlle also stood for all Colorado one-party government. A plural executive, sooner or later, would have to take in Blancos. This was the point that Manini, obdurately opposed to the Colegiado, constantly made when Batlle's plans, "a surprise to everyone," as Manini put it, were revealed.[49] Martín Aguirre, late Nationalist leader, had proposed a plural executive in 1903, specifically as a means of institutionalizing coparticipation.

Batlle, though, was confident his Colegiado, by electing only one member each year, would remain all Colorado. Once Uruguayans saw how well the Colegiado worked, they would be proud of it. When Batlle had proposed abolition of the death penalty, it had been resisted. In a country with a gaucho tradition where quarrels ended in knife duels and pistol shots, the death penalty was considered necessary. The death penalty had been abolished; society was not endangered; quite the contrary, Uruguayans boasted of their civilized state. Batlle had seemed out of touch with Uruguayan reality when he insisted that

Nationalist revolution was over if the Nationalists were handled right; events had borne him out. Don Pepe was confident that the same would happen with the Colegiado, once its novelty wore off.

Still, the Colegiado was risky. The likelihood that a future President would take Uruguay off the track it was now on came precisely because there was as yet no mass or powerful social-group support for the specifics of Batlle's programs. The Colorado Party supported its hero, Don Pepe Batlle. By insisting on the Colegiado, the hero might split the Colorados. If loyal Colorados, already uneasy at his radicalism, broke with Batlle over the Colegiado, they could unite with Nationalists, Colorado dissidents, ranchers and businessmen who considered Batlle dangerous and bring about exactly the derailment that the Colegiado was designed to avoid. The fact that Batlle's first major article on the Colegiado also praised the French cabinet system suggested that Don Pepe, the master politician, might be leaving himself a way out should opposition to the Colegiado become too formidable.

CHAPTER 11

Pressing Forward

If this presidency was going to end one year ahead of time, Batlle was even more determined to use continuing prosperity to press forward, so that the Colegiado would come in with bases set for it to follow in as many areas as possible. The Chamber authorized state purchase of two refrigerated cargo ships. There were perennial complaints that ships bypassed Montevideo for Argentina whose huge exports provided full cargoes; and now the refrigerated packing plants in Argentina and Uruguay were organizing in a shipping pool to control access to the British market by limiting cargo space. A State Merchant Marine could provide cargo ships for Uruguay and simultaneously reduce gold outflow.[1] And, a much more controversial issue, Batlle's strengthened eight-hour day bill was being readied for legislative debate.

Batlle, in conservative eyes, was not only doing too much, he was moving Uruguay in the wrong direction. In a year-end review of 1911, Martín C. Martínez warned of growing "social elephantiasis," while rural spokesman Irureta Goyena saw the state moving into stage three. In stage one it oppressed workers, in stage two it was neutral, in stage three it oppressed employers.[2] The Williman presidency, when the opinions of conservatives like Martínez and Irureta Goyena counted so heavily, seemed much longer ago than just one year.

I

Under Williman, though rural land values rose nearly 80 percent, land taxes, supposedly based on land values, actually decreased by

11,632 pesos. This was done, much to the pleasure of ranchers, by freezing the assessments on which land taxes were collected. Arena had already announced that Batlle's programs would require ranchers to contribute more heavily to the national Treasury. Don Pepe himself was careful not to say how much or exactly how ranchers would contribute, though he was moving chess pieces—the rural land survey, the exchange of Títulos de Ubicar Tierras Fiscales—in the direction he wanted to go. The Executive did announce that once the land survey was completed, the present system of assigning all properties in the same geographic zone the same value per hectare would be abandoned, and each property would pay, per hectare, taxes based on its actual appraisal value. This complex task could not be quickly completed, "not even during one administration."

For now the number of rural zones, in which each property paid the same per-hectare tax, would be increased to 267 from 139, and new assessments which would average 40 percent of actual land values would be established. To ease the impact, the rate would be lowered from 7.50 pesos to 6.50 pesos per thousand of assessed value. The Executive estimated that the result would be a "very reasonable" additional 540,000 pesos in revenue. The Chamber Committee believed that the Executive had underestimated the tax increase by 132,696 pesos, but it went along. And it went along with another Executive innovation which established Government expropriation of land in rural towns at tax evaluation plus 50 percent. This last provision, similar to one just instituted in Montevideo, worried Deputies. If landowners to keep taxes down tried to resist raised assessments, they opened themselves to lower payment in case of expropriation. The expropriation provision was approved by only one vote.

The bill cleared the Chamber in December and got quick Senate approval.[3] On January 12, 1912, the Executive issued a decree on individual, rural, landed-property assessment, preparatory to the shift from tax zones. The decree's introduction noted that individual property evaluation "is previous to and indispensable for preparing the final, rational, perfect, and fundamentally just solution of taxing the liquid return that the land is capable of producing."[4] This seemingly vague statement, comparable to but not quite as vague as "I was in Switzerland for three months and I found many people there who do not know the name of the President of the Confederation," contained one of Batlle's central programs to change Uruguay's structure of land tenure. Land would be taxed not on its sale value but on "the liquid return that land is capable of producing." People who owned land and let livestock graze on it while watching its sale value go up would have to pay taxes based not on present sale value, not on present income, but on what the land should produce if worked intensively. The profitability of land as an investment would go way down; improved pastures would then make economic sense to ranchers. Combined with State recovery of Tierras Fiscales, "the final, rational, perfect, and fundamentally just [land tax] solution" would profoundly alter the way Uruguayan land was used while greatly expanding the State's revenue.

II

Normally, the Senate, a very small body of nineteen Senators (one for each department, renewed by thirds every two years, with each Senator elected for a single six-year term and so outlasting the presidential administration during which he was elected), could be relied on to put a brake on radical bills passed by the Chamber. But this Senate, like the Chamber, was all-Colorado and a cozy Batllista club. In a single session the State Insurance Bank was approved in both readings. Arena wrote the Senate Committee report, which stated that "a monopoly exercised by a National Bank will substitute for the present monopoly exercised by some dozen foreign companies."[5] But the Executive signaled that it was going to use its governmental powers to put the private companies at a competitive disadvantage rather than immediately go to an insurance monopoly. The 1912 Montevideo business tax bill raised the fee payable by private insurance companies to 1,000 pesos annually, with a 50 percent additional tax for each type of risk insured.[6]

Don Pepe chose the Insurance Bank's Board of Directors with enormous care. Generally, he appointed professionals as key men in state enterprises and filled the other positions politically. The State Insurance Bank, a new enterprise in an untried field, had to overcome the suspicions of potential policy holders. For President, Batlle chose Luis Supervielle, a well known banker, and as Board members six other business and insurance men, several of whom were surprised at being named.[7]

Supervielle announced that he hoped to reach an "entente" with the private companies which would result in their eventual elimination, but that if conciliatory tactics, like reinsurance, failed, the Bank would compete, using all the advantages at its disposal. The Executive acted to favor the Bank. Companies with public works contracts had to take out workman's compensation insurance with the Bank. The Bank of the Republic expected its mortgages to have fire insurance from the State Insurance Bank. And Don Pepe criticized the critics. "Monopoly in law" had been delayed for reasons that should impel "all patriotically inspired Uruguayans" to insure with the Insurance Bank and produce a rapid "monopoly in fact."[8]

III

After Education Minister Blengio Rocca assured Deputies that girls who wanted to attend existing secondary and preparatory schools with males, "that is to say, girls who do not object to confronting promiscuity," could do so, the Chamber finally approved the Women's University in February, 1912.[9] In El Día, Don Pepe, using the pseudonym Laura—Petrarch's mistress—called for female suffrage to be included in the constitutional reform, so that Uruguay could be the first nation in America to allow women to vote.[10]

So far, Batlle was accomplishing what he had set out to do during this administration. He had only one serious worry. His daughter Ana Amalia, now seventeen, had come down with a cold after a dance. By April the diagnosis was tuberculosis. In May, Batlle cabled Rafael Di Miero, still busy in Paris buying furnishings for Piedras Blancas, to ship special medication urgently.[11]

IV

Don Pepe, though preoccupied with his daughter's health, continued the tremendous pace of his government. In Europe he had looked at many parks with Montevideo in mind, and now he moved on this. Private lands adjacent to the beachfront Parque Urbano were about to be subdivided. Batlle immediately expropriated these lands for "a great maritime promenade," easily accessible to the poor, and got legislative approval for the substantial outlay of 3,000,000 pesos, equivalent to about 10 percent of the government revenues for the year (this and other long-term expenditures would have to be financed by loans) as well as approval for expansion of the Prado, Montevideo's traditional promenade.[12]

Minister of Industries Acevedo was busy hiring foreign fishing, agronomy, and dry farming experts. Acevedo got Batlle's approval for bills to set up an Institute of Geology and Drilling and an Institute of Industrial Chemistry. Once more, Acevedo was very far-sighted. The Industrial Chemistry Institute would do industrial research, something unknown in Latin America; the other Institute would explore the Uruguayan subsoil for coal and oil, which now had to be imported, and prepare a geological map. Both institutes would do research and engage in operations. But, as usual with Acevedo's projects, the Institutes were very small: a director, one geologist, one mining engineer, and helpers in the Geology Institute; a director, three chemists, and helpers for the other institute. Even so, because there was no real industrial research and mining geology in Uruguay, deputies complained at this "exceptionally ostentatious" expenditure, and the bills were returned to committee.[13]

Uruguay did not produce oil, but it did produce alcohol, in a single French-owned distillery operating under heavy tariff protection. Batlle was anxious to expand industrial alcohol production as a market for Uruguayan maize and a substitute for oil. On March 7, 1912, El Día announced that "the government will ask the legislature for authorization to expropriate, with an adequate premium, the establishments at present producing alcohol or to end the tariff which presently weighs on this article if expropriation comes up against some of those insuperable obstacles which regularly complicate the progress of new nations unable to defend their rights." To the quick criticism that the government was raising the threat of tariff suspension to make the distillery's French owner come to terms, Don Pepe replied in El Día that tariff protection had existed for twenty years but instead of encouraging new factories had produced a monopoly. To end this, either end tariff protection "which creates this injustice or have the State take over the manufacture of alcohol."[14] And on March 21 the Executive sent its bill, calling for expropriation of the distillery at fair value plus 10 percent, to the legislature.

V

The pace of Batlle's government could be measured quantitatively in the national budget of 35.1 million pesos, approved in July after months of debate. During the administratively active Williman years the budget had risen 5 percent annually; in the year and a half of Batlle's administration the budget increased 27 percent. Indeed, Batlle and Serrato used this budget to fund activities usually requiring special legislation. Budgets for secondary schools in every one of eighteen departments, provisions for embassies in every Latin American country (Socialist Frugoni was furious at this "aristocratic" waste), four agronomy stations (Acevedo had wanted six but there was bickering over their locations)—all were included in the budget.

Gregorio L. Rodríguez, who had been a minister in old President Cuestas' cautious government and had a much more vivid memory of the economic crisis of 1890 than the young deputies, protested that this budget tried "to carry through in a single fiscal year all the improvements that they want for the country, and this is just not possible . . . the slightest setback in our production or any occurrence in Europe which causes a drop in the prices of our products can bring a substantial drop in public revenues and in consequence an intense crisis." Finance Minister Serrato disagreed and forecast that economic growth (using imports as a rule-of-thumb indicator, the 1911 growth rate had been a superlative 10 percent) would produce an "automatic increase" in taxes sufficient to balance the budget. The proud deputies stood and cheered.

Comparison of this budget with the 1904–05 budget showed how far Uruguay had progressed. That budget had carried 1,174,630 pesos for the Fomento Ministry. Since then Fomento had been subdivided into three separate ministries: Education, now budgeted at 3.2 million pesos; Industries, at 1.5 million; and Public Works, at 1.3 million— more than a fivefold increase. The War Ministry, whose budget had doubled to 4.7 million pesos because of army increases, was designed to assure the quick destruction of any Nationalist revolution and remained the largest, single, ministerial budget. Yet the army's share of the total budget at 13.39 percent was roughly the same as its 13.41 percent in 1904–05.

The big change had been the great easing of the burden of fixed expenses. The dark days of Uruguay's past had produced a heavy foreign debt to pay for budget deficits. In 1904–05 debt service and government profit guarantees to railroads accounted for 42 percent of the total budget. Since then, increased revenues had permitted many new undertakings, and debt service and railroad guarantees now took only 21.9 percent of the total budget. The change could be seen in the rubric Diverse Credits, which contained the start-up costs of new activities, public works, and the like. (Annual debt service on large-scale public works, not the much larger actual expenditures during the year, were included in the budget; that way, budgets were made to look smaller to foreign bondholders.) In the 1912–13 budget Diverse Credits were 7.4 million pesos, larger than any single ministry, compared with the modest 603,482 pesos for Diverse Credits in 1904–05.[15]

One important particular could be discerned in comparing the two budgets. Except for army increases (soldiers and War Ministry civilian employees were up to 12,022 from 6,482 in 1904–05), state employment had increased only minimally—2,972, an average of 425 additional employees per year—despite the great expansion of government undertakings. Batlle was consciously keeping down the growth of government employment. Bureaucratic seat warmers would mean expense and inefficiency. For government to continue to expand, it was necessary that Uruguayans believe in their government and its functional ability.

VI

Even while the budget was being debated, Batlle and Serrato took another major financial step. The Banco Hipotecario, the mortgage bank set up as part of the liquidation of the 1890 crisis, had been taken over by stock speculators. The Banco Hipotecario, which wrote about 20 percent of the mortgages in Uruguay, had a monopoly on issuing mortgage *cédulas* (bearer bonds of 25 to 100 pesos) sold through the stock exchange. The profitable Banco Hipotecario, which in its disastrous first years had a portfolio of overvalued mortgages, was now offering thirty-year mortgages on urban and rural property and had 20 million pesos in cédulas outstanding. Visions that the public, fearful of the bank's new management, would swamp the Montevideo money market with cédulas created alarm. At this juncture Batlle and Serrato pulled out a project they had already prepared but had kept secret to prevent stock market speculation—they sent a bill to the legislature nationalizing the Banco Hipotecario.

During Williman's administration Serrato, who had then been the Banco Hipotecario's Vice President, had proposed nationalization. Williman felt nationalization to be premature.[16] Now, when the issue was a speculative or state-run Banco Hipotecario, the normally expectable opposition to nationalization was muted.

The nationalized Banco Hipotecario would, the Executive pointed out, have the credit of the Uruguayan government behind it, be able to sell cédulas abroad, and provide mortgage loans in cash. Management's goals would not be profit—this was by now Batllista doctrine—but the supplying of credit at low rates "with the single and exclusive goal of favoring the public interest."

> Thus the Banco Hipotecario together with the Bank of the Republic will be the means by which the State, to the extent possible, will direct and orient bank credit, influencing the general direction of the economy, which cannot be left exclusively to private institutions.

To speed nationalization, the Executive offered to buy stockholders out at 115, the stock's price in May. The stockholders, mostly Uruguayans, held out for 121. Batlle and Serrato, as in their other major state enterprise projects, were very concerned about the Banco Hipotecario's future solidity. Over the years it would have to repay purchase costs out of earnings. With the Chamber Committee acting as mediator, a price of 117 was agreed to. By June 7, 1912 less than three weeks after the ferocious stockholders' meeting when the speculators took over, the Banco Hipotecario was legally a state bank.

Serrato, invoking Batlle's name to overcome the objections of some legislators, won approval for the Executive to negotiate short-term loans with the Bank of the Republic and local private banks to pay the Hipotecario stockholders. The Executive would then cancel the Montevideo bank loans by selling treasury notes abroad. Serrato expected to sell these low-interest, short-term treasury notes at close to par. Such sophisticated money management had never before been used by Uruguay.[17]

VII

Don Pepe had reopened his anti-Catholic campaign. He recalled Williman's Minister to the Vatican without even a protocol letter to present upon departure. To the outrage of Catholic sentiments, the Executive authorized Carnival on Ash Wednesday. Batlle devoted much effort to something he was very proud of, his articles in *El Día* on the fallaciousness of Catholic dogma. He didn't save the hundreds of other articles he wrote but clipped his "Reading the Bible" series and pasted them in a scrapbook he kept in his desk. [18]

The big, immediate anti-Catholic step in what for Don Pepe was a lifetime campaign was legislation to make divorce easier. Even though divorce could be granted at the mutual consent of the spouses with no further justification required, divorces did not reach 100 per year. [19] Senator Areco, the Batllista expert on moral legislation and author of the mutual consent clause now proposed that divorce be granted "at the will of only one of the spouses." Public opinion, not just Catholic opinion, was horrified, fearing that Uruguayan husbands, tired of their wives, would get rid of them in Moslem fashion. [20] *El Siglo* polled the country's lawyers, the major group in Uruguay's political elite: 2 were in favor of divorce at the request of either spouse, 214 opposed. Lawyers had signed their ballots, and among those opposed were all the law faculty but one. [21]

In order to get a majority that would bring the bill to the floor, the Senate Committee had to be restructured. Senator Espalter, Williman's Minister of Interior, one of the Committee minority whom Batlle had tried to win over, described "a long conversation" he had "a short time ago" with Don Pepe, though he would not directly name him.

> The institution of marriage—he told me—as it now exists among us, must be modified. The family is something like a feudal castle, closed in on all sides. It is hard to enter, because marriage is difficult and even harder to leave, because divorce is more difficult.
>
> It is necessary to do everything possible to encourage more marriages and it is also necessary to make divorce easy for those who are dissatisfied in marriage.
>
> The institution of the family with the stability and solidity which

our laws, and even our customs, give it produces innumerable evils to society.

The man who doesn't marry or is dissatisfied in his marriage, since he can only get out of it with difficulty, abandons himself to irregular unions and by his acts and disorderly conduct stimulates and increases the degrading vice of prostitution. And as for the woman, how much grief does her celibacy, so often involuntary, produce!

Maternity is a blessing in any form, even irregular—he continued—because how many times does a child redeem and regenerate his own mother!

When Espalter countered that a woman with a child born out of wedlock suffered,

No—my interlocutor answered—these reforms in the institution of the family should be accompanied by parallel reforms in the institution of property. The State, owner of all great fortunes or at least of a large part of them, will be able to support the woman and educate the child. . . .

I stopped talking, Mr. President. I found myself facing a utopian, a dreamer from Plato's Republic.[22]

Don Pepe was revealing some of his longest-term plans. When Uruguay was fully a model country, the State, "owner of all great fortunes or at least a large part of them" (through a tax program Batlle was carefully not explicit about), would provide for the needs of the less fortunate; marriage would then be of personal rather than societal concern. M. E. Tiscornia, the Catholic Batllista, insisted that this was Batlle's and "a few others" aspirations: to leave the State entirely out of marital questions and to allow people to live together and stop living together at will. Ultimately, if they succeeded, there would be no marriage and no divorce.

On July 31 Arena took the floor. He regretted that "the heavy cross of Christianity perturbed the judgment" of even religious liberals. As for the lawyers' opposition—so damaging to Areco's bill—they had been told divorce at the request of either spouse was indecent and without reasoning themselves had come out "on the side of decency where all the chic and interesting people of our society are." Science looked forward, jurisprudence backward, that was why revolutions occurred. He cited Socialist Frugoni's truth that divorce was unimportant to the poor. They had no property to divide, so they separated at will. Finally, on August 5, Arena came to the heart of the matter and introduced a compromise, "like all substitutes it has advantages and inconveniences." Article 7 of the divorce law would read, "Divorce will also result from the will of the woman."

It was his friend Carlos Vaz Ferreira, Uruguay's first original philosopher, "the most robust mind of my generation," who had convinced Arena that until the difficulties that might be caused women by divorce at the will of either spouse could be overcome, it was best to restrict divorce at the will of one spouse to the wife. Arena had resisted, arguing that divorce by mutual consent, now permitted, was frequently divorce at the hidden will of the husband, but had finally recognized that Areco's bill could not be passed. He had, of course, consulted Don Pepe. "My ties with señor Batlle y Ordoñez are so well known that it is inconceivable that I would not have conversed with him on a major conflict of ideas. . . . And Batlle told me immediately: I agree with you that Vaz is right. . . . It will take us where we want to go, since basically what we want is the liberation of women in marriage."

Espalter still could not accept the proposal. A woman dissatisfied in marriage now had the legal remedy of separation. Good social policy should not encourage remarriage by women who were failures as wives. Areco denied that there was any evidence that women who would take advantage of the new divorce law were unsuited for future marriages. Several Senators said they would not have voted for the original bill but would accept the compromise. As Senator Otero put it:

> We all know that this matter of divorce is going forward because the progressive and superior man who now occupies the Presidency of the Republic has thrown the weight of his influence in the balance, has won over many of his friends, has convinced some and gotten the votes of others, and after a hard fight is forcing this matter through by accepting modifications.

On August 21, 1912 the bill got its second affirmative reading and was passed to the Chamber.[23]

Espalter announced that he was taking a leave of absence. Tiscornia, the bill's other leading opponent, had resigned from the Senate to become a board member of the newly nationalized Banco Hipotecario. To be on the wrong side of Don Pepe was not a very agreeable position. Nevertheless, professional and social ridicule had kept even Don Pepe's supporters from voting for divorce at the request of either spouse. Don Pepe, the politician, had yielded on divorce at the request of the husband, at least for now. Was this what would happen to Don Pepe's even more troublesome vision, the Colegiado?

VIII

Divorce at the request of the husband could come later. Yielding on the Colegiado could mean fundamental political upheaval, and Batlle had no intention of yielding. He wanted to bring Uruguay toward the model country without violence; orderly constitutional reform was an ideal vehicle for that. It was also the safest. Batlle was leader of the governing party and expected to have a majority of Colegialist delegates elected to the Constitutional Convention, which would produce reform.

Constitutional reform was a cumbersome process. One reason why the Constitution of 1830 had never been reformed or amended was that it required reforms to have the approval of three successive legislatures. Traditionally, the Nationalists wanted constitutional reform as a means of institutionalizing their coparticipation in government. They had even proposed ways of overcoming the three consecutive legislature requirements, but when Batlle wanted to use such procedures to have a Constitutional Convention elected after the War of 1904, there were outcries from the Nationalists and the conservative classes. Constitutional reform under those conditions could have been a banner for revolution, and Batlle, instead, began a reform process that followed all the constitutional requirements. This was the third and final legislature whose approval was required.

Technically, the reform before the legislature was limited to changing the procedures for reform. The two previous legislatures had approved a series of options, among which this legislature must choose. This legislature had agreed on the new procedure: substantive constitutional change would be the work of a specially elected Constitutional Convention. Still at issue was the method of electing delegates to the Constitutional Convention. From Europe, Batlle had stated categorically that he opposed proportional representation; this information had been kept from Ramírez of *El Siglo*, who had made proportional representation for the constituent elections one of the major demands of his memorandum; and Ramírez now unleashed a furious press campaign accusing Batlle of duplicity.[24]

From December 1911 to May 1912 the Chamber debated whether to require proportional representation for the Constitutional Convention. Proponents insisted that without Nationalist participation (and the Nationalists were already abstaining from elections), constitutional reform could not be permanent. Only proportional representation could bring in the Nationalists. Rodó, Uruguay's famous intellectual, leading the fight for proportional representation, advanced another reason. "We all know—and it is nothing recent— that the Colorado Party, as governing party almost always rigidly follows the positions of those who govern." Everything which tended toward giving the Colorado Party "greater autonomy" from those in power "will be salutary." This was the real issue. Proportional representation would encourage anti-Batllista slates to stop the Colegiado. Years later Batlle, in marginal notes on his copy of a campaign biography, explained his opposition to proportional representation for the Constitutional Convention: "I feared the intervention of small groups, sometimes without clear ideas, moved by personal interests in an assembly whose power was going to be absolute." When the Chamber's vote on proportional representation finally came, there were only 19 in favor and 54 against. The outcome was no surprise, but there were several surprises among those voting in favor of proportional representation: Chamber President Lagarmilla, Oneto y Viana, originator of the divorce law, and Amézaga, Williman's confidante and ex-*El Día* editor.[25]

Inside and outside the Chamber, the opposition had consistently been depicting Batlle's constitutional plans as a device for his perpetuation in office. Batlle now sent Arena, who was everyone's friend, to Nationalist leader Martín C. Martínez. In the course of a visit to Martínez' law office, Arena told him and the other politicians gathered there what Batlle had been privately telling Colorado intimates. Batlle had "the firm intention" of not accepting any extension of his term or any reelection, or of serving on the Colegiado, should it be approved.[26]

In the Chamber those fearful of Batlle's power regrouped on the issue of ratification. Rodó moved: "The amendments or additions [to the constitution] will be submitted for the approval of the electorate two years after having been sanctioned by the Convention; but they will not go into effect until the Presidency following the one in which the Constitutional Convention concludes its sessions."

Rodó, who had once been the Chamber's official orator, explained his new motion. It was true that he had once favored quick constitutional reform without ratification. But that was under Williman "an Administration of moderation" and in the expectation that Nationalist participation in constitutional reform would produce "political conciliation." The present government had "radical and violent tendencies" and exacerbated hostility to the political opposition. There was every indication that consitutional reform under it would embody "the same extreme feeling for revolutionary and violent innovation," and was likely to provoke revolution. If the Chamber refused to approve his amendment, Rodó warned "in the present political circumstances the constitution should not be reformed, and to persist in reforming it will be a serious error and a menace of grave evils that we will all lament some day." Don Pepe's operatives now took over. In a standing vote, Rodó's motion was defeated. Julio María Sosa, one of Batlle's fastest rising protégés, moved that the convention be required to complete its deliberations within a year. This motion, previously defeated, required a two thirds vote for reconsideration. Of 53 deputies present, 36 voted for reconsideration, and the Chamber then approved Sosa's motion. On July 9, 1912, Chamber action on constitutional reform procedures was completed and sent to the Senate. When the Senate acted, the Constitution of 1830 would be formally amended. Thereafter for the constitution to be reformed, the Chamber of Deputies and the Senate, each by a two thirds vote, must declare the necessity of constitutional reform. The Executive must then convoke the election of a National Constitutional Convention "to be elected popularly." The Convention must conclude its deliberations and present its constitutional revisions within a year of its inauguration. Amendments and additions as a block must be submitted for popular approval. (That way the Colegiado could not be voted down separately.) "Voters will express themselves for 'Sí' or 'No.' "[27]

IX

Ana Amalia's tuberculosis was worsening. By July, she was in bed, coughing, with fever. Because she could not stand outside nurses, her family took turns looking after her. Batlle, in spite of the tremendous activity of his government, nursed her from midnight to early morning and kept a meticulous medical record for her physicians' use.[28]

X

On August 20, 1912, El Día announced that Manini was leaving on August 25 to head the Uruguayan delegation to the centenary of the Cortes of Cádiz in Spain. One third of the Senate was going to be elected in November, and Manini, who found being Minister of Interior—the traditional stepping stone to the Presidency—increasingly burdensome, had opted for a Senate seat. Manini's plan was to resign as Minister of Interior while in Europe, stay in Europe during the elections (the Nationalists were still abstaining, so Manini's election was a certainty) and not return until it was time to take his Senate seat. It had been a disillusioning year and half for Manini. First there had been the realization that Don Pepe had held the secret of the Colegiado from him in Europe; then there was the radicalism of Batlle's government, which went far beyond what Manini had anticipated. Worst of all was Batlle's insistence on the Colegiado, against everyone's advice. Manini believed Uruguay owed Don Pepe a tremendous debt. If Batlle needed more time in office, Manini, who favored a seven-year single term presidency, would go along. If Batlle wanted to name Serrato as his successor, though Manini preferred the more political Senate President Viera, Manini would go along. But Manini was convinced that radicalizing Uruguay under the Colegiado would ultimately bring down the Colorado Party, and this he must oppose.

Batlle had offered Manini a place on the first Colegiado, but Manini had refused. Batlle, who was the final arbiter on the six Senate seats to be elected in November, arranged one for Manini. The party commission in the Department of Flores had written Batlle in March advising him that a committee would visit him. "Would you, Sr. President, indicate to the Party Authority, the Candidate we should send to the Senate in the forthcoming elections . . .?" In August, Manini was nominated in Flores. Don Pepe expected that once young Pedro had cooled off, he would accept the inevitable and serve on the Colegiado.[29]

Everyone was careful to avoid the appearance of a break. Manini declined the honorary presidency of a dissident Colorado club, saying that the party was united in program and personalities. The day he left, Manini visited Don Pepe. All the Colorado dignitaries saw him off.[30] Serrato, whose hope to succeed Batlle as President was rising (surely Batlle would come to realize that the Colegiado was an impossibility), took over the Interior portfolio together with Finance, on an interim basis until Manini's cabinet resignation became official.

The Senate, in only two sessions, on August 21 and 22, had passed the Chamber of Deputies' constitutional reform bill and completed the amendment of the Constitution of 1830. On September 14, in a vote of fourteen to nothing, the Senate began the process of substantive constitutional reform by voting its "national convenience." Bachini's new newspaper, *Diario del Plata*, whose goal was to split Colorados from Batlle, lamented that if, as rumors had it, Batlle planned to eliminate the Senate, the Senate's recent actions demonstrated its uselessness. Three days later, the declaration of national necessity was before the Chamber of Deputies. Rodó spoke against it. The vote in favor was 67 to 4.[31]

All that remained was to pass the bill for electing the Constitutional Convention. The bill was no surprise: it had been presented to the Chamber on July 15, jointly by Julio María Sosa, increasingly Batlle's spokesman in the Chamber, and Antonio María Rodríguez, President of the Colorado Party National Executive Committee. To counteract "the old argument" that it was useless to run against the government, there would be a major innovation. Election to the Constitutional Convention would be by secret ballot. Each department would elect twice as many delegates as it elected Deputies to the Chamber of Deputies. Three fifths of the delegates from each department would go to the party which got the most votes; the remaining two fifths would be apportioned through proportional representation. This hybrid solution met Batlle's demand for a cohesive majority (three fifths of the seats in a department would go to the most voted party even if it drew less than half the votes), and it encouraged minority participation by offering proportional representation. In a sense, it divided up the two fifths of the seats the Nationalists could be expected to win among whoever ran, dissident Colorados, Catholics, Socialists, and Nationalists.[32]

The Nationalists dismissed both the Sosa-Rodríguez election bills and Arena's declarations that Batlle would not accept reelection, extension of his term, or a place on the Colegiado. Even without Batlle, the Colegiado would result either in "audacity, which could be dangerous," or, more likely, in domination by one member, "the one who would have the most solid base in the army." And as for elections to the Constitutional Convention under the Sosa-Rodríguez election bills, the National Party would be "culpable" if it took part.[33]

Batlle was not distressed. He had been elected President while the Nationalists abstained; he would supervise constitutional reform and the inauguration of the Colegiado while the Nationalists abstained. El Día announced that the election would take place soon and under the Sosa-Rodríguez bills: "constitutional reform will be made for all, not for specific parties or political groups, by all who want to make it."[34]

And Don Pepe was preparing the other half of his long range political program, the reformation of the Colorado Party, which would run Uruguay through the Colegiado. He noted in El Día that the Colorado Party, although well organized, still lacked "a sufficiently analytical exposition of its principles. This will doubtless be the work of the not-too-distant future. A program of its minimum aspirations, from which its members will not be able to depart, will be inscribed in its action program."[35]

CHAPTER 12 *Arazatí and Río Negro*

On September 21, 1912, in a long interview with Arena, *El Día* published Batlle's previously announced position that he would not be a member of the Colegiado after the constitution was reformed. He did not oppose limited reelection in principle, as in the United States. However, for himself "I declare that I would not want and would not accept either extension of my term of office or reelection." And, most important, he did not want the Colegiado compromised by accusations that personal ambition motivated him. "Since I put such weight on the transformation of the Executive, I feel it necessary to declare right now that I would not accept any position in the future government."

> Of all the ideals which I have cherished for the material and moral greatness of Uruguay, none is of such transcendental importance. One of the principal reasons which induced me to accept my present presidency was the expectation that, within my legitimate sphere of action, I would be able to influence the transformation of our presidential system, which I consider detestable. If that reform, together with the others which I have programmed and among which I put proportional representation in first place, is not accomplished during my government, I will consider my presidency to have largely failed, since its accomplishments, those of the last few years, and those that might come in the future could be sunk to the bottom the day after the always possible election of a disastrous president.[1]

The Nationalists were not convinced by Batlle's disavowals nor excited by the prospect of their longtime goal, proportional representation for the legislature once the constitution was reformed. "In a word, does Señor Batlle y Ordoñez remove himself from being in the first group of members of the Colegiado, does he remove himself from being on all the *septimos* [the seven man Colegiado] in the offing, or from a specific number of them?",[2] the Directorio newspaper asked.

The Directorio formally instructed departmental organizations to take no part in the November Senate elections, not even voter registration.[3] Batlle had chosen the six Colorado candidates. In addition to Manini, who would run in Flores, Varela Acevedo, Batlle's ex-secretary, would run in Rocha; in Tacuarembó, Antonio María Rodríguez, President of the Colorado Executive Committee and co-author of the official electoral bill for the Constitutional Convention, was the candidate; two old supporters would run in Treinta y Tres and Rivera; and Williman, back from Europe and named University Rector by Batlle, would be the candidate in Río Negro.

Río Negro was sticky. Ex-Senator Tiscornia had just resigned from the Board of the State Mortgage Bank and was going to run as anti-organization Colorado candidate for Senator in Río Negro, where he was a political power. His Colorado rivals for control of Río Negro, the Espalter brothers—Senator José Espalter had been Williman's Minister of Interior—were counting on Williman's candidacy to carry the department for them. Charges were pending against the departmental Jefe Político, and Don Pepe put a new Jefe Político in at the end of October to oversee the elections. Before the new man left for Río Negro, Batlle recommended to him that he support Williman's Senate candidacy.[4]

II

On November 5, Batlle's daughter began a diary: "It is six months and 17 days that I am sick! I am not sure what my sickness is but I think I know."[5] Don Pepe, seeing his daughter worsen, had decided to take her to the sea air at a ranch in Arazatí, San José, on the shore of the Río de la Plata. Her doctors did not oppose the trip, but neither did they recommend it. On November 7 overseas press services telegraphed the story that Dr. Frederich Friedman, a Berlin professor, had developed a successful serum which cured tuberculosis. Batlle immediately cabled the Uruguayan Minister in Berlin who saw Friedman. Friedman was confident he could cure the girl if she came to Europe.

Don Pepe decided to take "the first boat" to Europe, leaving November 23, unless before then Eurŏpean medical scientists advised that Friedman's serum was ineffective. Parisian experts were noncommittal. Berlin scientists considered Friedman something of a charlatan. Dr. Carlos Santín Rossi, a young Uruguayan physician representing the Batlle family, reported that Friedman had refused to see him and that Friedman's secrecy and doubtful cures made him unreliable. The best Berlin opinion, though, favored bringing the girl to Europe, where she would have "dietetic treatment in a favorable climate—North of Italy for the winter—Switzerland for the summer in a village rather than a sanatorium," but only if she was able to make the trip.

Once more her physicians warned Don Pepe that Ana Amalia was too weak; she was coughing blood, and seasickness could kill her. Batlle, who before had tried to get Friedman to come to Uruguay or send an aide with the serum, tried again. "Whatever I have, I will not spare monetary sacrifices," to pay for the trip.[6] Meanwhile, Batlle would take Ana Amalia to the sea air at Arazatí, where he hoped that she would either recover or become strong enough to be taken to Europe.

The news that Batlle was going to Arazatí, and might be going to Europe, stirred Uruguay. Rumors spread that revolution would break out as soon as Batlle left the capital. The Directorio newspaper had challenged the army to act: "How far would this passivity of the armed forces go? Would they accompany the President when, after making mincemeat of the old republican Constitution, he prepares to prolong his predominance indefinitely? Would they serve him as escort, when after completing all the plans attributed to him for the destruction of the family and weakening of property rights, he carries the false socialism of which he proclaims himself apostle to its ultimate extremes?"[7] This challenge was revealing, a new stage in the attempt to stop Batlle. It would be the army, recognizing the danger of Batlle's radicalism, which would oust him. The dissident Colorados, led by Bachini, and Carlos Travieso, "the father of the Uruguayan navy," had been complaining that Batlle neglected the army and promoted new

1904 officers ahead of veteran soldiers. Colonel Manuel Dubra had just resigned from the General Staff, publicly critical of Batlle's army policy. Nepomuceno Saravia was organizing a Nationalist demonstration across the border in Brazil. Arena wrote Manini in Europe, "something really serious" was coming; Batlle recorded his plan to take Ana Amalia to Arazatí in the notebook he was keeping on her health, but he added that he was preoccupied by "certain revolutionary plans that might impede the trip."[8]

Batlle moved the Ninth Cavalry, commanded by a trusted officer, to Montevideo and troops to the Brazilian border. Nepomuceno Saravia held his meeting on November 17. Two Directorio representatives were there to make sure that he did not play into Batlle's hands and invade. Two thousand Nationalists attended. The meeting became rough; a Brazilian police chief was killed, the meeting was suspended. Afterward Nepomuceno held a banquet for 200 special guests. There was no invasion and no military uprising in Montevideo.[9]

On November 20 an ambulance brought Ana Amalia to the pier with her mother and brothers. Don Pepe went first in an auto; another auto carried her cousin, Batlle's brother Luis' son, Luis Batlle Berres, her half-brother Carlos Michaelsson, and an intern. Her father was waiting at the dock and supervised her boarding the navy cruiser *Uruguay* on a stretcher. The trip was uneventful. At Arazatí the ship came close to shore and she was carried in a bed to a launch. On shore a tent waited; a high oxcart filled with straw and mattresses brought her to the ranch.[10]

III

If Don Pepe took a leave of absence to take Ana Amalia to Europe, the Senate president would become Acting President of the Republic. Senators could not be reelected; Senate President Viera's term was expiring, and a new Senate president would have to be elected in February. Williman, ex-President of the Republic, was the natural candidate. The prospect of Williman's return, *El Siglo* noted, was "welcomed with enthusiasm by the conservative classes and numerous independent groups."[11] In short, Williman, as Senate president, would, justifiably or not, give hope to the anti-Batllistas. Don Pepe now preferred that Williman's Senate candidacy be postponed until

24. Arazatí—the shore and the ranch. Photos by Milton I. Vanger.

another election, and although no one asked Williman to step aside, on November 6, while Batlle was in Montevideo still debating whether to go to Arazatí or Europe, Williman wrote the President of the Río Negro Colorado Commission that for "personal reasons" he was asking the Commission to find another candidate.[12]

The Río Negro Colorado organization, fearful that changing candidates on the eve of the election would give victory to Tiscornia—the Catholic Batllista, running as an independent Colorado—unanimously refused to accept Williman's resignation. Williman, now that he saw the Río Negro organization united behind him, telegraphed, "I am very pleased with your resolution which so honors me."[13] On November 19 El Día reported that the National Colorado Committee had endorsed the Río Negro Colorados' nomination of Williman.[14]

Serrato, interim Minister of Interior and in charge of running the elections (six departments were electing Senators but only in Río Negro were there rival candidates), was furious. He and Williman were personal enemies; Williman as Acting President of the Republic in Batlle's absence could be expected to veto Serrato as Batlle's successor. Serrato wrote a confidential letter to the Río Negro Jefe Político. The Río Negro Colorados' refusal to accept Williman's resignation "produced the greatest surprise here in Montevideo." Aguiar, the Jefe Político (as earlier instructed by Batlle) had been asking people to vote for Williman. Serrato instructed him to let people "and in particular the elements you are in charge of, vote as they see fit, for one candidate or another. Besides, I cannot refrain from telling you that as a result of what is going on there in Río Negro, I deeply desire the triumph of the faction which Dr. Tiscornia heads." And lest the Jefe Político be obtuse, Serrato sent him a revised list of rural police chiefs, of Tiscornia persuasion, to supervise the elections.[15]

The election took place on November 24. Its central issue was whether Williman or Tiscornia was Batlle's candidate. The Río Negro Intendente was so upset that he telegraphed Virgilio Sampognaro, Batlle's presidential secretary: "I consider Dr. Williman official candidate. I observe nevertheless Minister of Interior combats him with the powerful means at his disposal. Please advise President of the Republic of these facts."[16] Tiscornia, strong in Río Negro, had campaigned actively; Williman stayed in Montevideo. Both sides claimed victory. Then it was announced that two electoral districts had not functioned.

When these voted two weeks later, Williman's supporters—the Espalter faction—announced that he had carried the department with 390 votes to Tiscornia's 386, while Tiscornia announced that he would challenge the results in the Senate.[17]

The election, an intra-party fight involving only those intimately involved in politics, showed that Williman, as everyone knew, had no great popularity. From the Grand Hotel in Genoa, though, Senator José Espalter, Williman's Minister of Interior, who had left his brother, Deputy Ricardo Espalter, in Río Negro to oversee what he had assumed would be a routine election, oblivious to what had in fact happened, wrote Williman congratulating him on his victory. Espalter forecast that Williman would "occupy the presidency of the Senate . . . that your action in politics is destined to temper estrangements and disagreements, and to prepare a new political situation, because it is evident that Batlle's political personality is completely used up. Naturally as long as he is President he will have influence, but the day he leaves the presidency he will have no more than any other citizen of his distinguished qualities, and you, Doctor, without the slightest effort, will be able to do good for the country."[18]

IV

A special police telephone line had been installed at Arazatí to connect Batlle with Montevideo, and he planned to come to the capital weekly. Nevertheless, the same group of deputies who had fought the series of losing battles over proportional representation in the Constitutional Convention chose to attack Batlle now for not delegating the presidency to the Senate President. The Constitution required that when the President of the Republic was "absent," the Executive Power be exercised by the President of the Senate. The intent of the provision was that when the President was commanding the army in war—Rivera and Oribe, the first two Presidents, had done so—someone else would run the government. The protesting deputies argued, however, that any time the President of the Republic left the capital, he was constitutionally absent and must delegate the Executive power to the Senate President. Nobody raised this argument when Williman summered in Punta del Este, and a Nationalist attempt to invoke it when Batlle visited Paysandú in 1903 had been voted down. The deputies who were demanding now that Batlle turn over the Presidency were distinguished intellectuals, the historian Melián Lafinur and Rodó, but they were also allies of Bachini and the dissident Colorados. Batlle's supporters in the Chamber protested that "subtle superior spirits" were using "constitutional pretexts" to leave "a sediment of alarm in the country."

The day after the Senate elections and the day before debate on his absence was to begin, Don Pepe published an unsigned statement in *El Día* from Arazatí. He would travel to Montevideo regularly to meet with his Ministers.

> Señor Batlle y Ordoñez's personal interests, if he were to follow them right now, call for a leave of absence. But he believes it his duty to exercise presidential functions while he is President and since he believes that he can, without neglecting the public interest or violating the Constitution, he will exercise them in spite of the efforts of those who want him on leave.[19]

Socialist Deputy Frugoni dismissed the constitutional arguments but protested the trip's cost to the treasury. A whole cavalry regiment was quartered at Arazatí, a telephone "for the personal convenience of the President of the Republic, naval vessels at full steam, using up coal." What Frugoni did not know and what Batlle refused to reveal, for fear of stirring up alarm, was that he had received information that the Colorado dissidents, using their navy connections, were planning to kidnap him and force a change in government; the regiment was at Arazatí to repel kidnappers.

V

The second week in December, Arena and Senate President Viera visited Arazatí. Don Pepe, seeing his daughter dying before his eyes—a French anti-tuberculosis serum, administered at the ranch in Arazatí, had no improving effect on her—again wanted to gamble and take her to Europe. Arena wrote the absent Manini: "Batlle's preoccupation, his obsession, is to escape to Europe. But the doctors do not permit it, warning that death can assault her on the way." "You can imagine the nervous state of our little political world in the face of Batlle's voyage . . . but the truth is that Batlle is prepared to leave, confident of the solidity of the constitutional mechanism and disposed to delegate the presidency to Viera."[20]

Ana Amalia, who had just turned eighteen, was feeling the summer heat. Confined to bed, she wrote in her diary:

> Papá has conceived the idea of a five or six month trip to Italy, because he says there are places there where the climate is very good and where I would feel very well. First he proposed to mother and me that we go alone with the boys. That was rejected, but when he said he would ask for a leave and go with us, then the idea was quite well received. The trip was conceived so quickly, that we thought we would go on the 13th of this month.

Batlle made his third trip to Montevideo on December 16, accompanied by rumors that he was writing out his request for a leave of absence. He was back on the 18th, and the word was that he was leaving for Europe momentarily. But Ana Amalia's doctors told Batlle she was weakening and Europe was out of the question. Dr. Ricaldoni called in Dr. Juan B. Morelli—politically a furious anti-Batlle Nationalist—and they decided on a new treatment, a pneumothorax: forcing nitrogen down her lungs. The girl became frightened when she saw the doctors, their sleeves rolled up to their elbows, enter her room. Matilde, her mother, couldn't bear to watch. The doctors reassured her, her father held her hands. She suffered and cried: "Poor papá, pale and bathed in sweat, tried to smile and encourage me." Two days later, to Ana Amalia's terror, the treatment was repeated.

Melián Lafinur and Rodó could not get enough legislators' signatures to convoke the General Assembly (the Chamber and Senate meeting jointly) to judge Batlle. After allowing debate to continue for a month, the Chamber at 25 minutes after midnight on December 20, voted to reject the argument that the President of the Republic could not leave the capital without delegating the Executive Power to the Senate President. Years later, Don Pepe recalled that of all the opposition to him, this debate had been "undeniably infamous" and wrote down something he had refused to publicize at the time. He had paid the warship's coal costs "from my own pocket." As for Melián Lafinur, who had provoked the debate, "I have the worst opinion of his moral character." In family conversation, Don Pepe used what was for him strong language whenever Melián Lafinur's name came up: "I would spit in his face."[21]

VI

The lid was blowing on the Williman-Tiscornia Senate election. The Tiscornia-dominated Río Negro electoral commission had thrown out sixteen Williman votes and declared Tiscornia the winner.[22] For the Río Negro Colorado organization, whose control over the department was at stake, Serrato, acting Minister of Interior, had finally gone too far. On Christmas Day, Río Negro Deputies Ricardo Espalter and Jaime Herrera published an open letter. Serrato's interference in Río Negro, they began, was common knowledge. "Taking advantage of the sad circumstances through which the President is passing . . .," Serrato had held up promotions of public employees before the election, and after the elections promoted Tiscornia voters instead of those recommended by their office heads. To top it off, Serrato had just named the principal Tiscornia politicians to the municipal council of Río Negro's capital.[23]

The following day, *El Día* published an interview with Serrato. His only electoral actions in Río Negro had been to recommend "absolute liberty for each voter to vote the candidate of his choice." Had he wanted to intervene, he could have taken up departmental Colorado leader Ricardo Espalter's offer, repeatedly made, that Serrato name a Senate candidate to replace Williman.[24]

Serrato's counterattack was a mistake. To protect himself against Serrato's accusation of duplicity with Williman, Espalter now published damaging aspects of the story that he had previously held back. Ten days before the election, Antonio María Rodríguez, President of the Colorado National Executive Committee, had told Espalter to accept Williman's resignation and have the Río Negro organization nominate Juan Paullier. Espalter answered Rodríguez that he had got Williman to withdraw the resignation, had stopped in to see Serrato, and, knowing that Serrato was Tiscornia's friend, had got Serrato's pledge not to move public employees around before the elections. Lest his truthfulness be doubted, Espalter proceeded to publish two coded telegrams from Antonio María Rodríguez, President of the National Colorado Executive Committee, to Juan L. Bayeto, President of the Río Negro Colorado Committee.

Montevideo, November 13

Señor Juan L. Bayeto (coded)

Disregard previous telegrams; after publication of news of Doctor Williman's resignation, consulted President Batlle who charges me to tell you that Departmental Commission should accept resignation immediately, once accepted, members of Departmental Commission should be convoked to proclaim candidacy of Dr. Juan Paullier, assure the acceptance of the new candidate by all members of Electoral College by the most effective means or modify said Electoral College with respect to all members who may not accept the nomination. Urgent that you communicate results of your actions in regard to these recommendations of Sr. Batlle to me because he wants to know them and it is necessary to submit them to the National Commission for approval. Telegrams of Minister of Interior to which yours of today refers obey same instructions of señor Batlle: if difficulties should occur in preparing favorable opinion for the new candidate, concentrate efforts in nearest districts and avoid functioning of polling places in the rest by absence of some members of Election Boards, where elections would be held on following Sundays.

Funds requested will be sent after the recommendations complied with. Regards.

Antonio María Rodríguez

Montevideo, November 14—To Juan L. Bayeto

Last night Batlle sent for me to tell me that because rumors circulate here about efforts in favor of other candidates he recommends that you obtain signed pledge in favor of Doctor Juan Paullier from Electoral College and forward original to National Committee so that ballots new Electoral College can be printed with only those who have accepted that pledge and will send out printed ballots immediately.

Antonio María Rodríguez[25]

Publication of Rodríguez' telegrams was enormously damaging. Batlle appeared to be pulling the strings to force the Río Negro Colorados to do his will. The first telegram ordered interference with election boards, an illegal act. The second telegram's phrase "Last night Batlle sent for me" was made to order for opposition headlines and orators. Batlle, in Arazatí, waiting for Dr. Morelli to give the sinking Ana Amalia a third pneumothorax forcing of nitrogen gas, had to reply. In *El Día* on December 28, he explained:

The only thing the President of the Republic has done in that election is to authorize Dr. Antonio María Rodríguez, after the candidacy of Dr. Williman had been discarded due to the spontaneous resignation of that citizen, to recommend the candidacy of Doctor Paullier to the consideration of his [Batlle's] friends, understanding that in so doing he was only expressing his personal sympathies for that fellow citizen. Everything else alluded to in those telegrams is exclusively work of Dr. Rodríguez.

As for Rodríguez' "insinuation" that some electoral districts be kept from functioning by having election officials stay away, "Señor Batlle y Ordoñez is not and never has been in favor of putting obstacles in the functioning of electoral bodies, under any pretext."[26]

VII

Antonio María Rodríguez stated that Batlle's explanation was "rigorously exact." He, Rodríguez, had sent the telegrams because he was afraid that Ricardo Espalter had been holding back Williman's resignation so as to emerge as Senate candidate himself. Shortly thereafter, Williman told Rodríguez that "because of certain publications by Dr. Tiscornia hostile to his personality," he was withdrawing his resignation. With that, Rodríguez had convoked the Colorado National Executive Committee, which endorsed Williman's candidacy and sent electioneering funds to the Río Negro Colorado organization. So the hastily written telegrams in which "perhaps I went too far in some details" had been voided by later events.[27]

On January 2 a special Chamber committee was appointed to investigate Antonio María Rodríguez. Since his Chamber term was expiring at the end of the month, this was a way of defusing the issue. On January 4 Serrato had to face an embarrassing interpellation in the Chamber. Serrato's interpellations went so badly that the day before it resumed, Antonio María Rodríguez resigned as President of the Colorado Executive Committee: "if there is any error or impropriety in those communications, not on fundamentals but on details, all responsibility is exclusively mine and therefore I consider myself morally obliged to abandon the office of President of this high party authority."[28]

At 5 P.M. on January 7, Batlle, who had not been in Montevideo for nearly three weeks, arrived on the *Uruguay*, went to Government House, met with Ministers, Senators, and Deputies, signed decrees, left his office at 1 A.M., went to the port on foot—his presence could be reported the next day—and returned to Arazatí: It was routinely mentioned that he had also met with the Chief of Staff and other military officers in his office.[29]

Serrato had to endure further questioning in the Chamber. Ricardo Espalter accused Serrato of having taken advantage of disciplinary hearings that had been pending for eight months to dismiss police officials, rejecting the Jefe Político's recommendations for their replacements, and naming anti-Williman men as new rural police chiefs. Serrato had started disciplinary hearings of the Río Negro Intendent's office three days before elections, "so that employees and peons would realize that the Government and Minister of the Interior were combating Dr. Williman's candidacy." After the elections, Serrato had rejected promotions of those who voted for Williman (voting was by signed ballot) and "named all those who had voted for the opposition, even though they had not been proposed by their department heads, which meant that the Minister was using the National Budget to favor his friends, those who had joined him in supporting Doctor Tiscornia for election as Senator for Río Negro." What more proof did the Chamber want before condemning Serrato, that Serrato had ordered Williman voters beaten up—something he knew Batlle would not stand for?

Serrato, with a day's rest, replied. It was Batlle, not he, who insisted that police chiefs who had charges pending against them be dismissed before the elections. The new men named by Serrato, some of whom the Jefe Político had called "Tiscornia toughs," were in fact competent policemen. As for holding up promotions, four "insignificant" jobs, a porter, a sailor, a launch captain, and a customs clerk, were involved, jobs too insignificant for anyone really to consider them rewards or punishments. No coercion, no interference with voters had been demonstrated. "My conscience as a citizen and as a politician would have rebelled against such acts. Now it is up to the Chamber to judge my actions." Serrato's peroration was greeted with applause from the floor and gallery, and his day ended on a note of vindication.

Nevertheless, Cosio's motion that the Chamber declare itself satisfied with Serrato's explanations was opposed by Socialist Frugoni, who had called the interpellation: "a Minister should not, even in confidential letters, make political suggestions to the men whose personal situation in the Public Administration depends on his will." Cosio's motion was revised, and the Chamber, without mentioning Serrato, voted to pass to the order of the day.[30]

The interpellation had been ignominious for Serrato; his reputation as an incorruptibly able financial administrator now had a political taint. There was no indication, however, that Batlle's support of Serrato, the political capital that Serrato hoped would make him the next President, had weakened in the slightest. Areco, Viera's closest collaborator, had been named President of the Colorado Executive Committee to replace the resigned Rodríguez, and this encouraged the more politically oriented of the Batllistas, the supporters of Viera for President.[31]

The hullabaloo and disclosures about Río Negro, however revealing of patronage politics, changed nothing. *El Siglo* had thundered that Batlle and Serrato "would have been out in the street within two hours after the compromising telegrams became known in any nation really in control of its destinies,"[32] but Batlle was as much in control of Colorado politics and the Uruguayan government as ever. The Río Negro election itself had been fought over the question whether Williman or Tiscornia was really Batlle's candidate. When the Senate convened in February, five of Batlle's handpicked candidates would be seated, and then the Senate would decide whether Williman or Tiscornia would take the sixth seat. During this administration the Senate had been a Batllista club and the obvious meaning of the November Senate elections was that it would continue to be a Batllista club.

VIII

Batlle's last trip to Montevideo, when the strategy in support of Serrato had been arranged and routine government business transacted, had a sadder purpose. Ana Amalia was fading fast. The family privately believed that the pneumothorax treatments had pumped too

25. Batlle's house, Piedras Blancas, outside Montevideo.

much air into her lungs. Don Pepe was about to bring her home to Piedras Blancas to die. Even this could not be separated from politics. The attempt to kidnap him, Batlle had been warned, would come off on this final trip. Part of the crew of the navy cruiser *Uruguay* had been paid to do the job. The routine statement during Batlle's Montevideo stay that he had met with the Army Chief of Staff and other military officers concealed news that the meeting had involved investigation of the plot and plans to counter it. On January 16, without public announcement, Don Pepe and his family, with Ana Amalia, boarded the *Uruguay*. Colonel Dufrechou, in charge of Batlle's personal security during this Presidency, and his entire regiment also boarded. Don Pepe himself was armed. The voyage was uneventful.[33]

At Piedras Blancas, Ana Amalia's weakness and hard breathing anguished her family. The last two days she was kept alive by artificial devices. At 7:15 P.M. on January 24, her parents and brothers saw her die. The funeral the next day was attended by foreign diplomats and large crowds. On the way back, Don Pepe, that huge man with the gruff voice and impassive features, broke down in public and cried.[34]

APPRAISALS: II

Batlle's presidency was nearly half over—more than half if the Colegiado was going to shorten this administration by a year—and even though Batlle was holding back on some of his most radical proposals until after the Colegiado was inaugurated, the outlines of his vision of Uruguay as the model country were now much clearer and more public than they had been when he was elected on the "mature" Batlle image. He was using the nation's prosperity to push major economic transformation, rural and urban. Ranching would become intensive, agriculture would be expanded; industry would grow, both import-substituting industry and new industry, like fishing, industrial alcohol, and mining. New and expanded state enterprises would halt gold outflow while lowering costs to users. The State, "owner of all great fortunes or at least a large part of them," through taxation would be able to provide the minimum decencies of life for all. Education and culture would also be at the reach of all. (In contrast with later revolutionaries who want to end the gap between intellectuals and labor by forcing intellectuals to do manual labor, Don Pepe wanted to narrow the gap by giving workers an intellectual culture.) Women would be freed from the Church and the constrictions of male domination. The process of achieving the model country would be ongoing, under increasing democracy, run by the Colorado Party and assured by the Colegiado.

II

This summary of what Batlle was doing differs from most of the recent writing—beginning in the 1960's—about him. These writers see Batlle, because of a combination of his lack of awareness of rural matters and his political calculation, leaving ranchers alone, neglecting the interior, and concentrating his programs on Montevideo where his political support lay. Statements like "the nucleus of the problem—land tenure . . . had not yet reached the attention of the leader in the Presidency";[1] "though Batlle adopted a radical reforming posture in respect to a wide range of interests and institutions, it did not extend to the question of landownership";[2] "the Batlle government . . . operated in an almost completely urban context" are illustrative of what has become the conventional wisdom. "Batlle's bargain—urban reforms for rural status quo"[4] is seen as a "lateral path"[5] designed to expand urban consumption, "resolve social tensions" and so "not affect the traditional structures which he wished to preserve."[6]

Taken as a whole, these studies misinterpret Batlle's intentions, narrow the scope of his policies, and underestimate his radicalism. Rather than accepting the rural status quo, he was moving to force intensive land use and to reclaim government-owned tierras fiscales. Rather than operating in an almost completely urban context, his policies and politics were national. The agronomy stations, roads, state railroads, a still-to-be-announced new port on the Atlantic near the Brazilian border—all were designed to build up the interior; state bank credit and insurance served the interior as well as Montevideo; the State Electric Power System, which previously operated only in Montevideo, had just been expanded to operate all over the country; the new preparatory schools in every department were to bring the level of culture in the interior closer to Montevideo's.

Politically, Batlle presided over a national, not just Montevideo, party. The big political scandal of this administration had come over an election in the interior, in Río Negro. The Nationalists had abstained in 1910, giving the Colorados a national sweep, but even when the Nationalists had run in 1905 and 1907, Colorados won the majority in 14 and 15 of the 18 departments outside Montevideo.[7] To be sure, even though votes were counted honestly, the Nationalists, who had great difficulty getting their people to vote while Colorados benefited from the votes of public employees, were underrepresented, but that does not change the fact that Batlle's political support was national and not limited to Montevideo.

Nor is the view accurate that Batlle wanted to preserve traditional structures and relieve social tensions through lateral paths. A man who was moving to make the State "owner of all great fortunes or at least a large part of them" obviously did not want to preserve traditional structures. This misreading of Batlle's intentions and policies comes because these studies look back at Batlle from the vantage point of Uruguay's continuing post-1950's economic crisis, when consumption exceeded production, the country had a huge paper-shuffling bureaucracy, and deficit-producing state enterprises were breaking down.

The lateral-path argument places the beginning of these conditions in Batlle's second presidency. Batlle, in this view, intentionally expanded public employment, especially in the state enterprises, to increase the work force, Uruguayan consumption, and the market for goods.[8] But Batlle himself, as the analysis of his budgets indicated, was very careful to keep down the growth of public employment. Indeed, I have been arguing that the state enterprises developed by Eduardo Acevedo had too few employees to carry out their purposes. For Batlle, the function of state enterprises was to restrict gold outflow and to provide new and cheap services in the economic development program he was pushing on Uruguay. Filling state enterprises with excess employees would raise costs and prevent these enterprises from offering cheap services. Successful state enterprises justified new ones; inefficient ones would not.

When the State Electric Power System was expanded to operate in the whole nation, its board was given the right to fire workers even though public employees normally could be dismissed only with Senate concurrence. Legislators objected. Finance Minister Serrato answered that the State wanted its enterprises to be successful and "it must organize them as private industry is organized."[9]

III

The success of the State enterprises was remarkable. The Electric Power System had generated almost as much power in the last six months of 1912 as in all of 1910–11, and its profits in 1912 were a record 725,450 pesos. The new State Insurance Bank, even though it had not yet completed its first year of operations and was functioning without its monopoly, collected premiums of 354,152 pesos and was already profitable. The newly nationalized Banco Hipotecario (State Mortgage Bank) had taken advantage of government backing of its obligations to place four million pesos of its mortgage bonds abroad.[10]

Government finances were also in excellent shape. Despite all the increased expenditures of Batlle's new projects, Serrato forecast still another budget surplus—over a million pesos for fiscal 1912–13.[11] The government's scrupulous management of public funds remained its great strength among businessmen and ranchers. Even *El Siglo* acknowledged that "the present government does not steal. We believe that in this respect our country has not had and all of America does not have a government which surpasses it."[12]

Prosperity had not been aborted by Batlle's radicalism. Quite the contrary, the economy was booming. Using imports—the source of raw materials, machinery, and many consumers' goods—as the rule-of-thumb measure of economic growth, the healthy 5 percent growth rate of the prosperous Williman years had doubled to an annual 10 percent rate during the first two years of Batlle's administration. Serrato's official characterization of the state of the Uruguayan economy was "rapid development."[13]

There were two principal explanations for this. The first was that the prices for Uruguay's exports were excellent. Wool prices were holding high, while the quantity of wool exported had gone up from 46,990 tons in 1910 to 80,940 tons in 1912. Also 1912 cattle prices had reached an all-time high of 21.94 pesos per steer, and with Swift's new refrigerated packing plant and the expanded Frigorífico Uruguayo bidding up prices, the future of cattle raising was rosy.[14] The second explanation was the aggressive expansion of credit by the state-owned Bank of the Republic, a tremendous increase of 60 percent over 1910. As Serrato had noted, without the Bank's expansionary policies under its new charter, "the general business situation would be very different from the one we are enjoying."[15]

Nevertheless, there was concern because the Bank's gold holdings were dropping. They were now 43.03 percent of the Bank's combined demand deposits and banknotes over 10 pesos in circulation, close to the Bank's charter requirements of a 40 percent gold minimum, and this ratio had been secured only by the government's transferring its funds at the Bank from demand to time deposits. If the Bank's gold holdings did not rebound, it would be forced to tighten credit; indeed, complaints that the Bank was less willing to lend than it had been were already being heard.[16]

Financial experts explained that the slight tightening of bank credit in Montevideo was due to temporary external causes. The interest rate in Europe had risen because of the Balkan War which had begun in October 1912, and the interest rise had resulted in an outflow of deposits from Montevideo to Europe. Once the Balkan War ended, the European interest rate would drop and the gold would flow back to Uruguay.

Finance Minister Serrato was waiting for the drop in the interest rate so that he could simultaneously expand the Bank of the Republic's gold holdings and restructure Uruguay's public debt. Rather than floating new bond issues, Serrato had financed Batlle's many new projects with short-term debt, selling treasury notes abroad and borrowing from Montevideo banks. Serrato intended to float a massive bond issue at 4.5 percent interest abroad, the proceeds from which would almost double the Bank of the Republic's paid-in capital and would pay off the short-term debt and redeem Uruguay's outstanding 5 percent bonds.

The massive 4.5 percent bond issue would have been possible the previous year, but since then the rise in the London bank rate had made it impossible. (Early in 1912, the London bank rate was 3.5 percent and 5 percent Uruguayan bonds were selling over par; now, in early 1913, the London bank rate was 4.2 percent and the Uruguayan bonds were around 95, yielding investors 5.25 percent.)[17] As soon as interest rates fell, the operation would go into effect. The Bank of the Republic, its gold holdings substantially increased, would continue to provide the abundant credit which was underwriting Uruguay's prosperity. The cost of servicing Uruguay's public debt would be reduced. Uruguay would be in as favorable a financial situation as any new capital-importing country could expect to be. Serrato, the mud of the Río Negro Senate election washed off by this brilliant financial solution, supported both by Batlle and business, expected by then to be the candidate for the next President of the Republic.

PART III *Crises*

CHAPTER 13

The Apuntes

Batlle and Matilde took their daughter's death very hard. Misia Matilde was bewildered. Ana Amalia was the first child of better times—another daughter had died as an infant—[1] when the complications of her unhappy first marriage were over, when she had all her children with her, when her husband was establishing himself as a force in the Colorado Party. Matilde, for her husband's sake, had kept her composure the day Ana Amalia died, but as time passed, she could not control her sadness. She wanted to go to the cemetery but couldn't bring herself to go. Five weeks after the girl's death she came upon a diary begun, she noted, by "my poor Pepe" when the girl was six months old, and confided her anguish. "My God what would I give to see you, to bring you to my side again. With your going all our plans have been broken, you leave an emptiness that nothing will fill. You, daughter of my life, who are now an angel, send your mother consolation from heaven."[2]

Don Pepe was in scarcely better shape—their sons had never seen their parents like this and worried if they would be able to function in life again. Tears came to his eyes when he talked of her. He kept her diary together with the one he had kept when she was a baby, in his desk. The idea of going to Europe, always associated with Ana Amalia, was now ruled out forever.[3] Years later he began to write a memorial.

"I rested from the struggle contemplating her. She was the only pride of my life; she was my hope for a sweet twilight in my life."

While sick, Ana Amalia once had been passive. When her father pressed her to tell him what she was thinking about, she blushed and timidly answered: "I was thinking whether I am afraid of death." "Oh torture . . . I could not protect her, put my chest as a wall against what menaced her, proudly spill all my blood for her." Don Pepe had written an earlier version:

> I could not shout why should you fear if I am with you? If my strong arm protects you? Why, if I would shed all my blood for you? Why if your father, formidable to defend you, would put his breast as[4]

The draft stopped here for the idea that he had been helpless to save his daughter "the only pride of my life" went against his fundamental self-confidence, his belief that he could always do something to make things better. During the weeks of his mourning he started planning the moves that would finally bring the Colegiado to fruition. It took his mind off Ana Amalia's death; it would be his great contribution to Uruguay, something, as he later put it, "for our children and the children of our adversaries."

II

By mid-February, 1913, Batlle had ended his public mourning, and politics quickened. The newly elected Senators took their seats, without challenge to Antonio María Rodríguez, new Senator from Tacuarembó. On February 15 Otero, Batlle's choice for Senate President, was unanimously elected. Four days later *El Día* announced that Viera, whose Senate term had expired, would be sworn in that very afternoon at Piedras Blancas as Minister of Interior.[5] Finance Minister Serrato had been acting Interior Minister.

Viera, the new Interior Minister, showed no concern whatever about rumors that Serrato and other cabinet ministers were going to resign over the Colegiado. He allowed himself to be interviewed, announcing that his ministerial program was "to accompany Señor Batlle in his political-administrative acts." As Minister, he would be "a party man," "even in elections."

> I am completely in favor of constitutional reform, including reform of the system of government. I am convinced of the desirability of

the Colegiado, and the entire population of the nation will share this conviction—before the Constitutional Convention—if an effective and reasoned propaganda campaign is put together. . . .

When the nation is made to see the value and convenience of the Colegiado, first through constant theoretical preaching, then with the formula actually in operation, it is bound to accept it with pleasure.

The Nationalist Directorio's formal decision, made in January, not to take part in constitutional reform would not stop constitutional reform.

At the stage we have now reached, the problem is too far advanced toward solution to turn back. The Constitutional Convention, in spite of its large size, should be easily formed. There is plenty of time to form it and for it to complete its mission during the present presidency. The debates are not going to be long, and most of the constituent assemblymen are going to come with their opinions already formed on the principal points to be considered.

Viera and Serrato were the principal contenders to succeed Batlle as President, and Viera was asked about this.

Presidential Question? Next President? I believe there will be neither the first nor the second. The coming of the Colegiado will eliminate these questions.

As soon as Señor Batlle's term ends, by which time constitutional reform will be completed and the new system of government approved, the Collegiate Executive will be a fact and the nation will be fully prepared for this important reform.[6]

There it was. Hard as it might be to believe, and for all the maneuvering by presidential candidates and their supporters, after José Batlle y Ordoñez there would be no Presidents of the Republic. Don Pepe was trying to make the prospect attractive to his enemies. He again promised that speedy constitutional reform would result in a legislature elected during his administration under proportional representation. It would also get him out of office before his term otherwise would expire. The Constitutional Convention itself would set the date for the election of the new Executive and—"Of course the

26. Ana Amalia and Misia Matilde. (Misia is a respectful form of address, like Doña.)

present Executive Power will cease as soon as the Colegiado is elected."[7]

To ensure that the Colegiado was launched with the massive electoral support that would guarantee its acceptance, and to provide continuing victories in the annual elections which the functioning Colegiado would require, the Colorado electorate must be greatly expanded. On March 1, Batlle's eight-hour-day bill, first introduced seven years ago, was brought to the Chamber floor for debate. In June 1911, Batlle had submitted a new eight-hour day bill, far stronger than his original proposal. Though Manini had countersigned it, the message and even the law's articles were Don Pepe's work. All workers, including white collar workers—agricultural and ranch workers remained excluded—would work an eight-hour day, and no overtime would be permitted. Working mothers would get forty days off and be paid 20 pesos by the State until a pension system was enacted. Twenty-five inspectors would enforce the law. Instead of one day a week off, the bill proposed a rotating system of one day in six off—to abolish the Christian Sunday—although it intimated acceptance of an alternative, the English five-and-a-half-day week. Batlle's bill, introducing a reduced work day, would profoundly alter Uruguayan life. It would be easy to enforce, since it would apply to all businesses. Business and industry moved to prevent passage. Within two months of the bill's presentation, a petition opposing the eight-hour day because it "would significantly alter the costs of industrial production and radically change commercial customs" was sent to the Chamber committee. The 104 signatures represented the most impressive list of organizations, firms, and individuals that could be assembled in Uruguay: fifteen banks, foreign and local, the Italian and French Chambers of Commerce, the railroads, the trolleys, the gas and water works, Liebig's, the telephone company, port stevedores, the Chamber of National Products, the Manufacturers Association, the Retail Stores Association, the Rural Association.

The legislative committee, shaken but knowing that Don Pepe expected the bill's passage, used the classic technique to gain time. It asked the Executive to have the Labor Office provide statistics on the Uruguayan work day. The Labor Office report was not formulated until October 1912. It had surveyed Montevideo labor, not including white collar workers or the self-employed, in forty-four occupations, a total of 42,207 workers (probably one third of those who would be covered by the law). Of these, one third of those in private industry worked an eight-hour day; the rest worked more. It was likely that the percentage of those working more than eight hours would be substantially increased if the rest of the Montevideo work force could be included.

The statistics were no surprise—the bill would not have raised such resistance if it merely legalized the existing work day. The Chamber Committee, having delayed as long as it could, unanimously reported out Batlle's eight-hour bill. To simplify passage, it left for separate consideration the provisions on women's and children's work and the one day's rest in six. Don Pepe himself, to close off accusations of Godless crackpotism, acknowledged that the one-day-in-six provision was "an aspiration for the future,"[8] and agreed to the committee's procedures. The Chamber leadership knew what Batlle wanted, and the Chamber voted down requests for delay for additional documentation.[9]

In *El Día* on March 4 simultaneous with the publication of his Apuntes on the organization of the Colegiado, Batlle called for quick passage of the eight-hour day. The argument that the work day should vary with the physical demands of the job converted the worker into "a beast of burden." The right question to ask was, "Is the worker a man, a citizen?"

> If one admits that he is, it is necessary to agree that the worker should be in condition to carry out his duty to exercise his rights. He should have time to inform himself, to study social problems in which he has as much interest as an intellectual, so as to exercise his mission fully as a man in a true democracy.[10]

Batlle's conviction about the eight-hour day can be traced to the concept of the worker's right to leisure in the philosophical studies of Batlle's youth. His current emphasis, though consistent with his longtime conviction, was on the need of the worker as citizen for time off.

At the end of the general strike Batlle had looked ahead to the day when the worker "organizes politically, goes to elections, makes up a considerable part of the legislature" and would be listened to by government. Worker awareness had been heightened the past two years. The general strike, after all, had closed down Montevideo. Worker awareness, though, was not being channeled toward the increasingly discredited Anarchists,[11] who viewed strikes, even lost strikes, as useful training for the eventual revolutionary abolition of the wage system, or even toward the Socialists who, in August 1912, had only 476 enrolled members.[12] Four times as many workers as the total number of voters in 1910 would be benefited by the eight-hour day.[13] Don Pepe's emphasis on the worker as citizen opened the campaign to expand the Colorado vote for the Colegiado by bringing workers to the polls.

IV

On March 2 Manini, who had taken his seat in the Senate and for some days now had been secretly sounding out fellow Senators to stop the Colegiado, knowing the historic importance of his effort, began keeping a record.

Yesterday after the Senate session, which I was unable to attend, Arena came to see me at home. We talked almost entirely about professional matters in our law office but naturally we devoted a little time to politics.

It goes without saying that Batlle persists in his creation of the Colegiado. Arena confessed to me confidentially that Batlle no longer plans to decorate the Constitutional Convention with some opponents of that extravaganza. . . .

The contrary private indications that were made previously were probably meant to lull us into believing that we could influence the Constitutional Convention in favor of our ideas. It is essential for those people to manipulate us gently so that we let the Constitutional Convention come into being. Once that is resolved, they will treat us brutally as adversaries, do what they will and, what is more, laugh at our ingenuousness. Will some of my fellow Senators, opponents of the settimino [seven-man Colegiado], knowingly play the role of simpleton-criminals? Everything depends on them; the anti-reformist majority of the Senate has the institutional fate of the nation in its hands. Let us see if through weakness they commit the stupidity of turning their conviction over to the extravagant authoritarianism of Batlle. . . .

Batlle keeps calling Senators and Deputies to Piedras Blancas. The man, in spite of his conceit, smells danger and is trying on one hand to persuade and on the other to discover who his adversaries are.[14]

Manini had not talked seriously with Don Pepe since he left the cabinet.[15] Manini still acknowledged to himself that Batlle was a superior person, well above the ordinary political struggle, but even this had its disadvantage: "something that has not yet been publicly discovered: his unbridled ambition for personal glory." Batlle knew public opinion opposed the Colegiado, but it did not distress him. "On the contrary, the less public opinion supports his undertakings, which he believes to be eternal works of genius, the more he feels them become part of his own personality. They will be Batlle's accomplishments more than the nation's accomplishments. And this is precisely what flatters his arrogance."[16]

V

On March 4 Batlle, simultaneous with his article on the worker as citizen, published one announced the previous day. It was unobtrusively entitled "El P. E. Colegiado. Apuntes sobre su Posible Organización y Funcionamiento"—"The Collegiate Executive Power. Notes On Its Possible Organization and Functioning." The Apuntes in very quiet language publicly outlined Batlle's Colegiado plan.

"A Junta of citizens [Batlle made no mention of women suffrage in the "Apuntes" but he used the words "citizen" and "member," never "men"] which will be called the Government Junta of the Republic will exercise the Executive Power." Members would be directly elected for a nine-year term. In the first election voters would vote for a single list of nine citizens (so ensuring an all-Colorado Colegiado). The member at the top of the winning list would serve nine years, the second one eight years, on down to the ninth, who would serve one year. "Every year following a new member would be elected to substitute for the one whose term expires" (since only one member would be elected in every election, the victor would be Colorado, so assuring the continuity of the all-Colorado Colegiado).

The Junta, by absolute majority, would elect one of its members president for a two-year term, reelectable one or more times. The president would chair Junta sessions and formally represent the nation diplomatically, would propose army officer promotions to the Junta, would "exercise the immediate command of land and sea forces," and would "take prompt security measures in grave and unexpected cases of internal commotion or foreign attack, simultaneously convoking the Junta to give immediate account of the measures executed and adjusting his conduct to what the Junta resolves." The president's salary would be no greater than the other members, and he could be removed as president at any time without explanation by a two thirds vote of the Junta. The Junta would decide other matters by majority vote.

The Junta's functions, as outlined, were those of the present President of the Republic. There would be "one or more ministers designated by absolute majority of the members of the Junta and revocable by equal majority." These ministers would "exercise, in short, all the faculties which the Junta de Gobierno, in accord with its attributes, judges it wise to entrust to them to improve the operations of government."[17] Don Pepe was dividing the presidency among nine individuals. He had rejected any form of parliamentary government. Ministers would not need to be approved by the legislature; the legislature could not vote out a Junta. In response to arguments by Manini and Serrato and in the hope of winning their support, Batlle had expanded the Junta from seven to nine members and given the Junta President very limited power as Commander in Chief, but except for that, the Junta President had one vote, just like any other member.[18]

"We are aghast," was *El Siglo's* reaction to the "Apuntes." It had nothing in common with its presumed Swiss model. (The seven-member Swiss Federal Council was elected for a four-year term by the federal legislature, the legislature annually elected the Council's President and Vice President, and no canton could have more than one member on the Council.) It almost seemed that "by a Machiavellism of almost superhuman subtlety," Batlle was presenting a plan so monstrous that any later modification would make it tolerable. "But no, that is not the plan: the plan is another . . . it is the desire for perpetual domination." The Constitutional Convention under Batlle's "moral influence" would elect him to the first Junta, or else he would let a year pass and then enter. "Afterward, nine years of Batlle, and another nine, eighteen years of Batlle as President of the Junta de Gobierno reelected every two years, and so on, so long as Batlle lives." But no, Uruguay was not going to have perennial personal domination like Porfirio Díaz' Mexico:

> the nation repudiates the Colegiado . . . Señor Batlle y Ordoñez has all public opinion against it. His best friends reject such an idea, his own ministers oppose it. We will have reached the ultimate in our own villification if Batlle's own isolated, deranged will, blockaded by all civic forces, should succeed in imposing the Constitution that his extravagant authoritarianism has decreed. Others, no less audacious or autocratic, retreated in the past when confronted by public opinion, and he will have to retreat or be destroyed by it.[19]

Don Pepe kept his temper under control. *El Siglo* was absolutely right, the Colegiado was not a copy of the Swiss Constitution. It was not taken from any book. "Good or bad," it was an Uruguayan project, designed for "our own idiosyncracies." "It is also correct that it has aimed at organizing a stable government," to end revolution by suppressing personal arbitrariness. What was not correct was that the project was tyrannically aimed at securing the government for an Uruguayan Porfirio Díaz. "One does not go toward tyranny when one wants to divide the power now concentrated in one person among nine."[20] And the next day, Don Pepe noted that through an oversight the "Apuntes" had left out a requirement that Junta members could not be reelected until one or two years after their term expired. So much for the dark plot to keep the same men in power.[21]

Reasoned debate was required, and toward this debate Batlle made another concession. If there was fear that the President of the Junta would dominate it, he was willing to have the President removed by a majority vote of the Junta members, not by a two-thirds vote. But *El Siglo* would not debate. "When a concept is so absurd that only the mad can take it seriously, the sane do not waste time analyzing it." What was being presented was not a problem in political science but "a crazy attempt at personal domination." By pushing the Colegiado through before his term expired, Batlle would seat himself in it and claim he was not violating his promise not to serve on it once his term expired. The Nationalists had already set up a Protest Committee against Constitutional Reform. The Directorio newspaper proclaimed that the transparent reason why Batlle was making the Colegiado so powerful was "that he is preparing it for himself."[22]

CHAPTER 14 *Enough!*

Since the Apuntes, every day brought new rumors: army officers were being moved around; Serrato, Acevedo, Education Minister Blengio Rocca, and maybe others would resign from the cabinet; Batlle would have trouble with parliament. Manini, at the center of the still secret Senate operation to halt the Constitutional Convention, had one disappointment—Espalter, a natural ally, backed out, and a surprising convert, Antonio María Rodríguez ("Last Night Batlle Sent for Me") joined after an hour's talk. Batlle, alerted by Espalter, called in more Senators for talks. On March 10, 1913, Manini noted, there was "an unexpected and fortunate event." Senator Enciso, called to Piedras Blancas by Batlle for still another attempt to convince him of the advantages of the Colegiado, wearied and told Batlle he could stop wasting his time, "since the Senate majority resisting reform on the basis of rejection of the electoral law for the Constitutional Convention was already in existence and determined not to give way."

Manini, fearful that Don Pepe would put enormous pressure on waverers, met with Enciso that very night and proposed something that had already been discussed among the principals, namely the issuance of a signed public statement by the Senators explaining that they would reject

the electoral law for the Constitutional Convention, which means delay of constitutional reform until at least next year, after the general election of deputies is completed and in Batlle's last year of government, when his governmental influence will be substantially reduced.

By March 11, Manini had nine Senators pledged and expected two or three more.

On the afternoon of the 12th, Arena, as was his custom, entered Manini's office without knocking and discovered Antonio María Rodríguez and Varela Acevedo, who two days previously had turned down Batlle's offer of the Education Ministry. They were all old friends, but the meeting got hot. Varela Acevedo criticized Arena for not stopping Batlle before he reached the abyss. Arena said he couldn't stop Don Pepe, blurted out that Batlle would not accept any modifications in the constitutional reform procedures,[1] and followed that with the news that "in case the reform plan failed, Batlle would go resolutely to Viera's [presidential] candidacy." This last was a warning to Rodríguez, who detested Viera, as well as to Serrato's Senatorial friends who, to keep Serrato's candidacy alive, were joining the antireformists. Fear that Batlle would yet split the Senate majority impelled Manini and a group of five close political friends to get the signatures on paper. In two meetings on March 14, the document was agreed to, signed by ten Senators—with the Río Negro seat still unfilled, the total Senate membership was only 18—and carried for their signature to two others who were in the interior. Manini was sure one would sign and was hopeful of the other.[2]

Batlle, as he saw the Senate hardening against reform and faced with finding cabinet replacements for at least three ministers whose resignations were about to be made public, continued to defend the Colegiado in *El Día*. Why did *El Siglo* oppose the Colegiado? Because the Ramírez family, led by José Pedro Ramírez, the man responsible for the War of 1904, wanted to be President. Who was calling for the Chamber and the Senate "to obstruct constitutional reform as much as possible?" The Nationalists.[3] Don Pepe was relying on his basic strength, the Colorado Party. Those in the Senate who would stop constitutional reform were doing the bidding of the party's Blanco enemy and the bidding of the anti-Colorado power brokers who had hurt the party so much in the past.

Manini recognized the danger. Though he believed that Batlle's "party prestige" was "enormously diminished," he had to admit that "it is still considerable."[4] On the evening of March 14, having got ten Senate signatures on the document that afternoon, Manini appeared before the Colorado Club of the 7th Section of Montevideo, where he started his political career and whose Honorary President he still remained, to give his first open response to the "Apuntes." He did not claim that the "Apuntes" were designed to keep Batlle in power. For one thing, a Colorado Club would not have found anything wrong with keeping Batlle in power; for another, Manini knew that Batlle had no intention of serving on the Colegiado. Instead, Manini announced himself as both "a decided adversary of the Collegiate organization of the Executive Power" and "a Colorado, a member of this political situation, and co-author and collaborator" of Batlle's government. Manini favored constitutional reform, to discourage revolution by strengthening the legislature and thereby stimulating "the participation of all the political forces of the nation in the legislature and so give a vast legal sphere of action to party activities without causing the Executive Power to lose its present characteristics as jealous, rapid, and expeditious guardian of public order."

"Suddenly, when procedures for constitutional reform were almost complete, an unexpected formula was announced" which without strengthening the legislative power at all, would completely destroy the present Executive Power "even to the point where the stationing of troops would be subject to the deliberations of nine people." Such a reform would require long preparation before it could be considered.

> However laudable one of the purposes inspiring this reform may be, according to which, since we are not economically powerful enough to make an impact on the world concert, we should give the world the example of our advanced institutions, let us not forget that we run grave dangers in converting our native land into an experiment station for exoticisms or novelties and that our humble present, with the slow but sure steps we are taking toward the future, is worth more than illusory dreams of greatness and deceiving illusions of false glory, which we will never receive except as we are truly worth them.

Here was the heart of Manini's unhappiness. It was not just the Colegiado; fundamentally, Batlle's excessive radicalism, his converting Uruguay into an "experiment station for exotic novelties," must be stopped. "Slow but sure," was the real Uruguayan way, and in this Manini could expect substantial agreement, not necessarily from his listeners, but from Uruguay's political elite, deeply troubled at how far the country had departed from the cautious progressivism of the Williman years.

Manini went on to the substantive criticisms which should convince his Colorado listeners of the Colegiado's dangers. The party, now united, had given the nation a series of exemplary administrations. There was no compelling danger requiring an extreme change in the structure of government. Already Senator Espalter was advocating use of the Colegiado to provide the different Colorado factions a place in the government. The first effect of the Colegiado, then, would be "the disintegration" of the Colorado Party. But disintegration would not stop there.

> After all, I cannot conceive of any decorous pretext, once the institutional essence of the Executive Power is changed, by which we can deny the entry into it of representatives of the minority parties. If that Power loses its characteristic of absolutely executive functional indivisibility, and is transformed into a deliberative corporation, necessarily, fatally, distinct criterias, tendencies and orientations are admissible. With what justification can we impose upon the nation the obligation of designating all its members from the majority party?

This was the most telling attack a one-party government Colorado could make on the Colegiado. Sooner or later, either "to solve incidental political difficulties" or forced by a fundamental "movement of opinion," minorities would enter. And a Junta with Nationalists, Catholics, and Socialists would be charged with maintaining public tranquility! "Under such conditions it will be impossible for the Colorado Party to continue to exercise its historic mission as guardian of public order, a mission which up to now it has carried out for its own honor and the health of the nation." Even if, Manini went on, the Colegiado remained all Colorado, it would be vulnerable to overthrow by a caudillo. While its members debated what to do, some criollo Catiline would disperse this Roman Senate and set Uruguay back for decades, back to the militarist days of Latorre, with the Colorado Party split and morally discredited.

The Colegiado "divides us, everything else unites us . . . and for that reason I believe the wisest course would be to postpone it until full discussion determines the Colorado collectivity's definitive ideas about it."[5]

Manini's speech, announcing as it did great troubles for Batlle, also opened the kind of serious, honorable debate on the Colegiado that Don Pepe wanted. Manini, Batlle acknowledged, had been his closest collaborator. His public disagreement with the President of the Republic "honors the government of the country," because Manini knew "that the only arm that will be used in the contest will be reason and law and that the one who triumphs will be the one who employs the most persuasive arguments and brings the most supporters to his cause." To expect all citizens to accept any constitutional reform project was absurd; it would be enough if a majority approved. Nor was there merit in Manini's central argument, the need for delay so that Colorados would understand the implications of the Colegiado before deciding.

> The reform is simple. The entire plan consists of suppressing the president and replacing him with a commission. All the other laws will continue as they are. Now we all know what results the institution of the presidency have given in our nation's short political life, and the circumstance that there is no activity of any sort, except the Executive Power, which is not entrusted to a commission and not to a single man permits all of us easily to judge the applicability of collegiate bodies to the management of the common interest. . . . The time required to prepare the Constitutional Convention and the time the Convention will last will permit debate to clear up any remaining doubts.

But suppose Manini was right and that the Colegiado was difficult to understand. Then its supporters, who would have to overcome the bewilderment of the electorate, would be hurt by an immediate election. Manini argued that because the Colorado Party was united, there was no need to change the Executive Power. But "foresighted reforms" did not come under tyrannies; they came when those who had won unity after great difficulties made sure their successors did not have to repeat their arduous route. If the Colorado Party was united, "a simple discussion of theoretical principles" could not split it.[6]

In this debate on political philosophy between the ex-disciple and master while the ex-disciple was organizing a political upheaval to terminate the master's influence, Manini and Don Pepe had talked across the real issue. Manini had not confessed his confidence that if constitutional reform were delayed until the end of Batlle's presidency, Batlle's Colegiado arguments would have far less political impact. Batlle's argument that since the Colegiado was new, immediate election of the Constitutional Convention would be disadvantageous to its supporters, who would have difficulty convincing voters, ignored the advantage Batlle's "moral influence" as President would give the Colegiado. Don Pepe, though, had conveyed a crucial message to Manini. Let Manini advance his ideas and Batlle his. There would be no appeal to force by Batlle; but neither would he tolerate any appeals to force by his opponents. "So long as all the legal and constitutional requirements are respected, nobody will have any reason to reproach anyone for anything."

II

The same day Manini spoke, Serrato's resignation as Finance Minister was released, followed two days later by Acevedo's and Education Minister Blengio Rocca's. Acevedo's resignation was independent of the Colegiado—he had come to the Ministry of Industries with "an economic development plan which Your Excellency fully accepted because it formed part of your own presidential program" and having put it into effect with Batlle's "really limitless support" wanted to complete writing his historical vindication of the founder of Uruguay's independence, Artigas. Serrato and Blengio were resigning because they opposed the Colegiado. Both men's letters of resignation were flattering to Batlle; Serrato called himself Batlle's "enthusiastic collaborator," and Batlle who had already offered Serrato the first place, the nine-year post, on the first Colegiado, had *El Día* write laudatory accounts of all three Ministers' accomplishments.[7]

To be a Minister was the dream of almost every Uruguayan public man. Batlle's great difficulty in finding replacements—all three first choices turned the offer down because, *El Día* acknowledged, they had "ideas opposing the Colegiado project"[8]—showed how widespread opposition among the political elite to the Colegiado was. Viera and Arena were literally chasing potential candidates, and Arena later called it the "Ministers strike." Viera finally located a combative young man in Salto, Viera's home town, whom nobody had ever heard of and Batlle had never seen—Baltasar Brum. *El Día* misspelled his first name when making the announcement. Brum welcomed the idea of becoming Education Minister. Pedro Cosio, Serrato's protégé and Batlle's original second choice for Industries, was deciding whether to accept the prestigious Finance Ministry.[9]

Batlle continued to answer opponents of the "Apuntes." He was prepared to reduce the Colegiado's size from nine to seven, or five. He was even prepared to accept a Colegiado made up of a president and ministers so long as all measures were decided by majority vote and ministers who disagreed with the president stayed in the government, though he considered the "Apuntes" formula superior. Young Nationalist Washington Beltrán proposed that the Junta be elected by the Chamber, which would itself be elected by proportional representation, so that "in supreme moments of agreement, the independent groups coalesced could elect a list of candidates who represented the different shades of opinion." This was exactly what Manini feared, and Don Pepe was quick to reject it. Batlle stood for one-party government "which is now giving our country such beautiful results," and the "Apuntes" were designed to maintain one party government.

> The election of a single member of the Junta de Gobierno every year, has three different aims: to induce the parties to live constantly organized as is desirable in a democracy; to diminish the importance of each election so that the disturbances which suffrage occasions be less frequent and serious; and to avoid deals and conciliations based on mixed electoral tickets, which could give victory to citizens who represent no stable popular support whatever.[10]

Manini had not responded to Batlle's press campaign. His great effort with fellow Senators was coming to fruition. Senator Fleurquin, Serrato's friend, had returned on March 17 from the interior and signed the declaration. That afternoon Fleurquin and Varela Acevedo went to Piedras Blancas. Their unprecedented mission was to tell Batlle to his face that they officially represented the Senate majority, which would not vote for constitutional reform. They still hoped to persuade Batlle finally to forget the Colegiado—Varela Acevedo and Fleurquin were young men whose intelligence and morality Don Pepe respected. Manini accompanied them part of the way to Piedras Blancas and recorded:

> Fleurquin and Varela returned from Piedras Blancas disappointed and exhausted. Batlle, brutally stubborn, blindly arrogant, still expected to overcome us by forcing defections from our bloc through the use of means he knows how to employ when he sees himself hemmed in.
>
> He insinuated something we already suspected, according to which he would incite mobs of Colorado clubs to overwhelm us with electoral terror [según el cual incitaría asonadas de clubes colorados para imponérsenos por el terror electoral] and to top things off the manifesto that the dissident Colorados [Bachini's and Rodó's] group are preparing would serve him marvelously by making us appear like schismatics.
>
> We deliberated a very short time and decided in favor of immediate publication.

Fleurquin wrote a short letter to Batlle, attaching a copy of the document to it, so that Batlle would be the first to know.[11]

The next day every Montevideo newspaper published the statement signed by eleven Senators now sitting, an absolute majority of the Senate.

> The Senators who sign below consider that the reform of the Constitution of the Republic should be the unequivocal expression of national sovereignty and faced with the indisputable fact that the political atmosphere is not presently prepared to carry out reform under those conditions, reiterating their sentiments of solidarity with the present political situation and convinced that they are proceeding in the national interest and in the interests of the political situation itself:
>
> Declare that they will vote the indispensable prior laws only if new and ample electoral guaranties are offered and in the understanding that the election of the National Constitutional Convention will take place during the year 1914, at a date and under

conditions to be fixed by a special law dictated by the XXV
Legislature.[12]

Consumatum est! Manini recorded. "Honor to the Senate," head-
lined *El Siglo*. The Senate, which previously had dismissed Rodó's
arguments, had now come around to accepting them. Constitutional
reform must be delayed until the last year of Batlle's administration,
when he would be at his political weakest. Furthermore, the Senate
would not approve the official bill giving three fifths of the Constitutional Convention's seats to the majority tickets. It wanted "new and
ample electoral guarantees," presumably the proportional representation Batlle adamantly opposed. And all the while, the eleven Senators
claimed solidarity with Batlle!

The obvious meaning of the previous November's Senate election,
when five of Batlle's handpicked candidates won unopposed—the
obvious meaning that the Senate would continue to be a Batllista
club—had turned out not to be the real meaning. New Senator
Manini, who had stayed out of the country during the election, had
organized the bloc. New Senator Antonio María Rodríguez ("Last
Night Batlle Sent For Me"), co-author of the official bill on the
Constitutional Convention election, had joined, as had new Senator
Varela Acevedo. Without them there would be no Senate majority to
stop reform. Before accepting nomination to the Senate, none of the
three had told Batlle they planned to hold back constitutional reform.[13] But it was equally true that Batlle had not asked them.

Don Pepe, the political tactician, had made a gigantic political
mistake. He had kept a handwritten list of how the Senators stood on
the linked issues of the eight-hour day and the Colegiado. On the
eight-hour day he had 12 in favor, one doubtful, and nothing beside
the other five. On the Colegiado he had 7 in favor, 5 against, 6 blank.[14]
All five of the Senators he had down as against the Colegiado had
signed the eleven Senators' declaration. Where Don Pepe's intelligence had collapsed was on the blanks; 5 of the 6 signed. Manini had
won them over; the disciple had outwitted the master.

What to do? Batlle could invoke a constitutional argument—that
since both the Chamber and the Senate had already approved the
National Convenience of Constitutional Reform by two thirds votes,
the new Senate majority's refusal to implement that decision by voting

the election law was unconstitutional.[15] Batlle could have the Chamber of Deputies approve the electoral bill, call that sufficient, and convoke elections for the Constitutional Convention. In a situation like this, Old Cuestas, who had been President before Batlle's first administration, would have discovered a plot, exiled Manini and two or three other Senators, pressured the Senate to seat their first alternates, and pass the required electoral bill. And it could be imagined what the Mexican dictator Porfirio Díaz, to whom Batlle was being compared by the opposition, would have done to Senators whom he had picked and who then turned against him. Don Pepe had immediately ruled out such tactics. This was not the way to the model country, it was the way to counterrevolution. If Batlle warped the law or used force, Manini and his fellow Senators, who had many friends among army officers with whom they had fought side by side in the War of 1904, could reply in kind, and the Nationalist military might finally have army allies. Indeed Batlle's message to Manini after Manini's speech to the Colorados of the Seventh Section, that as long as controversy stayed within the law, no one would have any reason to reproach anyone, was also a warning to Manini not to subvert army officers.

Batlle could do what the eleven Senators so badly wanted, withdraw the Colegiado. The Ministerial crisis and now the Senate's action should have revealed to him that he had grossly underestimated the strength of opposition to it. Withdrawing the Colegiado would keep the party together, enable Batlle to finish out his term with legislative support, preside over noncontroversial constitutional reform, and as part of the package choose his presidential successor. Giving up the Colegiado would do for Batlle what supporting Batlle's candidacy had done for Williman: make governing easy. But the Colegiado was the means by which Batlle would achieve the model country. Without the Colegiado, Batlle's second term, which he viewed as only the beginning of the new model Uruguay, would instead be its culmination. Thereafter solidification, Manini's "slow but sure," would be dominant.

A third option was to follow the Senators' requirements to the letter, let constitutional reform come in 1914 with the Constitutional Convention elected by proportional representation, and, as President, run a slate of pro-Colegiado delegates in that election. Batlle had rejected this option when the danger of serious Colorado splits was remote; a Constitutional election under proportional representation now would surely bring many kinds of non-Colegiado and anti-Colegiado tickets. Such a Constitutional Convention might well be unmanageable, it would likely continue beyond Batlle's presidency into the next, and its potential for altering Uruguayan politics in dangerous ways was very real.

III

On the day the eleven Senators' declaration was published, Batlle asked Williman, with whom Manini had already talked, to visit him that same afternoon. Williman, accompanied by his son, went to Piedras Blancas. Don Pepe took him into the garden, Batlle's favorite place for solitary meditation, and alone, while Williman's son waited inside, the two had what *El Día* described as a long, cordial talk "on the present political emergencies."[16]

Before the disturbance produced by the eleven Senators' declaration, Don Pepe had already decided who would be on the first Colegiado. It was to be inaugurated with "first-line men," the best the Colorado Party could offer. There would be the Generation of 1904, Serrato, Manini, Viera, and Blengio Rocca. Arena, Don Pepe's spokesman, would be there, and so would Williman. As a means of uniting the party, Campisteguy, Batlle's first Minister of Interior, who had broken with Batlle over Williman's presidential candidacy and was now President of the Bachini-led dissident Colorado opposition, would be there too. It might now be possible to split the eleven Senators by changing the first Colegiado's membership. Arena, whose presence on the Colegiado would be the equivalent of Batlle's own, could be dropped; so would Manini, while some Senators among the eleven could be added.[17]

Batlle explained the advantages of the Colegiado to Williman and advised him that he would be a long-term member of the first Colegiado. Williman's Interior Minister, now Senator, José Espalter, had dropped out of Manini's group and two of the eleven Senators were believed to be obligated to Williman and likely to follow his lead should he come out pro-Colegiado. Williman didn't turn Batlle down, but neither did he agree to support the Colegiado or to influence

Senators. As Batlle put it, "We will not say that he is in favor of the Colegiado; but we insist that he does not reject the idea."[18]

Serrato insisted, some forty years later, that the day before he resigned from the cabinet, Batlle sent Julio María Sosa to offer him the next presidency with only one condition: Batlle would keep control of the Colorado Party and Serrato must keep his hands off. Don Pepe, more bluntly than he liked, was admitting where his power base lay; it was not in any middle class, he had yet to even mention such a group; it was not among the workers, though he was beginning open courtship of workers' votes; it was in controlling the Colorado Party.

For Serrato, whose dream was coming true too late, the offer was unacceptable. Serrato's anticolegialism was too public; if he became President now, the political world would know that he had sold out and Batlle would be his only source of support. Serrato did not want to be a puppet president, and neither did he want to face the moral and political crisis of accepting the presidency on Batlle's terms and then breaking with him. Serrato told Sosa that if he became President under Batlle's conditions, he would end either as "a poor devil or a traitor to Batlle." He declined the offer and then released his resignation as Minister of Finance.[19] It was about this time that Arena warned Manini in the presence of two other Senators that Batlle would make no concessions on the method of electing the Constitutional Convention and that if Batlle couldn't get constitutional reform through now, he would make Viera President.

Don Pepe had decided on his options even before the Senators' declaration was formally signed. He would try to produce defections—Williman's visit and some strategic offers of Colegiado places had that goal. Defections were conceivable. Senator Varela Acevedo later estimated that eight of the eleven were confirmed anti-Colegialists; the other three, sufficient to break the majority, might be swayed.[20] But splitting the Senate majority was extremely difficult. A Senator's breaking of the signed pledge would be a public confession of duplicity.

If the eleven Senators held together, then Batlle would simply wait them out. He would have the Colorado Party endorse the Colegiado, get the voters' mandate for the Colegiado by winning this year's elections to the Chamber of Deputies, win control of the Senate in the

1914 elections, and come to an understanding with Viera over the conditions of presidential succession. During Viera's term delegates to the Constitutional Convention would be elected. They would not be elected by proportional representation, they would be elected under the provisions of the bill now before the Chamber, so that three fifths of the seats would go to the winning ticket. Batlle, from his position in the Colorado Party, would head the pro-Colegiado ticket and lead the Colegiado delegates at the Constitutional Convention. The Colegiado, instead of coming in 1914 or 1915, would come four years later, but it *would* come.

CHAPTER 15

Regrouping

The unexpectedly difficult process of replacing the departed cabinet ministers was completed within two weeks of the announcement of their resignations. The three new Ministers were all substantial comedowns from their predecessors. In place of Acevedo, one of Uruguay's outstanding economists and publicists, Dr. José Ramasso, a little-known physician and businessman, took over as Minister of Industries. In place of Blengio Rocca, one of the most prominent Colorado leaders, Baltasar Brum, who had been discovered by Viera and would have to wait three months to reach the constitutionally required age of 30, would be Minister of Education. Brum, a lawyer and philosophy teacher, was a local politician in his native Salto, where his parents, who had emigrated from Brazil, were large land-owners. Pedro Cosio, Serrato's protégé, finally had agreed to accept the Finance Ministry. Cosio was an admirable person, a self-made man who had started as an apprentice furniture maker, gone to night school, got a job in the Rivera customs house, become an expert and professor in customs law, been elected Deputy, and attracted Batlle's attention when he led the Chamber debate on the State Insurance Bank. Cosio's dedication was unquestioned, but insiders considered him a good customs house man who would be in over his head as Finance Minister.[1]

Last November Batlle had asked Public Works Minister Sudriers to resign when he discovered that Sudriers' relatives stood to make speculative profits out of land purchase through inside knowledge of where public building would take place. Young Juan Carlos Blanco, Jr., son of Batlle's eminent Colorado rival for the 1903 presidency, was named Minister.[2] Viera had replaced Manini as Minister of Interior. By now, only two cabinet positions, War and Foreign Relations, were still being held by Ministers who had begun this administration.

In restructuring his cabinet, Batlle, as Brum noted later, had chosen "his collaborators from the young and even unknown element of the Colorado Party."[3] Cosio was not quite 40, Blanco was 34, Brum was not of age. This was the second time that Batlle was forcing a new Colorado generation. After the war of 1904, he had loaded the legislature with young men; Clemenceau, when he visited Uruguay, had been struck at seeing Senators in their twenties.[4] Batlle acknowledged that before, "the men who served with him were for the most part young men, and they easily obeyed his suggestions."[5] Now part of that generation, led by Manini, were fighting him, and Batlle again wanted bright young Colorados who would follow him through to the Colegiado.

The new cabinet was young, most of its members were obscure; even so, this cabinet of Batlle's resembled its predecessors. A trusted general was War Minister, a close Colorado associate was Minister of Interior. There was only one distinguished name, Juan Carlos Blanco, Jr., as once there had been Martín C. Martínez and Eduardo Acevedo; by chance there was now only one son of an immigrant, against three in 1911. Like Batlle's other cabinets, this was strongly Colorado. Viera's father had been an old Colorado soldier; Cosio's father had fought under the two great Colorado caudillos, Rivera and Flores; and Brum had been a Colorado youth leader. Manini was trying to convince Colorados that the Colegiado would threaten Colorado one-party government; Batlle had assembled a pro-Colegiado cabinet whose Colorado antecendents and enthusiasms matched or exceeded Manini's own.

II

None of the departmental Jefes Políticos had resigned. In Canelones, Jefe Político Berreta wrote Batlle that he was going through the whole department and could assure him that more than 8,000 Colorados would support his politics (only 3,200 had voted in 1910). As a sample, he enclosed a list of supporters he had got together in only two days, "all the best people the Colorado Party has in Canelones."[6]

With the cabinet crisis resolved, the process of regrouping moved to the Chamber of Deputies. Manini, still delighted with the reaction the Senators' statement had produced—a sense of "relief everywhere"—now received disquieting news. Areco, whose Senate term had just expired and who had been slipped into the Chamber as an alternate to be Batllista floor leader, was getting signatures from a majority of the Chamber of Deputies. Manini noted, "The signers are being told that the Deputies' document will be the way of finding out who is with and who is against Batlle, and it is being insinuated that only signers will be re-elected in November." The document was to be followed by Chamber approval of the electoral law for the Constitutional Convention.

> They surely believe that the Chamber's attitude will put pressure on some of our colleagues and make them defect or at least abstain. They will also increase the pressure with hordes from the clubs and telegrams from the departmental Colorado organizations.
>
> Their effort will be entirely useless. We would be idiots and criminals if we did not respond to the challenge by immediate rejection of the law on the part of the Senate.
>
> Therefore we will get together and agree right now to stand firm.[7]

On March 26, 1913, the same day the new cabinet was announced, the Deputies' declaration appeared, signed by 50 deputies and endorsed by three more. For the nation and the Colorado Party, they were responding to the Senators. The pending electoral law which permitted minorities proportional representation, two fifths of the seats in the constitutional convention, met the Senators' request of "new and ample guarantees for popular voting." There was no justification, therefore, for delay, and the Deputies, consonant with their "patriotic duty," intended to vote the law "immediately."[8]

III

The pressure that Manini anticipated was quickly mounted. The Montevideo Colorado Clubs began a call to convoke the Colorado Convention to decide the Party's position on "questions of the palpitat-

ing political present." Batlle in *El Día* enthusiastically endorsed convoking the convention and the clubs' decision not to vote on these
issues themselves. That way "the final decision will be more complete
and unanimous"; "reasons of party discipline" could also be adduced.
This did not mean that the clubs should not discuss the constitutional
controversy. Quite the contrary, in a "well organized democracy ideas
spread from the bottom upwards." Especially now, full debate with
the proponents of all positions heard, was essential. "Propaganda in
support of the ideas which are believed to be best and most adaptable
to our environment will thus gain in enthusiasm and ardor."[9] In every
section of Montevideo, parallel to the clubs, "popular commissions"
were being set up under a Central Committee to agitate for constitutional reform. "We will see what those who invoke public opinion to
oppose the patriotic effort for constitutional reform will say then."[10]

The eleven Senators held firm. Areco asked Chamber President
Lagarmilla, an anti-Colegialist, to act as intermediary in working out a
compromise which would permit quick constitutional reform. The
Senators met in Manini's house and advised Lagarmilla that "they
were determined not to vary even a single line of the document they
had signed."[11]

Pressure on the Senators was raised still higher. On April 3, on
Areco's motion, the Chamber took up the Sosa-Rodríguez bill for
electing the constitutional convention—secret vote, three fifths of the
seats to the winning ticket, the remaining two fifths distributed by
proportional representation. Debate and voting were over in a single
session. The vote in favor was 51 to 24. Julio María Sosa moved that
the elections be held the last Sunday in October 1913. This was
approved by voice vote. Then, as announced by *El Día* that morning,
Areco moved that debate on the final article appropriating funds for
the election be suspended, to avoid "the immediate rejection of this
law" by the Senate. Areco invoked "the possibility" that sometime
during the present year or else after the November elections, but
before the new Chamber was seated, "the attitude of the majority of
the Senate may be modified." That would be the signal to complete
passage of the bill and send it to the Senate.[12]

On April 6, the Montevideo Colorado organization met to debate
whether to ask the national commission to convoke the Colorado
Convention to approve the Colegiado. Manini spoke against it, asking

that the convention not be held until the end of the year so that convention members would be better informed. He pointedly remarked that there was no hurry because the Senate attitude meant postponement of reform. But, in the words of *El Día*, "the immense majority of those present" voted to convene the convention.[13] Batlle was quick to deny rumors that the convention would be asked to disqualify the eleven Senators. Expulsion from the party was a Nationalist procedure not authorized by the Colorado party charter, though, naturally, individuals who did not accept the party's "norms of action" could expect "to occupy positions which may not be the leading ones."[14]

Batlle was warning the Senators that their future careers would be in jeopardy if they persisted. Simultaneously, rather than pushing them into any irrevocable break, he was keeping open the doors for their return. Manini had just resigned as Honorary President of the Colorado Club of the Seventh Section, the club where he had given his first anti-Colegiado speech, because it had voted that the Colegiado did not violate the democratic ideals of the Colorado Party. Manini's resignation letter concluded:

> The accident that separates us does not, however, destroy the ties of the past that unite us and the duties that the future may solicit from us, and for my part I can say of myself that though my firm decision is to maintain myself in a position of combat, I do not forget that in problems of another order I am a soldier in the common cause.

The Club accepted his resignation but advised Manini that in the expectation that his separation would be of short duration, it was holding the position of Honorary President open for him.[15]

IV

El Siglo's poll of Uruguayan lawyers resulted in 19 in favor of the Colegiado, 238 opposed.[16] Anti-Colegiado Colorado youth were organizing a committee. The Nationalist Directorio was reconsidering going to the polls in November and had reopened the campaign to register Nationalist voters. By early April, clubs, committees, meetings, and drives pro and anti Colegiado were all over. The kind of political excitement which Batlle had hoped for, of bringing great issues to the people, was here.

The Socialist Party, pro-immediate constitutional reform, had since its formal organization in 1910 advocated the abolition of the presidency and the popular election of a council of ministers whose acts could be disallowed by the legislature, which could also convoke a public recall vote of the council. This proposal, patterned on the first Argentine Socialist party program of 1894, was far from the "Apuntes," but *El Día* nevertheless published the Socialist manifesto, commented that "constitutional reform was being held up by the reactionary forces of the country," welcomed Socialist support for Batlle's eight-hour day, and increasingly published articles by radicals and labor people who argued that it was ridiculous for workers to listen to revolutionary anarchists and not support Batlle's reforms.[17]

On April 7 pro-Colegiado Colorado youth held a mass meeting. Washington Paullier called for support "from the determined, from the workers, from radical intellectuals." "Firm in our aims . . . let us advance with faith in our success and in the powerful will of the citizen who leads us—our caudillo civil, Don José Batlle y Ordoñez!"[18] Nine days later the Colorado National Executive Committee met and on the motion of Julio María Sosa (who was taking over what used to be Manini's functions) voted to convoke the Colorado Convention on July 3. "As will be recalled, three years ago on the same date, that high party authority proclaimed the candidacy of señor Batlle y Ordoñez for President of the Republic."

Batlle wanted the Colorado Party governed from the botton upward, but he was orchestrating the constitutional reform campaign from the top down. He was advocating the Colegiado to decrease personal political influence of any one man, but his partisans were exalting him as "caudillo civil." Batlle himself made no political appearances—it was not considered proper for the President of the Republic to take part in partisan functions, although there was nothing to stop him—but the new strategy of open adulation was obviously his.[19]

Don Pepe also advocated convincing people through rational argument, and he kept up debate on the "Apuntes." To the opposition's claim that the Presidency of the Junta was a device by which Batlle would maintain power, he answered that originally he had set the

Junta's Presidency up this way to win Serrato's and Manini's support for the Colegiado. He had not succeeded; however, on thinking, he had decided to provide the Presidency of the Junta with some authority as a transition from the present regime. But the Presidency was a detail, and he would accept "an annual non-reelectable president and even a rotating president if desired so long as the right of the majority of the Junta to separate him from the post whenever they consider it necessary is retained." The "Apuntes," it was argued, gave the Junta too much veto power. As demonstration of his willingness to strengthen the legislature, expressed in his 1910 presidential program, he now "accepted the idea of submitting divergencies between the Executive and the Legislative Powers to plebiscites."[20]

V

No revisions of the "Apuntes" were going to satisfy its opponents. Attempts to reach an understanding with the eleven Senators had been "postponed."[21] This meant that consitutional reform could not be completed during Batlle's presidency, and that the next President of the Republic would be elected under the Constitution of 1830 by a majority of the legislators sitting in March 1915. The outcome of November's elections to the Chamber of Deputies would determine who the next President of Uruguay would be. And with the Colorados split three ways, pro-Colegiado, anti-Colegiado but in Manini's phrase "soldiers in the common cause," and the Bachini-led dissidents, Nationalist electoral chances were measurably brighter. The Directorio formally called on Nationalists to register to vote. "Abstention has already given all its fruits."[22] The dissident Colorados set up a committee to register anti-Batlle Colorado voters, with Juan Campisteguy, Batlle's 1903 Minister of Interior, as President. (Don Pepe still had Campisteguy in mind for the Colegiado; in El Día, Batlle was publicly lamenting Campisteguy's hostility to him.)[23] Colonel West, Williman's Jefe Político of Montevideo, was Vice President.

The Colegiado campaign was sharpening ideological differences between the contenders as they tried to expand their electorates. Batlle and his pro-Colegiado supporters were calling for the workers' votes. The Directorio newspaper urged the conservative classes to enter politics before it was too late. The dissident Colorados, who set themselves up a friends of the army, noted with pleasure that several wealthy ranchers were organizing against the government. The dissidents urged ranchers to bring their peons to the polls with them. But Batlle did not intend to be outmaneuvered. The jefatura of the department of Minas had just become vacant. *El Día* announced the appointment of a new Jefe Político, Santiago Salaberry," a powerful landowner in that region of the country."[24]

On May Day the Anarchists and Socialists held separate workers' meetings. Stones were thrown and windows broken. There were quick complaints that the police stood by and let "assaulting guerrillas" produce panic in Montevideo as part of the "demagoguery and anarchism on high." Several nights later the police broke up a Nationalist meeting. Interior Minister Viera was called to the Chamber to explain. He was unperturbed. Some 150 Nationalists, he said, came out of a meeting and congregated in front of the Teatro Solís, shouting "Down with the Reform! Death to Batlle! Viva the National Party!" Colorados ran out to confront them. The police chief intervened and prevented bloodshed. As for the May Day demonstration, five of the stone-throwers were under arrest. "The police could not suspend, I say, the workers' march because the workers have the right to assemble, they have the right to gather in the public plaza, they have the right to go to the streets, they have the right to demonstrate, and the police have the duty to protect those demonstrators."[25]

Viera was following Batlle's pro-workers line. His appearance had attracted a lot of attention because word had gone out that he was Batlle's candidate for President of the Republic. On May 10 *El Día* announced that there recently had been discussion about what to do if the Senate held up constitutional reform through Batlle's presidency. There was complete agreement on how to proceed:

> in the first place Consitutional Reform and the Colegiado; and in the second place in case this cannot be accomplished, the presidential candidacy of an avowed Colegialist.
>
> Doctor Viera's name, naturally, was in first place among the citizens who might be designated as candidate.[26]

VI

A pro-Colegiado demonstration brought together 40,000 people—*El Día* boasted it was the largest crowd in Montevideo's history and challenged the anti-Colegiado forces to equal it. On the evening of May 10 the Nationalists claimed they had put up to 25,000 in the streets, as a warm-up for a huge meeting on July 18—the anniversary of the Constitution of 1830.

The opposition dismissed the Colorado demonstrations as made up of public employees who had no alternative to participation. To refute these charges, Don Pepe wrote a characteristically skillful article, "Public Employees and the Colegiado." It simply was not true that public employees were being required to support the Colegiado. In fact, many opposed it. "With the Colegiado . . . the provision of jobs . . . and promotions . . . would be determined by criteria of justice and public utility, with the result that the most apt would always triumph."

> The instinct of self-preservation fatally requires many public employees who have achieved their present posts by illegitimate means to be furious enemies of the Colegiado.
>
> Meanwhile, for intelligent and hardworking employees, those for whom it is repugnant to beg for what by right belongs to them, the form of government which the great majority of the country desires would be the realization of a great deal of justice to which they always aspired.
>
> The President of the Republic, then, does not have to exercise pressure on his subordinates in the public administration. An unmistakable, unstoppable influence, which comes from human nature itself, attracts to his ideas the kind of men they need: the most intelligent, the most upright.[27]

Don Pepe was hiding a promise that the Colegiado would depoliticize public employment by turning reality around: employees who opposed the President were really dependent on the government for favors; public employees who supported the President and accepted the Colegiado demonstrated that they were independent, hardworking, intelligent and deserving of promotion.

VII

Arena was going to the littoral capitals for speechmaking and to advise local leaders that Viera would be the presidential candidate.

Arena had been hurt by the tensions and animosities of the past two years. His hands were shaking worse than ever: he was starting to hear voices; his marriage was breaking up. He was now Senator, *El Día* editor, and likely to be member of the Junta de Gobierno, but before the "Apuntes" appeared he had already written to a writer he admired: "Even though I have been something I never thought to be, I have been nothing I wanted to be," "an untroubled writer, somewhat bohemian, even a bit long-haired."[28] The split caused by the "Apuntes"—Manini was his law partner—had deeply disturbed Arena. He admitted publicly "that perpetual sacrifice of men imposed by service to ideas is repugnant to my somewhat sentimental personality."[29] Arena knew that Don Pepe, who felt family matters so deeply, considered political friends absolutely replaceable, and even he, Arena, was expendable. If Don Pepe believed in the Colegiado—he had kept it from Arena just as he had kept it from everyone outside his family—then Arena would quickly overcome his doubts. He admitted his first reaction had been "horror," but that he was quickly convinced by Batlle that the Colegiado was exactly what Uruguay needed.

Before leaving for the littoral, Arena tried his speech out in Montevideo. He spoke at a meeting in the Stella D'Italia, a theater near the university, on the evening of May 17. Shortly after he began, Viera entered and joined the audience.

Batlle is the author of the reform; Batlle is responsible for the reform, Batlle is the whole reform.

The idea that Batlle wanted to perpetuate himself in power was "an immense humbug." "For the public good, he sacrifices men, interests, affections, and he even sacrifices himself." Batlle found that the struggle over the presidency could divide the Colorado Party. Those who warned that the party would be damaged by the new form of government assumed that the party depended on the government. But it should be the other way around. "The Colorado Party should aspire to form Governments, to give Governments prestige, to support Governments, and if necessary to overthrow Governments." The fact that the Colegiado was not in the party program was unimportant. "If it isn't, we will put it in." Many new things must be put into the program. "The best chapters, surely, are still blank." The Colorado Party must make any Liberal (antireligious) or Socialist Party unnecessary in Uruguay. It must "assimilate all the human, all the practical, all the accomplishable that isn't utopian from the Socialist Party."

Arena was here giving his gloss on Don Pepe's new line. First, "Batlle is the whole reform." Second, under the Colegiado, the Colorado Party would determine government policy; the party would dominate the government, not as now, when the President dominated the party. Third, the Colorado Party must adopt the accomplishable goals of Socialism.

At the outset Arena warned that he would talk as long as his vocal chords held out and he spoke for nearly three hours. He expounded on the advantages of the Colegiado, on the unfortunate decision of the eleven Senators, among them "very good Colorados and very good Batllistas." But whether or not the eleven Senators came around, "I am absolutely certain the Colegiado will triumph." With that Arena went into his peroration, which during the next weeks was going to bring audiences to their feet and up and down the litoral:

> The Column is long
> It is already on the march
> Batlle leads it
> Sure that nothing or nobody will stop it.[30]

VIII

On May 21 there was a planning session for the 18th of July anti-Colegiado demonstration. In addition to the seven previously committed newspapers (they had united against Batlle's furious press attacks on José Pedro Ramírez, the dean of the conservative classes and the peacemaker of 1903),[31] the editors of the *Diario Español* (directed at Spanish residents) and the English language *Montevideo Times* were present, as were the presidents of the Nationalist Directorio, the recently formed Catholic Party, the president of the dissident Colorados, Campisteguy, and the presidents of two new Colorado anti-Colegialist committees. Ramírez of *El Siglo* proposed a provisional declaration, "constitutional reform in the present circumstances involves danger to public liberty and threatens the most vital interests of the nation." *El Día* reminded anti-Colegialists that this went beyond the eleven Senators' declaration. "Nobody can subscribe to the declaration without enrolling himself in the ranks of the opposition."[32]

On May 24 Manini spoke to the Central Committee of Colorado Anti-Colegialist Youth. This was Manini's first speech to fellow anti-Colegialists. He congratulated them in the name of the Colorado Party. "We are reformists . . . but we want reforms and not adventures." The Senate majority wanted reform to come from the people, not from "the man governing, however great his worth or illustrious his services." Using legal means, the Senate majority had produced "a wholesome postponement" of constitutional reform "preferring thus to avert, within the political situation of which it is a part and will continue to be a part, the dangers of the adventure we were risking." When anti-Colegialists reasoned this way, they were challenged by the argument that the Colegiado was an advanced formula included in the Socialist program. But

> Are we Colorados or are we Socialists?
>
> And let us give the answer clearly, categorically and definitively.
>
> The Colorado Party, liberal, advanced, evolutionary, shares some points of the Socialist minimum programs, beginning with all the laical religious solutions up to almost all the postulates for the legal improvement of the working class. But as a party, as a governing party of order and the defense of legality, it cannot share and does not share the postulates of social revolution that excite all Socialists.
>
> For them the transformation of the Executive Power into a committee is one of many means of annihilating government, something that is indispensable for them in reaching their ideal of transforming the present society, politically and economically considered.

Compared with the Apuntes Colegiado, the Socialist Colegiado was less dangerous, since it would be dependent on the legislature. "Nine persons endowed with an enormous amount of authority exercise a much worse despotism, because it is anonymous and clandestine, than that of a dictator who is known to be responsible for all his acts." Either despotism or anarchy would be the end result of the

Colegiado, and along the way would come, he again insisted, Colorado splits and minority entry into the Executive and the end of
one-party Colorado government. All this did not mean that the Colorado Party should stand pat on constitutional reform:

> We accept it and we favor it to make the institution of the presi-
> dency lose its excessive present predominance, by establishing
> strong and robust Legislative Bodies whose terms always extend
> beyond the Presidents, by full administrative decentralization
> which makes every public service or every important national
> institution into an autonomous organization . . . by creating really
> responsible ministers, tied to parliament. . . .
>
> Let us demonstrate to the Colorado Party that its historic mission
> never has been nor can be the creation of despotisms, unipersonal or
> collegiate but in the future as in the past to preserve liberty, the
> banner of Rivera and of Pacheco, of Suárez and of Garibaldi.[33]

While Manini in proposing an alternate constitutional reform continued to insist that the anti-Colegialists would remain part of the
governing Colorados, the anti-Colegialists were well on the way
toward an open split. The Nationalists were calling for the conservative classes to oppose Batlle, the dissident Colorados were calling on
ranchers to oppose Batlle. When Arena, Manini's law partner, called
on pro-Colegiado Colorados to adopt the accomplishable goals of
Socialism, Manini answered for the anti-Colegialists: "Are we Colorados or are we Socialists?" and concluded his speech with an
invocation to Colorado heroes which left out Batlle. Ideologically, if
not yet politically, the anti-Colegialists were already part of the opposition.

Batlle, as he did every time Manini spoke, responded personally
and over several days. The Colegiado, Batlle insisted, was no threat to
Colorado one-party government. Under the new constitution, elections would be held "under the most democratic procedures" which
would ensure "the legitimate predominance of the strongest party."
But even if (and here Batlle's 1917 political solution would coincide
with his present position) "the Junta de Gobierno should be integrated
with one, two, or three members of the minority, this could not
prevent the other eight, seven, or six members from carrying out
entirely one-party policies."

There was now no way for the party "to impose a program on the citizen who is to exercise the Presidency of the Republic." Under the Colegiado,

> The citizen who would enter the Junta de Gobierno each year would first be obliged to announce his action program, guaranteed by his word of honor. His influence, the ninth part of the influence of a probable candidate for the presidency of the Republic, would never be enough that he could avoid the requirement of a precise and clear exposition of his ideas. . . . And a simple majority of the members of the Junta de Gobierno pledged in this way to carry out the ideals of their party would be sufficient to assure the party's policies.[34]

Here was the heart of Batlle's reform, something already mentioned in Arena's "the Column is on the March" speech. All candidates would be pledged "to carry out the ideals of their party." Put another way, the party would "impose a program on the citizen" it elected to the Colegiado. No single member of the Colegiado would have great influence; therefore, the party program would guide the government instead of the reverse, as it now was. Under these conditions, even if Nationalists won a few seats, the Colorado majority on the Colegiado could exercise a far stronger and long continuing party government, as distinguished from the personal policies of an incumbent President of the Republic, than Uruguay had yet seen.

IX

The Chamber had been debating the eight-hour-day bill for three months. Although the galleries were packed with workers and Socialist Frugoni had furious exchanges with other deputies, what otherwise might have been the major political debate of this administration had been overshadowed by the eleven Senators. Still, debate was intense. Young anti-Colegialist Prando argued that the state need not intervene in the work day of adult males. Gregorio L. Rodríguez insisted that even though agricultural and ranch workers were exempt, the eight-hour day, by making the urban work day so short, would encourage rural exodus, make Uruguayan exports, all of which required some processing, more expensive, and ruin local industry.

Ricardo Vecino answered for the Committee that had reported the bill out. Most of the arguments against the eight-hour day were taken from Europe and the United States. "Our economic environment is much more simple," and in Uruguay the effects of the eight-hour day would be beneficial. As the work day shortened, employment patterns changed. Women, "less apt beings," took over the simpler jobs, while men moved to the more productive ones. So the argument that a fixed work day would hold back superior workers was inapplicable in Uruguay.

On May 28 Julio María Sosa won approval for permanent sessions until general debate on the bill concluded. Now Rodó, author of the Chamber committee report under Williman, which called for an eight-hour plus three-hour overtime work day, spoke. He stated doctrinal support for limiting the work day but "on the other hand I am opposed to the uniform, rigid and extreme character of the bill proposed by the Executive Power." A uniform eight-hour day would penalize the most able workers, and keep them from "rising above the mass and achieving higher positions in the social order." "Therefore those who share my views should, in my opinion, decide that this bill should not be voted at this time."

On May 31 the Chamber voted 44 to 8 in favor of approving the bill in general and going on to debate its individual articles. Batlle was anxious to get quick Chamber passage to build popular support for the Colegiado, and on June 5 discussion of the bill's articles began. Gregorio L. Rodríguez moved the Rodó committee clause permitting an additional three hours of overtime as an amendment. The bill's supporters warned that the overtime would be fictitious because workers were paid by the day, not the hour, and in practice this would mean the present work day at the same pay as now. Unions were too weak to prevent this. Socialist Frugoni admitted that "there are only four or five well organized trades" in all Montevideo. By voice vote—the result was sufficiently close for Rodríguez to call for a second voice vote—overtime was defeated. On June 14 the Chamber passed the bill, but before it could become law it needed Senate approval.[35] The Senate, though the majority claimed it still supported the government, no longer was a Batllista club. Manini, leader of the eleven Senators, had been cosponsor of Batlle's eight-hour-day bill when Minister of Interior, but now Manini was asking, "Are we Colorados or are we Socialists?" and what the Senate would do with the bill was a mystery.

X

The Senate majority, while no longer unconditional supporters of Batlle, did not routinely reject government projects either. On April 2 the Senate approved without debate the Chamber-passed Executive bill to appropriate 350,000 pesos for engineering studies of the port of La Coronilla, still entirely undeveloped, in the department of Rocha near the Brazilian border. La Coronilla had the potential of being a major Atlantic port, which would build up the East, take traffic for Brazil, and alter Uruguay's transportation network, all of which now flowed to Montevideo. The idea was not new, but it had been taken up by General Edward O'Brien, former American Minister to Uruguay, currently chairman of the local board of directors of the new Swift Montevideo refrigerated packing plant.

O'Brien proposed to build a port and a connecting railroad whose trunk line would cross all existing railroads and terminate at the Río Uruguay in Artigas, the opposite end of the country. The railroad would be built for the government and rented by the company, and the port would be financed by government guaranteed bonds. The plan fitted into Batlle's development program and attracting American capital to compete with English was appealing,[36] but Don Pepe wanted to be sure that O'Brien really had backers, that the terms would be favorable, and that the port would revert "to the power of the State" within a reasonable time. This appropriation for engineering studies would encourage O'Brien's efforts while determining La Coronilla's feasibility.[37]

One reason for Batlle's caution with O'Brien was the difficulty he was having with the English promoter Lord Grimthorpe over the Rambla Sur, a shore road in Montevideo. The project, a two-and-a-half mile road from the port to the beach, which dated from Batlle's first administration, had been taken over by Williman, who considered it the monument to his own administration. The contract, signed with Grimthorpe, provided that bonds not to exceed seven million pesos, guaranteed by the Uruguayan government, would be issued once sufficient construction had begun.[38]

Lord Grimthorpe, *The Times of London* reported, had formed "a powerful syndicate" to carry out what was "without doubt the most important English engineering enterprise" that Montevideo had yet seen. In fact, Grimthorpe's syndicate had no funds of its own, and Grimthorpe discovered that while bankers were willing to market the Uruguayan government bonds, he could not raise sufficient funds to start construction. In November 1911 Grimthorpe's City of Montevideo Public Works Company, Ltd., was declared bankrupt, with liabilities of £943,386 and assets of £68. The *Times of London* now reported "it was stated" that a principal reason for the company's failure "was attributed to the heavy expenses incurred in obtaining the concession."[39] Don Pepe felt Grimthorpe was claiming he had paid bribes to get the concession and refused to see Grimthorpe (who dismissed the bankruptcy as corporate reorganization) until a correction, something Grimthorpe could not arrange, was printed in the *Times of London.*[40]

Grimthorpe was in no position to build, but Batlle insisted that he meet all the contract deadlines. And instead of solving the problem for Grimthorpe by redesigning the Rambla so that it would cost only the seven million pesos covered by the Uruguayan government bonds— which was Grimthorpe's proposal—Batlle rejected the plans already submitted for the Rambla seawall and required a much stronger seawall and asphalted pavement on the road. Grimthorpe claimed the Uruguayan government, by exorbitantly increasing construction costs, was forcing him to give up the contract. The contract called for arbitration, but Grimthorpe, who had sold £281, 027 in debenture bonds to English and French investors before his first company went bankrupt, successfully campaigned in Europe for diplomatic assistance in getting compensation from the Uruguayan government, using the argument that Batlle's government had, as the British and French Ministers to Uruguay stated in a formal note delivered on October 9, 1912, "irremediably ruined" his company.[41]

The Uruguayan government made its side public by having the sympathetic pre-Apuntes Senate hear its position, which was that Grimthorpe had presented himself as the distinguished head of a strong group of capitalists but turned out to be a shaky promoter with shady financial connections who had plans to build a shoddy Rambla. Batlle's modifications were designed to assure that Uruguay got what Grimthorpe had promised, a strongly built Rambla with a first-class drive. Grimthorpe's recourse, Foreign Minister Romeu told the Uruguayan Senate, was not to diplomatic intervention but, under the contract, to the stipulated arbitration.[42] Strengthened by the Senate's support of its position, the government on April 27, 1913, presented to the English and French Ministers a formal memorandum concluding that when the English and French governments "know the true state of the affair . . . those governments will advise Lord Grimthorpe to desist from his exigencies."[43]

Batlle's government had to be very careful in resisting compensation to Lord Grimthorpe, just as it earlier had desisted from starting the insurance monopoly, because it was urgent that Uruguay have access to the European money market.

The Bank of the Republic's gold holdings were perilously close to the minimum of 40 percent of demand deposits and banknotes required by its charter. There had been an easing of credit in Europe as a result of the armistice in the Balkan War. The interest rate had not yet dropped to the point where Serrato's massive loan was possible, but a loan, on less favorable terms which would give the Bank gold, was. On April 23, four days before delivery of the Rambla Sur memorandum to the English and French Ministers, the Executive sent a bill to the Legislature authorizing the Bank of the Republic to negotiate a nine-million-peso loan abroad, the proceeds to go to increasing the Bank's paid-in capital.

The Senate's approval could no longer be taken for granted, so the bill, which ordinarily would first be passed by the Chamber, was instead first sent to the Senate for its consideration. The loan's form was unusual. Normally, the Executive negotiated a loan and submitted its terms to the legislature for approval. Here the Bank of the Republic was to be given legislative authorization to negotiate a loan without legislative control. The Senators understood the reason. If terms for this loan were specified, it would be very difficult to get better terms in the near future for the other Uruguayan borrowing (permanent funding of Serrato's short-term debt couldn't be put off for long). They, as much as the Executive, wanted the Bank of the Republic to continue to underwrite prosperity through credit expansion, and they approved the loan.

A second and more doctrinal issue was also involved. Batlle wanted all the Bank's profits, once debt service was met, to go to increasing its capital, and that the Bank not contribute anything to the national Treasury. State enterprises should reinvest profits to improve and cheapen services. Manini and Varela Acevedo, who were leading the debate on the Bank of the Republic loan, disagreed. State enterprises, once they were flourishing, should contribute to the Treasury and ease the burden of indirect (sales) taxes which raised the cost of living. Varela Acevedo proposed that the Bank of the Republic be allowed to retain profits until its effective capital reached 35 million pesos (25 million in capital, 10 million in reserves). When this figure was reached, probably six to eight years from now, a special law should determine profit allocations.[44]

Cosio, for the Executive, accepted the proposal. Varela Acevedo's compromise, while it demonstrated the Senate majority's independence from Batlle, had the immediate effect of allowing the Bank to reinvest all its profits. And Don Pepe was confident that by the time the Bank's paid-in capital reached 35 million pesos, the eleven Senators' bloc would have disappeared, the Colegiado would be functioning, and the Bank of the Republic, like all state enterprises, would, under law, be exempt from contributing profits to the national Treasury.

No agenda had been announced for the Colorado Convention to meet on July 3, 1913. On June 28, though, pro-Colegiado legislators met at Areco's house and "with absolute unanimity" agreed on four proposals for the Convention to approve: (1) The Convention would declare itself in favor of immediate constitutional reform and call upon Colorado legislators to pass the necessary electoral laws "without delay." (2) The Convention, recognizing that it was part of "the historic ideals of the Colorado Party," would resolve "to recommend to the future members of the Constitutional Convention the incorporation of the Collegiate Executive into the fundamental law of the Republic." The Convention would make two changes in the party charter: (3) any candidate for President of the Republic must agree in writing to carry out the party program, and (4) every legislative candidate must pledge in writing to vote for President of the Republic the candidate who had the votes of the majority of the Colorado legislators.[1]

So the eleven Senators were not going to be censured but were going to receive an implicit vote of no confidence. The next President of the Republic would have to pledge support of the Colegiado and immediate constitutional reform and all Colorado candidates for Deputy and then for Senator would have to pledge to vote for such a President of the Republic. But candidates for Deputy and Senator would not be required personally to support the Colegiado; anti-Colegialists could keep their principles and stay in the party organization. Don Pepe's long-range program of imposing party discipline on elected officials was being moved a few notches further along.

On the morning of the Convention the anti-Colegialists met in the Senate antechambers and 49 Convention delegates signed the following statement: "In view of the fact that the majority of the members of the Colorado Convention have resolved ahead of time to approve certain formulas which should have been the object of the deliberations of the said Convention, they consider that their attendance at the Convention meetings would be useless."[2]

The day before, July 2, Don Pepe gave a message to politicians who might be thinking of joining the anti-Colegialists in running separate electoral tickets in the November legislative elections. Teachers had been forbidden, since 1898, from, according to the decree, "becoming officers of political clubs, and in general from intervening in the militant politics of the country." In one of his first decrees as Education Minister, Baltasar Brum, who had now turned 30, ended the restriction. At the same time, similar restrictions on the police, which had been imposed by Williman, were also lifted.[3] It could be argued, as Batlle did, that the police had the same rights as other citizens. It could be further argued that Williman's restrictions were purely on paper. Still, shortly after the Río Negro Senate election disclosures, the political message was that police "moral influence" would be used for colegialist candidates and teachers would easily remember Don Pepe's explanation that the most intelligent and able public employees, those who could expect promotion, would be pro-Colegiado.

"In their character as delegates," the Ministers of Interior, Finance, and Public Works appeared at the Convention's inaugural session. Two hundred and thirty delegates attended. The stage was adorned with Uruguayan and Colorado flags; Rivera's portrait was in the center. The Colegialists were not going to let the anti-Colegialists appropriate the party's founder or traditions. The galleries were filled with claques or, as *El Día* put it, "with elements from the sectional clubs who desired to witness the discussion." At 9:30 P.M., Areco, President of the Convention, gave the opening address. It was three years to the day, he reminded the delegates, since the Convention had met to nominate for President of the Republic, "*the leading statesman of America*" and the "Chief of the Colorado Party," Batlle. Some "meritorious coreligionaries" were opposed to the Colegiado; Areco reminded them of "the essence of true democratic government: *the minority should accept the resolutions of the majority,* so long as the majority does not commit injustices, violate rights, or strangle liberty, things that cannot be conceived of in the Colorado Party." Committee reports on the four proposals were introduced. After a quota of speeches the delegates endorsed immediate constitutional reform—by acclamation.[4]

So far the Convention had been a carefully manipulated mass meeting. On the second day there was some discussion on how to deal with the absent delegates. Sosa quickly proposed a compromise. The Colegialists' preliminary meetings were no justification for anti-Colegialist inattendance. Therefore "the Convention announces its displeasure at the absence of distinguished coreligionaries who would have had the same rights in debate as the majority." Sosa's proposal having been approved "with great enthusiasm," he next answered an objection to the requirement that legislative candidates agree beforehand to vote the majority's candidate for President of the Republic—actually Batlle had introduced this as a secret requirement in 1905—by adding a clause, "when some very personal reason prevents the legislator from joining the majority, he can be forgiven by the party authorities." The Convention then approved the proposed changes to the party charter.[5]

The third session, on July 6, was crowded. This was the day the Colegiado would be approved, and delegates and gallery were expected to attend. Normally, Arena would make the speech, but he was recovering from an auto accident, and Francisco Simón, an indefatigable propagandist for the Colegiado, was given the honor. Simón was still going strong after speaking for two hours. The gallery could wait, or take, no more. It began its demonstration, the delegates joined in, and the Colegiado was voted by acclamation. The convention adjourned until July 14, when it would ratify the adopted resolutions and close its sessions.[6]

Ten of the eleven Senators had signed the nonattendance statement. The eleventh, Varela Acevedo, explained that while personally opposed to the "Apuntes" Colegiado, he was willing to discuss the matter. He still considered himself one of the eleven Senators, though he also considered that their pledge only bound signers until next

February 15, "after which date, each signer was absolutely at liberty."[7] Even if the Senate majority should disintegrate after February 15, 1914, an expectation of which could be read into Varela Acevedo's explanation if one chose, there still would not be time to complete constitutional reform during Batlle's term. Batlle thought the matter over very carefully, and on the morning of Monday, July 6, he sent his secretary, Virgilio Sampognaro, to Areco's house with the word that Viera's presidential candidacy should be proclaimed by the Convention when it reconvened on July 14. The delighted Areco, Viera's closest friend, had long been crippled but he could act quickly. A steady stream of delegates passed through his house to receive instructions.[8]

Viera's early nomination had many advantages. Colorado legislative candidates, instead of being pledged to vote an unknown for President of the Republic, would be pledged to vote for Viera, the Party's choice. Any postelection surprise maneuvers would be cut off, and it could be claimed, with some justification, that Viera was the voters' choice for President. Anti-Colegiado Colorado candidates in November would be campaigning not just against the exotic Colegiado but against Viera, a man with impeccable Colorado credentials. Early nomination and a long campaign would make Viera's ascension to the presidency seem routine—Batlle had built Williman up the same way—and simultaneously make the Colegiado familiar. Viera, instead of Batlle, would be the last President of the Republic. After him would come the Colegiado.

El Siglo did not see Viera's nomination that way. Batlle had put up Viera originally as a smoke screen for the Colegiado, but Viera's supporters had grown to such strength that they were using the Colegiado as a smoke screen to impose Viera on Batlle.

> The two antagonistic cheers "Viva el Colegiado" and "Viva Viera, future President of the Republic" cannot long live together. The second will rapidly kill the first. Actually, it already has, from the moment Viera's candidacy was announced.[9]

II

José Pedro Ramírez—dean of the conservative classes and long the object of a furious press campaign by Batlle blaming Ramírez' vote-buying in 1873 for bringing on militarism—was dying. Don Pepe personally wrote *El Día*'s transparently gloating coverage of Ramírez' condition.

> Confirming all the prognostications, Doctor José Pedro Ramírez has already entered the final crisis. There has been no hope of reaction for several days, but last night his doctors declared that the sick man's agony had already begun. In spite of that the life of José Pedro Ramírez had not yet been extinguished at 8:15 this morning. But given the medical opinion and the sick man's condition, the expected result cannot be far off.[10]

That day, in his seventy-seventh year, José Pedro Ramírez died. He had written Venancio Flores' proclamation for the *Cruzada Libertadora* in '63, had been one of those exiled to Havana in '75, had headed the Ministry of Conciliation which ended militarism in '86, been the peacemaker of '97 and '03; and was Uruguay's most distinguished lawyer. Under any other President, José Pedro Ramírez would have been given a state funeral, but Don Pepe, who had vetoed funeral honors for ex-President Julio Herrera y Obes when that old Colorado enemy died, sent no funeral message to the legislature. Five dissident deputies proposed a state funeral with the honors of a cabinet minister for Ramírez and a life pension for his widow. Speaking in the Chamber, Rodó eulogized Ramírez' "moral greatness": "the last survivor of a glorious succession of publicists and tribunes formed in the school of liberty, who defended it and preached it in the hardest times of our history." Whatever he had done, he had done for Uruguay.

> No one can expect the sower, the man who works the soil, to have the immaculate appearance of the pleasure seeker, of the idle, because everyone recognizes that if some mud sometimes splatters his clothes, it is because he has been casting seeds into the mud with both hands, seeds from which others will later benefit.

The Colorado deputies were embarrassed, and enough of them left the Chamber despite an order from chamber President Lagarmilla (a Manini man) to remain. There was no quorum to debate the proposal for a state funeral. That afternoon three of the deputies who had proposed funeral honors for José Pedro Ramírez called for a special

Chamber session to decide the question. Batlle was prepared for a confrontation, and a quorum was present at 6:30 P.M. Nobody took the floor to oppose a state funeral. Voting was by name. When it came his turn, Areco admitted: "I have profound respect and deep affection for Dr. José Pedro Ramírez but for reasons of political solidarity I vote for the negative." The vote was 24 in favor of a state funeral, 31 opposed.

Since the Chamber had refused a state funeral, the Senate, with the Colegialist Senators absent (the reverse of the Colorado Convention situation) voted its own honors. José Pedro Ramírez' body would be brought to the Senate antechambers, from which his funeral would depart. Manini, who had written the 1904 *El Día* articles accusing Ramírez of war guilt, now noted for the record that the vote was unanimous. The Senators rose and stood in respect for the deceased,[11] and there were applause and bravos from the gallery.

José Pedro Ramírez' funeral was long remembered. All business shut down. Twenty thousand attended. All the major Nationalists and all the remaining members of the old Constitutional Party were there. So was Manini. Williman was one of the pallbearers. At the cemetery eight men eulogized Ramírez. Then the students— Nationalist and anti-Colegiado Colorado—after having been refused the keys to the National Pantheon, broke down the doors and placed his coffin inside. Hours later the family removed the coffin and José Pedro Ramírez was buried in his family plot.[12]

Batlle's campaign against José Pedro Ramírez had been calculated. At the cost of outraging respectable opinion it reminded Colorados who their enemies were. (Ramírez, the peacemaker and power broker, had refused to confirm Batlle's version of the '03 peace pact, was blamed by Batlle for the War of 1904, and had stood aside when the Nationalists revolted in 1910.) But underneath Batlle's calculation was passion. His father's presidency had been ruined by the principists, led by José Pedro Ramírez. Lorenzo Batlle, preoccupied by the presidency, had neglected his family business and come out of the presidency a poor man. José Pedro Ramírez and his like talked of liberty but got large fees as lawyers and lobbyists. Don Pepe had been socially ostracized for years and Matilde still was, even though they lived an exemplary life together; José Pedro Ramírez, active nocturnally, kept up appearances, and had been a dignified presence in Montevideo society. Batlle, at the height of his campaign against him, had published what amounted to a justification of himself against Ramírez:

> Men who are ennobled by immaculate honesty, those who have preferred the pain of defeat to the splendor of an immoral triumph, those whose political conduct conforms to the most severe civic morality, those who have not bought votes nor sold their own, nor deceived public opinion, nor formed a reputation on the basis of mystifications,—all those men do not avoid the judgment of their contemporaries, they seek it out, because that pronouncement constitutes the greatest and purest of their triumphs.[13]

III

The Colorado Convention, completely ignoring José Pedro Ramírez' funeral that afternoon, met in the evening of July 14. A letter from Arena (that way Batlle preserved the fiction that the President of the Republic did not take overt part in partisan policies), who was still recovering from his auto accident, was read by the Convention secretary. Arena acknowledged that the Senate majority was blocking consitutional reform:

> Therefore, I move that this assembly resolve to support the candidacy of doctor Feliciano Viera should the election of the Executive Power have to be carried out in accord with the present Constitution.
>
> If we want to guarantee the triumph of the Colegiado, it is essential that the future president not only be in favor of the Colegiado but that his character, rectitude, intelligence, and party loyalty be sufficient assurance that the decisions of the Convention will be complied with without vacillations of any sort, and doctor Viera offers all those guarantees.[14]

Cheers from the delegates, then the necessary speeches, climaxed by Francisco Simón, whose Colegiado speech at the last session had been cut short by the impatient gallery. Viera, Simón proclaimed, was the man to continue Batlle's work.

> He is very popular in the interior, where he is known and appreciated. He is, today, among those who can aspire to the presi-

dency, the man with the greatest political following and the one
who would spontaneously win the greatest number of votes. A
decided colegialist, he and his friends are working with the greatest
enthusiasm for the triumph of the Colegiado,
     . . . we have faith in his political loyalty. . . .
     The Colorado Party is embarked on a program of national up-
building which . . . will make of our nation a modern Athens,
which shines for its culture, its moderation, its political education,
its love of liberty and justice and which shall be the pride of
America and the admiration of the world.

The Youth Committee pro Viera—formed that day—dropped
manifestos and Viera portraits from the balcony while Viera was
being nominated by acclamation. The delegates then ratified all decisions taken at the previous sessions and went home.[15]

"El Indio" Viera, the little fat, dark man from Salto, famous as an
eater and a good companion, President of the Republic! There were
stories that Batlle had once told intimates that Viera was not of
Presidential quality.[16] Viera had, insiders claimed, questionable
friends, the sort Don Pepe made it a policy to keep from the public
treasury. Don Pepe's brother Luis—whose political advice Batlle did
not usually take too seriously—had warned in a 1908 letter to Europe,
"Viera is a very good person, he couldn't be better, but he has the bad
judgment to have very bad friends, and of those around him, except
for Areco, there isn't one who is worth two cents."[17] Viera's colegialism was suspect. Fleurquin, Serrato's partisan and now one of the
eleven Senators, had seen Viera just after Batlle had called him in to
name him Minister of the Interior, and had told him, "I know you
have just swallowed the Presidency of the Republic." *El Indio*
shrugged his shoulders and answered, "Brother, what could I do?"[18]

Batlle would have preferred Serrato, the administrator. Viera was a
politician, and politicians in the presidency might be tempted to
control the Colorado Party. Don Pepe, however, prided himself on his
ability to judge men. Viera's outstanding political quality, mentioned
by Arena in his letter and Simón in his speech, was loyalty. If Viera
pledged to support the Colegiado and not challenge Don Pepe's control of the Colorado Party, he would keep his word. And Viera had,
again as Simón indicated, positive values as a candidate. The anti-
Colegiado Colorados were complaining that it was an exotic import,

but Viera was not. Except for his colegialism, Viera would have been the anti-Colegialists' candidate for President. In the manuscript Manini wrote in March, when he was organizing the eleven Senators, he remembered his own presidential ambitions, and went on: "I had accustomed myself to see Batlle's natural successor in Viera and looked forward to it, because *El Indio*, as we call him familiarly, in spite of the prejudices against him, in spite of his negative qualities, is loyal, calm, honest, and straightforward as a statesman, and I am sure that should he occupy the presidency, he would surround himself with good ministers, to whom he would give great freedom of administrative action while he reserved politics for himself, something he would know how to do, directly, nobly, and with fairness."[19] Viera's father, a hero in the War of 1904, had been one of the old Colorado gaucho military caudillos; two of Viera's brothers were now army officers. At a time when Batlle's opponents were looking toward the army to overthrow him, Viera's army connections would calm officers' opposition to the Colegiado. Viera was from the interior and was very well known to the Colorado politicians of the interior. His nomination was reassurance to them of Batlle's concern for national, not just Montevideo, interests. In sum, *El Indio* would provide reassurance that even if under the Colegiado, Uruguay became the new Athens, it would still be recognizable to good Colorados.

Viera himself was of the generation of 1904, one of the group of bright young men Batlle had brought to quick positions of importance. He had been a deputy through his father's influence and a pre-1903 supporter and presidential elector of Batlle; he had been returned to the Chamber after the War of 1904, then elected Senator and Senate President, and was now Minister of Interior. By the time he became President of the Republic, he would have occupied the two posts that traditionally led to the presidency: Senate President for six years and Minister of Interior for two. His specialty was back-room politics—he had been Williman's campaign manager—and he was considered more shrewd than deep, an operator who broke deadlocks, rather than an innovator. Yet he had long collaborated with Ricardo Areco, the most philosophical of the Batllistas, and Viera's own law doctoral thesis on "Liberty of Assembly and Association" had been published. Whatever the objections to his friends—the affable *Indio*, like the "Gringo" Arena, had no enemies—no one claimed that Viera, who lived modestly and scrupulously avoided representing anyone dealing with the government, was in any way dishonest. Viera, now 41, had married a hometown Salto girl; he was the father of nine children, and more were expected.

The opposition seized on Viera's nomination, "the death of the Colegiado," to cancel the mass demonstration scheduled for July 18 in favor of the Constitution of 1830. "Our meeting thus lost its object, since any danger of immediate reform and the Colegiado has disappeared." The real reason was different. The Serrato wing of the eleven Senators, five Senators led by Fleurquin, publicly declined to take part, preferring "a role as spectators." Viera's nomination effectively ended Serrato's chances of becoming President of the Republic, and his supporters, though reaffirming the maintenance of the Senate majority pledge, seemed to be having second thoughts about long-range politics. (Serrato himself had left for Europe after resigning as Finance Minister and had kept clear of anti-Colegialist politics. Batlle had just named him President of the State Mortgage Bank, and he had accepted, to take effect upon his return from Europe.) The Manini anti-Colegialists then also dropped out of the projected July 18 demonstration, disappointing opposition hopes that it would be the beginning of a joint Nationalist-anti-Colegialist Colorado electoral front in November.[20]

To throttle any further "death of the Colegiado" propaganda, *El Día* published an interview with Viera two days after his nomination. If he became President:

Reform would be one of the cardinal ideas of my government. I am absolutely convinced of the excellence of the Collegiate Executive. . . . At the beginning of this great contest of ideas I was dubious about the great initiative of President Batlle. I told him so clearly when he tried to spread his own enthusiasm for his magnificent project among his intimates. But I have no reason to hide the fact that later on I was unable to resist the overwhelming influence of Batlle's prestige and the suggestion of his powerful intellect. Perhaps I would not have become such a convinced propagandist for our ideas on the Colegiado had I not been induced by the serene and eloquent words of the only man who has exercised real influence on my public life. . . . And what contributes to that in the first

27. Viera and family. From *El Día*, March 1, 1915.

28. Feliciano Viera. By permission of División Fotocinematográfica, Ministerio de Educación y Cultura, Montevideo.

place is the admiration I profess for his fundamental virtues, his indisputable talent and the total integrity of his character, qualities which make him the leading patriot of our nation, and which show him to be an eminent statesman who is giving America an example it is unaccustomed to up to now—better to say, unknown up to now. . . . The triumph of the Colegiado will be due above all to his exceptional temperament . . . his tenaciousness.

Viera was very gentle with the anti-Colegialists, "temporary adversaries among whom are many men of talent and real intellect," who might yet be won over. Colorados should have no fear that the Colegiado would weaken the party. At most "our adversaries" could "delay the realization of the great enterprise a little."

Viera, as conditional candidate in case immediate constitutional reform was impossible, preferred to hold back his own program. He would, of course, act within the Colorado program:

> If I have any reason for desiring the Presidency of the Republic it would be to have the honor of being the continuer of the democratic and very advanced accomplishments of President Batlle. . . . His enormous activity has launched the nation on new and vast paths. His is the honor of having initiated that great set of liberal laws which have made our country, in social legislation for example, among the most advanced in America. . . .
>
> The evolutions suffered by the Colorado Party have made it virtually unnecessary for other modern groups to exist in our country. That is the case with Socialism, for example. The Colorado Party has the advantage over Socialism that it is in a position to carry out with practical efficiency the humanitarian principles which are nothing more than generous but platonic utopias in the latter. I believe this, too, is due to Batlle's influence. . . .

Viera was quick to reassure Colorado politicians, concerned with bread and butter patronage, that he would continue Batlle's Colorado one-party government. "One party government is more than a national convenience; it is a patriotic necessity."[21]

"Batlle, Batlle, and always Batlle. Batlle yesterday, Batlle today, Batlle tomorrow, Batlle forever." *El Siglo* agonized and stopped publishing editorials on Viera's nomination—which it had hailed as Batlle's defeat—until it could find some new way to handle it.[22]

With Viera's nomination, Batlle had virtually completed the regrouping he had been forced into by the eleven Senators. He had a new cabinet, he had the support of the majority of the Chamber, he had the support of the Colorado organization. He had handpicked his successor. Things were back under control. Don Pepe made still another move. He named Colonel Pintos, the Montevideo Jefe Político to the Military Appellate Tribunal and replaced him with Presidential Secretary Virgilio Sampognaro. Traditionally, the Montevideo police chief was a military officer; to install a civilian was an innovation. Two weeks after Viera's interview Sampognaro got his *El Día* interview.

> I am a Colorado. I have fought for my party and I will fight for it again every time the occasion presents itself. But I am not a petrified Colorado: one of the principal reasons for my Coloradismo is the evolutionary nature of the party. Within it, I declare myself Batllista, Colegialista, and Vierista. This last is very easy for me, since I have a close personal and political friendship with the candidate.

Was it true, as rumored, that Sampognaro was more or less a Socialist?

> Since I am a Colorado and not affiliated with any Socialist club, it is clear that I am not a Socialist. But if one means by Socialist, in the economic and ideological field, the improvement of the proletarian class, the suppression of privilege, the leveling of rights and duties, the protection of urban and rural workers, the solution of the agrarian questions, the greater participation of the people in the management of public affairs, etc., from that viewpoint how could I not declare myself a Socialist? What man of good will would deny it?[23]

Sampognaro's declarations were as striking as Viera's. The Montevideo police chief was the public official most involved with unions and strikes. Williman's police chief, Colonel West, had used the position to break unions. Now Sampognaro was proclaiming his proletarian sympathies and reminding everyone that he would be Batlle's man. He was even talking about rural workers and agrarian problems.

A line, begun with Batlle's worker-as-citizen article when the eight-hour day bill was brought out for debate simultaneously with the Colegiado Apuntes, united all recent Colegialist declarations. First was the cult of Batlle: Arena's "Batlle is the whole reform," Viera's "I was unable to resist the overwhelming influence of Batlle's prestige and the suggestion of his powerful intellect." Then came the argument that those who would be Socialists elsewhere should be Colorados in Uruguay. "I believe this, too, is due to Batlle's influence," Viera had just declared.

The cult of Batlle would hold Colorados to the Colegiado, though some, sharing Manini's fears that Batlle was pushing Uruguay into too many new paths, would drop away. They would be more than replaced by the new worker-voters. But the new political line had its risks, as Don Pepe well knew. Batlle, in defending his eight-hour-day project, had acknowledged that he "does this knowing that it creates resistance and antagonizes people who would be otherwise favorable to him—with the effective support that the worker element may supply more than problematical, given their predominant tendency not to exercise their political rights."[24]

CHAPTER 17 *Gold Crisis*

The Bank of the Republic had not yet been able to negotiate a gold loan abroad. Lord Grimthorpe's demands for compensation on the Rambla Sur contract, demands supported by the English and French governments, were an obstacle keeping European underwriters from accepting an Uruguayan loan. To remove the obstacle, Batlle's government in mid-June of 1913 proposed to England and France that the President of the United States, Woodrow Wilson, be named to arbitrate whether damages were due. The choice was shrewd; England and France, rearming and coming together against German rearmament, were anxious to win Wilson's sympathies and could not reject him. Wilson, advocate of moral diplomacy in Latin America, was likely to be sympathetic to the Uruguayan position, especially since its government was considered pro-American.[1]

But the Rambla Sur controversy was not the basic obstacle to the Bank of the Republic's floating a loan. The Balkan War armistice, which momentarily eased the European money market, had broken down. European governments, fearing major war, were making strenuous efforts to protect their gold supply. France formally forbade the issuing of foreign loans; the English government did the same, without formal order. Not only did European governments try to stop gold outflow, but they moved to repatriate gold by raising interest rates and tightening credit. The head offices of European banks, short of funds, were ordering foreign branches to hold down outstanding credit and send gold home, and in Montevideo this put even more pressure on the perilously low gold holdings of the Bank of the Republic.[2]

Uruguay was really hit when Glyn, Mills and Company, Uruguay's traditional London banker, refused to renew four million pesos in 5 percent Treasury notes coming due on July 8, 1913. Serrato, to pay for nationalization of the State Mortgage Bank, had sold these notes at par, part of his sophisticated money management preparatory to the large foreign borrowing he was planning. Serrato's successor, Finance Minister Cosio, now tried desperately to get new financing from Glyn, Mills. If they would not renew the Treasury notes, he proposed that they underwrite a loan of ten million pesos, which would be backed by the strongest Uruguayan collateral—mortgage bonds on the State Electric Power System. Cosio was turned down. Finally, after hard bargaining, Glyn, Mills agreed to renew half of the Treasury notes at 7 percent, to be guaranteed by Uruguayan customs receipts, but the other two million pesos, plus 162,000 pesos in charges, had to be deposited in gold immediately with the Montevideo branch of the Bank of London and South America for shipment to England.[3]

The devastating effect of the operation was not its high cost—the additional annual interest on the remaining two million pesos would be only 52,000 pesos—but the government's withdrawal of 2,162,000 pesos in gold from the Bank of the Republic,[4] which dropped the Bank's gold holdings to 39 percent of its banknote–sight deposit liabilities, just under the charter requirement of 40 percent.[5] The Bank's board of directors faced a very serious decision.

The Board might have asked legislative approval to lower the 40 percent gold requirement. The Bank of England got its gold requirements lowered in times of crisis; the very high 40 percent requirement had been introduced to assure the Bank's soundness when it was established in 1896. The Board's belief that the Uruguayan economy was sound and that only the unusual and presumably temporary situation of the European money market prevented it from increasing its capital by borrowing abroad, coupled with the Bank's seventeen years of sound management (its rate of bad loans was still well below 2 percent of all outstanding credit) could have been invoked to justify lowering the gold requirement. But to do this would be to admit that the Bank was in trouble and might have unexpected consequences.

(The Federal Reserve System of the United States was founded in 1913, the same year the Bank of the Republic faced its gold crisis. The Federal Reserve also had a 40 percent gold requirement. Samuelson comments that the founders of the Reserve "took it so seriously that part of the blame for the 1920 price collapse must be attributed to the fact that no one dreamed that Congress could lower the gold requirement at the time when the Federal Reserve was threatening to go below the 35 and 40 percent ratios that then legally prevailed.")[6]

Instead of making the Bank's troubles public, its Board decided to do nothing in the hope that the Bank's gold holdings would go up by normal gold inflow when the wool clip sales abroad began in October. But the two leading private banks of Montevideo, the locally owned Banco Comercial and the Montevideo branch of the Bank of London and South America, pursuing their own interests, ended any chance for a breathing period for the Bank of the Republic. The two private banks, the only ones to survive the paper money crisis of 1875, feared that the Bank of the Republic, like European banks, would impose a charge to convert its paper currency into gold; conceivably, it might even go to inconvertibility. The two had always considered the Bank an unwelcome competitor[7] rather than the regulator of Uruguay's credit; putting their own business interests over that of protecting the Bank of the Republic, they now converted their holdings of three million pesos of Bank of the Republic paper currency into gold.[8]

Uruguay's two leading private banks had acted on their behalf that the Bank of the Republic was in trouble. Montevideo was too small to hide this action, and individual holders of Bank of the Republic paper currency began to convert it to gold. The Bank of the Republic's gold holdings were now at 35 1/2 percent and going down. Finance Minister Cosio complained that the Banco Comercial and the Bank of London and South America had started "a real run."[9]

The Bank's board had to act to save the Bank and protect themselves from personal, even criminal, responsibility for violating the Bank's charter. On Saturday, July 26, 1913, the Bank of the Republic sent this circular to all customers who had lines of credit on which they were authorized to draw:

> Because of generally known reasons and as a transitory measure, we advise you that the credit which was authorized you is suspended.

In case you are a debtor, please reduce the amount of your debt as much as possible.[10]

The circular produced a panic. The public lined up at the Bank's teller windows to withdraw deposits and convert paper currency to gold. The bank had anticipated this and had large stocks of gold on display to assure everyone that its position was solid. Nevertheless, five million pesos in paper currency were converted into gold.[11]

Early that Saturday afternoon Finance Minister Cosio was interpellated by the Comisión Permanente, a Senate-Chamber Committee, which sat when the legislature was not in session. By then the government had announced a series of economy measures. It was suspending the purchase of the first government merchant ship (eliminating a source of gold outflow) and suspending expropriation of land for the Government Palace (eliminating additional emission of banknotes).

Cosio was reassuring; the Bank's circular was of "a transitory character." To avoid being unfair, it had been sent to all the Bank's customers, not just to the poorer risks. Nor was the Bank requiring immediate repayment of outstanding credit and loans, "which would really cause serious upheavals"; it was only asking repayment of "as much as possible." Repayment combined with the Bank's announcement that it would extend no new credit would soon bring the Bank's gold holdings up to the legal level.

Cosio then made a welcome announcement. Later that afternoon all the private bank managers were going to meet "with the aim of assuming an attitude of solidarity with the Bank of the Republic, that is, a decision not to carry out extraordinary conversion of banknotes as the Banco Comercial and London bank had done, to accept the banknotes of the Bank of the Republic, and even to convert them to gold." Cosio pointed out that the managers had no real choice because if the Bank of the Republic, whose basic condition was solid, was forced to liquidate its assets, it would be required to demand immediate payment of all outstanding debt, and this would bankrupt a great number of Uruguayan businesses (there were 86 million pesos in loans and discounts outstanding from all banks, of which the Bank of the Republic was owed close to 38 million),[12] and "necessarily that bankruptcy would have a disastrous effect on the portfolios of all those other banks." Cosio concluded "everything will settle down."[13]

At their meeting the bank managers did agree not to present paper currency to the Bank of the Republic for conversion into gold until the situation improved. They also issued a statement: "Those present expressed their conviction that there was no reason for alarm because the Bank of the Republic is the Bank of the Nation, which has always religiously met all its financial obligations and which is taking urgent measures at this very moment to clear up the monetary situation of the Republic completely. For these reasons the banks have decided to continue serving their customers, confident that the Government will very shortly remedy the inconveniences of the present moment."[14] To demonstrate their confidence, the banks made deposits with the Bank of the Republic.

Nevertheless, the run continued, and police were needed to control crowds at the Bank. Batlle's prestige was used to bolster public confidence in the Bank. The President formally gave the Bank's board a vote of confidence and in *El Día* Don Pepe explained why. Had the Bank continued operations in violation of its Charter while asking that the Charter be modified—this was the advice given confidentially by the private bank managers—more serious alarms would have resulted.[15]

By August 1 the run on the Bank of the Republic had ceased, and it was possible to get to the tellers' windows without waiting. The Bank's quick conversion of paper currency to gold, the abundant display of gold at the Bank, and the willingness of private banks to accept paper currency had cooled the panic. But the Bank's gold holdings, which had been 16,700,000 pesos in May, were now down to 7,500,000 and still falling slowly.[16] This loss of over half the Bank's gold meant that unless some new source was found, the Bank would have to continue its credit freeze, and such a freeze would have devastating effects on the economy.

II

The gold crisis puzzled Uruguayan economic commentators. During the debate on the budget, Gregorio L. Rodríguez had warned the Chamber "the slightest setback in our production or any occurrence in Europe which causes a drop in the prices of our products, can bring a substantial drop in public revenues and in consequence an intense crisis." Uruguay was now in an intense crisis, but with Europe building up its armies, the prices of meat, hides, and wool—Uruguay's exports—were soaring, not dropping. Some commentators therefore concluded that Uruguay was suffering a financial, not an economic, crisis.[17] But the financial crisis—that is, the credit freeze brought on by the Bank of the Republic's loss of gold holdings—was producing an economic crisis. The credit freeze meant that businessmen, unable to get credit to pay for imports, were sharply reducing imports, and since imports provided basic raw materials and consumption goods, Uruguay's economy had quickly and sharply contracted.[18]

Conservatives blamed Batlle for the gold crisis. His "sick passion for prodigality and lavishness," had overheated the economy and thereby produced excessive demand for imports, while his "persecution of foreign capital" had frightened off foreign investors, a principal source of the gold needed to pay for these imports. El Día, consistent with Batlle's views, answered that the reason for the gold shortage was that foreign investors had taken too many profits out of Uruguay, a minimum of 30 million pesos in gold since 1905.[19]

Conservative commentators and El Día were explaining different aspects of the gold crisis. Batlle's government program, especially its encouragement of credit expansion, had increased Uruguay's demand for imports and so produced pressure on the nation's gold supply. Uruguay's gold supply was substantially lower than it would have been if gold drainage abroad in past years had been prevented by reducing the profits earned in Uruguay by foreign business. But much more was involved in the gold crisis. In past years, new foreign investments, both in private business in Uruguay and in the purchase of Uruguayan government bonds—investments which had the ultimate effect of expanding the Uruguayan economy—had the immediate effect of increasing the nation's gold supply. Now, not because Uruguay was a less profitable place in which to do business or because Uruguayan government bonds were less safe but because of conditions in Europe, foreign investment had suddenly ceased, while foreign businesses in Uruguay continued to send profits abroad.[20] Indeed, they were not just sending profits abroad. Foreign bank branches and foreign-based businesses in Uruguay, pressed for more funds by their home offices, were converting assets or capital into gold and sending it home. Cessation of new foreign investment combined with maximum shipment of gold abroad (foreign companies' profits plus some capital) explained why Uruguay's gold holdings were falling even though its exports were selling at excellent prices.[21]

The gold crisis revealed, although contemporaries were not fully aware of it, that Uruguayan public men were wrong when they believed (in the 1910 words of veteran Professor of Political Economy Carlos María de Peña) that "we have achieved admirable economic power, which places us in the position of a consolidated nation." Uruguay had negligible economic power. Events in the major world economic powers, events over which Uruguay had absolutely no control, could suddenly change its economic prospects.[22] A later generation would say that Uruguay had a dependent economy.

For contemporaries, the gold crisis only reinforced previously held economic principles. Conservatives saw themselves vindicated. Foreign capital, that precious source of gold, must be encouraged. Ranchers, whose production paid for the imports that fueled the Uruguayan economy, must be left alone. Government must accept the economic facts of life and not do too much. The proper economic stance for Uruguay was, as Manini had so well said, "slow but sure." Batlle reacted very differently. Uruguay must have a more productive, more balanced, more national and less foreign-owned economy. Otherwise, Uruguay would never escape from its economic vulnerability. For Batlle, the gold crisis confirmed the correctness of his program.

Batlle had regrouped to absorb the effects of the political crisis caused by the eleven Senators. Now, virtually simultaneously, he had to absorb the effects of the gold crisis. The bank managers' statement had called on the government to take measures; the bank managers wanted the government to retrench. Serrato, whose decision to postpone a massive loan when it could have been floated had proved to be a terrible error, was still considered a brilliant financial manager because his cabinet resignation antedated the gold crisis; Finance Minister Cosio, who had to confront the results of Serrato's management, was blamed for the effects of the gold crisis. Cosio had announced that the government would postpone the purchase of the first government merchant ship and land for the Government Palace. Now, the run on the Bank of the Republic over, the Executive on August 14 asked the legislature to authorize a loan of 25 million pesos. Included in the loan was financing for merchant ships, the agronomy stations, the industrial chemistry and fishing institutes, road-building in the interior, and workers' housing in Montevideo. Don Pepe was rejecting retrenchment. The accompanying message pointed out that most of these expenditures had already been authorized by law "in accord with my government program."[23]

CHAPTER 18

Elections–November, 1913

The opposition dismissed the 25-million-peso loan. If the Bank of the Republic, with its financial connections, was unable to float a nine-million loan, how could Batlle's discredited government come up with 25 million? The government must retrench. Don Pepe gave another signal that he would not. In August 1913 he convoked the legislature to its customary extraordinary sessions, which were limited to debating bills included by the Executive in the convocation decree. Batlle headed the list with the eight-hour day. In second place was the compromise divorce bill passed by the pre-"Apuntes" Senate. This was the measure that authorized a wife to receive divorce at her own request without the necessity of providing reasons. (The original proposal had been divorce at the request of either spouse without the necessity of providing reasons.) *El Siglo* was furious. The convocation message demolished "any hope of sensible reaction" and demonstrated "our unbalanced President's inability to understand the effects of the acts with which he confronts the difficult situation in which he finds himself."[1]

In November there would be elections. The Colorado Convention's endorsement of the Colegiado combined with anti-Colegialist refusal to take part in the Convention had produced a situation in which an anti-Colegialist electoral challenge to Batlle was almost inevitable. With Manini leading the anti-Colegialists and asking, "Are we Colorados or are we Socialists?", there was no chance that the Senate would give Batlle an electoral issue by debating the Chamber-passed eight-hour day. The pre-"Apuntes" Senate, though, had already passed the divorce bill—and the Chamber, under considerable pressure from the Colorado leadership, voted it into law on September 6. On Areco's motion the approved bill was sent to the Executive immediately. Young Colorado anti-Catholic intellectuals could go satisfied into the elections. To assure the law's passage, the Chamber had refrained from changing even a line of the bill it had received. Even a single amendment would have required Senate concurrence, and this Senate now would pigeonhole any divorce legislation it got into its hands.[2]

II

Batlle could have made the eight-hour day, and the Senate's refusal to debate it, the central election issue, but he did not. The risk was too great that the additional workers' votes won by such a campaign would not make up for the loss of Colorados antagonized by Batlle's radicalism. There were more than enough Colorado voters now, if they could be kept from voting anti-Colegialist. Appeals to Colorado unity against the Nationalists, effective electioneering, and de-emphasis of divisive issues would be the victory strategy. To that end Batlle called in anti-Colegialist deputies and offered them reelection to the Chamber, telling them that running on the party ticket "did not have implications for the personal ideas that each one might have on certain problems."[3] Earlier, Batlle had refused to extend the registration period for new voters, even though this would have aided the effort to get nonvoting workers to the polls, because the Nationalists, who were moving away from abstention, wanted lengthened registration.[4] As always, Don Pepe, the Colorado advocate of one-party government, refused to do anything that could be considered a concession to the Nationalists.

Even so, soundings from the departments encouraged the Nationalist Directorio. As the department organization in Rocha put it: "The officialist Colorados can vote around 1,300; the independent Colorados, 800; the Nationalists, 1500. That is, should the party go to elections, we would be sure to obtain the minority [seats in the chamber for the department]; and under the reasonable supposition that the Colorado schism will show up at the polls . . . we would easily reach the majority."[5] The Directorio called a special meeting of influential Nationalists from all departments for August 26, to decide whether the party should participate in the elections. Batlle, the Directorio newspaper argued, did not want the Nationalists to vote and would use every trick to defeat them. The way to oppose Batlle was not to abstain, but to vote. The Directorio got what it wanted at the August 26th meeting—60 in favor of ending abstention, 28 opposed—and two days later formally voted that the National Party go to the polls.[6]

The Bachini-Rodó Colorado dissidents, delighted with the Nationalist decision to vote, floated the idea of "popular coalitions" of Nationalists and of anti-Batlle and anti-Colegialist Colorados. Otherwise, the election law, which gave the majority seats in the different departments to the most voted ticket in the department, would work in Batlle's favor.[7] The anti-Colegialists, who proclaimed themselves one-party-government Colorados, were not interested in becoming allies of the Nationalists, but neither would they stay on the official Colorado ticket. Almost daily meetings of the anti-Colegialist Senators and Deputies, and with the presidents of existing anti-Colegialist clubs, were climaxed by a public meeting in the Senate antechambers on September 27, to which more than 250 Colorados were personally invited.[8] Manini speaking for the provisional committee to a standing-room-only audience, announced the purpose of the meeting, "The definitive organization of anti-Colegialist forces," so that they could act politically and electorally from now "until the day before the reform of the Constitution."

Manini moved, and the meeting approved, the election of a 25-member anti-Colegialist Executive Committee. Its composition was a triumph for him. There were ten Senators on it (Varela Acevedo and Enciso of the original eleven were not on it but Senator Martín Suárez, an old follower of Batlle's, also elected in 1912, was), which meant that Manini had shamed the Serrato wing of the Senate majority into holding firm. President of the Chamber Lagarmilla, ex-Education Minister Blengio Rocca, Tiscornia of Río Negro, Amézaga, and other politicians Batlle could take little pleasure in seeing in opposition were also members.[9] Even so, by voting that the life of the organization was to end the day before the new constitution went into effect, the anti-Colegialists, "the Generation of 1904," were rejecting the Rodó-Bachini advice to complete their break with Batlle.

Manini, whose leadership ability was no surprise, was elected President of the anti-Colegialist Executive Committee and wrote its first manifesto, countersigned by all the other members and published on October 7. What previously had been Manini's personal views were now those of the anti-Colegialist organization. The "Are We Socialists or Are We Colorados?" question was again raised and answered. The only way the Colorado Party could absorb the Socialist Party, "a revolutionary group which conspires against the present social order," would be to adopt "the entire socialist program, and that would mean, in short, nothing more or less than the dissolution of the Colorado collectivity and its triumphant absorption by Socialism." But the manifesto was confident that by going separately to the polls—their belief in the efficacy of elections was what really separated the anti-Colegialists from the older and more skeptical Rodó-Bachini Colorado dissidents—the anti-Colegialists would bring the Colorado Party to its senses.[10]

III

Since a depressed economy should hurt government candidates, Batlle's opposition could take encouragement from the certainty that the elections would take place under the depressed economic conditions brought on by the gold crisis. It was still impossible to borrow abroad. Though the Second Balkan War had ended, the European powers continued to rearm and the European money market remained tight. The Bank of the Republic, unable to increase its gold holdings by foreign borrowing, had determined to bring its holdings up to the 40 percent charter requirement by reducing currency in circulation. In October paper currency in circulation was down to 13.6 million pesos, a brutal decrease of 43 precent from July. This had been accomplished by not renewing loans when they came due, granting no new credit, and requiring amortization of lines of credit. Money and credit contraction had forced business activity down. Imports, Uruguay's prime economic indicator, had dropped 13.3 percent in August from the previous year and were still falling. Despite his opposition to retrenchment, Batlle's government, faced with declining revenues from import duties, its principal tax, was suspending public works on the eve of the election and laying off temporarily hired peons.[11]

Private business was also reducing operations. To cut costs, the Algodonería Uruguaya textile factory had reduced wages by 40 to 50 cents a day and increased the workday to ten hours. The factory's workers went out on strike. In the small town of Puerto del Sauce, Colonia, textile workers were also on strike. On October 28, to support the textile strikers, the Anarchist-led Federación Obrera succeeded in calling a general strike in Puerto del Sauce, which meant the paper plant, the quarry, and the port workers. The Federación wanted the Puerto del Sauce strike backed up by a general strike in Montevideo, but the Socialists, who were running candidates in Montevideo, argued that in these depressed times Montevideo workers were not in a position to make a strike effective.

There was trouble in Puerto del Sauce, and troops were sent in. Public Works Minister Blanco acted as mediator, winning a wage increase and the rehiring of all strikers. But all strikers were not rehired, and the strike resumed. The owners then closed the textile factory. The only overt assistance the government could offer the locked-out Puerto del Sauce workers (*El Día* called them "forced strikers") was the right to fish with previously illegal hand nets. In Montevideo the officers of the Federación Obrera were criticized for lack of militance and resigned on November 17. No others were elected to replace them.[12] Thus the Federación Obrera, which had organized the great general strike of 1911 and which had preached that workers must not vote, had ceased functioning two weeks before the election.

VI

The Socialists, who wanted workers' votes, were obvious beneficiaries of the Anarchist decline. In their first independent campaign, they were running a slate of eight candidates for deputy in Montevideo. Their seven-part electoral program called for (1) reduction of taxes on consumption, (2) a progressive tax on land income, (3) constitutional reform (a council of ministers, instead of a President of the Republic, abolition of the Senate, political equality of the sexes), (4) labor legislation (an eight-hour day, a minimum wage, weekly rest, protection of women and children), (5) workers' housing and rent control, (6) army reduction, and (7) protection of rural workers.[13] There was no mention in the Socialist election program of socialization of the means of production, to say nothing of the dictatorship of the proletariat. Uruguayan Socialists, rather than the "revolutionary group which conspires against the present social order" pictured in Manini's anti-Colegialist manifesto, were actually advocating a reformist program that resembled Batlle's.

Now would have been the logical time for Viera, or Arena, to point out to workers that voting Colorado was the way to ensure enactment of the labor reforms that Socialists could only talk about. Now was the time for Don Pepe to explain the superiority of his programs over the Socialists' and his differences from theirs. None of these things happened. Instead, Emilio Basterga, a second-level *El Día* labor writer, was assigned to answer the Socialists. "We want workers without forgetting their class interests to vote for Batllista candidates because we judge that inspired by the doctrine and the actions of the Master, these candidates will continue what he has begun."[14]

The article fitted the new line that "those who would be Socialists elsewhere should be Colorados in Uruguay." (Batlle was the Master; Batllista candidates were Colorados.) Workers' votes were not being rejected but they were being de-emphasized. Workers were notoriously reluctant to vote by the signed ballots still required under the electoral laws, since their employers, or others, would know how they had voted. For this election the victory strategy remained: get out the committed Colorados and keep them from voting anti-Colegialist.

The Colorado organization that had worked so well since 1904 went into full electoral operation. On November 8 a huge Viera for President committee was formed. The day before, Viera, Minister of Interior, who would run the elections, sent a circular to all departmental Jefes Políticos, reminding them that under the July decree police were now able to engage in active politics.

I now believe it convenient to recommend to you the absolute necessity that such exercise of civic rights be effectuated in such form that your participation and that of your subordinates in electoral activities have no official character, and that suspicion of undue influences be completely avoided.

It is therefore indispensable that in no case should police buildings or property or anything belonging to offices under your supervision be used for political party functions and should only be employed in public service.[15]

This was a classic statement of Batlle's moral influence doctrine. In Canelones, Don Pepe's protégé and now departmental caudillo, Tomás Berreta, welcoming the Colorado departmental organization to the Jefatura just after nominations for deputy were announced, uncorked champagne and exchanged toasts. Berreta had not been reprimanded and had probably kept within the letter of Viera's circular. He could maintain that the champagne was not public property and the celebration was an after-hours, personal tribute. Complaints of police politics flooded in: harassment of anti-Colegialists in Florida, men called into rural police stations in Río Negro to ask them how they would vote. Manini, in the Senate, cited seven specific cases of police harassment of anti-Colegialists "keeping citizens from the polls instead of encouraging them to vote." Washington Beltrán, young Nationalist candidate for deputy, accused the Jefe Político and Intendent of Tacuarembó of offering jobs for votes. Don Pepe, as usual, turned such complaints around. Differing political ideas were respected, but efficient government could not operate "if a group of functionaries identify themselves with the infamous accusations of the political group to which they belong." The anti-Colegialist Executive Committee had refrained so far "from denying the legality of the government and its conduct or insulting its intentions, but other organizations dependent on it have made their insults so extreme that they appear to be ardent enemies of the present political situation rather than advocates of an idea, which could be good or bad without affecting the character of the government one way or another."[16] Public employees likely to be disciplined, then, were not the police but anti-Colegialist Colorados who challenged the political acts of their superiors.

V

Impelled by the present election law, which prevented rival tickets from pooling votes, and by their ideological coincidence, the anti-Colegialists and the Rodó-Bachini Independent or dissident Colorados came together in the "Colorado Concentration." They agreed to a joint single ticket in Montevideo and not to run lists against each other in the interior; the anti-Colegialists were going to run in at least five departments, the Independents in three; neither would oppose Ramírez of *El Siglo*, who was running in Rivera, sponsored by the

Nationalists.[17] But the anti-Colegialists, led by Manini, once more rejected the Bachini proposal for a coalition in Montevideo with the Nationalists, even though the arithmetic of the 1910 electoral law almost compelled it. The joint anti-Colegialist, Independent ticket had brilliant candidates for deputy—Chamber President Lagamilla, Batlle's resigned Education Minister Blengio Rocca, Bachini, Rodó and others—yet would win no seats at all unless it got more votes than the Nationalists, while a coalition with the Nationalists could result in as many as 16 seats divided among the participants. Surely, the Independent Colorados maintained, it could be explained even to "the most primitive and uncultured of the party masses" that the real struggle was not between Colorados and Blancos but one of "common hostility and protest against a regime which is, at bottom, not the expression of any party but rather that of an oligarchic circle divorced from all forces of public opinion."[18] The anti-Colegialists—strong, one-party government Colorados—wanted nothing to do with the Blancos, and once more refused.

The dissidents, their hoped-for broad coalition rejected, started a rumor campaign. The government, because of its straitened economic circumstances was going to pay government employees, vital Colorado electoral elements, not in cash but in treasury certificates, which employees would have to sell at a discount. New diplomatic reclamations were on the way. Batlle, in accord with the Anarchist Federación Obrera, had plans for a general strike on election day.[19]

In this charged atmosphere, Captain Lino Fernández, a veteran soldier in charge of the First Artillery Batallion in Montevideo advised Batlle that a military plot was under way. Military units stationed in Montevideo would rebel three days before the elections. To prevent reinforcements from reaching Montevideo, a warship was in on the plot. The dissident rumor campaign could well be a screen for plots. Now that the dissidents were allied with the anti-Colegialists, the Generation of 1904 who had army officer friends, Bachini's predictions of army revolts against Batlle might be coming true. Don Pepe transferred the suspected army units from Montevideo and replaced them with units from the interior. The Montevideo police were issued arms and munitions. A replacement army batallion was quartered in the building where Batlle would vote.[20]

The opposition claimed that Batlle was moving the military around

in preparation for the use of force during the election. The week before
elections was troubled. In Rocha, dissident Colorados tried to march
after an anti-Colegialist meeting. Police stopped them, tempers rose,
shots were exchanged. Five people, including the speaker, Colonel
Manuel Dubra, who shouted "Down with the Police—Death to
Batlle," were slightly wounded. Ramírez of *El Siglo* and a group of
bright young men were campaigning in Rivera under the banner of
"Partido Civismo Independiente." Colorado deputy Abellá y Escobar
fired his revolver at one of his old rivals, now supporting Ramírez.[21]

In Montevideo, a never-before-seen level of campaigning was going
on. The Nationalists had speakers all over the city. In the Stella
d'Italia where Arena had given his "the Column is on the March"
speech, Nationalist leader Vásquez Acevedo, having defined the
Nationalist election goal—stop Batlle, "the whole nation must vote
against him"—summarized the Nationalist electoral platform: "reduce the action of the State to its just limits, preventing it from
invading the proper sphere of private initiative."[22] So the Nationalists,
newly emerged from abstention and still led by cautious lawyers,
businessmen, and ranchers, were not trying to contest Batlle or the
Socialists for the labor vote. Rather, Nationalists urged Catholics to
vote Nationalist, and not waste their votes by voting for the Catholic
Civic Union.[23]

The Colorados were using new methods to get out the Montevideo
vote. A first-time-ever electric campaign sign at the Plaza Independencia flashed alternate messages: "To take votes from the Colorado
ticket is to Favor Enemies." "For the Party, for Batlle and Viera, for
Constitutional Reform." "United and Strong, Colorados to the Polls,
Viva Batlle." Speakers were at all the Colorado clubs. The clubs were
busy passing out Colorado ballots. (In the Uruguayan system of
public voting, the voter put his ballot, usually provided by his party,
in an envelope, signed the envelope, and dropped it in the ballot box.)
The Colorado Commission had hired twenty wagons, which drove
through Montevideo carrying the sign: "The Nationalists Are Going
to Vote. To Conquer Them All Colorados Must Vote the Party
Ticket. VIVA BATLLE!" and distributed hundreds of thousands of
handbills.[24]

Using mass electioneering, the Colorados were aiming at their own,
at the committed. They were saying, "Colorados must conquer

Nationalists"; they were not saying, "If you want the eight-hour day, vote Colorado." They were even deemphasizing the Colegiado, whose future this election should decide. The anti-Colegialists, unable to use the Colorado party label (*lema*), because then their votes would be added to those of the official Colorados, were running as the Partido General Fructuoso Rivera. Rivera was the founder of the Colorado Party and enemy of the Blancos, and the anti-Colegialists emphasized that they had rejected electoral coalitions with the Blancos. On election morning the anti-Colegialists called on all coreligionaries to vote for "the triumph of the ideals which constitute our program, concretely, resistance to the implantation of the Colegiado." "Colorados, When you vote for the *lema* Partido General Fructuoso Rivera you know that no alliance with the Nationalists is possible."[25]

VI

Election day, November 30, was warm, clear, and calm. Bars were closed and Montevideo streets were quiet. Rumors of government use of force proved groundless. There were no troops in evidence and few police. Political clubs opened early, with free food and music. Voters were driven to the polls by auto—another innovation. At 9 A.M. Batlle voted. His registry certificate listed his occupation as "Newspaperman who is occupying the Presidency of the Republic."[26] Later on, Viera voted. All day long autos and coaches hired by the different parties and flying party banners brought voters to the polls. The electoral board, which had been alerted for complaints, had little to do.

There was the same calm in the interior, with only two incidents in the whole Republic. In Rivera, the Colorados accused the coalition of fraud; in Minas one polling place had to be closed down. In Canelones and neighboring Montevideo, as in old times, Colorados and Blancos gathered in separate groups, roasting meat turned on spits on fires; caudillos gave ballots to their followers, and the men, wearing red or white ribbons in their buttonholes, cheered and moved off to vote.[27]

Even *El Siglo* expressed surprised satisfaction. "We must admit that when the moment came, the government did not reach the extremes that its preliminary acts forecast. Everything indicated that material violence would reign over all the Republic, but in general these predictions were not borne out."[28]

When election results came in that night, a happy crowd, waving Colorado banners, cheered in front of *El Día*. The official Colorado ticket had won a landslide victory, 60 percent of the national vote, in the largest voter turnout ever. Colorados had won in 17 of Uruguay's 19 departments and would have 68 deputies to the Nationalist 21. The anti-Colegialists and dissidents had failed to win a single deputy's seat.

The Colorado victory was impressive. It had come in the midst of an economic crisis brought on by the gold crisis and a depressed economy was an electoral situation inimical to a government party. It had come even though the anti-Colegialists and dissidents had taken away 13 percent of the Colorado vote. Even without these votes, the official Colorados had polled eleven thousand of the seventeen thousand votes cast in Montevideo. Of the total government Colorado vote, two thirds had come from the interior, outside Montevideo—a demonstration that Batlle still had a national, not just a Montevideo, movement. Viera was going to be President, and the Senate majority's blockage of constitutional reform could not last long.

In fact, the big losers were the anti-Colegialists. Nationally, they and the dissident Colorados had polled 4,981 votes, only 9 percent of the total cast. The government Colorados had 32,849 votes, up 20 percent from 1907, the last contested election. The Nationalists, even with some lingering abstentionism polled 15,577 votes, 9 percent higher than 1907. Don Pepe's hopes that the Nationalists were on the way to disintegration were being disabused. But the Socialists had won only 774 votes. Frugoni, the Socialist Deputy elected in 1910 with Colorado aid when the Nationalists abstained, had lost his seat. The Catholic Civic Union had polled the fewest votes, 381.[29]

The voting patterns established in the 1905 elections, immediately after the War of 1904, had persisted, and if they continued, the Colegiado would win when voters elected delegates to the Constitutional Convention. In this election, the total vote was up 23 percent from 1907, but only about one third of the eligible electorate had voted.[30] In the Constituent election, with the secret vote in effect for the first time, Uruguay should reach the voter turnout level of mass elections. That election over the Colegiado, an untried and ridiculed system of government, would be more difficult for Batlle to win than legislative elections had been. The secret ballot would encourage Nationalists, who now did not go to the polls because they did not want to get into trouble with the government; the secret ballot would also weaken Batlle's "moral influence" with Colorado government employees, and this should help Manini's anti-Colegialists. But Don Pepe also had a potential pool of voters who now stayed away from elections—namely workers. To the extent they had voted this time, they had not voted Socialist.[31] Uruguayans were still Colorados or Blancos. The Colegiado election was going to be decisive in Uruguay's future. With it would come mass voting, and Don Pepe expected, then, that he would get the worker vote.

VII

The anti-Colegialists had hoped to get 3,500 votes in Montevideo but got under 2,000. It developed that Bachini and Rodó, principal dissident Colorado leaders and candidates for deputy on the joint Montevideo anti-Colegialist-Independent Colorado ticket did not themselves vote. Having failed to convince the anti-Colegialists to join in a coalition with the Nationalists, Bachini and Rodó emphasized "the uselessness of electoral effort on the practical level" i.e., that their ticket could not outpoll the Nationalists and by increasing the total vote would only prevent the Nationalists from maximizing the number of minority deputy seats they would win. Bachini and Rodó recommended abstention, justified by the argument that honest elections could not be held with Viera, candidate for President of the Republic, running the elections as Minister of Interior. The anti-Colegialists, who wanted a strong showing in this election as a means of bringing the Colorado Party to its senses, rejected the recommendation. Bachini and Rodó, promising not to discourage their own followers, themselves abstained.[32] Now, the election over, the dissidents urged the anti-Colegialists to complete their break with Batlle. "Once and for all" the anti-Colegialists must decide whether they were "fundamentally part of the present governing group or fundamentally opposed." To stop Batlle, coalitions with the National Party, "with its large number of adepts and its support in the Conservative and moneyed classes" would be required.[33]

The anti-Colegialists held a postelection meeting and without committing themselves to specific future courses decided to continue their organization. On December 3, three days after the election, Manini, as President of the anti-Colegialist Executive, issued a circular that congratulated all anti-Colegialist party authorities "for the act of disinterested patriotism," in contesting the elections. Considering that the anti-Colegialist organization was less than two months old, Sunday's results were really encouraging. "We have not set ourselves up as an accidental group to win seats in the election. We have organized for the defense of ideas which, in our view, protect the public and party interest, and we must continue to be ready to struggle for them without feeling disappointments or experiencing weakness."[34]

Don Pepe, the real winner of the election, was immensely satisfied with the large turnout and absence of violence. Two days after Manini's election evaluation, he published his own. The election was a victory for democracy, constitutional reform and the Colegiado. The Colegiado, considerably deemphasized by the government Colorados during the campaign, had indeed been its central issue, and Don Pepe acted as if campaigning had made this clear. What also had not been made clear until now was that Batlle's understanding with Viera included a full four-year term for *El Indio*.

Don Pepe put it more delicately. The remaining year of his own government could be devoted to "exhausting" the debate over how to reform the constitution. "The government to follow can carry out the task and supervise it and complete it correctly, to the applause and with the assent of the entire nation."

> We should also state that we do not believe that the reform, once approved, should go into immediate effect. The purpose which the supporters of the Colegiado pursue, as we have stated on many occasions, is to spare the nation from the calamity of bad governments. The triumph of Doctor Viera's candidacy guarantees us four years of excellent administration, assured by the aptitude of the candidate and the unimprovable conditions under which that distinguished citizen will reach the first position of the nation. From that point of view, haste might also be unjustified because it might perhaps occasion the failure of the arduous effort at institutional reconstruction on which we are embarked.[35]

Don Pepe, during Viera's government, would head the Colegiado campaign. His original plan to retire permanently to Europe at the end of his term had been made obsolete by political events and his daughter's death. Well before the election, he had obliquely announced his post-presidential intention. Don Pepe acknowledged the truth of a story that Uruguay, because of gold-crisis budgetary stringency, had withdrawn from participation in the 1915 California Exposition in the United States. Where the story had erred, Don Pepe announced, was that he was to be the Uruguayan representative in California. "Such a thing would never have occurred to Señor Batlle, since he does not even intend to leave the country once his term is over."[36]

CHAPTER 19 *"Are We Colorados or Are We Socialists?"*

On December 5, 1913, Francisco Simón, Apostle of the Colegiado, who had made the nominating speech for Viera at the Colorado Convention and was a newly elected Deputy, gave the kind of radical *El Día* interview that had been deemphasized during the campaign. Simón, who had become very close to Batlle, favored "equalizing wealth"

> I think we should gradually apply the theory of Stuart Mill, according to which, as many are aware, the value of real property, when it is not the consequence of the personal effort of the proprietor, should go to the benefit of society.
>   . . . I also believe it desirable to accentuate the progressive tax on inheritance and other forms of capital, so as to keep those forms of wealth within a reasonable limit.
>   . . . that way the enormous differences that result in many able men living under miserable conditions while others who are worthless live in the most irritating opulence would largely disappear.

Simón also called for women's voting as soon as possible: "there cannot be true democracy in a country which denies the right of suffrage to half its inhabitants."

Simón, who had been talking with Don Pepe, was reopening the line that in Uruguay the Colorados would accomplish what Socialists elsewhere could only aspire to. But Simón was the first to be explicit about what Colorados intended to accomplish. And his equalitarian emphasis that society should give everyone an equal start and a decent minimum so that individual effort would be rewarded—"Personal effort, the only means which honestly and logically gives just title to enjoy property in the face of those who do not have property, can only create a limited personal fortune"—was radical but distinctly not Marxist.[1]

Don Pepe, whose article on the worker as citizen inaugurated the new party line that those who would be Socialists elsewhere should be Colorados in Uruguay so far had refrained from answering Manini's question, "Are we Colorados or are we Socialists?" Those with good memories, though, could recall that Batlle, just before leaving for Europe in 1907, had talked with the young Argentine socialist Deputy Alfredo Palacios about socialism. The Williman campaign newspaper, edited by Batlle's disciple Julio María Sosa, reported:

Above all, they spoke about Socialism. Señor Batlle told Doctor Palacios that he didn't know if he was Socialist—that his life had always been one of struggle, which had not permitted him to go deeply into that question. Nevertheless, señor Batlle y Ordoñez said, I have been, when a professor [desde la cátedra] an enemy of absolute individualism, and more than once I have tried to put into practice socialist ideas which appear to me to be very acceptable.[2]

Batlle's answer revealed a lack of self-assurance with foreigners that was going to reappear in Europe. It also revealed how far-sighted his political thinking was. In this case he was looking ahead to the current party line that those who would be Socialists elsewhere should be Colorados in Uruguay. Most of all, the answer revealed that Batlle had not really read Marx and authoritative socialist writers. Palacios then asked Batlle what book had influenced him most. Batlle thought a moment and replied, "the Course on Natural Law by Ahrens."[3]

Ahrens was a book of Batlle's youth. Recently, Areco, the Batllista expert on moral legislation, had presented Batlle with a copy, and on the title page Don Pepe had written:

This copy of Ahrens' work was presented to me by Areco. It is a gift I very much appreciate because in this great work I formed my view of the law, and it has served me as guide in my public life. JBO—1913[4]

Don Pepe when he was in his twenties had been a philosophy student. The military then governed Uruguay, and students, forbidden to discuss politics, debated philosophy. Batlle was one of the Idealist group headed by Prudencio Vázquez y Vega, who died young in 1883. Batlle nursed Vázquez y Vega while he lay dying of tuberculosis in Minas, brought the corpse back to Montevideo, and years later remarked "I venerate his memory." Vázquez y Vega, a Deist, insisted that man had innate morality and attacked Positivism because he blamed its relativistic morality for encouraging men to collaborate with military dictatorship. His own doctoral thesis, "Honorable Men Should Not Support Usurper Governments," emphasized the higher law and called on public employees to cease working for such governments. The resultant paralysis, he was confident, would bring down the military. Vázquez y Vega's articles stressed that absolute government and organized religion, especially the Catholic Church, prevented liberty of conscience and sovereignty of the people. "It is necessary to work endlessly to carry to the heart of the ignorant multitudes the blessed light of new ideas and to convince everyone, through the evidence of reason and the facts, of the falsity and inefficiency of Catholicism in our times." Thirty-nine years after Vázquez y Vega's death Don Pepe spoke in the town where he died. "Even today, so many years afterward, I ask myself why I am here advocating the same ideas we advocated then and he is not here."[5]

The great issue for the young philosophers was how to end military dictatorship and religious authority; they rarely got to what good governments should do. Vázquez y Vega, who identified government with repression, warned in one of his last philosophy lectures that one must "never forget that the individualist theory, which puts the least limits on individual activity, is infinitely superior than that other doctrine which assigns secondary missions to the State."[6] Here, Don Pepe, who succeeded Vázquez y Vega as President of the Philosophy Section of the Ateneo, parted with his friend, as indicated in his statement to the Argentine Socialist Palacios in 1907: "I have been, when a professor, an enemy of absolute individualism."

And here Ahrens entered. Heinrich Ahrens, a post-Kantian German follower of Karl Krause, had enormous success in Europe and America with his *Course on Natural Law*, which combined the history of philosophy and law with sections on economics and on private, public, and international law. It had gone through six editions, the last in 1868, and had been translated into French, Italian, Portuguese, and Spanish. For the Idealist anti-Positivist young Uruguayan philosophers, Ahrens' emphasis on innate human morality, which had made him so popular in Spain, combined with his opposition to both materialism and Catholicism, was just what the Uruguayan Idealist anti-Positivists needed in debates with their philosophical opponents. Ahrens argued that "the State cannot be simply a police institution protecting everyone in his rights; its positive mission is also to favor by positive means the perfection of good in every order of activity."[7]

Young Pepe was an avowed Idealist anti-Positivist. In 1880, during his student year in Europe, he wrote a relative that at home he had been able to exchange ideas with fellow students, but the Spanish-speaking friends he had made in Paris "have accepted the Positivistic ideas of Auguste Comte with a little haste, in my view, and this puts them in such a situation in respect to me, a believer in metaphysics, that every conversation degenerated into a discussion and every discussion into an argument." Young Pepe also had more difficulty understanding Ahrens than would be suspected from Don Pepe's confident 1913 notation "In this great book I formed my view of the law." He confessed in the same 1880 letter:

> My father has always reproached me, in part with a great deal of reason, with not being sufficiently methodical. He accuses me of reading many books. I, too, believe that if I find a good one and dedicate myself to grasping it fully, I would get a lot of benefit out of it, but what has always happened (and particularly just before I left Montevideo, with a course on natural law by a German author) when I read a good book carefully is that I get drawn into studies beyond my ability because of their extensiveness and the matters they treat, with the result that the remedy gives more energy to the sickness.[8]

Nevertheless, on returning to Montevideo in 1881 he noted in his diary: "I began reading my old book—Ahrens, natural law." A few days later, after noting that he had matriculated at the university, the diary entry was "I slept a lot—I studied little."[9]

Young Pepe had self-doubts. In Paris he had written his father, who feared that Pepe was "going to remain without a profession," that he,

Pepe, belonged to the group "of those who have an excess of high aspirations but are too weak to carry them out and are under no illusions in this respect."[10] No one who had watched Don Pepe get elected President twice or who now was watching him push the Colegiado would agree with this assessment. And Batlle himself no longer shared it. Immediately after his 1907 interview with the Argentine Palacios, where some of the intellectual uncertainties of his youth showed through, he had written in the journal he kept on the ship carrying him on his second trip to Europe: "Love of truth first brought me to study, love of justice then dragged me into the political struggle. No material interest of any sort determined these two orientations of my life." These were the comments of the mature, self-assured man.

The entry also paralleled Ahrens' definition of Kant's categorical imperative, "Do good for good itself, without consideration of reward or penalty."[11] Ahrens, though, found this concept insufficiently grounded in God. This was one of the many areas where Batlle departed from Ahrens. The young Uruguayans found Ahrens very useful in their desperate effort to rouse their people against military government, but Ahrens was addressing a very different public. Ahrens had lived through the Revolution of 1848 and the return of absolutism. His basic message, modeled on England, was that governments should cede enough to the demands of the "inferior classes" that both revolution and the absolutist reaction to it would be avoided. Ahrens' appeal to morality was an appeal to restraint. His section "Communist and Socialist Doctrines Considered as Aberrations in the Progress of the Philosophy of Law"—Marx was cited only in a footnote—warned that this extreme materialism appealed to "sensual appetites" and would deny the individual personality. Ahrens feared democracy, the tyranny of the majority, and political parties. "It would be against the ethical idea of the State to erect the party spirit into an electoral principle."[12]

Obviously, this was not what Don Pepe Batlle, the one-party government Colorado, had in mind when he noted on his gift copy of Ahrens that it had served as a guide in his public life. Ahrens' view that reforms should not outrun public opinion—"the State is not an experiment station for associations which, precisely because their theory is not yet ratified by practice, can easily propose goals contrary to the needs and true interests of the social order"—could easily be the anti-Colegialist motto, but not Don Pepe's.[13] Ahrens' Krausist concept of "organic harmony," which involved putting groups between the individual and the government to balance between revolution and absolutism (federalism, indirect elections, an upper house made up of representatives of different social groups) was opposed by Batlle's confidence that free elections would prevent abusive government.[14]

Where Ahrens' influence on Batlle became evident was in the analytic method Ahrens recommended for public men. The nature of man, given by God, enabled him through reason to deduce good. The public man would determine, from philosophy, the "ideal state, toward which social life must ever come closer," and from analysis of the history and present condition of his own country "the reforms for which the people are prepared by their previous progress and which can presently be realized." Ahrens himself in the introduction to the first 1837 edition of the book cautioned, "Do not believe that all the reforms explained in this course are susceptible, in the author's opinion, of being immediately applied"; and the underlying thesis of the book, advocating reforms in theory but denying them in practice, made it almost a bible for the Williman years.[15] Batlle deduced the reforms that he believed necessary—in a newspaper polemic on Socialism in 1917, he used language out of Ahrens, "Human nature in liberty, tends towards the good"[16]—but rather than waiting until reforms were so powerfully demanded that to resist them would create revolution, which was Ahrens' view, Batlle put through reforms as soon as he felt it was possible to enact them, making rather than following public opinion, arguing that because Uruguay was a new country, European impediments need not hold it back.

Ahrens' view of man's God-given nature brought him to advocate the end of the death penalty, the rights of illegitimate children, divorce, the banning of brutal sports like bullfighting, which mistreated animals. It was entirely understandable that Areco, the Batllista expert on moral legislation, should present his copy of Ahrens, whose views in all these areas were so influential, to Don Pepe. It was notable, however, that Batlle went further than Ahrens, who advocated divorce by mutual consent, surrounded by limitations; Batlle, on the other hand, wanted divorce at the request of either spouse. Ahrens wanted the father to support illegitimate children but denied them inheritance rights; the Batllistas were enacting laws concerning both. Ahrens argued that workers had the natural right to a limited work day and quoted Fichte's "right to leisure"; Batlle's message accompanying his eight-hour-day bill based it on every person's right to have enough time to himself to enjoy the life of civilization. Ahrens, though, considered that the eight-hour day went too far. He argued that everyone had the "right to subsistence." For Ahrens this meant that where an impoverished person's family or ex-employer failed him, the State should step in to keep him from starving. Don Pepe, consistent with his own analytical method, had plans, some to be announced very soon, some after the Colegiado assured their political possibility, to provide a decent minimum standard of life for every Uruguayan.

Batlle, with Ahrens as a point of departure, was carrying out a program to make Uruguay a model country; Ahrens, though he had an ideal for a just society, really was advocating sufficient incremental improvement to avoid popular revolution. Ahrens when discussing land ownership argued that "the general principle requires that land belong to the one who knows how to cultivate it." Use, not possession, justified ownership. He acknowledged that property values rose because of "industry that develops in a city or a new road or street," but he was reluctant to endorse solutions. [17]

The American Henry George, relying on the same economists that Ahrens read but reflecting on what he had seen in California and New York in the 1860's and '70's, concluded that land monopolization explained why poverty accompanied economic growth. Land values rose because of society, not the landowner, but the landowner, not society, took the increase for himself. If society taxed away the profits of land ownership but did not tax improvements on land, land prices would fall, land would be worked intensively, and government revenues would rise so much that no other taxes would be needed.

Uruguay, even more than California, suffered from people buying urban and rural land and holding it for the rise in land values, without improving it—close to half the ranch land in the country was rented. Taxing land heavily would force ranchers to improve their pastures or sell to farmers; it would force urban lot owners to build or sell. Don Pepe had been moving in this direction since his first administration.

Batlle's land tax ideas, though they stemmed from Henry George's were not identical, and Don Pepe was not a single taxer. [18] George, in the United States, was willing to see government operation of railroads and telegraphs but felt that economic growth was not a serious problem. Batlle, in underdeveloped Uruguay, had a much wider set of economic concerns.

But more than land taxes united Batlle and George. George anguished over "the injustice of society" and, in contrast with Ahrens, wanted to end it immediately. He saw the day when "no citizen will have an advantage over any other citizen save as is given by his industry, skill and intelligence; and each will obtain what he fairly earns." Ahrens talked of "inferior classes," but George talked of the "enormous wastes" of mental power "the present constitution of society involves." "How few are the thinkers, the discoverers, the inventors, the organizers, as compared with the great mass of the people! Yet such men are born in plenty; it is conditions that permit so few to develop."[19]

Don Pepe was a kindred spirit. Arena remembered Batlle's irritation at those who argued that workers' needs were few and therefore workers were satisfied with little. Arena recounted: "And as if he felt responsible for the tremendous injustice, he lived constantly turning it over in his mind, looking for the remedy."[20] Batlle would later advise a Socialist, "Señor Mibelli can read in George and Reclus how the modern conquerors starve the conquered to death."[21]

Elisée Reclus, the French Anarchist geographer, had lived in Colombia in 1855 and 1856 and saw in the racial mixture of South America the basis of its future greatness. Anarchist Reclus, who had been in the Paris Commune of 1871, rejected government and expected revolution—positions Batlle did not share. Reclus, though, believed workers understood things as well as professors did. He believed that "the evils that this society produces are infinite, and nevertheless it is possible to avoid them," and looked forward to future social peace based not "on the unquestionable domination of some and the hopeless servility of the rest, but on true and frank equality among comrades."[22]

Ahrens, George, Reclus, the Spanish feminist Concepción Arenal, the sources Batlle cited, were from his youth. These were authors widely read by his generation, but most of his generation had gone on to more pragmatic concerns as they matured. Those who went into politics did so part-time, exercising their professions as well. Don

Pepe spent all his time in politics and with his political newspaper, and he continued to think through the concerns first raised when he was a student. He became a thinker whose originality lay in his willingness to pursue positions beyond where their first expounders left them, and a politician with a remarkably cohesive program.

Batlle was an equalitarian—that really set him apart from Ahrens—who believed that morality was in human nature and good solutions attracted people of all classes. He would reject Marx's view that "the economic structure of society" is "the real foundation on which a legal and political superstructure arises and to which definite forms of social consciousness correspond."[23] When the Colegiado was safely installed, the Colorado Party would adopt Batlle's full program. Then Don Pepe would be ready to debate Socialists. To do so now could give new ammunition to the anti-Colegialists.

CHAPTER 20

Colorado Split

Batlle, the election over, on December 8, 1913, again tried to bring the anti-Colegialists back. Let the Senate pass the bill to elect the Constitutional Convention, let the anti-Colegialists vote by secret ballot for their own delegates to the Constitutional Convention.

> Reform would be completed in the first year of Doctor Viera's government, and submitted to plebiscite. If the vote were favorable, the new constitution would await the end of that government before going into effect, although some of the reforms adopted— for example, proportional representation—could be implemented before.[1]

Proportional representation would enable the anti-Colegialists to elect deputies in the next general elections.

Batlle was acting as though Manini's first public speech last March, when he argued that except for the Colegiado, anti-Colegialists were part of the governing party, still defined the political situation. But anti-Colegialist hostility had constantly grown, to the point where Manini in the Senate had accused Batlle and Viera of electoral illegalities (Manini accusing Don Pepe and *El Indio* of election violence was something still hard to believe), and Manini rejected Batlle's proposal. "It is not unification which is being sought, it is our disappearance from the political scene; it is the death of anti-Colegialism as an organization and an idea. It is capitulation." Manini warned that many Colegialist converts were more Socialist than Colorados: "Excommunicate us once and for all. It will be more comfortable for the new adepts to colegialism and . . for us as well."[2]

A test of whether the anti-Colegialists were ready for the open break with Batlle was at hand. The Executive had finally negotiated a foreign loan—not the Bank of the Republic loan, not all of the 25-million-pesos loan, but part of it, and the contract needed legislative approval. The loan was desperately needed. The Bank of the Republic still maintained the credit freeze it had begun in the July gold crisis. It had reduced commercial credit from 37.8 million pesos on June 30 to 28.8 million on December 31; paper currency in circulation was down to 16.2 million from 23.5 million. In six months the Bank had cut credit by 25 percent and paper currency in circulation by 30 percent.[3] Imports, the key indicator of economic growth, were down 14 percent for the six-month period. The Finance Ministry admitted that the economy was "paralyzed."

Export prices were still excellent, imports were down, and the Bank's gold holdings were rising. From a low of 6.2 million pesos they were back to 10.4 million pesos, and because of the Bank's sharply reduced operations, this equaled 50.89 percent of the Bank's combined demand deposits and currency in circulation, well over its 40 percent charter requirement. But the Bank was afraid to reopen credit, even though government employees were being paid with two- and three-week delays, because the last of Serrato's short-term debt, over 3 million pesos, was coming due in May and repayment would again reduce the Bank's gold holdings.[4]

The loan just negotiated would permit payment of the outstanding short-term debt and enable the Government to deposit additional gold in the Bank of the Republic and to activate parts of Batlle's program which had been stalled by the gold crisis. Finance Minister Cosio explained to the Senate how difficult it had been to float this loan. Though the Balkan Wars had ended, the world financial situation was uncertain. France forbade any foreign loans; England had raised the bank rate another half percent; attempts to borrow in the United States had been unsuccessful. In the circumstances the loan, with the obscure Ethelburga Syndicate in London, had been an achievement.

The loan was for ₤2 million (9,400,000 pesos) at 5 percent, but the

Uruguayan government would only receive 7,896,000 pesos of the proceeds—84 percent net—terms that would have been disgraceful before the gold crisis. Uruguay had to pledge part of its customs receipts to assure repayment and also that it would not issue any new foreign loans until October 31, 1914. Even worse, Ethelburga would not issue the loan all at once. It would issue it in four three-month installments during 1914 and reserved the right to cancel unissued installments in the event of war, outside or inside Uruguay. And Ethelburga would withdraw if the loan contract was not approved by the Uruguayan legislature no later than December 27.

The loan meant that the Bank of the Republic could reopen credit which would revive Uruguay's economy, and the Senate had to swallow Ethelburga's terms.[5] The Executive proposed to push economic diversification by using the loan's last installment, 2 million pesos, for Acevedo's Agronomy Stations, the Industrial Chemistry and Mining Institute, and the Fishing Institute, and to purchase two ships to inaugurate the State Merchant Marine. The Senate refused; the last installment must go to the Bank of the Republic.[6] When the Bank ultimately floated its authorized capital increase loan—which would have to be after Batlle's presidency—the then sitting legislature would decide the final disbursement of the 2 million pesos. The Senate approved the bill on December 22; the Chamber, which was busy passing Batllista legislation, namely easy recognition of illegitimate children and workmen's compensation, passed it the following day.[7]

The Senate majority had not given in to the election results. On the eve of the gold crisis, well before the election, the Senate had compromised with the Executive over the Bank of the Republic and Batlle got what he wanted, the Bank's right to reinvest all its profits. Now the Senate compromised and got what *it* wanted: denial of funds to the economic diversification projects. A state fishing institute which could not fish because it had no ship but which was legally compelled to pay the workers it had hired to crew the ship was not what Manini intended by his "slow but sure" economic policies. Nevertheless, it was an outcome of political stalemate; long-term political stalemate, something Don Pepe was confident he would prevent, could convert Batlle's model country into a multiplicity of such outcomes.

II

The Nationalist Directorio, delighted with the results of this election, was already thinking ahead to the next year's election of six Senators. On December 23 Directorio President Carlos Berro told the body "that in view of the political situation in which the Anti-Colegialist Colorado legislators find themselves [without any seats in the Chamber], it would be a good idea to have confidential discussions with them and offer them encouragement for their present attitude as well as encourage them in the patriotic necessity of maintaining it in the coming election of Senators, in which the National Party, for its part, will extend itself even more than in the recent elections."[8] Such talk of a national movement against Batlle had been advocated before the elections. Then the anti-Colegialists had rejected it, but now they were bitter and coming closer to the Colorado dissidents who favored collaboration with the Nationalists. Any such Colorado-Nationalist realignment raised the prospect of an army coup to get rid of Batlle. Ever since the October 1910 revolution, a coup had been in the background: fear of Batlle's assassination on inauguration day, concern that he would be kidnapped when his daughter was at Arazatí, information that army units and a navy ship would revolt three days before elections.

Batlle, who had lived through the militarist era, always took the danger of army coups very seriously, but he was careful not to be thought of as the army's enemy. He had encouraged army modernization during this administration: a French military mission, reorganized army administration, a geographic service, a radio service, a seamen's school, the beginnings of an air force. The army was now a small cadre of 39 units with 600 officers and 10,000 men, designed to be quickly expanded to as many as 80,000 men in the event of Nationalist revolution. Batlle's modernization directed them to new activities. The geographic service was doing mapping; the radio service was running the Montevideo port wireless; the seamen's school would provide crews for the new State merchant marine. And as the Nationalists moved into elections and away from revolution, the army's traditional mission of resisting Nationalist revolution became less urgent. Batlle was allowing the officer corps on active duty to decrease by attrition. The Ministry of War reported that in 1913, although there had been many promotions due to retirements and resignations, 57 vacancies, from colonel to lieutenant, or 22.53 percent of the vacancies, had not been filled, with results "favorable to the public treasury."[9]

Plotters might conceivably be working on officers who felt they should be promoted. In mid-January 1914 Batlle announced that he was leaving office hours open every week for army officers who wanted to see him. But much more dangerous than disgruntled individual officers was the effect on army officers as a group of Manini's anti-Colegialist preaching and warnings that Batlle was turning Colorados into Socialists. Comandante Moller de Berg, whom Batlle had put in charge of army administration, tried to argue the advantages the Colegiado would bring officers. Now the army was the arm of the President of the Republic who promoted officers on the basis of their political loyalty to him. The Colegiado would change this; officer promotions would be determined within the army itself, which would become fully professional. "The closed army register," promotion of officers exclusively determined within the army, "will never be achieved as long as there are Presidents who need the Army to maintain themselves in power."

> With the President gone, the essentially political role which the Army today plays will no longer have any reason to exist, and that is the fundamental reason why all true soldiers, all those who want the army organized on an indestructible basis should, within the limits established by our law, work for the Colegiado to become reality.[10]

Nevertheless, War Minister Bernassa y Jérez—the only member of Batlle's original cabinet still in office—had recently taken to late night inspection of the barracks. Two secret agents Batlle had sent out unbeknownst to each other, to discover what Colonel Dubra, implicated in the preelection coup, was up to, thought the other was a plotter and each reported back the other's plot talk: discontented army officers in collaboration with dissident Colorados led by Bachini and Travieso and supported by Nationalists would act before the Senate President, who would take over should Batlle be removed as President of the Republic, was elected on February 14. Ramírez of *El Siglo* was reported to have said, "I believe they won't even give me time to present my credentials as Deputy."[11]

On February 8 the Senate majority met for three hours without coming to an agreement on electing the Senate President. On February 9 *El Día* announced that an arms cache had been found in the department of Rivera—the department over which the War of 1904 had begun. Batlle received a note signed "A Soldier of order and decency" warning that "a coup against the present political situation is being organized by the Independent Colorados. They are waiting for the Vice Presidency of the Republic [the Senate President] to be in the hands of an anti-Colegialist. Leaders of the movement? Manini, West, Olave, and Dubra have been named to me and the perspicacity of Your Excellency will easily discover the others." The secret agents reported that the aide of Basilio Muñoz, the Nationalist military caudillo, was in on the plot. On February 11, three days before the Senate President was to be elected, *El Siglo* printed an editorial, "The President and the Army," which could be a signal: "A brutal policy of blind intolerance, of hermetically sealed exclusivism has produced an absolute divorce between public opinion and the government. The army shares the general feeling."[12]

The next day, February 12, Batlle ordered the arrest in Salto, of Colonel Dubra, Manini's tentmate in 1904. Dubra, Batlle had been warned, was plotting against the government. General Escobar, whose name had been invoked by Nationalist military in 1910 when they revolted expecting to be joined by the army, was put on leave. Alfonso Crispo. a reporter for Bachini's *Diario del Plata*, was brought to police headquarters on disembarking in Montevideo upon his return from Buenos Aires. Police Chief Sampognaro questioned him about a meeting that had taken place in a Buenos Aires law office between Crispo, Colonel Dubra, and Abdón Arósteguy, a Nationalist resident in Buenos Aires. When Crispo denied that any such meeting had taken place and insisted that he had unexpectedly met Dubra at the pier in Buenos Aires before embarking, Sampognaro asked Crispo to turn over all his papers, took them to another room, telephoned Batlle, and after a short while returned. "The President orders me to apologize for your detention, which has come about through a most serious error. You are, therefore, at liberty." Crispo, who had been held at police headquarters for an hour and a half, protested that he had been illegally arrested.[13]

On February 13 the eleven Senators met to decide on a candidate for

Senate President. Three of them were going to vote for Viera as President and apparently didn't want to vote for an anti-Colegialist Senate President. Without their votes there was no majority of the eighteen Senators sitting. Finally, it was decided that the names of all ten—Manini withdrew his name—be deposited in a ballot box and one name chosen by lot. The name was Blas Vidal, Williman's Finance Minister, an estimable person plotters were presumed to consider "worse than Batlle."[14]

Don Pepe, though he and the Colegialist Senators carefully avoided attacking the new Senate President,[15] blasted the Senate majority. They had turned the election of Senate President into a *tómbola* (charity raffle). Did this mean that the eleven Senators' pledge not to pass the law on Constitutional reform was renewed for another year? At first Don Pepe thought so, but after a few days, he reconsidered. "There has been nothing like this. The group has not been reconstituted."[16] The eleven Senators, clearly, were not working together smoothly; equally clearly, Batlle could count on only seven of the eighteen Senators sitting.

III

The Senate Presidency had changed hands without any upheavals, but Colonel Dubra remained under military arrest. The charge, signed by the Minister of War and dated February 12, two days before the Senate President was elected, stated: "this soldier was engaged in subversive efforts inside the army."[17]

The one solid piece of evidence was a statement Eduardo Dieste, a Spanish immigrant writer, had given to Batlle in December. Dubra had told Dieste, whom he had originally befriended on the ship bringing Dieste to Uruguay, that several army batallions were involved, an artillery park, and the navy. The movement would be in Montevideo and be over very quickly. Dubra insisted he knew nothing about plots. He had resigned from the army in December and demanded that his case be transferred from military to civil justice, where the evidence so far presented would be insufficient to justify keeping him under arrest.[18]

The evidence against Dubra all dated from November and December and had not then been considered strong enough to arrest him. Batlle evidently had arrested Dubra on a false lead. Here was an opportunity for the newly seated Nationalist deputies. They could excite the Nationalist mass with furious accusations against Batlle in the Chamber and get out the Nationalist vote in future elections.

On February 17 Washington Beltrán, just 30, a first-time deputy, reminded the Chamber that last week a distinguished independent newspaperman "was submitted to police brutality, violating the sacred rights of the citizen." Beltrán was talking about Crispo's detention at police headquarters, which Crispo claimed was for an hour and a half. The authorities said three quarters of an hour. Crispo's detention did not rank very high in world annals of government brutality, but the galleries, packed with Nationalists, cheered as Beltrán demanded that the Minister of Interior be brought to the Chamber to answer whether Police Chief Sampognaro acted on his own, "or has he committed this outrage on the person of a newspaperman by order of another newspaperman, who today occupies the Presidency?" Luis Alberto de Herrera, Nationalist firebrand, skilled at stirring things up, wanted the War Minister called to explain Colonel Dubra's arrest and the placing of the Captain of the warship *Montevideo* on inactive service. Juan Andrés Ramírez, Professor of Constitutional Law as well as *El Siglo* editor, insisted that the search of Crispo's papers was an illegal and serious infringement of his rights.

After letting debate go on for several days, Sosa, Batlle's Chamber spokesman, responded. It was unnecessary to call the Ministers of Interior and War: "the orders of arrest for both Colonel Dubra and Señor Crispo were given directly by the President of the Republic" in accord with Article 83 of the Constitution, which in an event "of the most urgent public interest" gave the President the right to arrest a citizen for 24 hours before turning him over to the courts. Crispo had been questioned and his papers checked because information had identified him as "the carrier of incriminating papers" for Colonel Dubra. Nothing remotely illegal had taken place. And "for the President of the Republic there are no enemies in the army, an institution for which he has the highest regard, except those, fortunately very few, who may be enemies of order and legality."

Herrera broke in. Batlle's government was collapsing. "Reclusion of the President in a rural wasteland under double lock and triple guard. . . . The army, divided, anarchized, broken . . . no longer offers assurance to this doomed regime, confirming once more the saying that bayonets are good for everything except sitting on them."

Finally on March 5, after two weeks of debate fully covered in the party papers—Colorado strategy had been to prolong debate so that the Nationalists could not claim they were being silenced—the motions to call the Ministers of War and Interior to the Chamber were defeated by voice vote.[19]

IV

The best news of early 1914 was that the Ethelburga Syndicate had quickly sold out the first £500,000 installment of the new bond issue, and 2,000,000 pesos in gold were deposited with the Bank of the Republic. The Bank now had gold holdings of 13 million pesos, the next Ethelburga installment would pay off the last of Serrato's treasury letters, and, with widespread popular approval, the Bank reopened credit to businessmen and ranchers, although as the Bank later put it, under "norms of severe discipline and prudence."[20] Batlle had been resisting retrenchment since the gold crisis broke, and the eased financial situation was quickly translated into new government action. On March 3 the Executive sent a bill to the Chamber creating 150 new first and second grade teachers. It was approved by March 28. Williman's school building program had been so successful—91,746 children were enrolled in public elementary schools in 1913 compared with 54,355 in 1903, the beginning of Batlle's first term—that teacher shortages made schools turn away pupils.[21]

The bill had been prepared by young Education Minister Brum. Don Pepe was delighted with Brum, a hard worker, an apt pupil, an enthusiastic Colegialist. Brum's only fault was a low boiling point. Barbaroux, whom Batlle had brought in as Foreign Minister to prepare arbitration on the Rambla Sur, had just resigned, and rather than appoint a new man for the year remaining in his government, Don Pepe added the Foreign Ministry portfolio to Brum's Education portfolio.[22]

On March 26, while approving the 150 new teachers, the Chamber brought out another Brum bill to establish public libraries in the capital city of every interior department. The bill, which would have pleased Ahrens, dovetailed with Batlle's program of secondary schools in every department; the libraries would be in the school buildings. Brum had prepared the library bill in July immediately on taking over the Ministry, but it had been held back because of the gold crisis. Though the sums involved were small, 54,000 pesos the first year, 10,800 thereafter, the Nationalists would not support the library bill. Herrera said that the Interior would prefer better mail service. Beltrán also opposed "these disorderly expenses." Even the senior Nationalists joined in. Vásquez Acevedo, an eminent educator, believed the general public would not use such libraries. Martín C. Martínez, ever cautious, wanted the opinion of the budget committee, but the Chamber passed it anyway.[23]

In April, Batlle, without much publicity and using general revenues, renewed other programs that had been suspended because of the gold crisis. The national orchestra was given funds to continue through the year. Autobuses, which Don Pepe hoped would compete with the British-owned trolleys, were restored to service, though only on asphalted streets (they broke down on Montevideo's cobblestones). And on April 14, this time with much publicity, the Chamber began debate on the first of a package of bills for a State railroad system.

A State railroad system was one of Batlle's prime goals for this administration. During his first administration neither public finances nor public opinion were favorable enough to support State railroads. Instead, he had required the British railroads to build a line to the Brazilian border ahead of traffic and at a less favorable profit guarantee. Under Williman the concession was rewritten to the railroads' satisfaction, and other concessions were approved. Back in power, Don Pepe refused to consider any new railroad concessions. Plans for State railroads ran into obstacles until Percival Farquhar, an American promoter who used French capital to build Brazilian railroads and who had tried to buy out all the British railroads in Uruguay as part of his Rio to Buenos Aires line, decided to cooperate with Batlle. In Uruguay, Farquhar now owned three feeder lines, two smaller lines, and a concession to build on the Atlantic, but the Central line, Uruguay's principal road and the one with the single route out of Montevideo with which all of Farquhar's lines connected, had eluded him.[24]

Farquhar's Rio to Buenos Aires project collapsed as a result of the effects of the gold crisis on Brazil. His whole railroad empire, badly overcapitalized, short on operating funds, and poorly maintained was near bankruptcy.[25] In these circumstances he was desperate to get something out of Uruguay, and during the past November had agreed to an extremely favorable contract with the Uruguayan government. Farquhar's Uruguay Railway Company would build 600 kilometers of railroad for the State. A trunk line from Montevideo to Florida would parallel the Central's main line (see map on p. 25). From Florida it would connect to Paysandú, so that Farquhar's littoral lines would have shorter and separate entry into Montevideo. MacArthur Brothers, an American engineering firm already involved in Uruguayan railroad building, would build another 400 kilometers from Florida Northeast to the Brazilian border, bisecting the Central Rivera and Melo lines. Farquhar, who now was stuck with a short line which went from the tiny Atlantic port of La Paloma 35 kilometers inland to Rocha and stopped, would sell this line to the State and build a branch line for the State west from Rocha, connecting with the State's Montevideo-Florida trunkline.

Within eight years, under the Farquhar and MacArthur Brothers contracts, the Uruguayan government would own a modern 1,000 kilometer railroad system which would both open new areas to railroads and force the Central to lower rates and improve service. Best of all, Farquhar and MacArthur Brothers were willing to accept payment in Uruguayan government bonds, thus getting around the restriction of the Ethelburga loan not to float new issues abroad for a year.

Ranchers disliked the British-owned Central railroad. They complained that its schedules were erratic, that it didn't send enough cars during peak livestock shipments, and that it charged too high rates. Farmers and those supporting agriculture were bitter that the Central did not, as Argentine lines did, offer rates low enough to permit cereal agriculture at any distance from Montevideo. And Don Pepe had seen the Central, Uruguay's one profitable railroad—send 2,699,607 pesos in gold abroad during 1912–13, coinciding with the gold crisis in Uruguay.[26]

So the Farquhar contract was enthusiastically welcome, even though the Central threatened diplomatic reclamations because the government railroad line would parallel its line out of Montevideo. Veteran Nationalist leader Rodríguez Larreta spoke for the committee and extolled the contract: "this bill has nothing to do with majority and minority. . . . Railroad construction is of such overwhelming national interest that we are all the majority."[27]

Martín C. Martínez, Uruguay's most respected attorney, went so far as to swallow his objection to State enterprises. He also dismissed the Central's claim that it should be recompensed because a rival line would be built. Neither its concession nor any other law of Uruguay gave it exclusive territorial rights. Martínez nevertheless doubted the wisdom of lining up with Farquhar against the Central. There simply was not enough traffic for two lines out of Montevideo; Farquhar's cost plus contract "can expose us to real surprises." (Farquhar had long experience in giving government inspectors stock in his railroads to approve poorly built railroad lines.) The Central, responding to what was happening, had offered to build lines for the State and accept rate regulation. Farquhar might be amenable today but not tomorrow; the Central, on the other hand, would be around for a long time. It was wiser to negotiate a deal with the Central.

Public Works Minister Blanco had prepared himself carefully. For the first time, Uruguay was going to have "economic control" of its railroads, now controlled from abroad. "The Executive Power desires that the Central Railroad of Uruguay, in accord with its concessions, prosper like all the companies active in the nation and respects foreign capital established in the nation so long as its profits are legitimate, just, and in accord with the law; but it can do no more. . . . The idea of State railroads and the nationalization of the same belongs entirely to the person now exercising the Executive Power," i.e., Batlle, and it was government policy that the Central must no longer keep the "key," exclusive entry to Montevideo. Competition would produce "lower fares, lower freight rates, increased comfort and speed—in a word benefit the nation." When the government railroad lines were ready, access roads would be built 15 to 25 kilometers around each station. The Montevideo port kept charges on shipping at a minimum, and the same policy would apply to the State railroads. Some European ports, Hamburg for example, ran at a deficit. "It won't matter that our railroads run at a deficit; we expect it, we will welcome it." The ideal was gratis railroad charges: "citizens should have no other obligation with the State than the taxes they pay . . . citizens contribute a quota and receive free passage and free haulage of their production."

Deficit operations of state enterprises represented a new departure for Batlle. Up to now his management policy was business-like operation and reinvestment of profits. State railroads with built-in deficits coming from low, even gratis, rates, so that agriculture finally would be profitable in the Uruguayan interior, might be a very great burden on the treasury, but railroads were universally popular, and such objections, as well as Martínez' arguments that Uruguay would be overbuilding its railroad system and his warnings that Farquhar was unreliable, were not persuasive.

During the debate, which lasted a month, Public Works Minister Blanco told the Chamber that the government had plans for an Atlantic port costing 10 to 12 million pesos at La Coronilla in Rocha, which would be the best deep water port in South America, would tie into the State railroads and end Uruguay's present centralization on Montevideo (additional evidence that Batlle's program was national, not centered in Montevideo). The port would benefit the interior and attract traffic from Brazil.[28] On May 19, 1914, the Farquhar contract was approved by the Chamber and sent to the Senate.[29]

CHAPTER 21 *Building a Platform for the Colegiado*

In May 1914, the Ethelburga Syndicate sold the second installment of the new bond issue. The funds were used in London to pay off the last of Serrato's treasury notes, and the Bank of the Republic was finally in the clear. Prosperity, though, had not returned. Because of the continuing effects of the gold crisis, imports, the principal determinant of the level of the Uruguayan economy and the principal source of government revenue, were still low. Finance Minister Cosio explained that continuing credit tightness in Europe caused suppliers there to restrict the traditionally extended terms of payment offered Uruguayan importers, and this counteracted the limited credit the Bank of the Republic was offering in Montevideo. Finance Ministers were professional optimists, and Cosio, basing his remarks on the still excellent prices for Uruguayan exports, predicted economic recovery within months, when the annual wool clip was sold and gold flowed in.[1]

Don Pepe had resisted retrenchment—Argentina and Brazil facing similar external problems had cut their budgets—when the gold crisis was acute, and now that it had eased, he was speeding up his program. In order to get around the external credit bottleneck, he had agreed, as noted, to pay the state railroad contractors with government bonds instead of cash, even though, as the Rambla Sur controversy had shown, this method made the State vulnerable if the contractor could not raise sufficient funds to begin construction. Still, building was better than waiting; building would provide employment and meet needs. Using the same financing technique as with the State railroads, the Executive proposed that four million pesos in Public Assistance bonds, originally part of the 25-million-pesos gold crisis loan that had not been placeable, be issued to builders of hospitals, asylums, and sanatoriums in Montevideo and the interior. The plan was particularly attractive because the goal was unobjectionable, construction workers would be hired, and the builders would be Uruguayan.

New taxes on betting, alcoholic beverages, theater tickets, and stock exchange transactions would pay for the Public Assistance bonds. The Public Employees Pension Fund proposed that the one percent tax on public employees' salaries, which now went to Public Assistance, be used to pay life insurance to the survivors of public employees. Gabriel Terra, author of the progressive inheritance tax during Batlle's first administration, proposed, to Nationalist consternation, that inheritance taxes be doubled to pay the life insurance and to provide additional revenues for public education.

Inheritance taxes, along with land taxes, were central to Batlle's thinking. They would provide revenue for expanded government services and reduce reliance on uncertain customs receipts. Their social function was of equal importance; land taxes would reduce property values, make for intensive land use, and open up land to new users; inheritance taxes would reduce the unfair advantages future generations of the well-off would have over the poor. Terra's first progressive inheritance tax had been greatly diluted by Nationalist Martín C. Martínez who had convinced the legislature that the tax should be on the individual heir's portion, not on the total estate (a 200,000-peso estate divided among four children was only taxed at 2 percent), with the result that the yield of the progressive inheritance tax to the government was only some 500,000 pesos a year.

To Nationalist Vásquez Acevedo's objection that the proposed increase in inheritance taxes would "raise them, in many respects, beyond the limits they have reached in any country in the world" and discourage "the spirit of saving, so lacking and at the same time so necessary in our country," Terra replied that because in Uruguay only real property paid inheritance taxes and real property was assessed at half actual value, of the 23 to 24 million pesos inherited annually in Uruguay, the state now received 1.5 percent, compared with 10 percent in England and 6 percent in France. Uruguay, now, was "the nation which, perhaps, pays the least amount of inheritance taxes in the world."

With Don Pepe's backing, things moved quickly. New articles revising the inheritance tax came out of committee. Urban property would be taxed at real value, rural property at real value less 20 percent; banking institutions were obliged to reveal deposits and securities owned by the deceased. Spouses and children would pay moderately increased rates, up to 8 percent of the value of the individual inheritance; for distant relatives the rates became steep, a maximum of 27 percent. Then came an innovation Don Pepe had advocated from Europe. In every bracket an heir "domiciled abroad" would pay an additional 8 percent. Martín C. Martínez protested this was "enormous and can discourage the entry of capital into the country and its remaining here." Terra dug in. As a lawyer he had seen "with real sadness" properties sold for three and four times what the deceased had paid for them and "enormous sums" sent abroad without additional taxes paid. "That is not just." Martín C. Martínez lost, and on June 30, 1914 the Public Assistance Bond–Public Employee Life Insurance Bill was approved by the Chamber. In the bill's form the tax revenue from inheritance would be tripled.[2]

II

The external credit bottleneck to Batlle's programs had an internal parallel in the Senate. Although the eleven Senators organized by Manini to block constitutional reform were not formally united (all were Colorado and eight were anti-Colegialist), neither had they really broken apart. They approved noncontroversial legislation like the 150 additional school teachers, but preferred not to discuss most of Batlle's projects. The famous Río Negro Senate seat, Williman versus Tiscornia, had still not been adjudicated nearly two years after the election; nothing was heard about Batlle's proposal to approve election legislation for the Constitutional Convention.

That Manini's hold on his Senate colleagues was limited was evident in June when another part of Batlle's package of State railroad bills was debated by the Senate, which had not yet considered those passed by the Chamber. Actually, the Executive's bill to take over the Ferrocarril y Tranvía del Norte (Railroad and Trolleys of the North) involved only 21 kilometers of railroad; it transported livestock from the northern boundary of Montevideo to the slaughterhouses. This short railroad line was valuable because it would provide the right of way out of Montevideo for the state railroad. The state now owned 40 percent of the Ferrocarril y Tranvía del Norte, as part of the liquidation of the 1890 crisis, while other creditors of a failed bank owned the majority of the stock and managed operations, which consisted of the railroad and 17 kilometers of horse-drawn trolleys through Montevideo. Don Pepe had eyed these trolley lines from the beginning of this administration; he intended the State to take over, extend, and electrify them, and compete with English- and German-owned Montevideo electric trolley lines.

The Executive's message acknowledged that the concession would revert to the State in 1928, but to wait until then would deprive it of "the large profits" electrification was certain to bring.

> Besides, horse-drawn trolleys offer the sad daily spectacle of the horses' martyrdom, hours and hours of dragging heavy weights; few of them survive the labor to which they are submitted . . . and the horses are subjected to brutal punishment which accustoms and familiarizes the public with barbaric procedures long since outlawed by all civilized nations.

The message never directly acknowledged that a major goal of the bill would be to force down the rates and thus the profits of the foreign-owned electric trolleys sent abroad. It did state:

> Finally, the State does not have the right to deprive the Municipality and the general public of the comfort and well being of a modern trolley line, with reduced fares on long routes which can be further extended, nor to deprive those owning property along the trolley right of way of the increased value to their properties nor to deprive the Treasury of the tax increases that logically will result from these increased values.

Instead of buying out the majority stockholders with cash, which the treasury did not have, or with bonds, which would accentuate the pressures on the Montevideo money market, the Executive had come to an agreement with the stockholders. It would take over the Tranvía del Norte, guarantee the stockholders 4.5 percent annual dividends plus a proportionate share of any additional profits, and would have

the right to purchase their stock at par whenever it seemed desirable.[3]
Manini, who as Batlle's Minister of Interior had been involved in the
earlier Tranvía del Norte negotiations, took the floor to oppose the
agreement. The stockholders were getting too much for a concession
that would end in thirteen and a half years and was yielding them only
3.5 percent.

Arena, still Manini's law partner, interrupted his friend and political adversary. Everyone knew why direct purchase or expropriation
was ruled out. The State didn't have the money. "Because we don't
have money, the merchant ships haven't been bought. Because we
don't have money the magnificent project to organize a fishing industry is suspended, a project which, as I see it, should be one of the
transcendent solutions for our country, a country so small and surrounded by so much water." To Manini's rejoinder to wait a few years,
Arena came back that it was easy for Senator Manini to wait "but all
the poor people who have to use the Tranvía del Norte daily . . . can't
wait."

Antonio María Rodríguez, one of the eleven Senators, spoke for the
Senate committee, which had reported the bill out favorably. He had
the greatest admiration for Manini, Uruguay's future Carlos Pellegrini
(the first son of an Italian immigrant elected President of Argentina),
but disagreed with Manini on this deal, which if not a brilliant
operation for the State, "is reasonable for both parties." State-
guaranteed 4.5 percent paper would sell at 56 to 60, not much above
Manini's estimate of the stock's present value. Nor were post-
electrification dividends likely to be significantly larger, since

> the new trolley policy which we all believe the Executive Power is
> pursuing, a liberal policy, a policy of low rates, can go into effect,
> not only to serve the public on this line but indirectly to oblige all
> the other trolley lines of Montevideo to lower their own rates, since
> this line is going to be a positive and effective competitor.

On June 12, Arena began his formal advocacy of the agreement:

> if we have reached, under the aegis of this Government, the place
> we have reached, the governments that come after it will continue
> day by day to move to more advanced positions, without which all
> our acts would be frustrated. . . .

. . . the goal of the Government cannot be the amassing of dividends, not for it, not for the Company. The goal of the Government must be to improve services, to make its trolleys a kind of trolley school, where the motorman, the conductors, all the personnel are treated better than anywhere else, paid better than anywhere else. The goal must be to develop a Company which reaches every part of the city, even where there are no immediate profits. Lower the rates, have low-cost trolleys for workers, not once in a blue moon like the ones now run by those delicious foreign companies, but frequently, regularly, so that not only workers but poor people can all use the cheap trolley.

The State trolleys were only one part of Batlle's state enterprise plan.

I invite the Senate to reflect a moment on what Uruguay would be like the day it had not one or ten, but hundreds of those organizations, run as well as any private organization—because the mechanism is the same, since each one depends on a totally autonomous Board of Directors—but which would have the immense, extraordinary advantage over similar private organizations because they would not seek profits for stockholders. Their only goal would be to serve the public well.

Arena was touching the reason for the renewal of Batlle's rain of projects even though it was the last year of his government and even though the economic situation forced patchwork financing that could well cause future trouble. Batlle did not intend this administration to be the peak of Uruguayan radicalism; if he had, he would have compromised with the eleven Senators so as to get more of his programs enacted. This administration was setting the positions the Colegiado would carry through "day by day to more advanced positions without which all our acts would be frustrated." Uruguay would have not just State banks, railroads, trolleys, and electricity, it would have hundreds of state enterprises, providing cheap services to counter the high prices caused by the growth of Uruguayan private industry operating under tariff protection. Uruguayan private industry would provide employment and reduce gold outflow; state enterprises would further reduce gold outflow while cheapening services. Together they would go a long way toward preventing future gold crises like the one currently crippling the country, make the Uruguayan economy less primitively based on cattle and sheep, and assure prosperous lives for Uruguayans.

On July 10 Senator Pérez Olave, another of the eleven, presented revisions he had negotiated with the stockholders and cleared with Viera, the Minister of Interior.[4] Pérez Olave had also prepared a charter for the Ferrocarril y Tranvía del Norte, patterned on the Bank of the Republic and the Electric Power System. The trolley's new board of directors was to propose electrification plans to the Executive Power, to be completed within three years, using trolleys "analogous or superior to those of the English-owned electrical trolley line." Manini acknowledged defeat and withdrew his motion to renegotiate the contract.[5]

III

On June 22 Don Pepe sent an old age pension bill to the legislature. Article One provided: "Every person who has reached the age of 65 or is absolutely invalid at any age, has the right to receive a minimum pension of 72 pesos a year from the State." Most Uruguayans were young; the 1908 Census listed fewer than 30,000 men and women over 65;[6] the Executive estimated that a 20-cent-a-month per-capita tax would yield pensions of eight pesos a month to the indigent aged, with small sums left over to build old-age hotels. Eight pesos a month was not a princely sum, but it was larger than any European pension and would begin at age 65, not the usual 70. "It should be understood that it only provides the bare minimum which society owes the individual who has reached the extreme situation of incapacity to work and lacks the means to live." Future legislation could expand on this bill.[7]

Don Pepe did not expect old age pensions to become law immediately. The bill was another setting of positions that would be advanced in the future. In the Uruguayan legislature bills once filed did not expire. This Senate would not approve old age pensions or the eight-hour day. Viera's Senate would. Old age pensions marked the beginning of the benefits of social legislation for rural Uruguayans. Everyone in Uruguay over 65, urban and rural, male or female, could benefit. The eight-hour day and old age pensions, part of Batlle's goal of a decent life for all Uruguayans, would also bring voters in for the Colegiado. Or, as El Día put it, "Passage of this old age pension bill by the end of this administration or in Dr. Viera's would mean that there would not be an old person in the nation over sixty-five who would not receive a pension which would serve to meet his necessities."[8]

IV

Batlle set another position, this one likely to be politically unpopular, when the Executive proposed that the Montevideo property tax be converted into a land tax, with buildings and improvements exempted from taxation. Batlle had been preparing for this since his first administration when Montevideo assessors had been ordered to separate land from buildings. Finance Minister Cosio, who had written the message, with "finishing touches" by Batlle, explained that "the uproar of the 1913 crisis did not give us time and liberty of spirit to think of tax reforms. We are now moving, slowly, with all the prudence that the seriousness of these questions requires, ready to take forward steps."[9] Taxes on land with buildings exempted were identified with Henry George and his Single Tax, but George was considered a crackpot and Cosio separated himself from Georgism. "Henry George himself was nothing more than an idealist, more a metaphysician than an economist"; Cosio's own favorite author on property taxes was de Greef. In fact, however, the Executive's message was saturated with Georgian views.

> Land is an obvious exception to the view that society may protect itself from increased costs of economic goods by the restriction of use or consumption, because the quantity of land is always limited and because man cannot avoid using it. Society has eminent domain over land, the exceptional nature of its situation being so marked that even the least advanced thinkers on economic and financial matters consider the levy on land to be more a social rent for use, more a right of *emphyteusis* [governmental rental] than, properly speaking, a tax.

Here, in legalistic language, was the kernel of what Don Pepe was to proclaim years later: "the land belongs to everyone." Society was the real owner of land; society could therefore determine how to use land; individual owners really were tenants of the government; the land tax was the government's way of collecting rents.[10]

The present proposal made no such sweeping changes. From now on, buildings would be exempt from the Montevideo property tax, which would be levied exclusively on land. At present, land and buildings combined paid taxes of 6.50 pesos per thousand of assessed value. (For example, a Montevideo property consisting of land valued at 30,000 pesos and a building valued at 30,000 pesos paid 390 pesos in property taxes annually; a vacant lot valued at 30,000 pesos paid taxes of 195 pesos annually.) The Executive proposed that buildings be exempted and the tax on land raised to 10 pesos per thousand of assessed value. (The empty lot which previously paid only 195 pesos would now pay 300 pesos, the land and building which previously paid 390 pesos would now pay only 300 pesos.) The State's revenue would not increase significantly (before, it received 585 pesos from both properties; now, it would receive 600 pesos)[11] but vacant lands and valuable lands with flimsy buildings on them would pay substantially more taxes and this would discourage speculators who held vacant lots waiting for their prices to rise and would put pressure on lot owners to build. The change should ease the high cost of living; a labor office survey indicated that a worker's family with four children paid 35 percent of its income in rent. By encouraging building, the bill would increase the supply of rental housing and reduce rents.

The Chamber committee enthusiastically endorsed the bill. The excessively high prices of Montevideo land caused high rents and also discouraged industry and commerce. Most of the report strayed from the issue at hand, Montevideo property taxes, to emphasize that the situation in the interior was worse. High land values resulted in growing latifundism, due "largely, to the unjust and antiscientific system of our land taxation." (A rancher did not have to be paranoid to see what was ahead. The traditional 6.5 per thousand tax was going up to 10 in Montevideo. Improvements had long been exempted from the rural land tax. Before long, using the arguments of this report, the rural land tax would be raised to 10 per thousand to bring it in line with Montevideo.)

Debate opened on June 3, 1914. Finance Minister Cosio spoke for the government. The purpose of the bill was to increase construction in Montevideo and encourage new housing. He didn't expect a building deluge to result from this law but did foresee some stimulus for construction companies to build on vacant lots: "this law will increase in some proportion the number of buildings."

Nationalist firebrand Luis Alberto de Herrera saw a wonderful opportunity in the bill to produce opposition between Montevideo property owners and Batlle. Herrera had been busy corresponding with ranchers and was about to relay to the Chamber their complaints of inadequate police protection against livestock thieves.[13] The country, he now shouted, was surviving in spite of the government.

I have always believed . . . that Government is an agent of the country's inhabitants and as such it cannot do everything it feels like doing. It must fit its policies to the exigencies of local society.

That is my position as a conservative, and I am pleased to be profoundly conservative against the demagoguery in power.

. . . the right of the State cannot go so far as to impose, in a form I consider legislatively despotic, upon someone who does not want to build, the obligation to do so against his interest or in violation of his liberty.

Herrera, having warmed up, went on to related issues not directly involved in the Montevideo property tax. He didn't like the campaign in government circles to push agriculture on ranchers. Improvements on rural land had been exempted from taxation since 1886 without increasing agriculture. "Let us leave those famous landowners alone; let them, enthusiastically serving their own interests, serve the interests of the nation by working their lands in the way most convenient to their pocketbooks." Ranchers were producing the wealth of the nation, and he resented their being called latifundists.

Herrera moved that the bill be returned to committee "to be studied from a point of view more in harmony with public needs and fiscal interests." Fellow Nationalist Rosalio Rodríguez made the same motion in more restrained form: it was now June 22 and the fiscal year began July 1. There simply wasn't enough time to study such a fundamental reform in the few days remaining. Let the present Montevideo property tax be extended for another year while this reform received adequate study.[14]

Cosio insisted that the reform must be voted, and *El Día* hit back at Herrera. The doctrine that primitive latifundists be left alone was obviously wrong:

That is why the men who are directing the present government, in this as in all things, have viewpoints contradictory to the Nationalists, who are backward and resistant to change by temperament and atavism—that is why the State, under the direction of these men, intervenes to establish industrial education which today is looked down upon, in the interior of the country, intervenes to spread knowledge of prevention and treatment of plant and animal diseases, intervenes to regulate by means of taxes the use or disappearance of the latifundia, which requires no labor and prevents our population growth, intervenes to encourage the improvement and growth of rural production, intervenes to foment the formation of farms on ranches.[15]

V

To those horrified at the way Batlle was shaking up Uruguay, it seemed that he was trying to remake the country all at once, but his program actually was a number of simultaneous stages. Some State enterprises, for example, were operating successfully, some were in process, some were suspended, some had not yet even been announced. External economic conditions and internal political splits had held Batlle back, but he was determined. He was using his last year in office to push projects so that they would carry through to the next government. But he was going much beyond that, building a platform from which the Colegiado would keep bringing Uruguay closer and closer to the ideal. External restraints had been greater than anticipated, but Uruguay could speed up when conditions changed. It was the internal situation that was crucial. Some of his projects, like the eight-hour day and old age pensions, should bring in more voters. Others, like property and inheritance taxes, affronts to the Church, and challenges to ranchers could bring voters to his opposition, where they would be welcome. It was clear that his opposition, both Nationalist and Colorado, was responding to his programs by emphasizing their conservatism. Batlle, in turn, was careful not to let the opposition infiltrate the army and always emphasized his own strong point, that he was the Colorado leader who had definitively defeated the Blancos, first in war and then in peace. There would be obstacles, expected and unexpected, but nothing that had happened had shaken Don Pepe's confidence that he had put Uruguay on the right path.

CHAPTER 22 *World War*

On June 26, 1914, four days after Finance Minister Cosio insisted that the Montevideo property tax bill exempting buildings and taxing only land must be approved, he startled the Chamber.

> The Government has been notified by the Ethelburga Syndicate of its decision to rescind the contract requiring it to issue bonds for £500,000 before the First of July. Naturally, this disconcerts the plans of the Government, since if the Government had been able to dispose of the £500,000 immediately, it would have been able to face a much longer delay in receipt of the Property Tax and consequently not fear the length of debate that might be required for complete passage of the law.
>
> In this situation, Mr. President, I am going to propose the extension of the Property Tax in effect for this fiscal year for the period 1914–15, so that the other project can continue to be debated with all the amplitude that may be necessary and to take effect in the fiscal year 1915–16.

Juan Andrés Ramírez, for the Nationalist minority, announced "the profound pleasure" with which they received Cosio's proposal. The Montevideo property tax was extended for another year without debate by the Chamber and approved by the Senate on July 2, and the decree authorizing its collection was signed by Batlle on July 5.[1]

The European credit market had suddenly tightened, Uruguayan bonds had fallen sufficiently for Ethelburga to invoke the cancellation clause. On June 28, two days after Cosio's unexpected announcement, newspapers carried stories, reported by the foreign wire services, that Archduke Francis Ferdinand, heir to the Austro-Hungarian monarchy, had been assassinated in Sarajevo. The distant event made no impression whatever in Montevideo.

Batlle's government, which had already spent 1.2 million pesos in anticipation of the two million it had expected on July 1, attempted to negotiate a loan with other London bankers and put through a bill increasing the duties on imported beer, wine, and whiskey. Batlle still refused to retrench. Negotiations to buy a merchant ship (the Senate majority had removed this from the Ethelburga loan), to be paid for with treasury notes, were close to completion. On July 9 the Chamber approved a three-year extension of the 300-peso monthly subsidy for scholarships for 50 students at the music conservatory.[2]

On July 14 the Chamber took up a bill Batlle had sent during Ana Amalia's illness. Article 1 provided: "In all the territory of the Republic boxing, simulated bullfights, pigeon shoots, cock fights, rat pit, and any other game or entertainment which would cause mortification for men or animals are prohibited," and Article 2 added: "Unjustified bad treatment of animals is also prohibited." The deputies, left to themselves, had forgotten about the bill but Don Pepe had not. He considered Viera an excellent person, but El Indio enjoyed bullfights, and Batlle wanted this bill approved before Viera took office. The Chamber passed it in a single session with only one change: boxing by individuals would be permitted, but not public bouts.[3] At that same session, Héctor Miranda, joined by three other Batllista deputies, formally introduced his bill to "Recognize that the women of the nation enjoy the same political rights that men enjoy."[4] Batlle included the bill, together with the eight-hour day, old age pensions, and paternity of illegitimate children, among bills to be considered in the legislative extraordinary sessions beginning in August.

II

A tremendous public demonstration pro Batlle-Viera and the Colegiado, with Uruguay's first use of movie cameras to record the event, was being planned for Viera's inauguration. Colorados were extolling the succession. Viera wrote a letter of appreciation to the authors of one such political pamphlet and released the letter on July 25:

> If I reach the Presidency, Batlle will be the most influential man of the political situation. This logical way of thinking must be clearly understood by honest men; and as for those who have expected or still expect felonies on my part, they will never weigh on my conscience. They would only be right if a cataclysm, which I do not expect, makes me lose my moral sense.[5]

Viera's open acknowledgment that Batlle would continue to head the Colorado Party infuriated anti-Colegialists and Nationalists. "The State is Don Pepe Batlle" was the Directorio newspaper's headline. Don Pepe, as usual, turned things around. The released letter was proof of Viera's "strong personality." What was the fuss about, was not Viera, now in Batlle's government, "the *most influential man of the political situation*"? "The man who proclaims in a loud voice that he accepts the influence of another does so because he feels strong enough to reject it when it becomes inconvenient or improper."[6]

Williman visited the Committee that was organizing the Viera inauguration the day Viera's letter was released, accepted a medal being distributed, and expressed confidence that Viera's administration would be honest, hardworking, and energetic.[7] Serrato was now President of the State Mortgage Bank, Acevedo had just been named by Batlle to the Board of the Bank of the Republic. Don Pepe did not expect these men to become propagandists for the Colegiado, but once constitutional reform was completed and they had saved their principles, he expected them to serve on the Colegiado.

III

July 31 was a Friday. News that Germany had sent an ultimatum to Russia produced considerable uneasiness in Montevideo and some withdrawals of funds from the banks. On August 1, Germany declared war on Russia, France mobilized, and England prepared to back France. Since it was Saturday, the banks were closed, but Finance Minister Cosio feared war-panic bank runs if banks opened on Monday. He consulted his mentor, Serrato, now President of the State Mortgage Bank, and Luis Supervielle, President of the State

Insurance Bank, and requested them to ask the private bank managers if they would support closing all banks and the stock exchange for a week while he prepared legislation to suspend gold conversion of Bank of the Republic paper money. Cosio, rather than call a meeting of the Bank of the Republic's board, polled the directors individually. The majority, fearful for the Bank's reputation and confident that they had enough gold to withstand another run, wanted to open on Monday. The private bank managers, especially the foreign branch managers who had been sending gold abroad on the order of head offices and were now operating with minimal reserves, were worried that they could not cover heavy withdrawals and welcomed closing and inconversion.

At 7 P.M. on Saturday Serrato advised Cosio that the private bank managers supported his proposal. At 8 P.M. Cosio telephoned Piedras Blancas and arrived there at 10:00. He explained to Batlle that he feared a "ruinous" bank run and proposed invoking the Constitution's "internal commotion" clause, previously used only during revolutions, to legalize the closings and inconvertibility. Don Pepe readily agreed to the closings but worried about paper money inconvertibility. His father's Presidency, he reminded Cosio, had suffered "grave difficulties because of inconvertibility." Don Pepe had been a young teenager during his father's disastrous presidency, and one of the strongest sources of his personal drive was to redeem his father's failures by his own successes. Cosio assured Don Pepe that this inconvertibility plan would prevent panic and keep paper money from depreciating; the traditional 40 percent gold backing would be retained, and to calm the public further, a limit to the amount of paper money [banknotes] in circulation could be established in the law.[8]

On Sunday Batlle brought the entire cabinet to Piedras Blancas. Cosio explained his plan; the message and decree closing the banks was signed by the President and each Minister. On Monday at 10:55 A.M., a little more than an hour before the banks were to open, the Chamber and Senate meeting jointly as General Assembly considered the decree, as required by the Constitution. Germany had just declared war on France and was invading Belgium. The legislators were stunned; the world of which Uruguay was such a powerless part was coming apart and Uruguay could be ruined economically without the Great Powers even being aware of it.

The Executive's message explained that the principal governments of Europe had declared a moratorium on payments for a month; European credit operations had ceased as had gold shipments. This had produced alarm in Montevideo's "banking and commercial environment" foreshadowing "the precipitant withdrawal of deposits from the private banks," which could create a panic of unmanageable proportions. To prevent this the Executive was ordering all banks and the Stock Exchange closed until August 8 and during that "truce to calm the spirit" would present a bill which would guarantee the stability of the banking system.

Areco immediately moved for acceptance. Martín C. Martínez doubted the legality of using the Constitution's "internal commotion" clause to justify closing banks, but his colleague, Juan Andrés Ramírez, *El Siglo's* editor, now officially a Nationalist, who had close ties to the bank managers, argued that urgency justified it. Gabriel Terra added that Cosio's solution, which was not in the textbooks, was being copied by Argentina and Brazil. The voice vote approving the decree was taken at 11:30 A.M. and the banks did not open. The bank managers met that afternoon, unanimously endorsed the government's measures, and assured it of their cooperation. In their considered judgment the war would not last more than two months.[9]

The next day, August 4, the day England entered the war, the Executive sent its banknote inconvertibility bill to the legislature. Bank of the Republic paper money could not be converted into gold for six months. This inconvertibility was very different, the message explained, from past *curso forzoso* (forced acceptance of paper currency) disasters. Then there was no gold; now there was gold and the purpose was to prevent panic-produced "disastrous dispersion" of gold. The 40 percent gold backing requirements would remain; the Bank charter's authorization to issue banknotes up to three times its effective capital, which enabled it to issue 36 million pesos, was reduced to a top of 26 million pesos; most important to business opinion, which usually feared inconvertible paper money as a means by which governments got around limitations on spending, the Government was authorized no additional drawing rights and, for the first time, the Bank of the Republic was authorized to rediscount private bank commercial paper.[10]

It was evident that in contrast with last year, when the gold crisis broke, this time the private banks, not the Bank of the Republic, were in trouble. (On July 31 the Bank of the Republic had 11,692,431 pesos in gold as reserves for 12,300,000 in deposits, and 16,200,000 in banknotes, while the private banks had half that gold, 5.7 million pesos, for approximately the same amount of liabilities, 28.9 million in deposits.)[11] It was common knowledge that some foreign branches had reserves so low that they could not meet any substantial withdrawals. José Irureta Goyena, the rural spokesman and attorney for the Banco Comercial, speaking for the private bankers, urged that foreign banks be accorded the same rediscount privileges as local banks. Serrato, invited by the Senate Committee, agreed. In the present critical situation, no bank, foreign or local, could be allowed to fail. Cosio's experience during the gold crisis had hardened him against foreign banks—in a book he wrote in 1920 he complained that foreign banks brought little capital with them and hoarded gold for shipment abroad. He now acceded to Irureta Goyena's request. On August 11 the banks and the Stock Exchange reopened without any runs or panic.

IV

Uruguay, though sympathetic with France, had declared its neutrality. England was blockading Germany, German submarines were attacking British shipping. The Royal Mail Steamship line, the principal shipper to southern South America, had suspended operations. How would Uruguayan meat, much in demand, reach its markets? Would European factories be shut down by the war and the wool and hides pile up unsold in Montevideo? Where would imports come from? Food prices, especially sugar, shot up. Since these supplies had been bought before the war, there were demands that the Government crack down on profiteers. The Bank of the Republic traditionally had its banknotes printed in Germany and was looking for an alternate source. Paper costs had risen; *El Día* was reduced to eight pages and the cost to vendors raised from a penny each to 12 cents for 10, but Batlle refused to allow its price to the public to be raised from the long-standing two cents. (*El Día* had been the first mass-oriented, street-sold newspaper in Uruguay.) *El Día* ran a notice: "*EL DÍA* is for the popular classes and it must reach their hands." Police had to disperse newsdealers trying to stop its sale.[13]

The war produced no perceptible influence on Batlle's control of politics. The opposition complained that the war had made Batlle's political machinations easier by preoccupying people with Europe and taking their minds off Uruguay.[14] For while Montevideo was tense with war concern, on August 23, at the formal request of sixteen delegates, the Colorado Convention convened to revise the Party Charter so that the internal government of the party at all levels would be by Colegiados. Viera, in person, accepted the Presidential nomination.

> If I become President of the Republic, distinguished delegates, I will not forget the basic reason why my Party has named me: to have assurance that the great reform, constitutional reform, will be accomplished. I do not forget, gentlemen, that my Party wants the Colegiado and that my Presidency is a means toward that end. I promise you that without violence, without pressures abhorrent to the liberal conduct of our Party, I will put all my personal influence at the service of that ideal. I will advise and ask friends and coreligionaries who are delegates to the Constitutional Convention to give our ideas life by substituting the Colegiado for the present form of Executive.
>
> The Colorado Party which has rallied around the present President . . . wants Batlle's work to continue; and I will not be the one to defraud such legitimate hopes.

The delegates demanded a speech from Arena and he improvised:

> I don't think Viera is another Batlle. If there were two Batlles in the country our administration would be less great and exclusive. . . . We will be satisfied if Viera makes us advance, even though step by step, along the many and wide roads Batlle has opened in our destiny. Above all, we will be satisfied if Viera supports us, encourages us, if he helps us achieve the Colegiado— that simple and democratic institution which is going to free the nation from the historic calvary in which presidentialism has always kept it.
>
> And if Viera, surpassing himself, accomplishes things as personal, as strong, as healthy as those Batlle has accomplished, better for Viera, better for us, better for the nation.

Cheers urged Arena on. Batlle's accomplishments and ideas led by the Colegiado would one day "bear fruit not only in Uruguay but in the soil of our fertile America . . . preparing in the New World, that future world without frontiers about which the great humanists dream!"

It is not strange, then, to believe sincerely that one day the nation will consider itself in debt to those who fought at Viera's side for the triumph and the spreading of the Batllista gospel.

For all its abhorrence of organized religion, the continuing cult of Batlle was taking on Christian symbolization, with Don Pepe in Christ's role. Arena's vision of Don Pepe's greatness was also being influenced by the destruction of Europe by the war. Civilization's center was moving to America, and Batlle's advanced Uruguay would be the model for America. Arena's immediate message, however, was that Viera was expected to follow Batlle, not strike out on his own.

On September 1 the Convention approved party reorganization. The party would be governed, from the clubs through the departments up to the National Commission, by committees of nine whose presidency would rotate every two or three months. Then came a surprise, an additional article to the charter proposed by Viera, Areco, Sosa, and eleven others, which was approved with cheers for Batlle, Viera, and the Colorado Party. In every party organization, from club to the National Executive Committee, where there were contested elections, the most voted list would get two thirds of the seats, the next most voted list, if it obtained one third the votes, would get one third of the seats. This, the election system for the Chamber of Deputies in its pure form, was explained by its sponsors as a means of permitting all Colorados "whatever the specific reasons which provoke their decision" to be represented in the party organization. The way was being prepared for the anti-Colegialists to come back home and still remain organized. [15]

V

The Germans had broken through Belgium and were heading toward Paris. The war, the most sanguine recognized, was not going to be over in another month. Bank credit remained tight, prices kept going up, building had just about stopped. Unemployment was high;

workers, fearful for their jobs, had ceased striking. There were only two strikes in 1914, compared with 41 in 1911, the first year of this administration, when unions held back by Williman felt safe with Batlle as President.[16] The refrigerated meat-packing plants had temporarily closed until transport could be assured.

Panic hit the interior when it was realized that with Germany occupying France and Belgium and England blockading Germany, Europe's factories, the market for Uruguay's wool and hides, might be unable to buy; over half this year's exports, 35 to 40 million pesos, wouldn't be sold. So far, cattle prices were excellent—the Allies needed meat—but every Uruguayan rancher, regardless of ranch size, grazed both sheep and cattle, and 1914's unusually heavy rains had produced devastating sheep mortality, up to 8 million head.[17] The wool clip would begin in October, and the inability to sell wool on top of the terrible loss of sheep would produce rural economic disaster.

Rural interests that had feared currency inconvertibility because they worried that Batlle would use it to pay for expanded government suddenly saw paper money as salvation. The Cámara Mercantil de Productos del País, the exporters' organization, after repeated meetings, voted to call upon the legislature to pass "a law that would authorize the Bank of the Republic to increase its banknote emission by 20 million pesos, to be used only to guarantee rural products, appraised at 50 percent of the export prices of these same products in the year 1913."[18] Ranchers or commission merchants would bring warehouse receipts to the Bank, which would advance them 50 percent of the value of the wool, hides, or other products warehoused, and these warehouse receipts would be the backing for the additional 20 million pesos. This would save the interior, put money into circulation, and create employment. The Asociación Rural endorsed the proposal, as did the Rural Congress then meeting.

Much of the political opposition to Batlle quickly espoused the warrants (paper money based on warehouse receipts).[19] Here was an issue which ranchers favored. That these dissident Colorado and Nationalist leaders had applauded Manini's denunciation of Batlle's turning Uruguay into an experiment station for novelties was forgotten in the prospect that leading the fight for wool-backed money could unite ranchers behind them against Batlle. Batlle was incensed:

Every time the Executive Power proposed passage of laws directed at the economic improvement of the most needy classes, these proposals were attacked in the name of absolute individualism. . . . To give the State intervention in the development of economic-social relations, was . . . to expose the nation to the disastrous consequences of inadmissible theories.

And now, when a moment of difficulty has arrived, they clamor for such measures, confessing that their adoption would ward off dangers of great, or not so great, magnitude.[20]

Don Pepe's point was that the wool was still on the sheep's back; the wealthiest sector in Uruguay was asking special consideration at a time when the government was attempting to keep the national economy from collapsing.

Imports had virtually ceased since the beginning of the war. Not only did this drop contribute to economic paralysis, but it produced an enormous decline in government revenues. To pay its obligations to December 31, the Executive asked legislative authorization to issue 3,500,000 in *Vales de Tesoro* (Treasury Notes). These treasury notes would be backed by specific taxes, sufficient to pay a high interest rate, 7 percent, and retire them within three years by amortizing a portion by lot at par every two months "so that they cannot depreciate and will be considered like a banknote." Public employees would be paid that part of their salary exceeding 150 pesos a month in these Vales, and Vales could be used to pay government bills. Included among the earmarked taxes was a new tax, expected to yield 300,000 pesos a year of .005 per kilo on meat exported by refrigerated packing plants.[21] Taxes on exports were traditionally considered economic errors and, since they were ultimately paid by ranchers, political dangers, but the message noted that "this tax, even assuming that the rancher ultimately pays it, comes when he is being offered very high prices for his livestock. In any event, it does not fall on the poor."

The message acknowledged unsettled economic conditions. It was absolutely impossible to transact business with Europe except in cash. But things could not go on like this. England, which had raised the interest rate to an unbelievable 10 percent, was lowering it to 5 percent and scheduling maritime shipping. The United States was buying meat. Europe was short of wool. Fears that wool and hides could not be sold would prove exaggerated. Legislation permitting warehouse receipts to be considered commercial paper upon which banks could lend money would be useful, and the Executive was including such a bill in this package. But commodity-backed money, as advocated by rural interests, was quite another matter. Since the world was on gold, attempts by individual countries to back money with anything else invariably failed.

This did not speak to ranchers' worries that they would not be able to sell their wool and that banks would not lend against warehouse receipts. The Executive also disappointed those who were calling for price controls. Batlle had much more sympathy for those forced to pay high prices for necessities than he did for schemes to supply money to ranchers who were selling livestock at record prices. Farmers' markets were opened in Montevideo, police stations were serving meals to the poor, there were plans to import low-priced bread from Buenos Aires, but none of these stopped the constantly rising prices, what the message called "the abuses of commerce." Nevertheless, the Executive limited itself to permitting municipalities to sell prime necessities to the public at cost. "The question of legislative limits on the price of goods has very serious economic consequences."

The hastily drawn package of bills had been sent on August 24. The Chamber Committee discovered that the *frigoríficos* (refrigerated meat-packing plants) enjoyed export tax exemptions and rewrote the law so that instead of the frigoríficos paying, "the tax will be paid by the seller of livestock," something even more unpalatable to ranchers. Within a week, however, the Committee had the bills on the Chamber floor.

Finance Minister Cosio spoke before anyone else could, warning that "local financial quackery" was intensifying the terrible uncertainty that paralyzed business. Credit, not money, was lacking, and credit was lacking because "anyone with something to lose" felt threatened by the schemes being floated.

Without pausing, Cosio speaking for Batlle, made the announcement that the Executive had been resisting since the gold crisis last year. The war, finally, had forced Batlle to accept retrenchment. The government was going to cut back. Sharply reduced import revenues required immediate budget cuts of 2,300,000 pesos. All public employees earning over 3,000 pesos a year would take a pay cut of 15 percent, starting with the President of the Republic, who, though on a fixed salary, would voluntarily reduce it by 15 percent. Only 300 functionaries were involved, and the savings of 50,000 pesos was more symbolic than important. No employees would be fired; instead, budgeted positions not now filled would be abolished. Each Ministry's budget had been scrutinized and cuts made, varying from 14,000 pesos in the War Ministry to 254,000 pesos in Finance (with the customs house inactive, few day laborers were needed). Since most of the cuts involved funds that might not have been spent, the real amount of budget cutting was less than the announced 2,300,000 pesos. The budget cut, Cosio announced, would permit issuance of an additional million pesos in Vales, to be used to hire the unemployed for road-building.

The Nationalists were delighted with Cosio's announcement, except that it didn't go far enough. Martín C. Martínez, always prudent, warned that the Executive had overestimated the yield of the inheritance and wine taxes, and that the proposed tax on livestock sold to frigoríficos was "extremely heavy." What was needed was a complete overhaul of the budget to produce more real and less illusory cuts. Herrera jumped in. Four fifths of Uruguay's financial troubles came from Batlle's stupidities. Who needed dramatic schools, fishing institutes, and the like? "Let them go fish somewhere else." Cosio countered that the government's proposals would meet financial needs until the end of the year. Things were too uncertain even for 1915 fiscal planning: "we depend exclusively on European solutions." But while debate went on, government finances worsened, and the Executive acceded to further cuts. Finally, on September 14, speaking for the Chamber Committee, Mora Magariños told his colleagues that in round numbers they had cut 2,700,000 pesos from the budget (about a 10 percent reduction from the prewar budget), and the budget cuts, new taxes, and Vales were sent to the Senate.[22]

The Senate was reluctant to tax livestock sold to the figoríficos for export. Cosio went to the Senate Committee, emphasized the desperate need for revenue[23] and the extremely high prices livestock were bringing, and worked out another compromise. A tax of .0025 per kilo on livestock going to frigoríficos[24] would be collected only if livestock sold for at least 10 cents a kilo. Instead of requiring the seller to pay, the bill stated: "This tax will be paid before the livestock leaves the yard," opening the possibility that ranchers could get the frigoríficos to absorb the tax.

Manini expressed opposition. The tax would hurt Uruguayan ranchers, unlike Argentine ranchers, who didn't pay any tax. Right now meat was Uruguay's only sure export and should not be tampered with. Cosio claimed that the tax would be paid by English consumers, that current prices were record prices, which was why he had accepted the minimum 10-cent-per-kilo selling price before the tax could be collected, "to cut the interminable discussions in committee, whose majority was hostile to the bill."

The Senate approved the tax on October 14; the Chamber Committee did not believe that the unheard-of price of 10 cents per kilo for livestock on the hoof could last. The government wanted authorization to increase the Vales de Tesoro in circulation to 6 million pesos. Without the livestock tax the additional Vales could not be amortized and might depreciate, creating more difficulties for the government and for public employees partially paid with Vales. The Senate had listened to ranchers' complaints, but the Chamber Committee "believes it would be unjust, that it would even be a demonstration of lack of national purpose, in the face of the most extremely exceptional circumstances, when the entire nation, even the most humble, is being asked to contribute so that the nation can get through these exceptional moments, that it should be those with the greatest ability to contribute who raise their voices opposing this tax."

The Nationalists called it a political double-cross. The Minister of Finance accepted a 10-cent-per-kilo minimum to get the bill approved by the Senate; his allies in the Chamber now required the tax to be collected regardless of the price ranchers receive. Gabriel Terra was unmoved: "Our principal tax, the import tax, is dropping enormously; we must tax wealth, and the only wealth which today brings a price is meat."

The Chamber's insistence on changing the Senate's bill brought the issue to the General Assembly (the Chamber and Senate meeting jointly), where even with the General Assembly's two-thirds majority requirement, the Chamber had enormous preponderance. Speaking for the Chamber, on October 15, Aragón y Etchert insisted that it disagreed with the Minister of Finance (who was not present). Speaking for the Senate, Martín Suárez—an anti-Colegialist—pictured the ranchers' difficulties. First there had been a drought, then too much rain with resultant heavy sheep mortality, capped now with a terrible shortage of money in the interior. Therefore, it would be only equitable to collect this tax when prices were exceptionally remunerative. The Chamber bill was then approved, and three days later the tax was being collected.[25]

VI

Batlle was being forced by the war to cut government spending, although Nationalists and anti-Colegialist Colorados complained that he wasn't cutting deeply enough. Nationalists and anti-Colegialist Colorados were the rancher's friends; they opposed export taxes on livestock and favored wool-backed money. Batlle rejected wool-backed money, put taxes on export livestock, and tried to keep his programs going despite revenue drops. Still, Batlle's opposition had yet to solve the problem of how to convert their support of ranchers' interests into votes.

CHAPTER 23 *Toward the Future*

The Senate majority, whose resistance to Batlle had stopped Constitutional reform and reordered Uruguay's politics, was altered by the election of six new Senators in November. The anti-Colegialist Colorados did not run any candidates. Only one Senator was elected in each department, and the anti-Colegialists, based on last year's vote, knew they couldn't win in any of the six departments. Nationalist politicians were a little more hopeful. The Directorio wanted to run everywhere but departmental Nationalist organizations could count and were reluctant to spend money and effort when they knew how many voters they had and how many the Colorados had. As the Salto organization explained, it was futile to contest these elections "given the numerical superiority of officialism . . . because there isn't even a minimal number of independent Colorados capable of intervening in the elections."[1] Only in two departments—Florida, where the rancher Gallinal was candidate, and Durazno, where Dr. Lussich, who had been Saravia's surgeon in the War of 1904, was running—were the chances of winning good enough to undertake a campaign. In the other four, the Colorado candidates were uncontested. In 1912 Batlle had made a tremendous mistake by running candidates he knew did not favor the Colegiado. This time every Colorado Senate candidate was a pledged Colegialist, and they were led by Areco, the Batllista specialist on moral legislation and Viera's closest friend, running uncontested in Viera's home department of Salto.

In part to excite Nationalist voters in the two departments, in part to disguise the party's electoral weakness, the Nationalist bloc in the Chamber mounted a furious campaign against government "scandals." On October 31, 1914, the paymaster of the Montevideo Customs House, who had been lending the Director and fellow employees money which he claimed was his own but which actually belonged to the Customs House, was caught short and fled the country. This "open sore on the sick body" of Batlle's government must be explained. Why, Nationalist Deputies demanded, had Batlle been so slow in moving against the paymaster, and why had he not fired the Director, Montevideo's largest deliverer of Colorado votes?[2]

The Nationalists kept up the "scandal" momentum. On November 24, five days before the Senate elections, Deputy Leonel Aguirre, son of the late Nationalist leader Martín Aguirre, moved that Interior Minister Viera be called to the Chamber to explain the contract for one million meters of asphalt paving in Montevideo. Legislation requiring the asphalting of Montevideo had been passed early in this administration, but Nationalists objected that the amount of asphalting was excessive. Buenos Aires had only 300,000 meters, Paris had 900,000; Montevideo already had 200,000 and was going for an additional million. Batlle liked the idea that Montevideo would have streets that were better paved than those of Paris. He wanted asphalting to modernize Montevideo and enable buses, which broke down on cobblestones, to keep running. Since the foreign-owned trolleys had to pay one third the cost of asphalting (benefiting property owners paid the other two thirds), the trolley companies were paying for the paving that would permit Uruguayan-owned buses to compete with them. Without financial pressure on the government, the contract would provide work for laborers, unemployed because of the economic paralysis produced by the European war. The Executive had contracted with an Uruguayan firm, in preference to a German firm that had submitted a lower bid. Nationalist Rodríguez Larreta complained that at 6.70 pesos a meter, "they are going to have to sell a quarter of Montevideo to pay for the asphalt." Nationalist Herrera interjected, "Property owners should resist."

Gabriel Terra answered for the Government that although the Uruguayan firm's bid was 6.70 pesos, to the German Neuchatel's 6.00 a meter, it was cheaper in the long run because it would use superior asphalt and maintain the pavement for twenty years. Buero, another

Colegialist, got to the heart of the matter. "Acquarone [the Uruguayan firm] is a local enterprise," which used mostly local materials. The era of "juicy foreign concessions" must end.

Young Nationalist Washington Beltrán responded. Now was not the time, what with the war's uncertainties, to burden property owners with the expense of asphalting. "I believe that the property owners of Montevideo should come together, form a property holders' league, and basing themselves on Article 41 of the Municipal Code, appear before the Courts of the nation to demand justice." So the Nationalists were not only the ranchers' friends, they were also friends of Montevideo property owners. Beltrán demanded that "the Minister of Interior candidate for President of the Republic . . . come to this Chamber and supply the information demanded by the people's representatives."

Terra, so useful to Batlle these days, reminded the Nationalists that he had opposed Batlle's election in 1910 and warned them against scandal mongering when there were no scandals. Were they remembering what had happened at the end of the administration of Don Pepe's father, Lorenzo Batlle? There were "barracks uprisings," "civil war, days of mourning and shame for our nation," provoked by false campaigns against a man of "high probity." The average property owner would pay only four or five pesos a month for five years. The ones really affected would be the foreign-owned, overly profitable trolley companies, obliged to pay 2 to 2.5 million pesos, long overdue. "It will be less money leaving the country."[3]

The Nationalists kept the debate on the asphalt "scandal" going all through the Senate election, which, on a small scale, was very successful for them. In Florida they got out 75 percent of their registered voters, in Durazno a startling 90 percent. The elections themselves, in the post-1904 pattern, were without incident; double the number of voters over last year's Chamber election voted. Uruguay was on the verge of mass elections. In Durazno, Nationalist Dr. Lussich, Saravia's surgeon, lost by 92 votes; in Florida the election was even closer, the Nationalists claiming victory for rancher Gallinal by 25 votes. The Colorados claimed that their man had won by 37 votes. The new Senate would decide whom to seat.[4]

The new Senate would have a Colegialist majority. Of the present eleven Senator majority, three whose terms were expiring would leave

and three would vote for Viera. The anti-Colegialists would be down
to five plus possibly one Nationalist out of nineteen Senators. Batlle,
now assured that the Senate would approve election of the Constitutional Convention, congratulated the nation in *El Día* on its "Election
day's work" while Bachini, who was giving up *Diario del Plata*, the
newspaper he had founded to rally Colorados against Batlle, was
bitter. His last editorial on "the uselessness of all free efforts in the face
of this voracious appropriation of the popular destinies" was echoed
by Juan Andrés Ramírez, who was leaving *El Siglo* to take over *Diario
del Plata*. Ramírez' farewell *El Siglo* editorial warned of the dangers
brought on "by the fatal perpetuation of a regime absolutely at odds
with national aspirations."[5] Revolution and army coups, not electoral
challenges, was the transparent message these two distinguished opponents of Batlle and the Colegiado were delivering.

II

By now the war in Europe had developed into a horrible stalemate
of indefinite duration, with thousands of men dying in trenches. But
Europe's stalemate was opening markets for Uruguay's exports at
sensational prices. The refrigerated packing plants were even buying
lean steers they previously had rejected. The Allies wanted wool for
winter uniforms, and the wool clip was being bought up. Fears that
wool would not be sold had evaporated, and with them demands for
wool-based money. Imports, though, continued to fall, and with them
government revenues.[6]

There was one potential source of government revenue that Don
Pepe had long been planning to tap—*tierras fiscales*, government lands
illegally occupied by private parties. Early in this administration the
Government had bought up outstanding *Títulos de Ubicar Tierras
Fiscales*, government certificates entitling the holder to claim Tierras
Fiscales, and the last extension on turning these títulos in had expired.
On December 3, immediately after the Senate elections, the Execu-
tive sent the legislature its long announced bill on tierras fiscales. The
Executive considered this bill of "transcendental importance" as a
means of producing "great revenues" for the State at a time when it
badly needed them. No one knew how much land was tierra fiscal.
Some authorities claimed as much as one fifth of the privately occupied lands were really tierras fiscales, which would mean lands

worth 130 million pesos, nearly five times the national budget, but many property owners had cleared their titles, and illegally occupied tierras fiscales were probably considerably less than one fifth of the nation's area.

In July the Chamber Committee had reported out a bill that considered lands occupied before 1830, the establishment of independent Uruguay, privately owned. *El Día* objected, explaining that the bulk of the tierras fiscales had been occupied between 1795 and 1830. Batlle's bill printed in full by *El Día* on December 8, 1914, went even further: there was no cut-off date. Illegally occupied tierras fiscales dating from the beginning of Spanish colonization belonged to the government.

> The prolongation for any additional time of territorial possession signifies nothing else but the indefinite gratuitous enjoyment of property belonging to the State, especially since these lands are usually left in their primitive state of natural pasture, and in the majority of the cases the State has not even received payment of the land taxes, taxes paid by those who own land legitimately.

Occupants could claim tierras fiscales within 60 days of the law's passage by paying the State 50 percent of the land's value. After that, third parties could "denounce" occupants of tierras fiscales and receive title by paying 70 percent of the land's value, or the State could take title by paying the denouncer 30 percent. The State could also denounce on its own, and the State could auction off reclaimed tierras fiscales.

The bill's goal was not to use reclaimed lands for agricultural colonization, although this was not prevented, but to use them for revenue. The bill acknowledged that it could not predict how much revenue would be produced, and suggested that the first priority be to "regularize the financial obligations of the State," and after that add to the capital of the Bank of the Republic and the State Mortgage Bank.[7]

Tierras fiscales were a legal morass, and Batlle's bill was much too sketchy. Claiming government rights to occupied tierras fiscales regardless of the date of occupancy was bound to infuriate ranchers who up to now had succeeded in preventing any legislation from reestablishing government ownership, to say nothing of such an extreme doctrine. The Chamber Committee would have to prepare a workable bill, and it would be Viera's administration before it could become law. But Viera had already announced that Batlle would be "the most influential man" during his administration, and Don Pepe was determined on tierras fiscales. Writing in *El Día*, he reminded the Chamber Committee:

> Restitution to the State of public lands unlawfully occupied by private individuals is one of the Executive's deepest preoccupations, since this transcendentally important matter fundamentally affects the vital interests of the nation.[8]

III

Don Pepe had pledged not to be on the Colegiado, and he intended never to run for public office again. Batlle would influence government from a place in the Colorado Party. Well before the Senate elections, the Colorado Party Executive Committee had been elected without contest. The last name on the list was José Batlle y Ordoñez. Under the new colegialist rules, the Committee's presidency rotated every two months but wherever he sat Don Pepe would be the center of power. (In a little noticed move, Batlle's eldest son, César, now thirty, was elected to the Montevideo Colorado organization. Don Pepe's father had been a Colorado virtually from the party's beginnings; his sons would carry on after him.)[9]

Don Pepe was very carefully naming people to run the government enterprises. For president of the newly nationalized Montevideo trolley line, the Tranvía del Norte, Batlle named Esteban Elena, former manager of the German-owned Montevideo Transatlántica trolleys. The rest of the board, though, were not trolley experts. The Vice President was José Romeu, whose embarrassment at investing in his niece's swindle had decided him in June 1913 to resign as Batlle's Foreign Minister. Four loyal Colorados and Héctor R. Gómez, ex-*El Día* editor, an anti-Colegialist close to Manini, made up the rest of the board. As president of the Electric Power System, Batlle named the brilliant young Uruguayan engineer Bautista Lasgoity. Lasgoity was a Nationalist, and Don Pepe ever afterward reminded critics of "moral influence"—that in naming Lasgoity he had put competence over party. Simultaneously, however, Batlle named as Treasurer of the Electric Power System a Colorado loyalist, Telémaco Braido, Jr.

A dinner honoring Braido was held, with tickets purchasable at Colorado headquarters. On that happy occasion Braido responded to well wishers with a speech:

Above all what has united us is that we all come from the ranks of Batllismo, which does not mean personal loyalty to a man but rather conscious solidarity with a regime, a regime which since it began back there around 1903, has initiated all the political advances, all the social progress, and all the economic conquests, with which the edifice of our national greatness stands out in the American world![10]

With the appointments of the expert, Lasgoity, and the politician Braido, Batlle perpetuated the system that was working so well. The experts ensured efficient operation of state enterprises, permitting their expansion; the politicians got out the vote, went along with Batlle's radicalism, and even, as Braido had just done, identified with it. Efficiency and political appointments were an unnatural partnership, but Batlle had managed it. As long as one-party government continued and elections produced very comfortable Colorado majorities, there was no need to exaggerate political patronage—Batlle and Williman had kept increase in government employment very low—and political appointees had to do a decent day's work if they expected to get ahead. If elections became very close and one-party government was replaced by some form of multiparty coparticipation the pressures to appoint excess public employees would become great, the ability to discipline public employees would weaken, and the unnatural partnership of efficiency and political appointments would become unmanageable. On the basis of the just held Senate elections and last year's Chamber elections, the unmanageability prospect was remote. The same political system that had won these elections should win the Colegiado elections. After that, Don Pepe had promised "the provision of [government] jobs . . . and promotions . . . would be determined by criteria of justice and public utility."[11]

IV

In mid-January, 1915 informants advised Batlle that the dissident Colorados, led by Bachini and Colonel Dubra (freed by civil justice and now in Buenos Aires) and the Nationalist military, were talking revolution.[12] That Bachini wanted a military coup was transparent. It was also obvious that intellectuals like Rodó and Juan Andrés Ramírez would rationalize it as the way of avoiding worse bloodshed, which would surely come later when Batlle and his radicalism were inevitably overcome.

Coup plots had not yet solidified, and this one did not, because the only hostile political group that army officers respected, the Manini-led anti-Colegialists, their companions in 1904 (virtually all army officers were Colorados, and soldiers usually wore red ribbons in their hats) were still legalists, and because Batlle, who had led the army in the War of 1904 and appointed most officers to their present commands, was always very careful to assure the army's loyalty.

The army had largely been spared from budget cutting and just recently had been further reorganized, adding four units while further reducing the size of all units. Even regiments would now be tiny, a maximum of 211 men, to be doubled in size during war. The Lilliputian size of units disturbed their officers, but more units meant more command posts, more promotions, more officers on active service, and fewer disgruntled officers. The new army would add 41 officers and have 305 fewer soldiers—an annual saving of 21,000 pesos. This was the first reduction in the army's authorized size since 1904. It would now have 9,300 soldiers led by 601 officers (and 10 bandmasters). The reduction was another demonstration that Batlle's concern about Nationalist revolution was diminishing. It also accentuated another concern of his: he had continually increased the number of army units so that it would be difficult for unit commanders to come together and plot a successful coup. The army would now have 45 units; it had come out of the War of 1904 with seventeen; in 1880, at the height of Uruguayan militarism, when army officers governed, the army had only seven units.[13]

V

Batlle had used the last months of his administration to build a platform for the Colegiado. His programs to tax land and not buildings, to recover tierras fiscales, and to provide railroad service below cost were revelations of the radical transformations he intended the Colegiado to accomplish. And he kept the tempo up to the very end of his government, usually a time when outgoing administrations relaxed. On January 21, only two months after receiving it, the Chamber opened debate on a controversial Batlle-Brum educational bill, making secondary education free and authorizing the Executive to end tuition in the University. Lost revenue would be replaced by doubling the property tax on property owners living abroad—already, heirs living abroad were to pay higher taxes, but now owners would pay double taxes, bringing to fruition an ideal Don Pepe had written Manini and Arena about from Europe in 1908. In *El Día* Batlle enthusiastically defended the new bill. "Young people of both sexes" who lacked funds but had talent should be educated. "Let the poor person, if he is born with talent, become a scholar, and the rich person, if he lacks it, let him plant potatoes." Don Pepe, echoing Henry George, went on to ask: "How many works of art are lost and how much the conquest of truth has lost because many people who were born with scientific or artistic potential did not receive the necessary education?"

> The thinking of the government is this: let all, without distinction of social class, receive the benefits of secondary education and let the most apt succeed, leaving for the less apt the less complicated and remunerative professions.[14]

Williman, who had done so much for primary education, feared the development of an intellectual proletariat and would have ended state-supported secondary education. Don Pepe had inaugurated liceos for every department, which now enrolled 1,250 students, and the Women's University, now attended by 225 girls, and encouraged public liceos in Montevideo, which now had 2,526 students. All told, students in public secondary and preparatory schools had doubled since 1903, and since public primary schools now taught 97,313 students, compared with 54,355 in 1903, secondary education, especially if encouraged, should expand very rapidly.[15] Batlle's and Williman's achievement was putting Uruguay well on the way toward ending illiteracy, and Batlle wanted education to go far beyond that.

The Batlle-Brum bill ended tuition for secondary school students—the seventh through the tenth grades. The Executive could end tuition for preparatory students—eleventh and twelfth grades—and university students when funds permitted. Secondary education came first "so as to raise the people's general culture." True, poor students could now ask that tuition, 32 to 44 pesos a year, be waived, but humiliating proof of indigency was required, and many nonindigent parents for whom fee payment meant "real privation" did not qualify.

Opposition centered less on ending fees—in a country moving toward mass elections the argument that primary and vocational education was all that workers needed was not easy to invoke openly—than on doubling the property tax for those living abroad. The Directorio newspaper protested that students would be saved 50,000 pesos in fees, while the tax brought in 500,000.[16] And Herrera on the Chamber floor shouted with his accustomed vehemence, "This bill . . . is not only directed against absent Uruguayans, basically, it tries to give a death blow to foreign capital . . . foreign capital has built up this country in large part."

Dr. Atilio Narancio, a Batllista with a future, spoke for the Chamber Committee. He admitted that foreign companies carrying on business in Uruguay, not just absent property owners, would be subject to the doubled tax, but only on real estate not used for the specific purposes of their tax concessions. True, Leibig's Meat Extract Company, an old preoccupation of Don Pepe's, would have to pay the doubled tax on the ranches it owned. Martín C. Martínez asked what would happen when tax concessions expired, as the Central Railroad's soon would. Narancio answered: "I believe that once the concession expires they will have to pay the double rate." The loss to foreign business would be the equivalent of only one-half percent in interest. Further, Narancio concluded, all the tax on absentee property holders would go to the University, not to general revenues.

When it came time to vote, a clause authorizing the abolition of tuition in the veterinary, agronomy, and normal schools, as well as the university, was added. Martínez tried to limit the tax increase to 50 percent. His motion was voted down. On January 30 tuition abolition and the doubled tax on absentee property owners was approved and sent on to the Senate.[17]

On February 14, with the newly elected Senators sworn in and the galleries packed with contingents from the Montevideo Colorado Clubs, Ricardo Areco, the Batllista closest to Viera, was elected Senate President. Four Senators voted for Manini; two were absent. *El Día* complained that the old Senate, even though it had important legislation before it, had met for a total of only 55 hours and 39 minutes during the past year.[18] The new Batllista Senate would be different.

VI

The political crisis provoked by Batlle's March 1913 Apuntes on the Colegiado was over; Viera would inherit a government with loyal majorities throughout. The gold crisis, whose causes were external to Uruguay and which culminated in the tremendous economic dislocations brought on by the beginning of the European War—of which the gold crisis was an early warning—was also over. Wartime European financing made it unnecessary or unprofitable to transfer to Europe working capital or assets invested in Uruguay. This had been signaled in November, when European holders of Uruguayan government bonds accepted Finance Minister Cosio's proposal that bond amortization be suspended. Uruguayan Consolidated Bonds were selling at 67 in London; holders preferred to keep them rather than have them amortized at market value.[19] Foreign subsidiaries and branch banks in Uruguay had probably reduced their working capital to minimal levels, as shown by the foreign branch banks' gold squeeze at the war's outbreak.

Capital repatriation from Uruguay to Europe, which had reduced Uruguay's gold supply, had stopped.[20] Even better, the war was proving to be an unbelievable bonanza for Uruguay's exports. Astronomical steer prices were joined by tremendous wool prices.[21] Uruguay was now able to pay for imports, but war restrictions on European exports made Uruguayan imports scarce. The result was the absolute reverse of the 1913–14 gold crisis: now gold for Uruguay was piling up in Europe. The European powers had forbidden gold export. To solve this problem, in February 1915 legislation was approved to count gold deposited in Uruguayan embassies abroad as part of the Bank of the Republic gold holdings, which in 1915 reached record levels (21.7 million pesos compared with 19.1 in 1909), a record that was eclipsed each year the war continued.[22]

With hindsight, Batlle's government had made two great blunders in monetary management. The first was Serrato's decision in 1912 to postpone massive borrowing abroad, which meant that Uruguay began the 1913 gold crisis with low gold holdings. The second was the Bank of the Republic's decision in 1913 to suspend credit in order to protect its remaining gold. The result was an unnecessarily brutal economic downturn. Using imports as a rule-of-thumb index, by 1914 there was an almost 25 percent drop in economic activity, compared with 1912.[23] While there were no estimates of unemployment and real wages for the period, the virtual cessation of strikes showed that these were hard times for workers. Using marriages as a surrogate index of Uruguayan well being, the negative effect of the 1913–14 economic downturn is striking. The marriage rate had risen from 4.77 marriages per 1,000 population in 1903 to 6.28 per 1,000 in 1912, a 32 percent increase in only nine years, but marriages dropped to 5.85 per 1,000 in 1913, and continued on down in 1914.[24]

Had Serrato realized in 1912 that a major European loan would be impossible in 1913, he would have negotiated one immediately; had the Board of the Bank of the Republic realized in mid-1913 that within a year and a half Uruguay would have abundant gold but imports would be in short supply, it would have kept business lines of credit open. Open credit meant maintenance of high import levels. Since raw materials and machinery were an increasingly large part of Uruguay's imports, maximum importation would have expanded the country's productive capacity and its ability to respond to the wartime economic situation.

Viera's government would inherit an improved but still perplexing economic situation. No one could predict how long the war would continue, or what the postwar international economy would be, even though most commentators anticipated it would be like the pre-gold crisis years. But as long as the war continued, exports would continue to sell at record prices, and imports would be very tight. With gold abundant, money and credit would expand. Uruguayan industries, protected by war shortages from foreign competition, could produce to the maximum of their capacity and were even beginning to export cloth and shoes to France. The problem would be to import raw materials and machinery in order to expand production enough to meet demand. A situation was emerging that was salubrious to Batlle. But government revenues, with taxes on imports still the principal source, would remain low. Finance Minister Cosio, whom Viera was going to keep on, predicted a 2-million-peso budget deficit for 1914, even after new taxes on cigarettes and drinking alcohol had been collected.[25]

For Martín C. Martínez and Manini the answer was to reduce government activities; after all, during a war boom the economy needed no government stimulus. But Don Pepe wanted to transform Uruguay, and many of his projects were in states of suspension. Some, like the state railroads, required imported equipment that might not be available, but others, like the agronomy stations, did not. Rather than cross arms until the war was over, Batlle wanted to take advantage of the war's opportunities.[26] The obvious source of revenue was exports but heavy taxes on steers and wool would infuriate ranchers. Quick action on tierras fiscales was another source of revenue, as well as raising land and inheritance taxes, but all these were tremendously controversial. Viera,[27] and Uruguayans in general, would have to confront Batlle's insistence on pushing them, on transforming the economy, on making Uruguay a model country. Challenging Batlle's vision was the slow but sure policy advocated by Martín C. Martínez among the Nationalists and by Manini leading the anti-Colegialist Colorados. For them Uruguay was a small country in an uncertain world, and the fewer risks it took, the fewer mistakes it would make. Close to but different from the advocates of slow but sure, and equally opposed to Batlle, Luis Alberto de Herrera had a different view. His Nationalist credentials were impeccable, and like Batlle he put all his time into politics. The Directorio considered him a useful crowd-rouser but too irresponsible to be a party leader. Herrera, in turn, considered the Directorio too stodgy to compete with Batlle in elections. He proclaimed himself a supporter of foreign capital, a Conservative, the ranchers' friend, the property owners' friend—and he didn't stop there. At the level of doctrine he argued that government must fit the "exigencies of local society"; at the level of action he said, "Let them go fish somewhere else." Don Pepe was pushing Uruguayans, frightening them with his rain of projects. Herrera raised no such frustrating standard. Instead, he advocated giving Uruguayans what they wanted, something much more electorally appealing than the Manini-Martín C. Martínez scrupulousness about what was prudent for government to do.

VII

Don Pepe kept pushing. To encourage agriculture he had just set up a school to train vegetable and poultry farm foremen; one of Acevedo's

29. Batlle, 1915, meditating under a favorite tree at Piedras Blancas.

agricultural colonization projects, a loan fund of 500,000 pesos, had the defect that it could only be used to purchase land. Batlle put through a bill authorizing use of some of these funds to buy equipment. On February 6, 1915 a bill freeing new industries from taxation went to the legislature. Another, "declaring the 12th of October, the discovery of America, a national holiday and removing Corpus Christi as a legal holiday," had already been received.[28] The "asphalt scandal" was settled by awarding a contract for the German firm to asphalt 50,000 meters (the Uruguayan firm would do one million meters), in exchange for which the Germans agreed to end all legal complaints against the State.

Don Pepe still had to settle with Juan Andrés Ramírez. In July 1911 Ramírez had challenged Batlle to a duel. Duels were illegal. Batlle as President of the Republic, refused, stated that Ramírez knew he would refuse—there had been a similar incident with the firebrand Herrera during Batlle's first presidency—and ridiculed Ramírez for cheap dramatics. In 1913 during the polemic over José Pedro Ramírez, Batlle announced that he would be available for duels once his presidency ended. On February 21, 1915, one week before the end of Batlle's presidency, Police Chief Sampognaro resigned for "personal reasons." On February 22 Batlle named him and General Dufrechou, who had been in charge of Batlle's personal security, as seconds and sent them with a letter to Juan Andrés Ramírez.

> I beg you to demand in my name from doctor Juan Andrés Ramírez a complete retraction of the offenses he has inflicted on me in the press during the last four years, or in its absence, settlement by arms.

Ramírez pondered Don Pepe's challenge for a day and then rejected it. If dueling was illegal three years ago, it still was today. How could Batlle, who had then threatened Ramírez' seconds with arrest, now "after becoming expert in the use of arms through practice during that long period," have the audacity to challenge him?

> These antecedents would justify my refusing any relationship of honor, now or ever, with someone who proceeds in this fashion, but I do not want to go to that extreme and limit myself to advising you that after the First of March if don José Batlle y Ordoñez wants

to have a duel with me he will have it, just as soon as he allows himself to put upon my personal dignity in the slightest way.

Don Pepe had not forgotten that in 1911 Ramírez tried to make him appear a coward. He had waited three years, practiced, and offered Ramírez a real duel, with potential for death, not a formality. Rumor had it that Batlle would have given Ramírez a choice of weapons. Police Chief Sampognaro, resignation withdrawn, was back on the job. Once Viera was President, he would order Sampognaro to stop any Batlle-Ramírez duel, the way Batlle had once stopped a Williman-Bachini duel. But in the last days of Batlle's presidency, with "resigned" Police Chief Sampognaro as a second, nobody could have stopped the duel. To get at Ramírez, Don Pepe had overcome his legalistic and anti-dueling scruples. (Until he challenged Ramírez, he had accepted challenges but had not challenged.)[29]

Misia Matilde, Don Pepe's wife, put Ramírez' letter rejecting the duel in a notebook which had belonged to their dead daughter. She wrote: "My dear Ana, I am putting the letter from Ramírez in your notebook, because I know what it would have meant to you to see the triumph of your father over that miserable man."[30]

VIII

Batlle's last days in office were those usual for the end of a presidential term. Batlle even appeared at the traditional reception for the diplomatic corps and received the customary album offered by business and commerce to outgoing presidents.[31] Despite efforts by the album's organizers, however, there were only 500 signatures, and none of the big business names were there.

The Nationalist legislators had announced that they would not take part in Viera's election, but that was an expected political gesture.[32] On February 27 Batlle received a real disappointment: Manini and four other Senators announced that they, too, would not vote for Viera or participate in his election:

It is not our intention to imply any offense with this attitude. On the contrary we would expect Dr. Viera to be inspired by the highest national and party interests and to recognize that the present political problems are intimately related in their effects to the economic and financial situation of the nation, which requires all the attention of the branches of government.[33]

In 1913 Manini had argued that public opinion was not ready for constitutional reform; now he argued that wartime economic conditions required its postponement. He no longer was in a position to hold back the reform, but he still opposed the Colegiado. Manini was confirming that the anti-Colegialists would not come home, they would run their own states of delegates for the constitutional convention. In 1911 Manini had favored Viera as Batlle's successor in 1915, with himself in line for 1919. Now, he would not even vote for *El Indio*.

Two days later Batlle would put the Presidential Sash over Viera's shoulders, and the two would step out on the balcony of Government House to review the largest political demonstration ever held in Uruguay; the Committee pro-Viera had been working on it for months. The column would be led by the Colorado legislators who had just elected Viera. Trains were bringing Colorados from the interior to join the Montevideo contingents. Additional film and more movie cameras had been brought from Buenos Aires, so that the demonstration could be seen forever after. Medals, thirty thousand of them, would be handed out to the demonstrators. One side carried Batlle's bust, the other Viera's. Viera was looking toward the right, Batlle toward the left.

APPRAISALS: III

When Batlle put the Presidential Sash over Viera's shoulders on March 1, 1915, it looked as though Don Pepe had assured the coming of the Colegiado. Instead, in an enormous surprise, when the secret ballots cast in the July 30, 1916, election of delegates to the Constitutional Convention were counted, the Nationalist and anti-Colegialist Colorado vote exceeded the Colorado Colegialist vote. The era of strong one-party government had ended and the era of putting together governing majorities through the politics of consensus had begun. Batlle salvaged a mixed Presidential-Colegialist government out of the new Constitution, which went into effect in 1919, organized the Batllista Party as a separate party within the Colorado Party and, still Uruguay's central public figure, then fully revealed and kept pushing his programs to make Uruguay the model country, right up to his death in 1929. After his death the Batllista Party and outlook remained the spinal column of Uruguayan politics and life, certainly until the 1960's, and subterraneously, perhaps, to this day. But the post-1916 era of consensus was hostile to audacity, and in the great anomaly of Uruguayan history, Batlle's second administration, which he had seen as the completion of a platform from which future new waves of projects would be launched, is instead considered to be the peak of Uruguayan governmental radicalism.

I intend to write about the period 1915 to 1929 in the future. For now, the very fact that the Batllista Party never won an absolute electoral majority and that Batlle, to his death, had to engage in complex electoral arrangements with other Colorado factions to forestall, by ever smaller margins, Nationalist electoral victories, should give pause to the standard explanations of Batlle's success. If Batlle was supported by the middle class, the working class, and, as a recent scholarly argument claims, the political elite—that is, the majority of the electorate and their political leadership—the failure of the Colegiado in 1916 and the subsequent Batllista disappointment would be close to inexplicable.[1] But if we look at the situation closely, by the end of Batlle's second presidency it is evident that no such class and elite support for him existed.

In spite of the still widely accepted statement that "by the time that Batlle had completed his second term in 1915 the middle sectors had firmly established their political predominance,"[2] there was, during this administration and in the 1913 and 1914 elections, virtually no mention of an Uruguayan middle class, classes, or sectors. Batlle himself, so far as I know, never referred to an Uruguayan middle class at any time during this government. Public men did make rare references to an Uruguayan middle class. During the last year of Batlle's government Gabriel Terra spoke of "the middle class of my country, made up largely of public employees" on the floor of the Chamber of Deputies, and no one challenged this restrictive definition.[3] It is reasonable to conclude that if a survey had been taken in 1915, heads of families, except for public employees, would have been as puzzled by the question "Are you a member of the middle class?" as they would have been in 1910.

This lack of reference to a middle class is very significant. At the theoretical level self-identification or class consciousness is an important element in political affiliation. At the practical level, in post World War II Uruguay, electoral appeals to the middle class and praise for its virtues were a political staple. The absence of such appeals and praise during Batlle's second administration argues for the absence of middle-class based politics.

It is nevertheless conceivable that Batlle tailored his programs to fit the aspirations of those who, because of their occupations, were, so to speak, middle class without knowing it. It can be argued that the principal beneficiaries of the end of tuition in secondary schools and university education were members of the middle class. The message accompanying the bill ending tuition, written and countersigned by Brum but approved and signed by Batlle, emphasized the benefits to the indigent but acknowledged that some who were not legally indigent, "modest employees and small industrialists," would also benefit. There is, here, the embryonic concept of a lower middle class. Yet Don Pepe himself, when defending the bill in *El Día*, saw an Uruguay where "all, without distinction of social class," received advanced education, and the talented poor became scholars while the untalented rich planted potatoes.[4] Batlle was identifying himself with the poor, not with a middle class.

Batlle's industrial protectionism is usually cited as evidence of his allegiance to the middle class. Across the river in Argentina, however, protectionism was weak, and this antiprotectionism has been attributed to a middle class similar to the Uruguayan.[5] In this case and similar ones, a policy is cited as evidence of the existence of a class, though the class is defined to fit the policy. But even the most tortured definition of a middle class would probably accept the premise that family and property are central to middle class values. Yet Batlle was moving to alter the family and weaken property. Divorce at the request of either spouse; high inheritance taxes; rights, including inheritance, for illegitimate children; taxes on land, not improvements; preparations for heavy land taxes based on the principle that the State, representing society, is the only legitimate owner of land— all demonstrate that just as the evidence of politics argues against a Batlle based in the middle class, so does the bulk of the evidence of government policy.

There was one Uruguayan social class, recognized by Batlle, by Uruguayan politicians, and by themselves, to which Batlle was appealing by the end of his administration. They were the workers. This was in sharp contrast to his attitude at the time of his reelection, when the directors of his campaign kept labor issues out and when the Anarchist-led Federación Obrera called on workers not to vote. Batlle's return to government opened the way for a sharp increase in the number of strikes, most notably the General Strike of 1911, and strikers benefited from Batlle's benevolent neutrality. But Anarchist misuse of strikes, which resulted in the workers losing strikes, combined with unemployment coming from the gold crisis and the outbreak of World War I, made workers fearful of striking, weakened unions, and resulted in Federación Obrera's suspending operations. Workers' class consciousness, shown by the General Strike, had risen during Batlle's administration; Anarchist leadership, which called on workers not to vote, had sharply weakened; workers were not voting Socialist. Batlle began the "Those who would be Socialists elsewhere should be Colorados in Uruguay" campaign, designed to bring in new voters, a campaign whose success would be determined in future elections.

Batlle did not sponsor union legislation. In the Uruguayan climate of suspicion that unions were foreign-led revolutionary cells, those who proposed to legalize unions intended to restrict union activities by setting up obligations for leaders and members. Batlle gave no support to such legislation, and none passed. Nor did Batlle try to replace Anarchist union leaders with Colorados or to set up Colorado sponsored unions. Unions were too weak, hostility to them was too great. To set up Colorado unions would play into anti-Colegialist "Are we Colorados or are we Socialists?" hands. Instead, Batlle's legislation was directed at the whole working class, only a small part of which was unionized, and he pushed measures, especially the eight-hour day and old age pensions, that would benefit all workers, not just the unionized minority. But Batlle never emphasized the appeal to workers over the appeal to Colorados. Indeed, in the worrisome 1913 elections, appeals to workers were deemphasized, because workers were a future rather than a present source of support.

So the widely accepted view that Batlle's political support came from a dynamic middle class in coalition with a militant working class diminishes, on investigation, to the potential for future workers' votes. Nor is a recent corollary to the middle class–working class argument persuasive. This position claims that Batlle's programs responded to a political elite which believed in economic nationalism, wanted social justice, and had tremendous self-assurance. The elite's outlook is summed up in the phrase "We could do anything."[6] The corollary is not yet fleshed out with evidence, and a composite biography of the Uruguayan political elite during Batlle's reelection and second presidency surely is needed.[7] What can now be said with considerable confidence is that the bulk of the political elite was increasingly fearful at the direction of Batlle's policies. Most political leaders were lawyers, and the two surveys of the opinions of lawyers taken during this government, on divorce at the request of either spouse, and on the Colegiado, showed that lawyers were massively opposed to Batlle. The breakaway of the eleven Senators, the cabinet resignations, and Don Pepe's forcing of a new political replacement generation all confirm the political elite's increasing fear. Though in 1907 Batlle himself wrote, "We can accomplish miracles," this sentiment was not representative of the political elite. Juan Andrés Ramírez' horror at the insurance monopoly, Rodó's opposition to the eight-hour day, Manini's "slow but sure" are much more authentic expressions of the Uruguayan political elite's outlook than "We could do anything."

The political elite's increasing fear of Batlle's radicalism paralleled that of business and ranchers. In contrast with unions, business and ranchers were well organized. The Rural Association's opposition to

Williman's bill that would have doubled the land tax on ranches which had no agriculture was sufficient to prevent that measure from even being debated by the legislature. The Peace League, quickly organized in 1910 to oppose Nationalist revolution, had the support of the Rural Association, the Stock Exchange, the Chamber of Commerce, and the Center of Retail Shopkeepers. Business and ranchers were appealed to with the "Batlle is better than war" campaign. To ranchers, "the Correspondent" reported, "Batlle does not recognize the existence of an agrarian problem which calls urgently for government attention," and business was assured by "the Correspondent" that Batlle "recognized . . . that the labor problem in our country does not have the same character or the same gravity it has in European countries."

The expectations raised by the "mature Batlle" campaign image were destroyed by Batlle once in power. The same business organizations that had supported the Peace League opposed the State insurance monopoly and the eight-hour day. By 1915 business wariness of Batlle had turned into opposition to Batlle. No major business firm, as noted, was willing to sign for Batlle the traditional album given to outgoing Presidents. The threat Batlle posed to ranchers, prosperous and well organized in 1915 as they had been under Williman, had materialized in overt action. Batlle was pushing ranchers; he had programs to force the intensive use of land, to raise inheritance taxes, to recover privately occupied tierras fiscales. When World War I began, Batlle rejected ranchers' demands for wool-based money; instead, his government instituted a tax on livestock sold to refrigerated packing plants for export. Ranchers were even more prosperous in 1915 than during Batlle's reelection campaign, business was still suffering from the gold crisis and the economic dislocation brought on by the outbreak of World War I, but the most striking change between Batlle's reelection campaign and the end of his administration was in businessmen's and ranchers' perception of the danger Batlle presented to them. By 1915 "the Correspondent's" reassurances could no longer be invoked.[8] In 1916, during Viera's administration, ranchers organized the Federación Rural to oppose the Colegiado.

A sociopolitical structure far different from the one conventionally postulated has been described here: minimal evidence of middle class politics, a weak labor movement, a political elite adhering to "slow but sure," well off and well organized business and ranching interests, yet government policies of economic transformation, reduction of foreign economic influence, expansion of the State's role, provision of a decent minimum of life for all. It should be obvious that explanations of such policies based on discerning class coalitions favorable to them must be flawed, even if the dominant consensus in writing on Latin America is that the discerning of such coalitions is the principal task of political history. And the most obvious flaw is that there is no place in such analysis or explanation for Batlle as a political leader using the Colorado organization and tradition to bring about the model country.

Yet what would have happened in Uruguay had the mine designed to assassinate Batlle during the War of 1904 gone off under his coach instead of exploding immediately ahead of it? The most likely result would have been the continuation for the foreseeable future of the Colorado-Blanco armed rivalry and political instability that held back the economy. And if, somehow, this instability could have been resolved, the best possible result would have been a government like Williman's, honest, well-intentioned, and devoted to "slow but sure."

In 1905, Serrato foresaw a future in which the "governing classes" of Uruguay would be middle class, but in 1910 Serrato assured Batlle he would be reelected by "the great majority of the country based on the Colorado Party," and Batlle's 1913 offer of the Presidency of the Republic to Serrato had one important proviso, Serrato must keep his hands off the Colorado Party. Socialist Frugoni, looking back later on Batlle's second presidency, criticized Batlle for not abolishing the traditional parties then and setting up a class-based party.[9] Frugoni's view, one that makes sense to later analysts who assume that strong class-based support for Batlle's programs existed, would have been considered ridiculous by Batlle. The Colorado Party was his father's party, it was his wife's father's party, it would be his sons' party. But beyond that it was his power base in an Uruguayan society close to overwhelmed by his transformation program. And the Colegiado, which seems like Batlle's aberration to those who consider him the leader of a class coalition, was his means, through the Colorado Party, of keeping Uruguay on the track toward the model country in the absence of strong class support for his programs.[10]

II

In the good, democratic time of *Uruguay feliz* (happy Uruguay), the years immediately after World War II when the country had high levels of employment and a cosmopolitan life style without Cold War tensions, Batllistas claimed that modern Uruguay was *obra de Batlle*, Batlle's doing. When the high prices for Uruguayan wool which were the basis of those good days ended after the Korean War and the country could not adjust to the resulting unfavorable economic situation, a new view of Batlle—who had died in 1929—emerged. He was responsible for Uruguayans' preference for the "easy life," their inability to produce as much as they consumed. The most subtle of this 1960's school of explanation was Carlos Real de Azúa's *The Impetus and Its Brake*. While blaming Batlle for what came later, he acknowledged Batlle's "imposing" accomplishments. Since Real de Azúa specifically ruled out the possibility that Batlle's programs "merited a more complete reception" the book really could not explain why the impetus was braked. If Batlle represented "the immanent tendencies" of Uruguayan society, especially its middle class, why did this society not continue his reforms? Why did it instead shift to consumption?[11]

Uruguay's foundering continued; economic stagnation and hyperinflation produced political cynicism and urban guerrillas. The process culminated in the 1973 military coup, which put down politics but has not ended economic stagnation. In these circumstances, new views of Batlle are starting to emerge. If Uruguay is now in such disastrous condition, Batlle could really not have accomplished as much as earlier generations believed. José Pedro Barrán and Benjamín Nahum are beginning to downplay Batlle's accomplishments—in some ways they are the reverse of the obra de Batlle school, which gave him credit for all of Uruguay's successes. They still see Batlle as based in the middle and working class, but it is a conservative instead of a progressive middle class, and a timid instead of militant working class. The logic of their approach makes them conclude that "the innovating enthusiasm of Batllismo" had been braked by 1913[12] when, in fact, Batlle continued to build the platform for the Colegiado and by the end of his presidency in 1915 was perceived by Uruguayans to be more radical than they had realized when he was elected in 1911. In sum, Real de Azúa couldn't explain the brake; Barrán and

Nahum are forced to do violence to the actual historical situation and postulate a tamed Batlle.

One conclusion coming out of this review of the most important explanations of Batlle since the 1960's is that historians who base their analyses on the predominance of new classes have great difficulty explaining political change after these classes predominate. A more obvious conclusion is the perennial one, that changed present circumstances make historians reevaluate past eras. It is predictable that when Uruguay emerges from its present military control and economic stagnation, new views of Batlle will also emerge.

My focus has been on Batlle in the context of his reelection and presidency, but some discussion of later implications is in order. Even without the benefit of hindsight, it is true that after 1904 Blanco ranchers, who now owned valuable livestock and land, were decreasingly willing to go as far as revolution, and without them revolution could not succeed. Contemporaries, nevertheless, who had seen Saravia disprove this assertion in '97 and '04, believed otherwise. Even Don Pepe, who belittled the likelihood of revolution, did so to prevent concessions to or appeasement of the Nationalists. The continued expansion of the government army until 1914 shows that Nationalist revolution was preceived as a continuing threat. And the growth of the army and its budget brought a new threat, a threat Batlle was constantly alert to—a threat combined with assassination and kidnapping—the threat of an army coup. Had a coup occurred, the Nationalists would have joined it, the political elite would have justified it as necessary to prevent worse bloodshed in the future, and the kind of electoral democracy that Uruguay developed and that, after World War II, withstood twenty years of economic crisis until 1973, would have been sidetracked.

Few would still proclaim that electoral democracy is an inevitable result of economic progress, and in the Uruguayan process of strengthening electoral democracy the struggle between Batlle and the eleven Senators led by Manini played a key role. Batlle's colossal political error, his failure to assure their support of constitutional reform when he handpicked six Senate candidates in 1912, permitted Manini to organize an anti-Colegialist Senate majority. Had the Senate bloc not been formed, Constitutional reform would have come in 1914, and with the Nationalists abstaining, Batlle's original Colegiado would have governed Uruguay. Batlle had confidence that when Uruguayans experienced the benefits of the Colegiado, they would enthusiastically support it. Batlle's plans for Uruguay's economic transformation would have coincided, once the post-World War I world economy recovered, with the prosperous 1920's. This is the Batllista scenario. Alternatively, it can be argued that since Batlle's programs lacked strong class support, the Colorado Party would have split over them, even under Batlle's original Colegiado. Since proportional representation was part of the Colegiado package, the split would have required negotiations for the construction of legislative majorities and Nationalist cooperation in government, the same sort of consensus politics that hamstrung reform after 1916.

Whatever the potential outcomes, the 1913 Colorado split brought the Nationalists back to the ballot boxes that year; the revolutionary road had been blocked, the electoral road, even with Batlle's "moral influence" on public employees, was promising. And this was Manini's hour. He, who had good support among army officers, believed in elections and rejected coup insinuations. Batlle, in turn, rejected any plan to muzzle the eleven Senators. By rejecting or closing the alternatives to elections, Batlle and Manini moved along the cumulative process of Uruguayan electoral democracy.[13]

For Batlle's opponents, their victory over him in 1916 opened the era of true electoral democracy. From the vantage point of our times, Uruguay paid a great price when it thereafter preferred government by consensus and suspended Batlle's economic transformation program. Batlle's plans for intensive use of land so that more livestock could be pastured and agriculture developed, his goals of expanded industry, of new industries like fishing, his programs for new ports and railroads—all of them pushed Uruguayans too hard. Batlle combined the twin goals of economic transformation and a decent minimum life for everyone. A decent minimum was politically popular; economic transformation was not. Instead, the politics of consensus combined the slogan "Let them go fish elsewhere," i.e., leave ranchers and businessmen alone, with the promise of a decent minimum.

To provide the decent minimum, consumption went up, and with it imports, paid for by fixed volumes of exports from the nontransformed rural economy. Uruguay was more vulnerable than before to price changes for its exports, a vulnerability exposed in the 1950's and 1960's when export prices fell. Then economic diversification plans—many of them seemed almost the Batlle-Acevedo-Serrato projects dusted off—were formulated, but the political will to transform was still lacking. This lack of political will brought on the Tupamaro urban guerrillas and in reaction, the military coup of 1973. It is an open question whether that special combination of coercion and belief in a free market economy that characterizes the post-1973 governments can solve Uruguay's economic problems.

This is not to say that had Batlle's economic transformation programs been carried out, Uruguayans would have lived happily ever after. Much of his program was admirable. Why shouldn't Uruguay be a model country, not a follower? Why shouldn't Uruguay do its own industrial research and develop new products for the world as Acevedo and Batlle planned and not just import technology? But some of his optimism proved excessive. For example, programs that were so heavily based on long-term continual tax increases could expect sooner or later to run into taxpayers' revolts. Also, the ability of foreign enterprises, supported by their governments, to thwart Batlle's economic nationalism was greater than he had expected. The doctrine that foreign companies replaced by state enterprises must be compensated for the loss of future profits is today a museum piece nostalgically remembered only by the oldest members of London clubs, but it was successfully invoked then. Uruguay's ability, under Batlle, to play one foreign country against another was exceedingly limited. Batlle contracted with the *United States* promoter Farquhar to build state railroads to compete with the *English*-owned railroads. After Farquhar's bankruptcy, the *French* Minister to Uruguay warned Farquhar's *American* receivers: "Mr. Leferre states Uruguay is hostile to any foreign interests. Is doing and will continue to do its best to put foreign interests out of business. Is endeavoring to get B Ry [Brazil Railway—the principal Farquhar company] to parallel existing roads which are now paying [making profits] in order to cripple them and buy them in."[14] The rules of the game were against Uruguay. Even if England's economic predominance faded, and in 1915 this was not in evidence, successor sources of foreign capital were going to drive the same hard bargains.

None of this alters the conclusion that Uruguay paid a very high price for suspending Batlle's program of economic transformation. Foreign resistance to economic nationalism and changes in the world economy over which Uruguay had no control, like the gold crisis and World War I, made economic transformation more difficult but not impossible. To be sure, Uruguay would still have had to face the Great Depression and later changes, many of which have been decidedly unfavorable, but it would have faced them with a more productive and less vulnerable economy.

During Batlle's time the State enterprises were successful and their success justified the State's expanded economic role.[15] In the 1960's and 1970's, Uruguay's State enterprises, greatly expanded after World War II, virtually collapsed. They failed to deliver services, ran huge deficits, and symbolized the State's incompetence. Did Batlle have any responsibility for the later disaster? The answer, in summary, is that he did not foresee that governments like his would not continue indefinitely, and he organized the State enterprises on the assumption that such governments would continue. (1) Though Batlle expected the State enterprises to be run in business-like fashion, he also expected them to operate "within the ideas and plans of the Government."[16] This failure to insulate State enterprises from central government became pernicious when later governments saw these enterprises as enormous opportunities for political patronage. (2) Batlle expected workers in the State enterprises to put in a day's work, but he also expected them to vote Colorado. Batlle appointed experts to the State enterprises, but he also filled the other Board seats with political appointees. Later this balance between efficiency and politics was first altered and then destroyed. (3) Batlle assumed that Acevedo's pilot programs—fishing, industrial chemistry, mining, agronomy stations—would be strengthened by later governments. They weren't, and became mere bureaucratic offices. (4) The patchwork financing forced by the gold crisis for the State Railroad System and electrification of the State trolleys came apart. Later governments did not favor these undertakings. The result was that the State Railroad System was never built (had it been built, it would have tested the effects on efficiency of below-cost service, an innovation in Batlle's goals for State enterprises.) Instead, the State operated some short feeder lines that went nowhere and produced deficits. And to Don Pepe's great anguish, horses continued to draw the Tranvía del Norte trolleys through Montevideo until the line was mercifully suspended in the mid-1920's. These trolleys carried few riders and produced heavy losses.

Much the same might be said of Uruguay's experience with the mixed Presidency and Colegiado from 1919 to 1933 and with the second Colegiado from 1952 to 1967. An institution that Batlle had designed to work for a Colorado Party with clear electoral mandates was undermined by the politics of consensus.

III

Batlle was not a natural politician, one who enjoys being with crowds, shaking hands, patting backs, giving speeches. He was ill at ease with people he didn't know—especially non-Uruguayans—and hid this behind formal manners and old-fashioned clothes. His family concern and affection were intense. The deaths of his brother and his daughter affected him enormously; he brought his brother's sons to live with him. This intense family affection compensated for the absolutely calculated way he treated political associates. His statement to visitors in Europe, "in politics I do not have friends except for those who believe in the same ideas I do," was later confirmed when he was unmoved by the departure of his closest followers over the Colegiado. Arena literally had the shakes, but Don Pepe simply fashioned replacements.

Obviously, Batlle had resolved the self-doubts of his youth. A likely psychobiographical hypothesis is that he had determined to redeem his father's political failures by his own success; he was carrying out the Colorado one-party government his father had failed to achieve. Batlle's personality was combative—remember his attacks on the Ramírez family, members of which had contributed to his father's failures. Psychologically, Batlle sublimated his combativeness by fighting for a model Uruguay where everyone's worth would be recognized.

Uruguay today is far from the model country Batlle intended it to be. Military government, which he fought in his youth, is back. What would Don Pepe do if he were alive today? One thing is certain. He would calculate the prospects and then act. Though he had fought military governments, he took part in the government of General Tajes, which returned Uruguay to civil rule. When Tajes died in

1912, Batlle was criticized for his own earlier involvement with him. Don Pepe responded: "For Señor Batlle political action means the constant effort to move from one political state to another better one. At every moment, even the one which appears to be the most desperate, something can be done. Sometimes it will be abstention, sometimes revolution, sometimes taking part in a regime capable of evolving, at others the open, decided, and enthusiastic support of governments based on public opinion which are determined to carry out the national interest and aspirations."[17]

NOTES

PART I. CIVIC DREAMS

1. TO PARIS

1. The journal is not really an intimate diary, and Batlle may have intended to use it as a source for later articles. It is in the Batlle Archive in possession of the Batlle Pacheco family, Montevideo.

2. Batlle, Paris, to Domingo Arena, May 7, 1907, Batlle Archive.

3. "El Sr. Batlle en París," *El Día*, June 22, 1907. "Del Dr. Juan C. Blanco (hijo)," *El Día*, June 25, 1907.

4. Batlle, Paris, to Domingo Arena, May 7, 1907, Batlle Archive.

5. "Del señor Batlle y Ordoñez," *El Día*, July 7, 1907. The article quoted from a letter dated June 11. Batlle soon forbade publication his private letters.

2. THE WILLIMAN YEARS

1. Exports, the official prices of which underestimated market prices by 15 to 20 percent, rose in official prices to 40,935,635 pesos in 1910, up from 29,442,205 pesos in 1900. Imports, where there was no great difference between official and market prices, were 40,814,161 pesos in 1910 and 23,978,206 pesos in 1900. The peso's exchange value was 96.6 U.S. cents. Dirección General de Estadística, *Anuario Estadístico de la República Oriental del Uruguay, 1918* (Montevideo, 1920), 487. Luis Carlos Benvenuto, *Breve Historia del Uruguay* (Montevideo, 1967), 78, 93–94, has constructed a table of Uruguayan per capita income in constant United States dollars by decades for 1832–1932. It is based on export figures, on the assumption that exports

represented a constant 15 percent of Gross Domestic Product throughout the whole century. This central assumption, which if erroneous will produce unreal numerical results, is not explained. Since official export figures differed from market figures differently at different times, using official export figures introduces another source of error, as does Benvenuto's assumption of unchanged Uruguayan internal prices from 1832 to 1913.

2. Reginald Lloyd and others, eds. *Impresiones de la República del Uruguay en el Siglo Veinte* (London, 1912), 87.

3. Dirección General de Estadística, *Anuario Estadístico de la República Oriental del Uruguay, 1908* (Montevideo, 1911), II, Part III, lxx-lxii (hereafter cited as *Anuario Estadístico*). *Anuario Estadístico, 1907–1908*, II, Part I, xli. The census, titled *Censo General de la República en 1908*, was published as Vol. II, Part III, of *Anuario Estadístico, 1908*.

4. *Diario de Sesiones de la H. Asamblea General*, XII, 71 and 129 (hereafter cited as *Asamblea General*). *Anuario Estadístico, 1915*, 454, 467–468.

5. Juan Oddone and Blanca Paris, *La Universidad desde el Militarismo a la Crisis* (1885–1958) (4 vols., Montevideo, 1971), IV, 268. The original appeared in *Anales de la Universidad* [Montevideo], XX (1910), 71 ff.

6. J. C. Williman, Williman's son, has published a filial biography, *El Dr. Claudio Williman, Su Vida Pública* (Montevideo, 1957).

7. *Diario de Sesiones de la H. Cámara de Representantes*, CIII, 529–531; CCX, 328–330 (hereafter cited as *Cámara*). *Asamblea General* XII, 146. *Anuario Estadístico, 1907–1908*, II, Part III, xxviii.

8. Ibid., II, Part III, vii-viii.

9. José Pedro Barrán and Benjamín Nahum, *Historia Rural del Uruguay Moderno (1851–1885)* (Montevideo, 1957) 546. This is the first of a seven volume study completed in 1978.

10. Federación Rural, *Informe Producido ante el Congreso Rural Anual de 1910 por el Doctor Daniel García Acevedo en nombre de la "Comisión de Estudios para mejorar la situación de la Gente Pobre de Campaña"* (Montevideo, n.d.), 45–46.

11. Lloyd and others, *Impresiones*, 213–216. "La Propiedad Rural," *El Día*, September 8, 1908. *Anuario Estadístico, 1907–1908*, II, Part II, Apéndice 79; II, Part III, 1126–1127. Barrán and Nahum, *Historia Rural del Uruguay Moderno*, VI: *La Civilización Ganadera Bajo Batlle (1905–1914)*, 269–281.

12. This question has been brought up forcefully by José P. Barrán and Benjamín Nahum, first in *Historia Rural del Uruguay Moderno: IV, Historia Social de las Revoluciones de 1897 y 1904*, 63–76, where they argue, with qualifications, that the "pobrerío rural," the rural poor, formed the basis of the revolutionary army of 1904. They have continued to argue this, for a wider time period and without qualifications, in later volumes, for example in

Vol. V, *La Prosperidad Frágil* (1905–1914), 14: "the Blanco revolutions based on the rural 'poor.' " Their original analysis relied on a 1903 newspaper article listing the size of the contingents from each department (Uruguay is divided into 19 departments) in Saravia's revolutionary army formed that year. They conclude that 73 percent of the soldiers came from four departments, especially from two frontier departments in which the 1910 Rural Congress survey indicated high numbers of rural poor. Assuming the correctness of the newspaper article for 1904, the fact that these departments supplied the bulk of Saravia's army does not tell us whether the soldiers were peacetime peons, police, unemployed rural poor, etc. Barrán and Nahum argue that the pobrerío rural decreased by at least 50 percent from 1900 to 1910, VI: *La Civilización Ganadera Bajo Batlle (1905–1914)*, 381. Once more their numerical argument is indirect. Prosperity created jobs, and some of these jobs must have been filled by the rural poor. However, continuing ranch modernization may have thrown more peons off the ranches and into the rural poor, so that what actually happened to the numbers of the rural poor during these years is still uncertain. The point, however, is that these departments were still strong Blanco departments after the rural poor decrease claimed by Barrán and Nahum. In the crucial 1916 elections in every one of these departments the Blanco vote was greater than the combined Colorado vote. *Asamblea General* XIII, 197. Testing these departments for political sentiment therefore produces the same or more positive results as testing for the presence of rural poor. The social composition of Saravia's revolutionary armies, both the soldiers and the officers, is still to be researched. The outcome of this research will go part of the way toward understanding revolutionary goals. Another part will be research on the motivation of soldiers and officers. As against Barrán and Nahum's assertions that Saravia's wars were a "revolutionary strike" by their soldiers, the recollections of the poet Emilio Oribe offer an alternative hypothesis. In the years before the War of 1904, Oribe was a child along the Tacuarí, in the revolutionary bastion of Cerro Largo, among men who would fight in 1904. He recalled: "I know that these beings were strong and good; they were also *Blancos*." *Rapsodia Barbara* (Montevideo, 1953), 5.

13. *Asamblea General*, XII, 79–80. *Cámara*, CCII, 526, 548, 584. The Chamber did not print the bill, but it was printed by the Montevideo press.

14. "Fomento de la Agricultura," *El Siglo*, December 21, 1909. *El Día* supported the bill in "Colonización," on December 10, 1909, and the author of the Rural Association petition, José Irureta Goyena, answered with a series of articles titled "Por el Progreso Natural," *El Siglo*, May 11, 13, 14, 15, 17, 18, 1910.

15. *Asamblea General*, XII, 79–80.

16. "El Caso Carballo," *La Democracia*, July 24, 1907. "Movimiento Obrero," *El Día*, February 6, 1908.

17. *Anuario Estadístico, 1908*, II, Part III, xlvi–xlviii, 956–965. Germán W. Rama, *Las Clases Medias en la Época de Batlle* (Montevideo [1963?]), 6–8, reprinted from *Tribuna Universitaria* No. 11.

18. *Anuario Estadístico, 1909–1910*, I, Apéndice, cxv.

19. *Anuario Estadístico, 1911–1912*, 717.

20. Strike news was carried daily in the Montevideo press from February 7, 1908, to April 5, 1908.

21. "El Conflicto Ferrocarrilero," *El Día*, April 5, 1908. Francisco R. Pintos, *Historia del Movimiento Obrero del Uruguay* (Montevideo, 1960), 85.

22. Williman, *El Dr. Claudio Williman*, 756.

23. *Cámara*, CXCIII, 594–596. Ibid., CXCIV, 570–571. Ibid, CXCV, 155–161. *Senadores*, XCIV, 292–294. *Asamblea General*, XII, 3.

24. Georges Clemenceau, *Notes de Voyage dans l'Amérique du Sud. Argentine–Uruguay–Brésil* (Paris, 1911), 194–195.

25. Lloyd and others, *Impresiones*, 87–92. J. Fred Rippy, *British Investments in Latin America, 1822–1949: A Case Study in the Operations of Private Enterprise in Retarded Regions* (Minneapolis, 1959), 132–149. W. H. Koebel, *Uruguay* (London, 1911), 276. Barrán and Nahum, *Historia Rural del Uruguay Moderno*, V: *La Prosperidad Frágil (1905–1914)*, 32–34. On railroad contract negotiations, see *Cámara*, CXC, 595–605. Ibid., CXCII, 656–696, and esp. CXCVII, 484–490.

26. *Cámara*, CXCII, 300–829, passim. *Senadores*, XCVII, 181–192. Eduardo Acevedo, *Anales Históricos del Uruguay* (6 vols., Montevideo, 1933–1936), V, 494.

27. *Cámara*, CCXXIII, 152–175. José Batlle y Ordóñez, Paris, to Domingo Arena, April 17, 1908, Batlle Archive.

3. POLITICS DURING THE WILLIMAN YEARS

1. James Bryce, *South America: Observations and Impressions* (New York, revised edition, 1921), 359.

2. Milton I. Vanger, *José Batlle y Ordóñez of Uruguay: The Creator of His Times (1902–1907)* (Cambridge, 1963), 171–178. Though the two-thirds, one-third seat formula had resulted from Saravia's revolution of 1897, political tension had made contested elections too dangerous; 1905 was its first electoral test.

3. Martín C. Martínez, leading Nationalist conservative, wrote ten articles on this in *El Siglo* under various titles on April 25, 26, 27, 28, 30, and May 1, 3, 7, 8, 9, 1907. Juan Andrés Ramírez reviewed electoral legislation from a Nationalist point of view in "Sinopsis de la Evolución Institucional," in the

commemorative volume *Diario del Plata, Uruguay–1930* (Montevideo, 1930).

4. The interview was reprinted in *El Día* as "La Situación Uruguaya," May 28, 1907.

5. *Cámara*, CXCI, 415–417. *Senadores*, XCI, 11–14.

6. "Los Torneos del Trabajo," *La Democracia*, September 3, 1907.

7. "Sueños y Realidades," *El Día*, September 7, 1907.

8. "Las Cláusulas Secretas," *La Democracia*, October 10, 1907.

9. "Cosas de la Tierra," *El Día*, October 16, 1907.

10. *Asamblea General*, XII, 123. "La Derrota Nacionalista," *El Día*, November 27, 1907, contains vote breakdowns by party in each department for 1907 and 1905. "Música Celestial," *La Democracia*, November 27, 1907. *Anuario Estadístico, 1907–1908*, II, Part III, XLIII.

11. *Asamblea General*, XI, 434.

12. A copy of the secret speech came into the possession of Uruguayan diplomats and was published in Brazil in 1908. It is reprinted in Cuadernos de Marcha, *El Río de la Plata*, Montevideo, No. 20 (December 1968), 33–50.

13. Williman, *El Doctor Claudio Williman*, 625–640. Eduardo Acevedo, *Anales Históricos del Uruguay* (6 vols., Montevideo, 1933–1936), V, 317–319. Cuadernos de Marcha, *El Río de la Plata*, 25–26.

14. [Antonio Bachini], "Verdades Ignoradas," *Diario del Plata*, March 7, 1912.

15. Juan José Amézaga, "Un Capítulo de Historia Internacional. El Uruguay y el Brasil," *Revista Nacional* [Montevideo], XIX (August, 1942), 161–197. Eduardo Acevedo, *Anales Históricos del Uruguay*, V, 423. Williman, *El Doctor Claudio Williman*, 696–698.

16. Angel Cárcano, "Ensayo Histórico sobre la Presidencia de Roque Sáenz Peña," in Academia Nacional de Historia, *Historia Argentina Contemporánea, 1862–1930* (4 vols., Buenos Aires, 1965–1967), I, Segunda Sección, 176–177. Jacobo Varela Acevedo, *Recuerdos de Mi Actuación en el Ministerio de Relaciones Exteriores (1907)* (Montevideo, 1949), 16. Cuadernos de Marcha, *El Río de la Plata*, 87, publishes a British 1967 note referring to the 1908 protest. [Bachini], "Verdades Ignoradas," *Diario del Plata*, March 7, 1912.

17. "Informes Diplomáticos de los Representantes del Imperio Alemán en el Uruguay, 1902–1911," *Revista Histórica* [Montevideo], XLIII (March, 1972), 421–422.

18. Williman, *El Doctor Claudio Williman*, 654–655. "La Cuestión del Plata," *El Siglo*, June 9, 1908.

19. Cárcano, "Ensayo Histórico," 176–177, summarizes a letter from Zeballos written after his resignation to Sáenz Peña on Zeballos policies as foreign minister. "Argentina–Uruguay," *El Siglo*, June 21, 1908.

20. *Cámara*, CCI, 214–222.

4. BATLLE IN EUROPE

1. The code is in the Batlle Archive.

2. Williman first offered the appointment to a former Nationalist Foreign Minister and to Julio Herrera y Obes, the pre–'97 Colorado leader, as conciliatory gestures. The instructions sent to the delegation, while emphasizing Uruguay's interest in arbitration, did not call for the delegation to do more than act decorously. "La Conferencia Williman–Herrera," *El Siglo*, April 18, 1907. Batlle, Paris, to Jacobo Varela Acevedo, May 30, 1907, Jacobo Varela Acevedo Archive (in family possession). Instrucciones á que deberán ajustar su conducta los Señores Delegados del Uruguay á la Conferencia de Paz que se reunirá en La Haya el 15 de Junio de 1906 [sic] Williman, Jacobo Varela Acevedo, Batlle Archive. *Cámara*, CXC, 423–426.

3. Batlle, Brussels, to Arena, November 6, 1907, Batlle Archive.

4. Telmo Manacorda, *Itinerario y Espíritu de Jacobo Varela* (Montevideo, 1950), 49.

5. Batlle, Brussels, to Arena November 6, 1907, Batlle Archive. In August, Matilde, Batlle's wife, wrote their sons in Paris that Pepe was disgusted with the Conference. "You know how his conscience is and how he gets upset because he says nothing is being done." "I imagine that more than once he must have regretted accepting the position because if he had done something for his country the bad moments would have meant nothing." Matilde Pacheco de Batlle y Ordoñez, Scheveningen, to los muchachos, August 3, 12, 1907, Batlle Archive.

6. James Brown Scott (Director), *The Proceedings of The Hague Peace Conferences, Translations of the Official Texts. The Conference of 1907* (3 vols., New York, 1920–1921), II, 905. I have followed the revisions on this translation made by the Delegation of Uruguay to the Fifth General Assembly of the United Nations. [E. N. Oribe, editor], *United Action For Peace. Unidad de Acción en Favor de la Paz. Action Concertée en Faveur de la Paix* (New York, 1950), 7–8. *El Día* published the Declaration in Spanish in "La Conferencia de La Haya," on July 6, 1907.

7. Batlle, Brussels, to Arena, November 6, 1907, Batlle Archive.

8. Scott, *Proceedings*, II, 269.

9. Batlle, Brussels, to Arena November 6, 1907, Batlle Archive.

10. Scott, *Proceedings*, II, 156–158. "The complete ruin of the North American project gave me the theme for the speech and spirit to deliver it. I delivered it almost at the end of the Conference. My recondite intention was to make it clear that if our motion could be considered utopian, the North

American project was even more utopian." Batlle, Amsterdam, to Jacobo Varela Acevedo, October 26, 1907, Jacobo Varela Acevedo Archive.

11. Manacorda, *Itinerario y Espíritu de Jacobo Varela*, 49–50.

12. Batlle, Brussels, to Arena, November 6, 1907, Batlle Archive.

13. Manacorda, *Itinerario*, 49. Batlle, Amsterdam, to Jacobo Varela Acevedo, October 26, 1907, Jacobo Varela Acevedo Archive. Batlle, Brussels, to Arena, November 6, 1907, Batlle Archive. Batlle, Amsterdam, to Arena October 25, 1907, Batlle Archive.

14. "Nuestra Delegación en La Haya," *El Día*, December 26, 1907.

15. Batlle, Paris, to Arena, November 20, 1907, Batlle Archive.

16. Batlle, Paris, to Arena, December 23, 1907, Batlle Archive.

17. Batlle, Paris, to Arena, January 3, 1908, Batlle Archive. Batlle, Paris, to Arena, March 21, 1908, Batlle Archive.

18. Batlle, Paris, to Arena, January 3, 1908, Batlle Archive.

19. Batlle, Paris, to Arena and Manini, January 28, 1908, Batlle Archive. Batlle, Paris, to Arena, February 25, 1908, Batlle Archive.

20. Batlle, Paris, to Arena, November 20, 1907, Batlle Archive.

21. Luis Batlle y Ordoñez, Montevideo, to Batlle, January 6, 1908, Batlle Archive.

22. Batlle, Paris, to Arena and Manini, February 7, 1908, Batlle Archive.

23. Luis Batlle y Ordoñez, Montevideo to Batlle, February 27, March 11, 1908, Batlle Archive. "Los Toros," *El Siglo*, March 31, 1908.

24. Batlle, Paris, to Arena, December 6, 1907, Batlle Archive.

25. Batlle, Paris, to Jacobo Varela Acevedo, December 8, 1907, Jacobo Varela Acevedo Archive. "El Conflicto Internacional y el señor Batlle y Ordoñez," *El Día*, January 19, 1908.

26. Batlle, Paris, to Arena, December 23, 1907, Batlle Archive.

27. Batlle, Paris, to Arena and Manini, January 29, 1908, Batlle Archive.

28. Batlle, Paris, to Claudio Williman, March 6, 1908, Fondo Documental Dr. Claudio Williman, Archivo General de la Nación, Montevideo, Caja 3, 1908, 1a. 226, Documento 92.

29. Batlle, Paris, to Arena, begun March 21, completed March 27, 1908, Batlle Archive. Batlle was less insignificant to European governments than he realized. Their diplomats in Montevideo were aware that Batlle was expected to be president again, wanted him to be friendly, and alerted their foreign offices to his presence in Europe. The problem was that Batlle didn't act the part of ex-President, and the chancelleries were unsure how he would receive an invitation. When Batlle left for Europe, the German Minister to the Plata had suggested that he be invited to Germany, warned his Foreign Minister about "the somewhat tough personality of the ex-President, his socialistic

inclinations, and his preference for family life," and suggested that the German embassies in France and England watch the reception those governments offered him before acting. The German embassy in Paris reported that Batlle was living "exclusively like a tourist," but that the President of France might well offer him a lunch at the Élysée. When the Germans discovered Batlle's fortification mission, the question of how best to invite him to military maneuvers reached the Kaiser. "Informes Diplomáticos de los Representantes del Imperio Alemán en el Uruguay 1902–1911" Revista Histórica [Montevideo], XLIII (March, 1972), 370, 375–376, 393–399.

30. Luis Enrique Azarola Gil, Ayer. Memorias y Perfiles (Montevideo, 1957), 79–80.

31. Batlle, Paris, to Arena, May 11, 1908, Batlle Archive. Williman, El Doctor Claudio Williman, 657–658.

32. Batlle, Paris, to Arena, April 17, 1908, Batlle Archive. Arena on August 14, 1907, wrote to Batlle and Manini, then at The Hague, over his first difficulties with Williman on labor matters. Batlle Archive.

33. Batlle, Paris, to Arena, May 11, 1908, Batlle Archive.

34. Batlle, Paris, to Arena, July 6, 1908, Batlle Archive.

35. Batlle, Paris, to Arena, July 29, 1908, Batlle Archive.

36. Domingo Arena, Montevideo, to Batlle, August 27, 1908, Batlle Archive.

37. Batlle, Montbarry, Switzerland, to Arena, August 8, September 10, 1908, Batlle Archive. Batlle, Lausanne, to Arena, September 29, 1908, Batlle Archive. Batlle noted that Concepción Arenal's book was some thirty years old and he must have been referring to The Woman at Home, published in 1875. In her earlier book, The Woman of the Future (1864), she opposed women's suffrage because in Spain there was too much ignorance and women's vote would mean two votes for husbands. In the later book, basing herself on the United States experience, where it was claimed that women's suffrage moralized politics, she leaned toward women's suffrage in Spain. Suffrage was only part of her general argument that women should take part in the wider world. La Mujer del Porvenir and La Mujer de Su Casa are published together as Volume IV of the Obras Completas de Concepción Arenal (Madrid, 1916).

5. TIMING THE RETURN

1. Domingo Arena, Montevideo, to Batlle, October 20, 1908, Batlle Archive.

2. Arena, Montevideo, to Batlle, November 12, 1908, Batlle Archive.

3. Batlle, Paris, to Arena, December 28, 1908, Batlle Archive.

4. Batlle, Sens, to Arena, February 10, 1909, Batlle Archive. Batlle, Paris, to Fermín Silveira, January 21, 1909, Batlle Archive.

5. Domingo Arena, Montevideo, to Batlle, January 29, 1909, Batlle Archive.

6. Batlle, Cairo, to Arena and Manini, April 9, 1909, Batlle Archive.

7. Batlle, Naples, draft of letter to José Serrato, May 24, 1909. Batlle Archive.

8. Batlle, Athens, to Arena, May 6, 1909. Dora Isella Russell, "Tres Cartas de Batlle," *El Día, 1886–Junio–1961* (Montevideo, 1961).

9. Batlle, Rome, to Arena, letters dated June 5, 7, 1909, Batlle Archive.

10. Batlle, Naples, draft of letter to José Serrato, May 24, 1909, Batlle Archive.

11. Batlle, Paris, to Arena, July 11, 1909, Batlle Archive.

12. Batlle, Paris, to Arena, August 27, 1909, Batlle Archive.

13. Arena, Montevideo, to Batlle, August 7, 1909, Batlle Archive. Manini, Montreux, to Arena, August 2, 1909, Batlle Archive. Feliciano Viera, Montevideo, to Batlle, September 22, 1909, Batlle Archive.

14. Manuscript written by Manini, March 2–24, 1913, Carlos Manini Ríos, *Anoche Me Llamó Batlle* (Montevideo, 1970), 233.

15. Batlle, London, to Arena, November 3, 1909, Batlle Archive.

16. Batlle, Paris, to Arena, November 28, 1909, Batlle Archive.

17. Ariosto D. González, *José Serrato. Técnico del Estado* (Montevideo, 1942) 99. Batlle, Paris, to Arena, December 6, 1909, Batlle Archive.

18. Batlle, Paris, to Arena, December 11, 1909, Batlle Archive.

19. Rodolfo Vellozo, Montevideo, November 20, 1909, to Batlle, Batlle Archive.

20. Batlle, Paris, to Arena, December 11, 1909, Batlle Archive.

21. Manini, Paris, to J. J. Amézaga, December 11, 1909, Batlle Archive.

6. PRESIDENTIAL NOMINATION

1. "Nacionalistas: a votar," *La Democracia*, September 25, 1909. "Alto Exponente Democrático," *La Democracia*, September 26, 1909. Archivo del Partido Nacional, *Notas del Directorio*, Series III, VII, 17. "Una Carta Política del Dr. Rodríguez Larreta," *La Democracia*, October 21, 1909. "Sobre Unificación Nacionalista," *La Democracia*, December 15, 1909.

2. "Las Alarmas," *La Democracia*, December 18, 1909.

3. *Diario de Sesiones de la H. Comisión Permanente*, XII, 136–137 (hereafter cited as *Comisión Permanente*).

4. María Julia Ardao, "Alfredo Vásquez Acevedo. Contribución al

Estudio de Su Vida y Su Obra," *Revista Histórica* [Montevideo], XXXVI (December 1965), 103. Partido Nacional, *Actas del Congreso Elector del Directorio*, Series VII, III, 117–139.

5. "La Convención del Partido," *La Democracia*, December 31, 1909.

6. "El Gran Triunfo de la Justicia Internacional," *El Siglo*, January 6, 1910. "El Protocolo," *El Día*, January 7, 1910. "Los Rumores Tremendos," *El Día*, December 25, 1909.

7. "Los Sucesos," *El Día*, January 19, 1910. *El Día* ran daily stories during the revolution under this title.

8. Partido Nacional, *Actas del Directorio*, Series I, VII, 26–28. "Los Sucesos de Actualidad," *La Democracia*, January 27, 1910. *Comisión Permanente*, XII, 139–145.

9. "Los Sucesos," *El Día*, January 27, 1910. *El Día* published the exchange of presidential telegrams on January 25.

10. Claudio Williman, Montevideo, to Batlle, March 10, 1910, Batlle Archive. Williman, *El Dr. Claudio Williman*, 539–540.

11. Interview, César Batlle Pacheco, June 27, 1952.

12. Batlle, Paris, to Arena, February 17, 1910, Batlle Archive.

13. "Mar Revuelto," *El Siglo*, February 10, 1910.

14. Antonio Bachini, "Una Réplica al Señor Batlle y Ordoñez," *Diario del Plata*, December 13, 1913.

15. "El Ministro Bachini," *La Democracia*, February 11, 1910.

16. Pedro Manini Ríos, Montevideo, to Batlle, February 13, 1910, Batlle Archive. interview, José Claudio Williman, September 1, 1952.

17. "La Subversión de Una Hoja Suelta," *El Día*, February 11, 1910.

18. José Serrato, Montevideo, to Batlle, January 13, 1910, Batlle Archive. Ariosto D. González, *José Serrato. Técnico del Estado* (Montevideo, 1942), 99.

19. Batlle, Paris, to Arena, February 17, 1910. Batlle, Paris, to Arena, February 23, 1910, Batlle, Archive.

20. Batlle, Madrid, to Arena, March 18, 1910, Batlle Archive. Batlle, Barcelona, to Luis Mongrell, Paris, May 1, 1910, Batlle Archive. Hugo Mongrell, *Luis Mongrell (1858–1937). Político, Revolucionario y Periodista, Cabañero y Ruralista* (Vigo, 1958), pp. 680–681.

21. Batlle, Barcelona, to Claudio Williman, May 11, 1910, Archivo del Dr. Claudio Williman, Archivo General de la Nación, Montevideo, 1910; Caja 10, Documento No. 18.

22. Claudio Williman, Montevideo, to Batlle, March 10, 1910, Batlle Archive.

23. Manini, Montevideo, to Batlle, March 13, 1910, Batlle Archive.

24. See above, Chapter 2, note 12.

25. Ramírez reported this in a later polemic, "Nuestra Verdad frente a la de Batlle," *El Siglo*, January 19, 1912.

26. Arena, Montevideo, to Batlle, April 12, 1910, Batlle Archive. Arena, Montevideo, to Batlle, April 22, 1910, Batlle Archive.

27. "El Comité Nacionalista de Propaganda Cívica," *La Democracia*, March 4, 1910.

28. "Un generalismo que habla," *El Día*, April 11, 1910.

29. "La Unificación del Partido," *La Democracia*, May 8, 1910. "¿Directores o Dirigidos?" *El Siglo*, May 17, 1910.

30. "La Liga de la Paz," *El Siglo*, April 21, 1910.

31. "Liga de la Paz," *El Siglo*, May 12, 1910.

32. "El gran acto cívico del domingo," *La Democracia*, April 26, 1910.

33. Manini, Montevideo, to Batlle, May 7, 1910, Batlle Archive.

34. Manini, Montevideo, to Batlle, one letter dated May 20, 21, 24, 1910, Batlle Archive.

35. "La Cuestión Presidencial," *El Día*, May 24, 1910.

36. "La Cuestión Presidencial," *El Día*, May 27, 1910.

37. Héctor Miranda, "Batlle," *El Día*, May 27, 1910.

38. Ricardo Areco, Montevideo, to Batlle, June 1, 1910, Batlle Archive.

39. "De Don José Enrique Rodó," *El País*, June 1, 1910.

40. Carlos M. Rama, "Batlle y el Movimiento Obrero y Social," [Acción] *Batlle. Su Obra Y Su Vida* (Montevideo, 1950), 46.

41. Milton I. Vanger, *José Batlle y Ordoñez of Uruguay: The Creator of His Times 1902–1907* (Cambridge, 1963), 185.

42. For these reasons, the Directorio newspaper published Lasso de la Vega's manifesto as "La Candidatura de Batlle," *La Democracia*, April 3, 1910, while *El Día*, the newspaper Lasso wrote for, did not. *El Día* did not approve of a Labor Party; workers should vote Colorado. *El Día* did publish an article by Félix Ramos, "El Sr. Batlle y Ordoñez y los Obreros," on June 17, 1910, which argued that "we workers should accompany the party which proclaims the candidacy of the citizen Batlle y Ordoñez."

43. Manini, Montevideo, to Batlle, single letter dated May 20, 21, 24, 1910, Batlle Archive.

44. Feliciano Viera, Montevideo, to Batlle, May 28, 1910, Batlle Archive.

45. Manini, Montevideo, to Batlle, March 13, 1910, Batlle Archive. Manini, Montevideo, to Batlle, June 30, 1910, Batlle Archive. Manini Ríos, *Anoche Me Llamó Batlle*, 199.

46. *Cámara*, CCIV, 155–167. In its final version the bill provided that the minority would get 2, 3, 4, 5, or 8 out of 24 seats in Montevideo depending on whether it got one twelfth to one third of the votes cast; one or 2 seats out of 8

in Canelones and one out of 4 in 10 departments if it got one fourth of the vote; one out of 3 in 4 departments if it got one third of the vote; one out of 2 in 3 departments if it got one third of the vote.

47. José Espalter, *El Problema Nacional* (Montevideo, 1905), 59–69.

48. For example, under existing law in a department where four Chamber of Deputies seats were up for election and 4,000 voted, of whom 2,800 voted Colorado, 950 for the Directorio Nationalist ticket, and 250 for the Radical Nationalists, the Nationalists would get no seats, since no Nationalist ticket had got one quarter of the votes cast—1,000 being the minimum necessary to win the minority seat. The Colorados would get all four seats. Under the double simultaneous vote, the two Nationalist tickets votes would be pooled, reaching 1,200, well over the one-quarter requirement of 1,000 votes, and the department's minority seat would be awarded to a Directorio Nationalist because that ticket was the minority ticket with the most votes. There were other provisions to protect the Directorio—of course, if the Radicals were the most voted minority, they would get the new law's benefits—and vote pooling was also permitted the majority party.

49. *Cámara*, XXIV, 167–246, passim. *Senado*, XCVII, 288–296, 333–342.

50. "Circular del Directorio á las Comisiones Departamentales," *La Democracia*, June 29, 1910. Partido Nacional, *Actas del Directorio*. Series I, VII, 56–60.

51. "Estaba Escrito," *El Día*, July 1, 1910. "Las Dos Tendencias," *La Democracia*, July 6, 1910.

52. "La Convención," *El Día*, July 2, 1910. "Los Sucesos Uruguayos," *La Prensa* (Buenos Aires), January 26, 1910. The Directorio newspaper claimed all but 10 of the 160 delegates drew some income from the national budget. "La Soberanía Popular en la Convención Colorada," *La Democracia*, July 6, 1910.

53. "El gran Acto de Ayer," *El Día*, July 4, 1910.

54. Cable, July 4, 1910, signed Viera, Batlle Archive.

55. Rafael Di Miero to Director of *El Día*, April 22, 1912, Batlle Archive. The letter was intended for publication.

56. Antonio Bachini, "Una Réplica al Señor Batlle y Ordoñez," *Diario del Plata*, December 13, 1913.

57. Recollection of Rafael Batlle Pacheco.

58. Matilde Pacheco de Battle y Ordoñez, Milan, to Hijos, June 6, 1910, Batlle Archive. Serapio del Castillo, Paris, to Batlle, July 4, 1910, Batlle Archive. Serapio del Castillo's outline of the Ramírez memorandum is in the Batlle Archive.

59. Manini, Montevideo, to Batlle, June 24, 1910, Batlle Archive. "Batlle Hablará," *El Siglo*, May 29, 1910.

60. Batlle, Genoa, to Arena and Manini, June 3, 1910, Batlle Archive.
61. Eduardo Iglesias, Montevideo, to Batlle, March 14, 1910, Batlle Archive.
62. Batlle, Paris, to Claudio Williman, July 6, 1910 (Copy), Batlle Archive.
63. El Corresponsal, "Batlle y Sus Ideas," *El Siglo*, July 31, 1910. When Roberto B. Giúdici and Efraín González Conzi published *Batlle y El Batllismo* (Montevideo, 1928), they transcribed the interview on pp. 406–408 into the first person and said that in it "Batlle gave the fundamental bases of his ideas of government." The result is that the statement "Batlle does not recognize the existence of an agrarian problem" now appeared as "I do not recognize." Later commentators, relying on the transcription, seized on this statement as evidence of Batlle's explicit disavowal of concern with agrarian problems. El Corresponsal's interview cannot be taken as an authoritative account of Batlle's 1910 views.
64. "La Palabra del Señor Batlle," *El Siglo*, August 2, 1910.
65. El Corresponsal, "Batlle y Sus Ideas," *El Siglo*, July 31, 1910.

7. REVOLUTIONARY REACTION

1. "Ocasos Sombríos," *La Democracia*, June 21, 1910. "Nunca, Ni en Ninguna Forma," *La Democracia*, July 8, 1910. "La Muerte de Batlle," *La Democracia*, July 28, 1910.
2. J. C. Williman, *El Dr. Claudio Williman. Su Vida Pública* (Montevideo, 1957), 555–556. "La Policía y la Política," *La Democracia*, July 14, 1910.
3. "Semana Política," *La Democracia*, July 31, 1910.
4. Partido Nacional Archivo, *Actas del Directorio*, Series I, VII, 64.
5. María Julia Ardao, "Alfredo Vásquez Acevedo. Contribución al Estudio de Su Vida y Su Obra," *Revista Histórica* [Montevideo], XXXVI (December, 1965), 626–627.
6. "El Nuevo Directorio," *La Democracia*, September 7, 1910. Partido Nacional Archivo, *Actas del Directorio*, Series I, VII, 67–69. Partido Nacional Archivo, *Actas del Congreso Elector de Directorio*, Series VII, III, 158–165. "Congreso Elector," *La Democracia*, September 6, 1910.
7. Batlle, Paris, to Arena, July 18, 1910, Batlle Archive.
8. Batlle, Paris, to Arena, August 10, 1910, Batlle Archive. Carlos Manini Ríos, *Anoche me Llamó Batlle* (Montevideo, 1970), 219–220.
9. Manini, Montevideo, to Batlle, September 19, 1910, Batlle Archive.
10. Claudio Williman, Montevideo, to Batlle, September 10, 1910, Batlle Archive.
11. "El Ministro Bachini," *El Día*, September 14, 1910.
12. Manini, Montevideo, to Batlle, September 11, 1910, Batlle Archive.

13. Batlle, Paris, to Manini, July 18, 1910. Batlle Archive. Williman, Montevideo, to Batlle, September 10, 1910, Batlle Archive.

14. Luis Enrique Azarola Gil, *Ayer. Memorias y Perfiles* (Montevideo, 1957), 85.

15. See Chapter 3, p. 20.

16. This idea went back to Don Pepe's youth. During his return from his first trip to Europe in steerage on a German ship in January 1881, Pepe noted in a diary he was keeping that all the South American nations had navies, even Uruguay, which was too poor. *"Wouldn't it be more rational if the American nations used the capital they spend on these naval squadrons in buying and maintaining steamships destined to transport a select immigration to their virgin and fertile territory . . .?* I dreamed a little, a short time ago, about this idea. I dreamed that my country had been the first to put it into practice and that in a few years it had reached first place among all the neighboring nations, for its population, for its products, and for its intelligence." Batlle Archive.

17. In March 1910, from Milan, Florencio Sánchez, the playwright, wrote his uncle: "It is quite possible that after I premiere here I will return to Montevideo. Batlle, with whom I have spent two weeks here in continuous contact, has told me that he needs me and that I should return with him when he begins his government." Angel Curotto, "Recordando a Florencio Sánchez en el Cinquentenario de su Muerte," *El Día–Suplemento*, November 6, 1960.

18. "La Respuesta del Sr. Batlle a La Convención Colorada," *El Día*, September 28, 1910.

19. "El Programa," *El Siglo*, September 28, 1910. "Política de Coparticipación y Política de Partido," *El Siglo*, September 30, 1910. "Las Dos Grandes Bases del Programa de Batlle," *El Siglo*, October 1, 1910. "El Programa del Sr. Batlle y la Reforma Constitucional," *El Siglo*, October 4, 1910.

20. Arena, Montevideo, to Batlle, undated, Batlle Archive.

21. "La Palabra del Directorio," *La Democracia*, September 28, 1910. "La Política de Batlle," *La Democracia*, October 1, 1910. It dismissed the nonpolitical parts of Batlle's program as routine generalities. Partido Nacional Archivo, *Actas del Directorio*, Series I, VII, 86–87.

22. Archivo del Partido Nacional, *Notas Recibidas por el H. Directorio*, Series II, XII, 231–288.

23. "La Concurrencia á la Urnas," *La Democracia*, October 12, 1910. Partido Nacional, *Actas del Directorio*, Series I, VII, 90–91.

24. Manini, Montevideo, to Batlle, October 21, 1910, and Maruni [Manini], Montevideo, to Batlle, October 24, 1910, cable, Batlle Archive.

25. *Diario de Sesiones de la H. Comisión Permanente*, XII (Montevideo, 1937), 169. Hereafter cited as *Comisión Permanente*.

26. "Los Sucesos de Actualidad," *La Democracia*, October 25, 1910.

27. Nepomuceno Saravia García, *Memorias de Aparicio Saravia* (Montevideo, 1956), 614. Arturo Ardao and Julio Castro, *Vida de Basilio Muñoz* (Montevideo, 1938), 161.

28. "Los Sucesos," *El Día*, October 27, 1910.

29. Williman, *El Dr. Claudio Williman. Su Vida Pública*, 684.

30. "La Disolución del Directorio," *La Democracia*, October 27, 1910. Partido Nacional Archivo, *Actas del Directorio*, Series I, VII, 94.

31. "La Renuncia del Sr. Bachini," *El Día*, October 28, 1910. Interview, José Claudio Williman, September 1, 1952. Williman, *El Dr. Claudio Williman*, 558–559.

32. "La Insurrección," *El Siglo*, November 8, 1910. Julio Herrera y Obes, the pre–97 Colorado leader, had reorganized his forces and come out violently against Batlle—"limited intelligence . . . insane self-preoccupation which inevitably makes him believe he is infallible"—and for "political temperance and concord," but Herrera y Obes had lost all appreciable Colorado influence when he sat out the War of 1904. Julio Herrera y Obes, "Las Promesas de Un Candidato," *La Democracia*, October 1, 1910. "Un Manifiesto Colorado," *La Democracia*, September 2, 1910.

33. "Los Jefes Nacionalistas al País," *La Democracia*, November 19, 1910. Saravia García, *Memorias de Saravia*, 613–614. "El General Galarza y la Candidatura de Batlle," *La Democracia*, July 29, 1910. "El Redentor Colorado," *El Día*, February 10, 1910. Washington Lockhart, *Vida de Dos Caudillos: Los Galarza* (Montevideo, 1968), 89, 149–150. No evidence was ever presented that the two generals, Pablo Galarza, the hero of Tupambaé, whom Batlle supposedly had distrusted until well into the War of 1904 because of Galarza's involvement in the preelection murder of a newspaperman in 1887, and José Escobar, reported to have been badly treated by Batlle in 1904, were in fact involved.

34. Arturo Ardao and Julio Castro, *Vida de Basilio Muñoz*, 161–163. Saravia García, *Memorias de Saravia*, 614. "Los Sucesos," *El Día*, November 7, 1910. Carlos Burmeister, Montevideo, to Batlle, December 2, 1910, Batlle Archive.

35. When the revolution broke out, Viera sent Batlle a coded cable "Situation not serious." Don Pepe was confident it would soon be over. Viera sent Batlle a second cable: "2,000 rebels attacked Nico Pérez defended by 150 soldiers. After two days of combat our capitulation honorable. Revolutionaries had 180 casualties, army 50." Batlle, alarmed, cabled that he wanted to return. Williman, while no longer openly opposing Batlle's return, did not favor it, so a third coded cable went out from Viera: "Within two weeks you will receive Arena's letter. Wait before deciding on return. Rebels pursued

closely by General Justino Muniz and Basilisio [a Colorado Saravia]." The Viera coded cables are in the Batlle Archive. Arena, Montevideo, to Batlle, November 12, 1910, and Batlle, Paris, to Arena, November 16, 1910, Batlle Archive.

36. Saravia García, *Memorias de Saravia*, 615.

37. "¡Hacia La Paz!," *El Siglo*, November 6, 1910; "Los Sucesos," *El Día*, November 7, 1910.

38. Viera coded cable to Batlle sent November 5, 1910, Batlle Archive. The code, a number to letter code, is also in the Batlle Archive.

39. "La Insurrección," *El Siglo*, November 11, 1910.

40. "Los Sucesos," *El Día*, November 2, 8, 1910.

41. "La Candidatura Batlle Frente á la Guerra," *El Día*, November 8, 1910. "La Candidatura Batlle," *El Día*, November 10, 1910.

42. "Frente á la Guerra," *El Siglo*, November 8, 1910.

43. "Los Sucesos," *El Día*, November 14, 1910. Williman, *El Doctor Claudio Williman*, 563–567. Saravia García, *Memorias de Saravia*, 615–616. "Sobre las Condiciones de Paz," *El Día*, November 19, 1910.

44. Received in Montevideo November 20, 1910. Williman, *El Dr. Claudio Williman*, 574.

45. *Cámara*, CCVII, 251–259, 290–337. "El Aumento de Fuerzas," *El Siglo*, November 26, 1910. José R. Usera, "El Ejército" in Reginald Lloyd and others, editors, *Impresiones de la República del Uruguay en el Siglo Veinte* (London, 1912), 172.

46. *Comisión Permanente*, XII, 173–174. *Cámara*, CCVII, 267–286.

47. If Williman's term expired before elections could be held, Viera, the Senate President would become Provisional President until elections took place. Viera and Manini argued that the elections must be postponed until after the revolution ended. Serrato, fearing Viera's provisional presidency, argued that the elections should be held even during revolution. Williman had not committed himself; Feliciano Viera, Montevideo, to Batlle, November 17, 1910. Arena to Batlle, November 12, 1910, Batlle Archive.

48. *Cámara*, CCVII, 230–235.

49. "El Directorio," *La Democracia*, December 11, 1910. Partido Nacional *Actas del Directorio*, Series I, VII, 96. "Preparando Asesinatos," *La Democracia*, December 10, 1910. "Los Legisladores Nacionalistas," *El Día*, December 6, 1910.

50. "Los Próximos Comicios," *El Día*, November 29, 1910. "Sobre lo Mismo," *El Siglo*, February 25, 1911. Williman, *El Dr. Claudio Williman*, 588.

51. "La Iniciativa del Comité Colorado," *El Siglo*, December 3, 1910. "Las Integraciones en las Listas Coloradas," *El Día*, December 5, 1910. Eduardo

Acevedo, *Anales Históricos del Uruguay* (6 vols., Montevideo, 1933–1936), V, 431.

52. "Los Cívicos Católicos Están por Batlle," *La Democracia*, December 10, 1910. "Frente al Comicio," *El Día*, December 7, 1910. Celestino Mibelli, "Los Liberales y las Elecciones," *El Día*, December 9, 1910.

53. Carlos M. Rama, "Batlle y el Movimiento Obrero y Social" in [Acción], *Batlle. Su Vida, Su Obra* (Montevideo, 1956), 46. Aurelio del Hebrón [pseud. of Alberto Zum Felde], *El Uruguay ante el Concepto Sociológico* (Montevideo, 1911), 44.

54. Rama, "Batlle y el Movimento Obrero y Social," 46–47.

55. "Los Socialistas y la Insurrección," *El Día*, November 30, 1910.

56. "La Renuncia del Sr. Bachini," *El Día*, November 24, 1910.

57. "La Actitud de los Colorados Tradicionales en los Comicios Próximos," *La Democracia*, December 15, 1910. "Los Autónomos," *El Siglo*, December 11, 1910.

58. "Informes Diplomáticos de los Representantes del Imperio Alemán en el Uruguay (1902–1911)," *Revista Histórica* [Montevideo], XLIII (March, 1972), 469–470.

59. "Permanente," *La Democracia*, December 15, 1910. "La Salud de Batlle," *La Democracia*, November 29, 1910. "Los Toqueteos en el Ejército," *La Democracia*, November 22, 1910. "¿El doctor Williman Envenenado?", *La Democracia*, December 10, 1910.

60. *José Batlle y Ordoñez. Proclamación de Este Eminente Ciudadano a la Presidencia por el Comité de Propaganda de la 4a Sección. December 9, 1910* (Montevideo, 1911), 11. Club "Santiago Vázquez," *Al País* (Montevideo, 1910), 5–13.

61. *Cámara*, CCVIII, 158. The Chamber debates on disputed elections are a mine of information on electoral practices.

62. The official 1910 results were published in Williman's February 15, 1911 message, *Asamblea General*, XII, 123, and can be compared with 1905 and 1907 results in "La Derrota Nacionalista," *El Día*, November 27, 1907. Colorado assistance to Frugoni, and whether police voted for Frugoni, was a source of perennial dispute beginning with "La Enseñanza de Ayer," *El Día*, December 19, 1910. "Bajo la Fuerza y contra la ley," *La Democracia*, December 20, 1910. [Batlle], "Distingamos," *El Día*, December 31, 1913. Frugoni later maintained that he had not asked for these voters and if they voted for him to stop the Catholics, they ceased being Colorados, either temporarily or permanently; "La Carta que no Publicamos," *El Día*, January 12, 1959. Carlos Manini Ríos, *Una Nave en la Tormenta* (Montevideo, 1972), 231–232.

63. Arena, Montevideo, to Batlle, November 12, 1910, and Manini, Montevideo, to Batlle, November 18, 1910, Batlle Archive.

64. Batlle, Berlin, to Arena, January 14, 1911, Batlle Archive.
65. Pedro Figari, *El Momento Político, 1910–1911* (Montevideo, 1911), 3–71. "Actualidad," *El País*, January 12, 1911.
66. "El Sr. Batlle y Ordoñez," *El Siglo*, January 5, 1911.
67. "El Año que Empieza," *La Democracia*, January 1, 1911.

APPRAISALS: I

1. John J. Johnson, *Political Change in Latin America: The Emergence of the Middle Sectors* (Stanford, 1958), 44. Johnson used the term "middle sectors" instead of "middle classes" to indicate weaker social cohesion. Germán W. Rama, *Las Clases Medias en la Época de Batlle* (Montevideo, [1963 ?] reprinted from *Tribuna Universitaria*, No. 11), 9, 10. Peter Winn, "British Informal Empire in Uruguay in the Nineteenth Century," *Past and Present*, No. 73 (November, 1976), 124–125.

2. Francisco Bauzá, *Ensayo Sobre la Formación de Una Clase Media* (Montevideo, 1876). Reprinted in Francisco Bauzá, *Estudios Sociales y Económicos. Colección de Clásicos Uruguayos*, Vol. 140 (Montevideo, 1972), 3–67. The quote appears on page 4 of the reprint. Germán W. Rama, *El Ascenso de las Clases Medias. Enciclopedia Uruguaya*, No. 36 (Montevideo, 1969), 104.

3. *Senadores*, LXXXIV, 514.

4. *Memoria del Ministerio de Hacienda, 1904*, (Montevideo, 1905), 28.

5. *Cámara*, CCXXXI, 192.

6. Germán W. Rama's *El Ascenso de las Clases Medias*, 102–120, illustrates the problems involved in this type of analysis. Rama replicates the technique used by Germani in Argentina and concludes, using the Uruguayan census of 1908, that 28.8 percent of the active population were middle and upper class. What he has done is add up the occupations he considers to be middle class, but he has not shown that the people identified as middle class identified themselves as middle class and acted politically in accordance with that identification. In fact, the technique does not permit him to distinguish the middle class or classes from the upper class and leaves the implication that the middle classes should be considered part of the upper class. Rama glosses over this inability to locate the middle class by saying the middle classes consider themselves a "group in movement," not a social class. Having made this distinction, it is ignored, as is the quantitative inseparability of upper and middle classes, for the study immediately goes on to talk of an Uruguayan "political formula of middle classes supported by workers sectors," 116–118.

Rama explains the rise of the middle classes as a result of late nineteenth-century Uruguayan urbanization and immigration, which in turn were produced by the transformation of the ranching economy that tied Uruguay much more intensively to the Atlantic economy. It is true that about 30 percent of the Uruguayan population lived in Montevideo in 1908; it is also true that immigrants were about 30 percent of Montevideo's population. But neither urbanization nor immigration were new phenomena in Uruguay. At independence in 1830 Montevideo had about 20 percent of the nation's population; by 1868 it had reached the 30 percent figure it sustained until 1908. Immigration shows a pattern even less conforming to Rama's analysis. In the period from 1835 to 1840, upward of 40 percent of Uruguay's population were immigrants; by 1861 immigrants were down to 33.5 percent and by 1908 further down to 17.3 percent. There were fewer foreign-born residents of Montevideo in 1908 than there had been in 1889. (Alfredo Castellanos, *La Cisplatina, La Independencia y la República Caudillesca, 1820–1838* (Montevideo, 1974), 97. José Pedro Barrán, *Apogeo y Crisis del Uruguay Pastoral y Caudillesco, 1838–1875* (Montevideo, 1974), 11, 106. *Anuario Estadístico* 1902–1903, I, 116. *Anuario Estadístico* 1907–1908, II, Part III, *Censo General de la República en 1908*, vii–viii.) Though Rama cites similar statistics, he does not see them as raising questions about his analysis. But if urbanization and immigration are not a new development in late nineteenth-century Uruguay but rather were longtime conditions of Uruguayan life, they do not explain the postulated formation of a new middle class. Put another way, they suggest that Uruguayan social transformation was much less abrupt than analysts have argued.

7. Benjamín Nahum, *1905–1930 La Época Batllista* (Montevideo, 1975), 30. Serrato, who in 1905 had forecast that the Uruguayan middle class would "provide the governing classes of the future," made no mention of a middle class when he wrote Batlle in January 1910 advising him to come home before the November elections. He saw "some merchants and industrialists" opposed to Batlle because they feared revolution and the loss of the "paradise" they enjoyed under Williman in regard to labor. Serrato, though, was confident that Batlle had the support of "the great majority of the country based on the Colorado Party." José Serrato, Montevideo, to Batlle, January 13, 1910, Batlle Archive.

8. [Batlle] "Tremenda Inconsecuencia," *El Día*, June 2, 1913.

9. John J. Johnson, *Political Change in Latin America: The Emergence of the Middle Sectors*, 50.

10. The origins and spread of the term "conservative classes" deserves further research. Eugene W. Ridings, "Class Sector Unity in an Export Economy: The Case of Nineteenth Century Brazil," *Hispanic American Historical Review*, 58 (August, 1978), 447, notes its use in Brazil.

11. Benjamín Nahum, *1905–1930 La Época Batllista*, 25.

12. Careful reading of Batlle's messages and newspaper articles during the last two years of his first administration reveals the outlines of his positions: on moral legislation, his polemic with Rodó over removal of crucifixes from public buildings; on social legislation, the eight-hour day message; on state enterprises, the message on expansion of the state-owned Montevideo electric power system; on foreign capital and enterprise, his veto of export tax reduction for Leibig's and his *El Día* explanation of that veto. Milton I. Vanger, *José Batlle y Ordoñez of Uruguay: The Creator of His Times 1902–1907* (Cambridge, 1963), 244–250, 255–258. On agrarian questions, Giúdici and González Conzi's conversion of the Correspondent's "Batlle does not recognize" to "I do not recognize the existence of an agrarian problem" has been seized upon by commentators to demonstrate his disinterest in rural matters. But even during Batlle's first administration, the idea was government policy that increases in land value which did not come from the labor of the owner came from society and should be taxed by the state. *El Día* carried articles attacking latifundia, and in the Chamber of Deputies Arena invoked Batlle to support setting up an experimental colony for the rural poor. Vanger, 105, 195, 211–212, 259. In 1908 Arena went to Tacuarembó and delivered a speech calling on ranchers to grow forage and intensify their operations to provide employment for the rural poor and to subdivide their lands so as to increase the size of the rural population; "Exposición de Tacuarembó," *El Día*, October 26, 1908. He wrote Batlle that the speech had "many of our ideas" in it. Arena, Montevideo, to Batlle, October 29, 1908, Batlle Archive.

PART II. RAIN OF PROJECTS

8. SECOND INAUGURAL

1. "Batlle en Montevideo," *El Día*, February 14, 1911. *El Día* reported Batlle's reply in the third person.

2. "El Futuro Presidente," *El Siglo*, February 12, 1911. [Batlle], "Ni lo ha Dicho, ni lo Piensa," *El Día*, February 16, 1911. Batlle's *El Día* articles, except when signed with one of his pseudonyms, have to be identified stylistically.

3. "Las Prisiones," *El Día*, March 2, 1911. "Las Medidas del lo. de Marzo," *El Día*, March 4, 1911.

4. "Espectativa," *El Siglo*, March 2, 1911. "¿Es Este un País de Asesinos?", *La Democracia*, March 3, 1911.

5. *Asamblea General*, XII, 161–170. A draft of Batlle's surprise oath is in the Batlle Archive. The idea was not new to Batlle. In 1892, when he was an obscure deputy, he had moved that the invocation to God be removed from

an oath of office. Arturo Ardao, "Ideas Filosóficas de Batlle" [Acción] *Batlle, Su Vida, Su Obra* (Montevideo, 1956), 31–32.

6. "La Transmisión del Mando," *El Día*, March 2, 1911. There is a copy of Williman's speech in the Batlle Archive.

7. "La Transmisión del Mando," *El Día*, March 2, 1911.

8. Serrato had just opened an engineering office. To overcome his expressed reluctance, Batlle told him, "You must accompany me. If I had known you would not I would not have accepted a second presidency." Interview, José Serrato, September 21, 24, 1952. Jacobo Varela Acevedo, Batlle's first choice for Ministry of Industries, declined, and recommended his cousin Eduardo Acevedo; Jacobo Varela Acevedo, interview, April 18, 1952. Juan Bernassa y Jérez, Montevideo, to Batlle, March 3, 1915, Batlle Archive. "El Ministerio," *El Siglo*, March 4, 1911. "Los Nuevos Ministros," *El Día*, March 6, 1911.

9. "El Chauffeur del señor Batlle," *El Día*, February 22, 1911.

10. The Río Negro, too shallow for serious navigation, divides the nation in two. The bill, as passed, called for a foreign loan of some three million pesos to deepen the river, to be paid for by modest contributions from landowners within 15 kilometers of the river. Arena wrote the laudatory committee report. *Cámara*, CCVIII, 498–507, 559–575, 596–601.

11. *Senadores*, XCVIII, 428–608, passim.

12. "Los Toros," *El Día*, March 24, 1911.

13. El Niño de la Bola [Juan Andrés Ramírez], "Croniquilla," *El Siglo*, March 26, 1911.

14. "Hacia Otros Rumbos," *El Siglo*, March 26, 1911.

9. GENERAL STRIKE

1. "El Gran Mitin de Ayer," *El Día*, March 27, 1911. "Movimiento Obrero," *El Día*, March 25, 1911. "Los Alquileres," *El Día*, April 13, 1911. "La Huelga de Enfermeros," *El Día*, April 12, 1911.

2. Francisco R. Pintos, *Historia del Movimiento Obrero del Uruguay* (Montevideo, 1960), 93. Carlos M. Rama, "La Cuestión Social" in Cuadernos de Marcha, *Montevideo entre Dos Siglos (1890–1914)*, No. 22 (February, 1969), 66. Héctor Rodríguez, *Nuestros Sindicatos (1865–1965)* Montevideo, 1965), 14–15.

3. "El Congreso Obrero," *El Día*, May 2, 4, 5, 1911.

4. Pedro H. Alfonso, *Sindicalismo y Revolución en el Uruguay* (Montevideo, 1971), 33.

5. "La Huelga," *El Siglo*, May 12, 1911.

6. "La Huelga del Día," *El Día*, May 12, 1911.

7. "La Gran Huelga," *El Día*, May 19, 1911.

8. "La Gran Huelga," *El Día*, May 17, 1911. "La Huelga," *El Siglo*, May 20, 1911.

9. "¡Al Fin!," *El Día*, May 22, 1911. "Fin de la Huelga," *El Día*, May 22, 1911.

10. "La Gran Huelga," *El Día*, May 26, 1911.

11. "Otra Vez En Plena Huelga," *El Siglo*, May 23, 1911. *El Siglo* explained that Batlle "spoke the following words more or less."

12. *Cámara*, CCIX, 456–525.

13. "Resonancias . . .", *El Día*, June 2, 1911.

14. "Una Revolución de 48 horas," *La Democracia*, May 27, 1911. "La Huelga de Tranvías," *La Democracia*, May 23, 1911.

15. "Sinopsis de la Huelga," *El Siglo*, May 27, 1911. [Batlle], "Explicación," *El Día*, May 27, 1911. "Movimiento Obrero," *El Día*, May 30, 1911.

16. [Batlle], "Entretenimiento," *El Día*, June 5, 1911.

17. [Batlle], "Pequeño Balance de la Huelga de Tranviarios," *El Día*, May 30, 1911.

18. "El Embargo de los Tranvías," *El Siglo*, June 3, 1911. Dirección de Rodados, Montevideo, to Intendente Ramón V. Benzano, June 5, 1911, Batlle Archive.

19. *Cámara*, CCIX, 654–660. *Cámara*, CCX, 14–33.

20. *Cámara*, CCX, 277.

21. These figures, adapted from José P. Barrán and Benjamín Nahum, *Historia Rural del Uruguay Moderno*, V: *La Prosperidad Frágil (1905–1914)* (Montevideo, 1977), 44–45, do not support their conclusion that cattle raising because of the stagnation of the tasajo market, was far less profitable than sheep-raising, nor the consequences that they draw from this conclusion, the supposed political weakness of the "rural upper class." Ibid., 152.

22. *Memoria del Ministerio de Industrias, 1911* (Montevideo, 1912), 30–32. *Memoria del Ministerio de Industrias, 1912* (Montevideo, 1913), 170. "La Industria de Carnes," *El Siglo*, May 17, 1911. "Un Importante Ofrecimiento," *El Día*, May 13, 1911.

23. Esteban F. Campal, *La Pradera* (Nuestra Tierra 28) (Montevideo, 1969), 14–23, Osvaldo del Puerto, *Hierbas del Uruguay* (Nuestra Tierra 19) (Montevideo, 1969), 17–19.

24. Juan Ángel Álvarez Vignoli, *Tratado de Economía Rural* (Montevideo, 1922), 220, 244–245. *Cámara*, CCIX, 681.

25. *Anuario Estadístico, 1913–1914*, 419. Uruguay's first agronomist, Álvarez Vignoli, *Tratado de Economía Rural*, 63, in a course he gave around 1912, argued that 50 percent of the ranching operations were on rented land. The

economic conservative, Martín C. Martínez, *La Renta Territorial* (Montevideo, 1918), 193, using 1916 census figures, put the rented land at 35 percent. The 1908 census listed 12,353 ranches operated by owners, 5,264 by renters, 862 by owners and renters, 1,266 unspecified. *Anuario Estadístico, 1907–1908*, II, Part III, *Censo General de la República, 1908*, 1126. Carlos A. Arocena, "Ganadería y Agricultura" in Reginald Lloyd and others, editors, *Impresiones de la República del Uruguay en el Siglo Veinte* (London, 1912), 233, concluded that rural land rented at 3 to 5 percent of estimated market value. Though rents were low in relation to land market value, they rose as land values rose.

26. Barrán and Nahum, VI, 109–110. *Memoria del Ministerio de Industrias, 1912*, 145.

27. Even though Uruguayan ranchers were not innovators, it is not necessary to explain their refusal to invest in artificial pastures as the result of their precapitalist "archaic mentality," which made them prefer to buy more land for reasons of prestige rather than improve the land they already had. Even today it is an open question whether investment in artificial pastures is as profitable as investment in additional land; Instituto de Economía, Facultad de Ciencias Económicas y de Administración, *El Proceso Económico del Uruguay*, 2nd edition (Montevideo, 1971), 111–122. "Es Mejor Negocio Comprar Campo que Reinvertir Para Mejorarlo," *El Día*, June 3, 1978. Estimates of ranch profitability for 1905–11 are offered in Barrán and Nahum, VI, 27–42. Until researchers grounded in accountancy use actual ranch records, such estimates will continue to be subject to wide margins of error.

28. "Los Ingenieros Agrónomos Nacionales," *El Día*, May 27, 1911. Eduardo Acevedo, *Anales Históricos del Uruguay* (6 vols., Montevideo, 1933–36), V, 571. La Comisión de Agrónomos enviada por el Gobierno a Europa, Norte América y Australia, *Lo Que Desearíamos Hacer por Nuestro País* (Montevideo, 1912).

29. *Memoria del Ministerio de Industrias, 1911*, 17–19.

30. *Cámara*, CCIX, 680–683. *Cámara*, CCX, 275–285, 308–319, 348–352. *Senadores*, C, 221–225.

31. "Fomento Agro-Pecuario," *El Día*, June 26, 1911.

32. *Cámara*, CCIX, 688–689. *Cámara*, CCX, 115–117, 322–364.

33. *Cámara*, CCIX, 684–685. *Cámara*, CCX, 369–374. "Buen Fin, Pero Malos Medios," *La Democracia*, April 18, 1911.

34. *Cámara*, CCX, 409–417.

35. *Cámara*, CCX, 119–127. *Cámara*, CCXI, 140–154, 246–260, 343–348. *Cámara*, CCXII, 3–16.

10. THE MODEL COUNTRY

1. *El Banco de la República Oriental del Uruguay en el XXVo Aniversario de Su Fundación, 1896–24 de Agosto–1921* (Montevideo, 1921), 30–63. "Movimiento Bancario de Abril," *El Siglo*, May 19, 1905.

2. José Pedro Barrán and Benjamín Nahum, *Historia Rural del Uruguay Moderno*, II (Montevideo, 1971), 505–508. José Serrato, "Don José Batlle y Ordoñez" in [Acción] *Batlle. Su Vida. Su Obra* (Montevideo, 1956), 6.

3. *El Banco de la República Oriental del Uruguay 1896–24 de Agosto–1917* (Montevideo, 1918), 115, 130–137, 244–245.

4. Until actual capital reached 12 million pesos, the Bank would add to capital its annual profits after paying the debt service on the loan to found the Bank, whether or not there was a government budget surplus; between 12 and 20 million pesos, half the profits would go to capital, half to the national treasury. The banknote emission increase was for banknotes of 10 pesos and over. Smaller denominations were unchanged; their emission remained limited to half the bank's paid-in capital.

5. *Cámara*, CCXI, 74–101, 354–355. *Senadores*, XCIX, 554–571.

6. *Cámara*, CXCIV, 453–455.

7. José Serrato, "José Batlle y Ordoñez y el Banco de Seguros del Estado," *El Día*, May 21, 1955. In 1914 Gabriel Terra in a Chamber speech said that a German economist, Wagner, author of a three-volume history of taxation, had inspired the law. Presumably, Serrato had consulted this work when preparing the bill. *Cámara*, CCXXXI, 189–190.

8. "El Monopolio y El Principio de Indemnización," *El Día*, July 24, 1911.

9. *Cámara*, CCXII, 79–82.

10. The list, undated, with the heading "Sobre el Banco de Seguros," is in the Batlle Archive.

11. *Cámara*, CCXII, 82–87, 93–110.

12. *Hansard's Parliamentary Debates*, Fifth Series, XXIX, Column 1898–1899.

13. A copy of the letter was sent me by the Librarian of the Foreign Office, London, through the British Consulate, Boston, Massachusetts. The telegram dated August 17, 1911, same source, from the Foreign Office to Minister Kennedy read: "Your telegram Commercial (of July 29th). Insurance Monopoly. You should make a firm but courteous communication to the Uruguayan Government, either in writing or verbally as may seem best to you, pointing out the disadvantages which would accrue to the Uruguayan public if they were debarred from continuing to enjoy the maximum benefits and minimum rates ensured to them by free competition between Insurance Companies. You should mention the possibility of claims for compensation

being brought against the Uruguayan Government if the British companies are compelled to cease operations in the Republic through the Bill becoming law.

"As the contemplated legislation would probably cause European firms to lose confidence in the stability of commercial and financial conditions in the Republic, you should draw attention to the effect of such feeling on the Uruguayan trade, and advance any other considerations which, after consultations with the Insurance Agents, you may consider likely to have weight."

14. D. C. M. Platt, *Finance, Trade, and Politics in British Foreign Policy, 1815–1914* (Oxford, 1968), 70. John Fischer Williams, "International Law and the Property of Aliens," *British Yearbook of International Law*, IX (1928), 1–30. Alexander P. Fachini, "Expropriation and International Law," *British Yearbook of International Law*, VI (1925), 159–171.

15. Batlle had written on these ideas in 1906, before leaving for Europe: "There is no doubt that it is to our country's advantage to import capital at 5 percent, so long as the capital is employed in productive tasks. . . . But is it equally unquestionable that capital which extracts 20 percent leaves us real profits?" N. [Batlle] "Sobre Liebig," *El Día*, July 24, 1906. Historians who believe that Batlle's concern with balanced budgets and strong currency prevented him from fully carrying out his economic nationalism or that reliance on foreign loans meant heightening Uruguay's dependency should consider the foreign capital replacement aspect of these policies.

16. Herbert Feis, *Europe: The World's Banker, 1870–1914* (New Haven, 1930), explains that although in England there was no formal mechanism requiring government approval for the floating of foreign loans, there were a variety of informal mechanisms, and when "important objects of British policy . . . were touched, the British Government renounced its attitude of nonintercourse between itself and the financial forces of the country," 85–87.

17. "La Coincidencia Aquella," *La Democracia*, August 23, 1911. "Dura Lección," *El Siglo*, August 23, 1911.

18. Frutos [Batlle], "Dura Lección," *El Día*, August 24, 1911.

19. *Cámara*, CCXII, 169–259.

20. Robert J. Kennedy, Montevideo, to José Romeu, September 11, 1911; Foreign Office letter No. 36276:11, September 19, 1911. Both were sent me by the Librarian of the Foreign Office, London. "Uruguayan Insurance Monopoly, Attitude of Great Britain," *The Times*, London, September 22, 1911.

21. *Cámara*, CCXII, 318–354.

22. "Promesas Que Se Esfuman," *El Siglo*, June 8, 1911. "El Cuento de la Representación Proporcional," *El Siglo*, June 18, 1911. Luis Carlos Berro, *Breve Campaña. Artículos Aparecidos en "La Acción"—Mayo–Agosto 1911* (Mon-

tevideo, 1911), 38. "Defensa Social," *La Democracia*, July 9, 1911. Eduardo Víctor Haedo, *La Caída de un Régimen la. Etapa. Las Crisis del Partido* (Montevideo, 1936), 203.

23. Partido Nacional Archivo, *Actas del Directorio*, Series I, VII, 128–129. Nepomuceno Saravia García, *Memorias de Saravia* (Montevideo, 1950), 616.

24. "Circular a las C. Departamentales," *La Democracia*, September 26, 1911.

25. Saravia García, *Memorias de Saravia*, 617. "La Circular Famosa," *El Día*, September 29, 1911.

26. *Cámara*, CCXII, 364–495. "El Célebre Monopolio," *La Democracia*, October 10, 1911.

27. *Anuario Estadístico, 1915*, 97. Cámara Mercantil de Productos del País, *El Uruguay en la Exposición de Bruselas* (Montevideo, 1910), 87–99.

28. "La Refinación del Petróleo," *El Día*, October 11, 1911.

29. *Cámara*, CCXI, 359–364. *Cámara*, CCXIII, 190–214. *Senadores*, XCIX, 599. The committee report and documentation on bottles assembled by the contending parties are an extremely valuable case study on the cross currents of protection.

30. *Cámara*, CXII, 499.

31. *Senadores*, C, 349.

32. *Cámara*, CXII, 500–540, 544–590. "La Moral de una Sanción," *La Democracia*, October 20, 1911.

33. *Senadores*, C, 349–356. "La Fabricación de Sarnífugos," *El Día*, November 16, 1911.

34. "Partido Colorado," *El Día*, June 20, 1925.

35. Alberto A. Márquez, *Bosquejo de Nuestra Propiedad Territorial. Tesis Presentada para optar al grado de doctor en Jurisprudencia* (Montevideo, 1893), 229–389. José P. Barrán and Benjamín Nahum, *Historia Rural del Uruguay Moderno*, IV (Montevideo, 1972), 17–18.

36. *Asamblea General*, XII, 422. *Senadores*, C, 277–284, 315–323. "Partido Colorado," *El Día*, August 21, 1925.

37. José Serrato, "José Batlle y Ordoñez y el Banco de Seguros del Estado," *El Día*, May 21, 1955.

38. *Cámara*, CCXIII, 3–23, 31–51, 61–69.

39. Reginald Lloyd and others, editors, *Impresiones de la República del Uruguay en el Siglo Veinte* (London, 1911), 89.

40. Students from interior *liceos* would be able to enter the University faculties of Business, Agronomy, and Veterinary Medicine but would need to go to the preparatory division of the University before entering the prestigious faculties of Law, Medicine, and Engineering. The departmental *liceos* would be simple. A Director and five professors were budgeted for each.

41. *Cámara*, CCXIII, 143–144, 171–176, 320–345.

42. "Nuestras Mujeres," *El Día*, June 27, 1911. "Los Empleos Públicos y las Mujeres," *El Día*, April 10, 1911.

43. *Cámara*, CCXIII, 176–189, 345–387, 390–411, 457–484. Domingo Arena, "Anécdotas de Excepcional Valor Documentario," *Biblioteca "Batlle,"* Montevideo, I (1942), 166; originally published in *El Día*, October 20, 1937.

44. José Serrato, "José Batlle y Ordoñez y el Banco de Seguros del Estado," *El Día*, May 21, 1955.

45. "Silencio Inútil," *El Siglo*, December 10, 1911.

46. [Batlle], "El P. E. Colegiado," *El Día*, December 18, 1911.

47. Domingo Arena, "Conferencia dada por el Dr. Domingo Arena sobre reforma constitucional, en el teatro Stella D'Italia, la noche del 17 de Mayo de 1913," *Biblioteca "Batlle,"* I (Montevideo, 1942), 29–30.

48. Interview, Rafael Batlle Pacheco, July 15, 1952. Interview, César Batlle Pacheco, July 16, 1952. Arena tried to give the impression in later years that Batlle had taken him into his confidence on the colegiado from Europe, but the supposed letter he cited was, in fact, the sentence from "The Correspondent's" interview. "Desde Montevideo, Una Conversación con el Senador Arena," *La Vanguardia* (Buenos Aires), February 12, 1916. It was now evident that Batlle's reluctance to announce his presidential program, revealed in his July 18, 1910, letter to Manini from Paris, came because he knew that he could not include the centerpiece of his planning, the Colegiado, in it and that the omission would be thrown up to him ever after. [Batlle], "Batllistas y Riveristas Con el Doctor P. Díaz," *El Día*, July 29, 1919. Batlle's European statement to Manini which Manini recounted in a 1913 private manuscript, appears in Carlos Manini Ríos, Anoche Me Llamó Batlle (Montevideo, 1970), 233.

49. "Se Despeja una Incógnita," *El Día*, July 25, 1919.

11. PRESSING FORWARD

1. *Cámara*, CCXIV, 397–425. Peter H. Smith, *Politics and Beef in Argentina: Patterns of Conflict and Change* (New York, 1969), 41, 57–70.

2. Martín C. Martínez, "La Elefantiasis Social," and José Irureta Goyena, "Divagando," *El Siglo*, December 31, 1911.

3. *Cámara*, CCXIV, 252–309, 457–480. *Senadores*, C, 534–627.

4. "El Registro de la Propiedad Raíz," *El Día*, January 23, 1912. "Empadronamiento de la propiedad raíz-rural," *La Democracia*, January 20, 1912.

5. *Senadores*, C, 410–443.

6. *Cámara*, CCXIV, 212–233, 431–446. *Senadores*, C, 493–534.

7. *Cámara*, CCXIV, 379–381. Leopoldo Caravia, to Batlle, January 5, 1912, Batlle Archive. Domingo Arena, prologue to Luis Batlle Berres, editor,

El Batllismo y el Problema de los Combustibles (Montevideo, 1931), 5. "El Banco de Seguros," *El Día*, January 6, 15, 1912.

8. [Batlle], "Hoy lo Mismo que Ayer," *El Día*, March 13, 1912. "Los Puntos Sobre las Íes," *El Siglo*, March 21, 1912.

9. *Cámara*, CCXV, 20–42.

10. [Batlle] Laura, "El Voto de las Mujeres," *El Día*, March 14, 1912.

11. Dora Isella Russell, "Ana Amalia Batlle Pacheco," *El Día–Suplemento*, February 3, 1963. Rafael Di Miero, Paris, to Batlle, May 10, 1912, Batlle Archive.

12. *Cámara*, CCXV, 262–286, 345–372. *Cámara*, CCXVI, 129–140. *Senadores*, CI, 70–71, 159–160, 204.

13. *Cámara*, CCXV, 57–65, 173–183.

14. "El Monopolio del Alcohol," *El Día*, March 7, 1912. [Batlle], "El Estanco del Alcohol," *El Día*, March 15, 1912.

15. *Cámara*, CCXVI, 263–326, 361–392, 469–494, 524–552. *Cámara*, CCXVII, 7–35, 94–123, 126–151, 227–252, 347–359, 366–396, 538–563. *Cámara*, CCXVIII, 12–26, 30–58, 74, 105–162, 190–227, 233–317, 322–404, 411–493. *Cámara*, CCXIX, 47–65. *Senadores*, CII, 184–187, 318. *El Siglo*, after "patient investigation," reported on the number of public employees in the 1912 budget in "El Funcionario en la República," *El Siglo*, April 18, 1912. The data on the 1904–05 budget is from *Anuario Estadístico, 1907–1908*, I, 912. The Gregorio L. Rodríguez quotation is in *Cámara*, CCXVIII, 290.

16. "Banco Hipotecario del Uruguay," *Industria y Comercio*, Montevideo, III (July 21, 1908), 501–502. "Lo del Banco Hipotecario," *El Día*, July 3, 1908. Barrán and Nahum, VII, 109–118.

17. *Cámara*, CCXVII, 216, 255–295. *Senadores*, CI, 328–352, 438–457. Banco Hipotecario del Uruguay, *25 Años, Banco Hipotecario del Uruguay, 1912–1937* (Montevideo, 1937), 49–72.

18. In "The Catholic God," Don Pepe rejected the doctrine of eternal damnation. "The God of the Catholics the way they picture him cannot be loved. He is a being of incurable evil, an evil which surpasses every limit and still overflows filling the universe with evil." [Batlle] "El Dios Católico," *El Día*, April 2, 1912.

19. *Anuario Estadístico, 1920*, 23.

20. In fact, Areco's bill had provisions against divorce by whim. Divorce at the request of either spouse could not be invoked until after two years of marriage, the divorce process would take one and a half years, and the husband could be required to pay alimony. Nevertheless, a husband or wife who wanted a divorce would get it without demonstrating any reason.

21. "El Divorcio Ad-Libitum Juzgado Por el Foro Nacional," *El Siglo*, June 16, 1912.

22. *Senadores*, CI, 540–542. Arena in 1935 gave a similar, though sanitized, description of Batlle's divorce views: Domingo Arena, "El Humanitarismo de Batlle," *Biblioteca "Batlle,"* I (Montevideo, 1942), 145–146, originally published in *El Día*, October 20, 1935.

23. *Senadores*, CI, 367–387, 422–503, 540–553, 594–615. *Senadores*, CII, 35–58, 69–91, 109–122, 130–143, 159–168, 192–205, 217–258, 284, 318–331, 335–357, 373–388, 394–427, 430–443.

24. "El Cuento de la Representación Proporcional," *El Siglo*, June 18, 1911.

25. *Cámara*, CCXIII, 423–526. *Cámara*, CCXV, 110–158, 202–241, 289–333, 379–408, 429–446, 470–591. *Cámara*, CCXVI, 3–25, 85–121, 170–196, 336–356, 427–463. The Rodó quote is in *Cámara*, CCXV, 393. Batlle notations to Giúdici biography, 432, Batlle Archive. [Batlle], "El Desastre," *El Día*, May 13, 1912.

26. "Las Declaraciones del Señor Batlle," *El Día*, August 20, 1912.

27. *Cámara*, CCXVII, 48–52, 160–177, 400–414, 468–481. *Cámara*, CCXIX, 28–41, 120–139, 154–178. *Senadores*, CII, 410–411.

28. The notebooks are in the Batlle Archive.

29. [Batlle], "Batllistas y Riveristas Con el doctor Ramón P. Díaz," *El Día*, July 26, 29, 30, 1919. Pedro Manini Ríos, March, 1913, manuscript in Carlos Manini Ríos, *Anoche Me Llamó Batlle* (Montevideo, 1970), 233. [Batlle], "Reforma Radical," *El Día*, March 29, 1913. "Del doctor Manini Ríos," *El Siglo*, September 5, 1913. Santiago A. Grezzi, Trinidad, to Batlle, March, 1912, Batlle Archive.

30. "La Delegación á Cádiz," *El Día*, August 20, 1912. "El doctor Manini Ríos," *El Día*, August 24, 1912. "La Delegación Uruguaya en el Centenario de las Cortes de Cádiz," *El Día*, August 26, 1912. "La Cartera de Interior," *El Siglo*, August 23, 1912.

31. *Senadores*, CII, 454–456, 462–463. "El Senado y la Reforma Constitutional," *Diario del Plata*, August 29, 1912. *Cámara*, CCXX, 288–302.

32. *Cámara*, CCXXIX, 512–529. Where the majority won more than three fifths of the vote, its "excess" ballots would go toward winning additional seats from the minority two-fifths seats distributed by proportional representation. Vote pooling of separate ballot lists of the same party in a department would be permitted where three fifths of the candidates at the top of the ballot were the same. The likely effect of both these provisions was to increase the Colorado majority in the Constitutional Convention.

33. "Compás de espera," *La Democracia*, August 21, 1912; "La Reforma y el Dr. X," *La Democracia*, August 30, 1912.

34. "La Reforma," *El Día*, August 31, 1912.

35. [Batlle], "Concepto de la Política," *El Día*, June 19, 1912.

12. ARAZATÍ AND RÍO NEGRO

1. "La Reelección Presidencial," *El Día*, September 21, 1912.

2. "A cuenta . . . Las Declaraciones del Sr. Batlle," *La Democracia*, September 22, 1912. "Impresiones y Dudas," *La Democracia*, September 24, 1912.

3. "Con los Colegas," *La Democracia*, September 6, 1912. Partido Nacional Archivo, *Actas del Directorio*, Series I, VII, 154.

4. Manuel Herrera, Fray Bentos, to Claudio Williman, September 8, 1912, and Colonel Orlando Pedragosa, Fray Bentos, to Claudio Williman, September 14, 1912, Archivo del Dr. Claudio Williman, Archivo General de la Nación, Montevideo, Caja O (hereafter cited as Archivo Williman). "Garantías Electorales," *Diario del Plata*, October 29, 1912. "Preparativos Electorales," *El Día*, October 31, 1912. "La Gran Tormenta en un Vaso de Agua," *El Día*, January 9, 1913.

5. Diary of Ana Amalia Batlle Pacheco, Batlle Archive. Dora Isella Russell, "El Diario de Una Agonía," *El Día–Suplemento*, January 23, 1966.

6. The notebooks Batlle kept on Ana Amalia's health detail these developments. The notebooks, cables from the Uruguayan ministers to Germany and France, and drafts of Batlle's responses from November 1912 to January 1913, are all in the Batlle Archive.

7. "Filosofía de los Ascensos," *La Democracia*, September 13, 1912. "Los Sueldos en el Ejército," *Diario del Plata*, July 24, 1912.

8. "Actualidad," *El Siglo*, November 10, 1912. Arena to Manini, undated, written December 1912, in Carlos Manini Ríos, *Anoche Me Llamó Batlle* (Montevideo, 1970), 31, 200.

9. "La Asamblea de Bagé," *La Democracia*, November 19, 1912. Nepomuceno Saravia García, *Memorias de Saravia* (Montevideo, 1956), 616–617.

10. "El viaje del Sr. Batlle," *La Democracia*, November 19, 1912; Diary of Ana Amalia Batlle Pacheco, Batlle Archivo. "El Desembarque de Batlle en el Arazatí," *La Democracia*, November 24, 1912. The Directorio newspaper had the best coverage because Dr. Juan B. Morelli, a Nationalist leader, assisted in Ana Amalia's case.

11. "Williman y La Influencia Oficial," *El Siglo*, November 26, 1912.

12. Williman, *El Dr. Claudio Williman. Su Vida Pública*, 821.

13. J. C. Bayeto, Fray Bentos, to Williman, November 12, 1912. J. D. Bayeto, President Comisión Departamental, Fray Bentos, telegram to Williman, November 16, 1912. Santiago Fabini, Montevideo, to Williman, November 15, 1912. Williman, telegram, Montevideo, to J. C. Bayeto, November 16, 1912. All are in Archivo Williman.

14. "Las Senadurías," *El Día*, November 19, 1912.

15. Copy of letter José Serrato, Montevideo, to Juan José Aguiar, November 18, 1912, Archivo Williman.

16. Ramón Orozco, Fray Bentos, to Williman, December 27, 1912, Archivo Williman.

17. "Después del Comicio," *El Día*, November 25, 1912. "La Elección de Río Negro," *El Siglo*, December 14, 1912.

18. José Espalter, Genoa, to Claudio Williman, December 6, 1912, Archivo Williman.

19. [Batlle], "Insistiendo," *El Día*, November 25, 1912.

20. Arena to Manini, undated, written December 1912, in Carlos Manini Ríos, *Anoche Me Llamó Batlle*, 31, 60–61, 200.

21. *Cámara*, CCXXI, 399–517. *Cámara*, CCXXII, 13–22, 26–95. Batlle notations to Giúdici biography, 437–438, 311, Batlle Archive. Conversations with Anita Chervière de Batlle Pacheco, June–September 1966.

22. "Las Elecciones de Río Negro," *El Día*, December 7, 1912. "La Elección de Río Negro," *El Siglo*, December 15, 1912. "Las Senadurías," *El Día*, December 9, 10, 1912. "La Senaduría por Río Negro," *El Día*, December 14, 16, 21, 31, 1912.

23. "Los Diputados Herrera y Espalter," *El Siglo*, December 25, 1912.

24. "Sobre Las Elecciones de Río Negro," *El Día*, December 27, 1912.

25. "Corriendo o Veo," *El Siglo*, December 28, 1912.

26. [Batlle], "La Elección de Río Negro," *El Día*, December 28, 1912. [Batlle], "Sobre Cosas Electorales," *El Día*, December 30, 1912.

27. "La Elección de Río Negro," *El Día*, December 31, 1912.

28. "En la Comisión N. Colorada," *El Día*, January 7, 1913.

29. "El Presidente de la República," *El Día*, January 8, 1913.

30. *Cámara*, CCXXII, 133–369.

31. "En la Comisión N. Colorada," *El Día*, January 13, 1913. "Notas Breves," *El Siglo*, January 19, 1913. "La Presidencia de la Comisión Colorada," *El Día*, January 20, 1913.

32. "Que se Callen," *El Siglo*, December 31, 1912.

33. Carlos Travieso, the supposed leader of the kidnapping, indignantly denied, then and later, having anything to do with plots. Carlos Travieso, Montevideo, to Batlle, February 3, 1923, Batlle Archive. Rafael Batlle Pacheco, interview, June 9, 1952.

34. "Ana Amalia Batlle Pacheco," *El Día*, January 25, 27, 1913. "La Ceremonia Fúnebre de Ayer," *Diario del Plata*, January 26, 1913. Dora Isella Russell, "Ana Amalia Batlle Pacheco," *El Día–Suplemento*, February 3, 1963.

APPRAISALS: II

1. José Pedro Barrán and Benjamín Nahum, *Historia Rural del Uruguay Moderno*, VII, *Agricultura, Crédito y Transporte Bajo Batlle 1905–1914* (Montevideo, 1978), 42.

2. M. H. J. Finch, "Three Perspectives on the Crisis in Uruguay," *Journal of Latin American Studies*, 3 (November 1971), 189–190.

3. John Kirby, "On the Viability of Small Countries: Uruguay and New Zealand Compared," *Journal of Interamerican Studies and World Affairs*, 17 (August 1975), 279.

4. Peter Winn, "British Informal Empire in Uruguay in the Nineteenth Century," *Past and Present*, No. 73 (November 1976), 123.

5. Ricardo Martínez Ces, *El Uruguay Batllista* (Montevideo, 1962), 45–46.

6. Finch, "Three Perspectives," 184.

7. "La Derrota Nacionalista," *El Día*, November 27, 1907.

8. A similar view to Martínez Ces' lateral paths is developed by Carlos Real de Azúa, *El Impulso y Su Freno: Tres Décadas del Batllismo y las Raíces de la Crisis Uruguaya* (Montevideo, 1964).

9. *Cámara*, CCXX, 309–391.

10. *Asamblea General*, XII, 422–425.

11. *Asamblea General*, XII, 414.

12. "El Año a Vuelo de Pájaro," *El Siglo*, January 1, 1913.

13. *Anuario Estadístico, 1916*, 472. *Asamblea General*, XII, 413.

14. Roque Faraone, *Introducción a la Historia Económica del Uruguay (1825–1973)* (Montevideo, 1974), 95.

15. *Asamblea General*, XII, 285.

16. Banco de la República Oriental del Uruguay, *1896–24 de Agosto–1917* (Montevideo, 1918), 320–321, 335, 337, 354. *Asamblea General*, XII, 414. Barrán and Nahum, VII, 99–103, argue that the Bank did not lend appreciably to new and small producers. Their proof is indirect—the Bank's limited mortgage lending. They do not attempt to measure the effects of the Bank's massive credit expansion upon new and small business.

17. Pedro Cosio outlined Serrato's plan in *Senadores*, CVI, 428–429. A. G. Ford, *The Gold Standard, 1880–1914 Britain and Argentina* (Oxford, England, 1962), 176–177. *Anuario Estadístico, 1915*, 333.

PART III. CRISES

13. THE APUNTES

1. Conversations, Anita Chervière de Batlle Pacheco, June–September, 1966.

2. The diary that Batlle kept from April 4 to May 10, 1894, with the entry by Matilde dated March 15 [1913], is in the Batlle Archive.

3. Domingo Arena, "Los Últimos Días de Batlle," *Biblioteca "Batlle,"* Montevideo, I (1942), 205. Originally published in *El Día,* October 20, 1930.

4. The drafts are in the Batlle Archive.

5. *Senadores,* CIII, 232, 247–249. "El Ministerio del Interior," *El Día,* February 19, 1913. "Gobierno de Extramuros," *El Siglo,* February 20, 1913. [Batlle], "Costumbres Democráticas," *El Día,* February 22, 1913.

6. "Importantes Manifestaciones del doctor Viera," *El Día,* February 22, 1913. "El Directorio del Partido," *La Democracia,* January 15, 1913.

7. [Batlle], "¡Y Cómo nó!" *El Día,* March 1, 1913. "¡Lo que Faltaba!" *El Siglo,* February 13, 1913. "Las Elecciones Generales," *El Día,* February 18, 1913.

8. [Batlle], "El Día de Descanso Obrero," *El Día,* July 24, 1911.

9. *Cámara,* CCXXIII, 143–290. A bound notebook with the eight-hour day message and law project, handwritten by Batlle, is in his Archive.

10. [Batlle], "Las Ocho Horas," *El Día,* March 4, 1913.

11. On May Day, 1912, the Federación Obrera proclaimed its lack of confidence in eight-hour day legislation. "Workers: let our slogan and our chant in the First of May manifestation be: Down With the Wage System." "Cuestiones Obreras," *El Día,* April 25, 1912.

Because most Uruguayan workers were unskilled, easy to replace, and had no savings, employers could either wait out strikers or hire replacements. After a failed strike, workers often deserted the union. This meant that labor leaders had to be very careful in deciding whether to call strikes. But their Anarchist outlook encouraged them to strike. For example, they called La Commercial's trolley workers out a month after the general strike; only 200 of the company's 1,120 workers struck. There were 41 strikes in 1911, of which 16 were won; in 1912 strikes were down to 24, of which 6 were won. The 1911 Congress of the Federación Obrera claimed to represent 7,000 workers. In 1912 no figures were released, and a special committee was assigned the task of reorganizing dissolved unions. *Anuario Estadístico, 1909–1910,* I, Apéndice XCV. *Anuario Estadístico, 1911-1912,* 717–718. Francisco R. Pintos, *Historia del Movimiento Obrero del Uruguay* (Montevideo, 1960), 93, 97. "Cuestiones Obreras," *El Día,* October 15, 1912. "Otra Vez . . .," *El Día,* June, 20, 21, 1911. "Los Huelguistas de la Comercial," *El Día,* June 22, 1911. "En los Tranvías," *El Siglo,* June 20, 1911. "Movimiento Obrero," *El Día,* June 8, 1911.

12. Pintos, *Historia del Movimiento Obrero del Uruguay,* 89.

13. The 1908 census employment figures for all Uruguay, excluding

agriculture, ranching, professions, domestics, and public employees, added up to 242,499, of whom 31,247 were women and 77,969 were aliens. *Anuario Estadístico, 1907–1908*, II, Part II. *Censo General de la República*, XXXIV.

14. Manuscript written by Pedro Manini Ríos, March 2–24, 1913, printed as Documentary Appendix V in Carlos Manini Ríos, *Anoche Me Llamó Batlle* (Montevideo, 1970), 227–234. Hereafter referred to as Manini manuscript.

15. [Batlle], "Se Despeja Una Incógnita," *El Día*, July 25, 1919.

16. Manini manuscript.

17. [Batlle], "El P. E. Colegiado, Apuntes Sobre Su Posible Organización y Funcionamiento," *El Día*, March 4, 1913. Though the Apuntes concentrated on the collegiate executive, the article outlined Batlle's "total plan" for Constitutional reform. The plan called for a Senate with double its present membership (of 19) and no change in how it was elected. The Chamber of Deputies (89) would also be doubled, "but it would be elected by the most perfect system possible of proportional representation." Under the reformed Constitution Supreme Court justices, now appointed, would be directly elected as vacancies occurred. The expansion of both houses fitted Batlle's long-expressed preferences for large assemblies to avoid accidental majorities. The Senate, as Don Pepe was finding out, was vulnerable to this, and the danger of minority coalitions converted into majorities was built into proportional representation. The expanded houses and the election of Supreme Court justices would popularize politics, and the potential for divisiveness in the Chamber, to be elected by proportional representation, would be counteracted by the large number of loyal party members who would vote party positions.

18. [Batlle], "El 'truc' del Porfirismo en la Junta de Gobierno," *El Día*, April 23, 1913.

19. "El Acabóse," *El Siglo*, March 5, 1913.

20. [Batlle], "Razones y No Gritos," *El Día*, March 6, 1913.

21. [Batlle], "La Junta de Gobierno," *El Día*, March 7, 1913.

22. [Batlle], "Sí, Siempre en lo Mismo," *El Día*, March 6, 1913. [Batlle], "La Junta de Gobierno," *El Día*, March 7, 1913. "Con Don Porfirio," *El Siglo*, March 8, 1913. "La Gran Mistificación de don Pepe Batlle," *La Democracia*, March 8, 1913. "Contra La Reforma," *La Democracia*, March 9, 1913.

14. ENOUGH!

1. Manini recorded this in a way damaging to Batlle. Arena "in one of his habitual outbursts of frankness confessed to us that Batlle would not accept any modifications in the reform procedures because he was convinced that an open consultation with the people meant the failure of his project and he must do good for the people even against their will." This sounds, however, more

like Manini's sentiments about Batlle than anything Batlle would ever admit, even to Arena. It may have been produced by Manini's pressure on Arena for proportional representation in the constituent election (which Manini had formally proposed in 1910, *Cámara*, CCVI, 375) as a means of open consultation with the people. Manini manuscript.

2. Manini manuscript.

3. [Batlle], "Consejo Saravista," *El Día*, March 12, 1913. [Batlle], "Táctica Vieja," *El Día*, March 14, 1913. [Batlle], "Sobre el Colegiado," *El Día*, March 10, 1913. [Batlle], "Los Enemigos del Gobierno Colegiado," *El Día*, March 11, 1913.

4. Manini manuscript.

5. Comité Central de la Juventud Colorada Anticolegialista, *Documentos Políticos de Propaganda anti-Colegialista del Dr. Pedro Manini y Ríos* (Montevideo, 1913), 4–14. The speech is reprinted in Manini Ríos, *Anoche Me Llamó Batlle*, Appendix IV, 223–227.

6. [Batlle], "La Unidad Colorada," *El Día*, March 15, 1913.

7. José Serrato, interview, September 21, 24, 1952. "El Ingeniero Serrato," *El Día*, March 14, 1913. [Batlle], "El Documento Inconsulto," *El Día*, March 19, 1913. "Los Ministros de Industria é Instrucción Pública," *El Día*, March 17, 1913.

8. "Las Carteras de Hacienda y de Industria," *El Día*, March 14, 1913.

9. Domingo Arena, untitled article first published in *El Día-Suplemento*, October 20, 1933. *Biblioteca "Batlle,"* Montevideo, I (1942), 155. Domingo Arena, "Baltasar Brum," *El Día-Suplemento*, April 1, 1934, republished *El Día*, March 31, 1953. "El Ministerio de Instrucción Pública," *El Día*, March 15, 1913.

10. [Batlle], "La Junta de Gobierno," *El Día*, March 12, 1913. [Batlle], "El Gobierno Colegiado y los Acuerdos de Ministros," *El Día*, March 14, 1913.

11. Manini manuscript.

12. "Un Documento Extraordinario," *El Día*, March 18, 1913.

13. [Batlle], "Los Testimonios de la Historia," *El Día*, April 2, 1913. [Batlle], "El Documento Inconsulto," *El Día*, March 19, 1913.

14. The list is in the Batlle Archive.

15. [Batlle], "El Veredicto Colorado," *El Día*, December 8, 1913.

16. "El Doctor Williman," *El Día*, March 19, 1913. Manini manuscript.

17. [Batlle], "Batllistas y Riveristas Con el doctor Díaz," *El Día*, July 30, 1919. Batlle disclosed that he had these men in mind in a press polemic in which the charge that he planned the Colegiado as a means of staying in power was repeated. To demonstrate that nobody could have dominated in the Colegiado, he wrote: "What list? The one which would have been calculated by Señor Batlle y Ordoñez when he presented his project, before

the anticolegialist resistance developed, the one he would have sponsored had this resistance not developed; the one of the first line men in government.

"That list—let us agree that señor Batlle y Ordoñez would be on it [dando por sentado que el señor Batlle y Ordoñez figuraría en ella]—would almost certainly have been the following: Batlle y Ordoñez, Serrato, Williman, Soca, Viera, Campisteguy, Arena, Manini Ríos, Blengio Rocca." Carlos Manini Ríos, *Anoche Me Llamó Batlle*, 58, sees this article as proof that Batlle intended to be part of the first Colegiado; but in context "let us agree that Señor Batlle y Ordoñez would be on it" was a debating tactic to demonstrate that not even Batlle could have dominated the planned Colegiado, not an admission that he planned to take part in it.

In the Batlle Archive, on the back of the letter from Dr. Carlos Santín Rossi to Batlle on Friedman and bringing Ana Amalia to Europe, there is a list in Batlle's handwriting: Serrato, Williman, Viera, Otero, Soca, Blengio, Espalter, Varela Acevedo (crossed out). The list is similar to the one published by Batlle in 1919, but there are three new Senators on it. Arena, Manini, and Campisteguy do not appear. The list seems to be a tentative revision by Batlle of intended members of the first Colegiado and may explain Espalter's unexpected separation from the eleven Senators.

18. [Batlle], "Noticias Falsas," *El Día*, May 13, 1913. Shortly after the Batlle-Williman meeting, stories by Dr. X. appeared in *La Razón* on May 10 and 12, 1913, that Batlle had offered Williman the next presidency if the Colegiado did not materialize and that Williman had rejected the offer. José Claudio Williman, interview, September 1, 1952, said that first Batlle offered his father the presidency if he would accept the Colegiado, and when his father refused, offered it if he would not oppose the Colegiado, and his father again refused. Batlle on May 12 and 13, 1913, in *El Día* publicly denied that he had offered Williman the presidency. There is no documentation that Batlle did offer Williman a place on the Colegiado, but this interpretation is consistent with Batlle's intentions and the fact that Serrato and Manini acknowledged that Batlle had offered them places.

19. José Serrato, interview, September 21, 24, 1952. José Serrato, "Don José Batlle y Ordoñez" in [Acción], *Batlle. Su Vida Su Obra* (Montevideo, 1956), 7. Ariosto D. González, *José Serrato, Técnico del Estado* (Montevideo, 1942), 126. Although the quotes come directly from Serrato, I have surmised his reasons for rejecting the offer, and the surmise may do him an injustice. In the September 1952 interviews he did say that Batlle, earlier, had asked Fleurquin, Serrato's friend and now one of the eleven Senators, to convince Serrato to support constitutional reform. Fleurquin, without saying why, gathered 25 or 30 of Serrato's political supporters, who unsuccessfully tried to

convince Serrato. When Fleurquin reported this to Batlle, Batlle was angry and put in a call to Viera. I have the impression that had Fleurquin explained to Serrato that the presidency was at stake, Serrato would have allowed himself to be convinced, as Viera had been convinced.

20. Jacobo Varela Acevedo, interview, April 18, 1952.

15. REGROUPING

1. "Integración del Ministerio," *El Día*, March 26, 1913. Juan C. Quinteros Delgado, *Vida y Obra de Pedro Cosio* (2nd edition, Montevideo, 1937), 3–46. Wifredo Pi, *Una Realidad Internacional, El doctor Baltasar Brum y la Política Exterior* (Montevideo, 1918), 25–34. Juan Carlos Welker, *Baltasar Brum. Verbo y Acción* (Montevideo, 1945), 17–74. "Ministros!," *La Democracia*, March 27, 1913. "Cómo Somos Aristocráticos," *El Siglo*, April 2, 1913.

2. Gabriel Terra later claimed that he, acting as attorney for Sudriers' relative, had suggested the location, totally unaware that the Government intended to build there. *Cámara*, CCXXXVII, 376. Interview, Rafael Batlle Pacheco, July 1, 1952. "La Renuncia del Ministro Sudriers," *El Día*, November 28, 1912. "El Ministro de Obras Públicas," *El Día*, November 27, 1912. Blanco, though not an engineer, headed the Montevideo port works office and shared Batlle's concerns. Just before being nominated Minister of Public Works, Blanco called for a Congress on Roads. "If freight rates are lowered—and doubtless the State railroad network will contribute to this—and low-cost, easy-maintenance, all-year-round roads are built, we will solve a great problem. Land subdivision will be accentuated, the interior will be industrialized, and caudillaje, the result of our almost uninhabited latifundios, will be ended": "Caminos," *El Día*, October 17, 1912.

3. Baltasar Brum, "Aspectos de la Obra de Batlle," *Biblioteca Batlle*, II (Montevideo, 1942), 8. The article was first published in *La Nación* (Buenos Aires), October 1929.

4. G. Clemenceau, *Notes de Voyage dans l'Amérique du Sud. Argentine-Uruguay-Brésil* (Paris, 1911), 194–195.

5. [Batlle], "Reforma Radical," *El Día*, March 29, 1913.

6. Tomás Berreta, Jefatura Canelones, to Batlle, April 1, 1913, Batlle Archive.

7. Manini manuscript.

8. "Al País y al Partido Colorado," *El Día*, March 27, 1913.

9. [Batlle], "Actividades Partidarias," *El Día*, March 28, 1913. "La Reforma y la Juventud Colorada," *El Día*, March 27, 1913.

10. "En Favor de la Reforma," *El Día*, March 28, 1913.

11. "Una Aclaración," *El Día*, April 2, 1913. "La Maniobra Aquella," *El Siglo*, April 1, 1913. "Las Negociaciones Fracasadas," *El Siglo*, April 3, 1913.

12. *Cámara*, CCXXIII, 534–546. "La Elección de la Constituyente," *El Día*, April 3, 1913.

13. "La Convención Colorada," *El Día*, April 7, 1913. "La Convención Colorada," *El Siglo*, April 6, 1913.

14. [Batlle], "Lo de la Descalificaciones," *El Día*, April 7, 1913.

15. "Del doctor Manini Ríos," *El Día*, April 1, 1913. "El Club de la 7a y el Dr Manini," *El Día*, April 15, 1913.

16. "La Idea Avanza," *El Siglo*, March 23, 1913.

17. Emilio Frugoni, *Los Nuevos Fundamentos* (Montevideo, 1919), 159, 174; Jacinto Oddone, *Historia del Socialismo Argentino*, Vol. 1 (Buenos Aires, 1934), 225–226. Un Socialista, "El Septimo," *El Día*, August 20, 1912. "La Reforma Constitucional," *El Día*, April 1, 1913. "Los Socialistas y la Reforma," *El Día*, March 27, 1913. "Por las Ocho Horas," *El Día*, April 7, 1913. "El Mitin de Anoche," *El Siglo*, April 6, 1913. "Celo para Obreros," *El Día*, April 10, 1913. Emilio Basterga, "Los Trabajadores y la Reforma," *El Día*, April 11, 15, 1913. Ángel Falco, "Las Instrucciones del año XIII y la Reforma," *El Día*, April 15, 1913.

18. "La Gran Demostración de Anoche," *El Día*, April 8, 1913. Washington Paullier, *El Ejecutivo Colegiado y la Reforma Constitucional* (Montevideo, 1914), 11–33.

19. [Batlle], "Prestigios Positivos," *El Día*, April 22, 1913.

20. [Batlle], "El 'Truc' del Porfirismo en la Junta de Gobierno," *El Día*, April 23, 1913. [Batlle], "Consecuencia de Ideas," *El Día*, May 2, 1913.

21. "Colegialistas y no Colegialistas," *El Día*, April 22, 1913.

22. "Resolución del Directorio," *La Democracia*, April 30, 1913.

23. [Batlle], "Reforma Radical," *El Día*, March 25, 1913.

24. "Comité Central Colorado," *El Siglo*, May 7, 1913. "Indiferencia Culpable," *La Democracia*, April 23, 1913. "Los Hacendados y la Política," *Diario del Plata*, May 1, 1913. "El Jefe Político de Minas," *El Día*, May 3, 1913.

25. "El 1° de Mayo," *El Día*, May 2, 1913. "La Actitud de la Policía en los Últimos Mítines Populares," *El Día*, May 5, 1913. "El 1° de Mayo en Montevideo," *El Siglo*, May 3, 1913. "El Escándalo del Jueves," *El Siglo*, May 3, 1913. *Cámara*, CCXXIV, 112–113, 161–193.

26. "La Candidatura del doctor Viera," *El Día*, May 10, 1913.

27. [Batlle], "Los Empleados y el Colegiado," *El Día*, May 13, 1913.

28. Antón Martín Saavedra, *La Comedia de la Vida. Carta Epílogo de Domingo Arena* (Montevideo, 1917), 117–121.

29. Domingo Arena, "Conferencia dada por el Dr. Domingo Arena sobre reforma constitucional, en el teatro Stella D'Italia, la noche del 17 de Mayo de 1913," *Biblioteca "Batlle,"* Montevideo, I (1942), 25.

30. Arena, *Conferencia* . . ., 21–70. The peroration had the mark of another writer Arena admired, Émile Zola (*J'accuse*). "Truth is on the march and nothing will stop it."

31. "El Gran Homenaje al Doctor José Pedro Ramírez," *El Siglo*, April 10, 1913. "En el Día del Homenaje al Doctor José Pedro Ramírez," *El Siglo*, April 9, 1913. "Resonancias," *La Democracia*, April 11, 1913. [Batlle], "Permanente," *El Día*, April 13, 1913. "La Prensa y El Presidente de la República," *El Siglo*, April 17, 1913. [Batlle], "La Palabra del Contubernio," *El Día*, April 16, 1913.

32. "Preparando el Mitin," *El Siglo*, May 21, 1913. "Una Declaración Contubernial," *El Día*, May 23, 1913.

33. Comité Central de la Juventud Colorada Anticolegialista, *Documentos Políticos de Propaganda Anticolegialista del Dr. Pedro Manini y Ríos* (Montevideo, 1913), 19–31.

34. [Batlle], "Partidismo y Colegialismo," *El Día*, May 27, 1913. [Batlle], "El Momento Propicio," *El Día*, May 26, 1913.

35. *Cámara*, CCXXIII, 290–513 passim. *Cámara*, CCXXIV, 3–618 passim. *Cámara*, CCXXV, 8–13, 30–48, 54–113.

36. Batlle was not a blind enthusiast for American capital. When he proposed a State insurance company to Manini and Arena from Europe in 1908, he noted that "at a single swoop, the country would save many hundreds of pesos that now go to North America." Batlle, Paris, to Arena, February 25, 1908, Batlle Archive.

37. *Senadores*, CIII, 340–341. *Cámara*, CCXXIII, 327–328. Eduardo C. O'Brien, Montevideo, to Batlle, February 22, 1911. O'Brien, Montevideo, to Batlle, February 16, 1912. unsigned memorandum O'Brien, Montevideo, to Batlle, April 2, 1912. O'Brien, Montevideo, to Francisco J. Ros, April 4, 1912. All are in the Batlle Archive. "Crédito y Ferrocarriles," *El Día*, September 13, 1911.

38. *Senadores*, XCVII, 598–622. *Cámara*, CCVI, 400–410. J. C. Williman, *El Doctor Claudio Williman. Su Vida Pública* (Montevideo, 1957), 455–460. The contract provided that guaranteed bonds would not be issued until construction representing the difference between the project's total cost (to be agreed upon) and seven million pesos was completed. Sale of valuable lands which would be created by filling in the shoreline of the Rambla would provide funds to repay the bonds and also produce profits for the syndicate and the Uruguayan government.

39. "Uruguay: A Great Embankment Scheme," *The Times-London*, No-

vember 30, 1910. "Montevideo Public Works," *The Times-London*, September 22, 1911. "City of Montevideo Public Works Corporation Ltd.," *The Times-London*, July 26, 1911.

40. Grimthorpe, Montevideo, to President of the Republic, March 25, 1912, Batlle Archive.

41. *Senadores*, CIII, 265–269. "Uruguayan Finance," *The Times-London*, June 10, 1912. "A Propósito de la Rambla Sud," *El Día*, November 26, 1912. "Intervenciones Deprimentes," *La Democracia*, October 11, 1912.

42. *Senadores*, CIII, 258–286.

43. Memorandum submitted April 27, 1913, to Legations of France and Great Britain, Batlle Archive.

44. *Senadores*, CIII, 478–504, 510–513. *Cámara*, CCXXV, 273–294. [Batlle], "Factores de Progreso," *El Día*, April 28, 1913. Banco de la República Oriental del Uruguay, *1896–24 de Agosto-1917* (Montevideo, 1918), 247–248.

16. PARTY DISCIPLINE—VIERA

1. "Los Legisladores Colegialistas," *El Día*, June 30, 1913.

2. "La Convención N. Colorada," *El Día*, July 2, 1913. "La Convención Colorada," *El Siglo*, July 4, 1913.

3. "Los Maestros y la Política," *El Día*, July 12, 1913. Lorenzo Vicens Thievent, "Derechos Políticos," *El Día*, July 8, 1913. Police were forbidden to vote but were given a discharge on election day to get around the prohibition. A bill to authorize police voting had been submitted by four Colorado deputies in 1911, debated on the floor, and returned to committee. *Cámara*, CCXII, 127–145, 339. "El Voto de los guardias civiles," *El Día*, July 8, 1911. Batlle comments to Giúdici biography, p. 141, Batlle Archive.

4. "La Convención Nacional Colorada," *El Día*, July 4, 1913.

5. "La Convención Nacional Colorada," *El Día*, July 5, 1913.

6. "La Convención Nacional Colorada," *El Día*, July 7, 1913.

7. "Del Doctor Varela Acevedo," *El Día*, July 5, 1913.

8. "La Proclamación del doctor Viera," *La Democracia*, July 9, 1913. "En la Convención Colorada," *La Reforma*, July 9, 1913.

9. "La Nota del Día," *El Siglo*, July 9, 1913.

10. [Batlle], "El Doctor José Pedro Ramírez," *El Día*, July 12, 1913.

11. *Cámara*, CCXXVI, 427–439. *Senadores*, CIV, 307–308.

12. "El Gran Homenaje a José Pedro Ramírez," *Diario del Plata*, July 15, 1913. "El Sepelio del Doctor José Pedro Ramírez," *El Siglo*, July 15, 1913.

13. [Batlle], "Un Hombre al Agua," *El Día*, March 21, 1913.

14. "La Proclamación de Anoche," *Diario del Plata*, July 15, 1913.

15. "Convención Nacional del Partido Colorado," *El Día*, July 15, 1913.

16. "Batlle y Viera," *La Democracia*, July 10, 1913.

17. Luis Batlle y Ordoñez, Montevideo, to Batlle, Paris, February 18, 1908, Batlle Archive.

18. Interview, José Serrato, September 21, 24, 1952.

19. Manini manuscript, Manini Ríos, *Anoche Me Llamó Batlle*, 233.

20. "Suspension del Mitin," *Diario del Plata*, July 16, 1913. "La Muerte del Colegiado," *El Siglo*, July 15, 1913. "El principio del Fin," *El Día*, July 11, 1913. "Los Triunfos del Colegialismo," *El Día*, July 15, 1913.

21. "Con el doctor Feliciano Viera," *El Día*, July 16, 1913.

22. "Los Propósitos de Don Feliciano," *El Siglo*, July 17, 1913. "Espectáculo Insólito," *Diario del Plata*, July 19, 1913.

23. "Con el Nuevo Jefe Político," *El Día*, August 2, 1913.

24. [Batlle], "Tremenda Inconsecuencia," *El Día*, June 2, 1913.

17. GOLD CRISIS

1. Foreign Minister Romeu, an Acevedo Díaz Nationalist and not much of a diplomat, had just resigned over a family scandal. Batlle replaced him with Emilio Barbaroux, a non-Batllista Colorado and a young man who had been Williman's interim Foreign Minister and was now Uruguayan Minister to Belgium. Barbaroux prepared the Uruguayan arbitration proposal, which was that the arbitrator must first decide whether Grimthorpe had to accept the arbitration required by the contract (one arbitrator chosen by him, one by the Uruguayan government, the two to choose a third member from among the justices of the Uruguayan Supreme Court). This had been the Uruguayan position; Grimthorpe, supported by England and France, demanded immediate compensation. Only if the arbitrator ruled against the Uruguayan position would he make the second decision of assessing damages and awarding compensation to Grimthorpe. "La Renuncia del Dr. Romeau," *El Día*, June 13, 1913. "Informes Diplomáticos de los representantes del Imperio Alemán en el Uruguay," *Revista Histórica*, Montevideo, XLVI (February 1975), 140–143. "El Ministerio de R. E.," *El Día*, June 14, 1913. "La Cartera de Relaciones Exteriores," *El Siglo*, June 15, 1913. "El Nuevo Ministro," *Diario del Plata*, July 15, 1913. "Misterios de Cancillería," *Diario del Plata*, June 29, 1913. Draft Convenio, Proposiciones del Uruguay, undated, Batlle Archive.

2. "La Situación de la Plaza," *El Siglo*, June 20, 1913. A. G. Ford, *The Gold Standard, 1880–1914: Britain and Argentina* (Oxford, 1962), 176. Banco de la República Oriental del Uruguay, *1896–24 de Agosto–1917* (Montevideo, 1918), 94–95, 122.

3. "La Operación de Cuatro Millones," *El Día*, July 7, 1913. "El Negociado Financiero," *El Siglo*, July 8, 1913.

4. The operation involved a loan from the Bank to the government of

1,162,000 pesos—under the Bank's charter the government had the right to draw up to two million pesos from the Bank—to be repaid weekly from customs receipts, and government withdrawal of 1,000,000 pesos from funds it had deposited in the account to build the Government Palace.

5. Banco de la República Oriental del Uruguay, *1896–24 de Agosto—1917*, 95, 136–137. Pedro Cosio, *La Conversión y los Problemas del Crédito* (Montevideo, 1920), 57. Octavio Morató, *Surgimientos y Depresiones Económicos en el Uruguay a Través de la Historia* (Montevideo, 1938), 43–45.

6. Paul A. Samuelson, *Economics: An Introductory Analysis* (Fifth Edition, New York, 1961), 358.

7. The Bank of the Republic had exclusive rights to issue paper currency, was the government's banker, and did banking business directly with the public. It was not a central bank controlling or regulating private banks.

8. *Comisión Permanente*, XII, 203. David Joslin, *A Century of Banking in Latin America to Commemorate the Centenary in 1962 of the Bank of London and South America Limited* (London, 1963), 52–59, 111–112, 133–138. Joslin, unfortunately, does not discuss the bank's Uruguayan operations in the 1913 crisis. The Banco Comercial's official history, *El Banco Comercial A Través de Un Siglo 1857–1957* (Montevideo, 1957), unpaged, in its brief description of the Banco Council's actions during the 1913 gold crisis does not mention this conversion.

9. Morató, *Surgimientos*, 43–48.

10. "En el Banco de la República," *El Día*, July 28, 1913.

11. *Comisión Permanente*, XII, 203–205. Banco de la República Oriental del Uruguay, *1896–24 de Agosto—1917*, 98, 123.

12. "Permanent Committee in the United States of America in the hope of increasing the knowledge of our people concerning this interesting country . . .," *Uruguay* (n.p., 1915), 31–32.

13. *Comisión Permanente*, XII, 203–205.

14. "El Asunto del Día," *El Siglo*, July 29, 1913.

15. Banco de la República Oriental del Uruguay, *1896–24 de Agosto—1917*, 96–97; [Batlle], "La Conducta del Directorio," *El Día*, August 1, 1913.

16. Banco de la República Oriental del Uruguay, *1896–24 de Agosto—1917*, 123.

17. Eduardo Acevedo, "No Hay Crisis!" *El Día*, August 15, 1913.

18. Of course, the credit freeze had restrictive effects beyond contracting imports.

19. "La Situación Económica," *El Siglo*, July 29, 1913. "El Delirio de las Grandezas," *El Siglo*, August 12, 1913. "Moraleja," *La Democracia*, July 31, 1913. "Espejismo Financiero," *Diario del Plata*, August 12, 1913. Martín C. Martínez, "La Situación—Económica Financiera," *El Siglo*, August 30, 1913.

Morató, *Surgimientos*, 43–48. "El Estado de la Ganadería Nacional," *El Siglo*, July 3, 1913. In *El Día*'s gold outflow estimate, five million pesos were for government debt services. "La Situación Económica—Financiera," *El Día*, July 21, 1913.

20. British investment, the largest in Uruguay, had increased by 48.4 million pesos from 1900 to 1913, according to the estimate of J. Fred Rippy, *British Investments in Latin America, 1822–1949: A Case Study in the Operations of Private Enterprise in Retarded Regions* (Minneapolis, 1959), 67, 142.

21. The extent and composition of capital repatriation from Uruguay still needs to be studied. John Maynard Keynes' *Indian Currency and Finance* (London, 1913), published during the Balkan War credit uncertainties, noted that the Bank of England was able to bring gold to England by raising the interest rate, which resulted in British banks repatriating short-term loans abroad (18–25). The inability of Uruguay to renegotiate short-term loans precipitated the gold crisis, but more than short-term loans were involved. While it is true that the bulk of foreign investment in Uruguay was in long-term bonds and fixed capital—i.e., railroads and railroad equipment— and therefore not readily repatriable, the total amount of foreign investment was so much greater than the country's gold holdings (something on the order of twenty-five times the amount of gold in Uruguayan banks—see page 18) that repatriation of small proportions of fixed and operating capital could cause acute problems of gold outflow.

22. The crisis was not limited to Uruguay. The *Economist* of London's Buenos Aires correspondent reported on July 16, "Trade continues depressed . . . due to the restriction of discounts by banks and numerous [business] failures . . . 500,000 pesos Gold withdrawn from the Caja Today." Ford, *The Gold Standard, 1880–1914: Britain and Argentina*, 170–172.

23. *Cámara*, CXXIX, 251–256. "El Futuro Enpréstito, *El Día*, August 11, 1913. The loan, separate from the 9-million-pesos loan authorized for the Bank of the Republic, would be issued in series over 12 to 18 months. Of the proceeds, 5 million pesos would consolidate debts resulting from the acquisition of the State Mortgage Bank; 4.5 million would be to pay for the expansion of the Electric Power System; 2.2 million to pay for acquisition of Montevideo park lands; 5 million to the Montevideo municipality, including workers' housing; 4 million for the Public Assistance Agency for hospitals, orphanages, etc.; 2 million for roadbuilding in the interior; 1,090,000 to complete the agronomy stations; 300,000 for the Industrial Chemistry and Fishing Institutes; and one million for acquisition of merchant ships. The message stated that all but 400,000 pesos in annual debt service, a sum that the national treasury could easily handle, would be assumed by the benefiting individual government organizations. The feasibility of the loan was based on

the easing of the European credit market because the Second Balkan War had just ended.

18. ELECTIONS—NOVEMBER, 1913

1. "Inconsciencia," *El Siglo*, August 6, 1913.
2. *Cámara*, CCXXVII, 4–7, 62–63, 77–80, 127–142, 146–167, 170–191, 194–215, 221–243.
3. [Batlle], "Entrevistas Políticas," *El Día*, August 19, 1913.
4. Partido Nacional Archivo, *Actas del Directorio* Series I, VII, 221–223. "Admirable!," *La Democracia*, June 22, 1913. [Batlle], "La Prórroga de la Inscripción," *El Día*, June 24, 1913. [Batlle], "Un Pedido Improcedente," *El Día*, June 25, 1913. *Cámara*, CCXXV, 25–29, 119–135, 222–270, 294–304, 440–464. "El Rechazo," *La Democracia*, June 29, 1913.
5. Partido Nacional Archivo, *Actas del Directorio* Series I, VII, 246–248.
6. "Concurrencia a las Urnas," *La Democracia*, August 30, 1913. "Datos Para el Problema," *La Democracia*, August 3, 1913. "Cuestiones Partidarias," *La Democracia*, August 23, 1913. "Actividades Partidarias," *La Democracia*, August 27, 1913. Partido Nacional Archivo, *Actas del Directorio* Series I, VII, 248–265. "El Otro Camino," *El Día*, August 27, 1913.
7. "Acción del Momento," *Diario del Plata*, August 31, 1913.
8. "Los Legisladores Anticolegialistas," *Diario del Plata*, September 11, 13, 23, 1913. "Fracaso Presidencial," *Diario del Plata*, September 12, 1913. "Los Anticolegialistas," *El Día*, September 24, 1913. "Anticolegialismo," *El Siglo*, September 26, 1913.
9. "La Gran Asamblea Anticolegialista," *El Siglo*, September 28, 1913. [Batlle], "Entre los Anticolegialistas," *El Día*, September 30, 1913.
10. "Anticolegialismo," *El Siglo*, October 7, 1913.
11. Banco de la República Oriental del Uruguay, *1896–24 de Agosto–1917* (Montevideo, 1918), 122–123. "La Renta de Aduana," *El Día*, September 5, 1913. *Cámara*, CCXXVII, 272–297, 361–377. *Senadores*, CIV, 418–452.
12. "La Huelga de Tejedores," *El Día*, September 17, 1913. "El Paro General," *El Siglo*, October 24, 1913. "Contra la Huelga General," *El Día*, November 1, 1913. "La Huelga en Lacaze," *El Siglo*, November 6, 1913. "La Huelga del Sauce, *El Día*, November 11, 13, 17, 26, 1913. "La Cuestión Obrera," *Diario del Plata*, November 18, 1913. Francisco R. Pintos, *Historia del Movimiento Obrero del Uruguay* (Montevideo, 1960), 100–102. Pintos, who does not mention the government's mediation, blames the Federación Obrera for accepting "an employers' proposition" and criticizes Batlle for sending troops: "The strikers had serious difficulties even in holding meetings."
13. "Entre Socialistas," *El Día*, October 22, 29, 1913.

14. Emilio Basterga, "Con 'El Socialista,' " *El Día*, October 22, 1913. During the Puerto del Sauce strike, *El Día* did read the Senate majority a lesson: the strike showed that social problems existed and that enactment of the eight-hour day was necessary. "El Actual Conflicto Obrero," *El Día*, November 3, 1913.

15. "Las Elecciones," *El Día*, November 7, 1913.

16. "Influencia Moral," *El Siglo*, November 4, 1913. "La Influencia Moral de la Policía en Campaña," *El Siglo*, November 11, 1913. "Indignos Enjuagues," *La Democracia*, November 18, 1913. *Senadores*, CV, 16–17. [Batlle], "Los Empleos y la Política," *El Día*, November 19, 1913.

17. "Movimiento Político," *El Siglo*, November 20, 1913.

18. "Coalición Popular," *Diario del Plata*, November 20, 1913. The election law of 1910 gave the majority seats in a department to the most voted ticket, and the minority seats to the next most voted ticket. Other tickets got no seats. In a hypothetical case, 21,000 vote in Montevideo, of which 13,500 vote for the government Colorados, 4,000 vote for the Nationalists, and 3,500 vote the anti-Colegialist-dissident Colorado ticket. If there is no coalition, the anti-Colegialist-dissident ticket gets no seats, the Nationalists get 4 seats (1/6 of 24), and the government Colorados get 20 seats. If there is a coalition, it reaches one third of the total vote and divides 8 seats among Nationalist and anti-Colegialist-dissident Colorados, while the government Colorados win 16 seats instead of 20 seats. The coalition would win 16 seats only if it outvoted the government Colorados.

19. "¿Bonos de Tesorería?" *Diario del Plata*, November 14, 1913. "La Situación Financiera," *El Siglo*, November 18, 1913. "El Alcohol Extranjero," *Diario del Plata*, November 20, 1913. "La Cuestión Obrera," *Diario del Plata*, November 18, 1913.

20. "El Proceso Militar," *El Día*, February 17, 1914. "Tomando Precauciones," "Distribución de Armas," and "Movimientos de Fuerzas," *El Siglo*, November 26, 1913.

21. "El Suceso de Rocha," *El Día*, November 29, 1913. "Fraude, Coacción y Sangre," *El Siglo*, November 29, 1913. "De Rivera," *El Siglo*, November 30, 1913. Adolfo Tejera, *Retrato de Un Ciudadano, Apuntes Para la Biografía de Juan Andrés Ramírez* (Montevideo, 1945), 144–153.

22. María Julia Ardao, "Alfredo Vásquez Acevedo, Contribución al Estudio de su Vida y su Obra," *Revista Histórica*, Montevideo, XXXVI (December, 1965), 672–674. "Plataforma," *La Democracia*, November 30, 1913. The Nationalist election platform also promised that their deputies would resist the President, resist Batlle's constitutional reform, insist on electoral liberty, substitute the national guard for the regular army and allow

citizens to arm themselves, oppose new taxes and government spending, protect property, and protect the disinherited rural poor by encouraging "industries at the level of their abilities."

23. "Los Católicos," *La Democracia*, November 30, 1913.

24. "La Actualidad Electoral," *El Día*, November 29, 1913.

25. "Movimiento Político," *El Siglo*, November 30, 1913.

26. The registry certificate, dated March 13, 1913, is in the Batlle Archive.

27. "Las Elecciones de Ayer," *El Siglo*, December 1, 1913. "Desarrollo General del Comicio," *El Día*, December 1, 1913.

28. "Las Elecciones de Ayer," *El Siglo*, December 1, 1913.

29. The election figures given here are the official results published in *Asamblea General*, XIII, 3. Earlier figures, before challenged votes were decided, appear in "Después de las Elecciones," *El Día*, December 2, 1913.

30. The 1908 Census listed 171,898 men eligible to vote. *Anuario Estadístico 1907–1908*, Vol. II, Part III, xliii. According to the Constitution, male citizens, native and naturalized, could vote if they were age twenty and over, literate, and not day laborers. Two restrictions were not enforced: electoral literacy meant the ability to sign one's name; no one was classed a day laborer, since the electoral definition of that term was a man hired by written contract, and written contracts were not used for day laborers.

31. It would be most useful to know whether the approximately 10,000 additional voters over 1907 were first-time voters or those who had not voted in 1907 but had voted earlier, with their occupations, ages, and party preferences. Quantitative election analysis of this period will be difficult because the registry lists were later destroyed, but other data should be available.

32. "Reportajes de Actualidad," *Diario del Plata*, December 2, 1913. "Intimidades Ignoradas," *Diario del Plata*, December 4, 1913.

33. "Deber de los Partidos," *Diario del Plata*, December 4, 1913. "Sobre el Anticolegialismo," *Diario del Plata*, December 13, 1913.

34. "Momento Político," *El Siglo*, December 4, 1913.

35. [Batlle], "Los Comicios y la Reforma," *El Día*, December 5, 1913.

36. [Batlle], "Una Verdad y Una Inexactitud," *El Día*, August 8, 1913.

19. "ARE WE COLORADOS OR ARE WE SOCIALISTS?"

1. "Los Nuevos Representantes del Partido," *El Día*, December 5, 1913.

2. "El doctor Alfredo Palacios," *La Prensa*, March 10, 1907.

3. Arturo Ardao, "Ideas Filosóficas de Batlle" in [Acción], *Batlle. Su Obra y Su Vida* (Montevideo, 1956), 35, reports that Palacios told him this about an interview he had with Batlle "years before 1913."

4. Arturo Ardao, *Batlle y Ordóñez y el Positivismo Filosófico* (Montevideo, 1951), facing 176, publishes a photograph of the Ahrens page with Batlle's notation. The original is in the Batlle Archive.

5. Batlle's own Deism had weakened over the years. He no longer referred to God, and now spoke of destiny and the designs of nature where others would use God. He did not rule out an afterlife. Arena wrote that some months after Ana Amalia's death, a butterfly perched on Batlle's extended hand and Batlle speculated that it might be a message from his daughter. Domingo Arena, "Los Últimos Días de Batlle," *Biblioteca "Batlle,"* Montevideo, I (1942), 215–219. The article was originally published in *El Día,* October 20, 1930.

6. F. Fernández Prando, editor, *Escritos y Discursos de Prudencio Vázquez y Vega* (Montevideo, 1958), 11–25, 68–93, 112, 174.

7. E. Ahrens, *Curso de Derecho Natural ó de Filosofía del Derecho completado en las principales materias, con ojeadas históricas y políticas* (Sixth Edition, Pedro Rodríguez Hortelano and Mariano Ricardo de Asensi, trans., Paris/Mexico, 1880), 56. Hereafter cited as *Ahrens–Derecho Natural.*

8. Batlle, Paris, to Guillermo Young, July 2, 1880, Batlle Archive. Ardao first corrected the view that Batlle as a result of his European trip became a Positivist, and this letter reinforces Ardao's position.

9. The diary, begun in Europe on January 1, 1881, describes the trip home in steerage and the first days back in Montevideo. Batlle Archive.

10. Lorenzo Batlle, Montevideo, to José Batlle y Ordóñez, March 13, 1880. Pepe, Paris, to Lorenzo Batlle, July 5, 1880, Batlle Archive.

11. *Ahrens–Derecho Natural,* 51.

12. *Ahrens–Derecho Natural,* 81–92, 286–287, 570.

13. *Ahrens–Derecho Natural,* 325.

14. *Ahrens–Derecho Natural,* 321–322, 327–331, 575–577. Organic harmony required governments to expand "social goods," "like roads, parks, libraries, museums, beneficent institutions, etc." and disseminate culture: "it is of the greatest importance that in every province there be a center of advanced education, a university, and if possible an academy of arts and a polytechnic institute" (*Ahrens–Derecho Natural,* 346, 603). Ahrens influence on Batlle here is clear. Organic harmony also required a balanced national economy of agriculture, industry, and commerce, but governments must limit themselves to setting the economic rules: "the State cannot be banker, lender, partner or associate in an economic enterprise" (*Ahrens–Derecho Natural,* 518). Batlle wanted a balanced economy, but state enterprises were central to its achievement.

15. *Ahrens–Derecho Natural,* 23–25, XVII.

16. [Batlle], "Cuestiones Sociales," *El Día,* July 15, 1917.

17. *Ahrens–Derecho Natural*, 360, 347–348.

18. Goran A. Lindahl, *Uruguay's New Path: A Study in Politics during the first Colegiado, 1919–1933* (Stockholm, 1962), 257–260, 345. Batlle gave the fullest exposition of his ideas on land taxes in 1925. His goal, he then pointed out, was not land subdivision but intensive land use. "Partido Colorado," *El Día*, July 3, 1925.

19. Henry George, *Progress and Poverty. An Inquiry into the Cause of Industrial Depressions and of Increase of Want with Increase of Wealth . . . The Remedy*, First Edition New York, 1880 (New York, 1971), 141, 421, 469.

20. Domingo Arena, "El Humanitarismo de Batlle," *Biblioteca "Batlle,"* Montevideo, I (1942), 140. The article was originally published in *El Día*, October 20, 1935.

21. [Batlle], "¡Abajo las Armas!," *El Día*, July 31, 1917. Batlle's polemic with Celestino Mibelli, who would be Uruguay's first Communist deputy, went on in *El Día* from May through July 1917 and deserves reprinting.

22. Elisée Reclus, *Evolución, Revolución y Anarquismo*, A. López Rodrigo, trans. (Buenos Aires, 1969), 34, 46. Reclus, *Mis Exploraciones en América*, A. López Rodrigo, trans. (Valencia, n.d.), 5–7.

23. Karl Marx and Friedrich Engels, *Selected Works* (2 vols., London 1950), I, 328–329.

20. COLORADO SPLIT

1. [Batlle], "El Veredicto Colorado," *El Día*, December 8, 1913.

2. "El Anticolegialismo," *El Siglo*, December 13, 1913.

3. These percentages are for the Bank of the Republic and do not include private banks, which had also curtailed credit, or gold coins in circulation.

4. Banco de la República Oriental del Uruguay, *1896–24 de Agosto–1917* (Montevideo, 1918), 97, 108, 127, 335. *Asamblea General*, XIII, 15–16, 19. "El Vencimiento del 5 de Diciembre," *El Siglo*, November 14, 1913.

5. The Senate did get Ethelburga to revise the loan cancellation clause to "If during the execution of the contract, war should occur in Uruguay or in Europe, or a financial crisis, if any of these causes a drop of five points in the 1905 [Uruguayan] Conversion Bonds from their average price during the first two weeks of December 1913, the Syndicate will be able to rescind the contract."

6. Of the rest of the loan, 3 million pesos would go abroad to pay off treasury notes coming due, and the balance would go to the Bank of the Republic as government deposits and in repayment for government drawing on the Bank in the purchase of the State Mortgage Bank and Montevideo park lands.

7. *Senadores*, CIV, 558–571. *Cámara*, CCXXVIII, 166–176, 348–360, 400–413.

8. Partido Nacional Archivo, *Actas del Directorio* Series I, VII, 305–306. "Triunfo," *La Democracia*, December 14, 1913.

9. *Asamblea General*, XIII, 67–68. [Batlle], "Sobre el Ejército," *El Día*, March 11, 1914. Segundo Bazzano, Montevideo, to Ministro de Guerra y Marina, August 7, 1913, and Juan Bernassa y Jérez, Montevideo, to Batlle, March 3, 1915, Batlle Archive. José R. Usera (Secretary of the General Staff), "El Ejército," in Reginald Lloyd and others, editors, *Impresiones de la República del Uruguay en el Siglo Veinte* (London, 1911), 172.

10. "Del Comandante F. Moller de Berg. El Ejecutivo Colegiado y El Ejército," *El Día*, May 24, 27, 1913.

11. Captain Sandes, an army officer on active duty, posed as a plotter. He found no army officer on active duty who acknowledged being in on the plot. He did encounter Juan Carlos Jentschik, who said he was Ramírez' nephew and who gave him information. There is also an unsigned memorandum on the stationery of the Secretaría de la Presidencia de la República relating a visit from JCJ [Juan Carlos Jentschik?], mentioning Captain Sandes as a plotter and informant. The reports are in the Batlle Archive.

12. The reports and anonymous warning are in the Batlle Archive. "El Presidente y el Ejército," *El Siglo*, February 11, 1914. "La Vice Presidencia," *El Siglo*, December 20, 1913.

13. "Actualidad," *El Siglo*, February 13, 1914. "La Prisión del Coronel Dubra," *El Día*, February 13, 1914. "El Asunto del Día," *El Día*, February 14, 1914.

14. [Batlle], "¡Tómbola!," *El Día*, February 14, 1914. "La Presidencia del Senado," *El Siglo*, February 14, 1914.

15. Francisco Accinelli, Montevideo, to Pedro Manini Ríos and José Astigarraga, February 14, 1914, Batlle Archive. "Protesta," *El Día*, February 16, 1914. *Senadores*, CV, 84–85, 88, 333.

16. [Batlle], "¡Tómbola!," *El Día*, February 14, 1914. [Batlle], "El Compromiso del Senado," *El Día*, February 21, 1914.

17. "La Prisión del Coronel Dubra," *El Día*, February 13, 1914.

18. "El Proceso Militar," *El Día*, February 17, 1914. Eduardo Dieste Montevideo to Batlle, December 28, 1913, and Carlos Travieso, Montevideo, to Batlle, February 3, 1923, Batlle Archive. "Actualidad," *El Siglo*, February 13, 1914. "Del Coronel Dubra," *El Siglo*, February 21, 1914. "El Coronel Dubra," *El Día*, November 7, 1910. Travieso, furious at being followed by police spies, recalled that Arena had greeted him with "So calm and conspiring," to which he had answered, "I wish I could bury you all head first."

19. *Cámara*, CCXXIX, 44–212. "Temor Infundado . . ." *La Democracia*, February 19, 1914. [Batlle], "Desatinos Parlamentarios," *El Día*, February 21, 1914.

20. "El Empréstito," *El Día*, February 13, 1914. Banco del la República Oriental del Uruguay, *1896–24 de Agosto–1917* (Montevideo, 1918), 136. *Asamblea General*, XIII 1–2, 15, 19. "El Año A Vuelo de Pájaro," *El Siglo*, January 1, 1914. "Lo Que Se Olvida," *Diario del Plata*, February 8, 1914.

21. *Cámara*, CCXXIX, 256–270, 290–301, 348–363.

22. Domingo Arena, "Baltasar Brum," *El Día-Suplemento*, April 1, 1934. Barbaroux had voted for Independent Colorados in November. His resignation was voluntary and may have come because he felt he had not been consulted on the foreign aspects of the Dubra arrest. "El Ministro de Relaciones Exteriores," *El Día*, February 14, 1914; "La Crisis Ministerial," *Diario del Plata*, February 15, 1914. "Informes Diplomáticos de los Representantes del Imperio Alemán en el Uruguay," *Revista Histórica*, XLVI (February 1975), 160–161.

23. *Cámara*, CCXXIX, 409–438, 481–495, 506–525.

24. Charles A. Gauld, *The Last Titan: Percival Farquhar, American Entrepreneur in Latin America* (Stanford, California, 1964), 167–239. Simon Hanson, "The Farquhar Syndicate in South America," *Hispanic American Historical Review* (August 1937), 314–326.

25. W. Cameron Forbes, Receiver, Brazil Railway Receivership Journals 1914–1919, Baker Library, Harvard University, Mss 724, 1914–1919, B 827. I, 194–209, XXIII, 3–15.

26. *Anuario Estadístico, 1915*, 579–585. Although the Central was profitable, the feeder lines were not, and the government still had to pay them profit guarantees. The State railroads would both receive and increase feeder line traffic, and this should reduce or eliminate government payment of profit guarantees to them.

27. There is no evidence in these debates for the frequently advanced view (for example, Peter Winn "British Informal Empire in Uruguay in the Nineteenth Century," *Past and Present* No. 73, November, 1976, 122) that Batlle favored railroad expansion so as to suffocate Nationalist revolution more easily. Nationalist enthusiasm for railroad expansion suggests that war use of railroads was not a serious concern of theirs, either.

28. As part of the Nationalist campaign to discredit Batlle, Beltrán charged in the Chamber that General O'Brien, ex-United States Minister to Uruguay, was being overpaid by the government for taking soundings at La Coronilla. In fact, O'Brien was concerned that the State railroads would eliminate his own project for railroads and colonization out of La Coronilla.

Cámara, CCXXX, 379–381, 629–631. *Cámara,* CCXXXI, 49–82, 85. Eduardo (sic) C. O'Brien, Montevideo, to Batlle, June 13, 1914, July 9, 1914, Batlle Archive.

29. *Cámara,* CCXXIX, 561–585, 595–615, 622–642. *Cámara,* CCXXX, 7–29, 431–455, 497. The contract left it to the Executive to decide whether to rent the State railroads to the Uruguay Railway Company or operate them "in the form it esteems preferable." The Chamber immediately took up and approved the second in the package of State railroad bills, liquidating the Pan American railway concession, renewed and expanded in 1909 under Williman. The concession called for a railroad to traverse Uruguay from Carpintería on the Brazilian border to the river port of Colonia. The original promoter, an American, Bright, had been unable to fulfill the contract and had been jailed in the United States for stock fraud. He claimed that to get the concession, he spent large sums for bribes. (Williman's two great public works projects, the Rambla Sur and the Pan American railway, had very messy consequences.) MacArthur Brothers, which had built the only actual trackage, 45 kilometers from Trinidad to Durazno, had taken over the expired concession. Their legal rights could delay the State railroad, and Batlle's solution was to buy back the concession for 200,000 pesos, buy the trackage that had been built, and have MacArthur Brothers build the Northeast branch of the State railroad, approximating the original Pan American route, 400 kilometers from Florida to the Brazilian border. *Cámara,* CCXXX, 498–552, 574–596, 634–662. *Cámara,* CCXXXI, 85–101, 150–151.

21. BUILDING A PLATFORM FOR THE COLEGIADO

1. *Cámara,* CCXXX, 570–574. "Con el Ministro de Hacienda," *El Día,* May 29, 1914.

2. *Cámara,* CCXXIX, 256–270, 290–301, 348–363. *Cámara,* CCXXX, 37–61, 91–97, 108–126, 285–298, 663–669. *Cámara,* CCXXXI, 151–175, 179–196, 318–337, 383–404, 457–476, 558–606. *Cámara,* CCXXXII, 39–94.

3. To satisfy the Montevideo municipality, which had disagreements with the company over meat haulage rates and had refused to approve trolley electrification, the Executive granted the municipality 190,000 pesos and deeded it the choice plot of land the Executive had bought for the Government Palace. The plot, at 18 de Julio and Ejido, was to be the anchor of a great avenue cut through the center of Montevideo connecting the Government—now Municipal—Palace with the soon-to-be-built Legislative Palace, a building Batlle intended to be monumental.

4. Stockholders would exchange their stocks for new government certifi-

cates yielding 4.5 percent plus up to 2.5 percent more if Tranvía del Norte profits permitted. The State could amortize the certificates at par or a lesser agreed-upon value. If it did not, the certificates would expire in 75 years. Adolfo H. Pérez Olave, Montevideo, to Feliciano Viera, July 4, 1914, Batlle Archive.

5. *Senadores*, CV, 333–346, 367–382, 384–399, 402–416, 420–431, 436–451, 459–472, 474–489, 533–542, 553–570. *Senadores*, CVI, 10–23, 41–80, 88–117, 189–195. *Cámara*, CCXXXVI, 317–319. Adolfo H. Pérez Olave, Montevideo, to Feliciano Viera, July 4, 1914, Batlle Archive.

6. *Anuario Estadístico*, 1908, Vol. II, Part III, *Censo General de la República*, xxxiii.

7. *Cámara*, CCXLVI, 168–172.

8. "Pensiones á la Vejez," *El Día*, June 18, 1914. Batlle had announced that an old age pension bill would be a companion to the eight-hour day in his 1906 eight-hour-day message.

9. Pedro Cosio, "El Impuesto á la Tierra," *El Día*, March 27, 1914.

10. "Partido Colorado," *El Día*, June 20, 29, July 2, 3, August 21, 1925.

11. The Executive's message stated that the new law would result in revenues of 2,103,143 pesos, compared with the 2,102,896 pesos that would be produced under the existing legislation.

12. "Con el Ministro de Hacienda," *El Día*, May 29, 1914.

13. *Cámara*, CCXXXII, 340–381.

14. *Cámara*, CCXXXI, 118–147, 222–247, 290–311, 409–445, 518–551.

15. "Un Programa Nacionalista," *El Día*, June 26, 1914.

22. WORLD WAR

1. *Cámara*, CCXXXII, 11–18. *Senadores*, CVI, 27–38.

2. *Cámara*, CCXXXII, 94–109, 164–168, 223–240. *Cámara*, CCXXXIII, 28–36, 82–90, 301–317. The offer to sell the merchant ship "Priestley" is in the Batlle Archive. "Los Trasportes Nacionales," *El Día*, June 26, 1914. El Trasporte Nacional, *El Día*, July 4, 1914. *Senadores*, CVI, 265–266. *Cámara*, CCXXXIII, 19–21.

3. *Cámara*, CCXXXIII, 39–40, 254–280. Bullfights were already forbidden, but "simulated bullfights," where the bull's horns were padded and the bull was not killed, were legal.

4. *Cámara*, CCXXXIII, 228–250.

5. "Una Carta del Dr. Viera," *El Día*, July 25, 1914. Washington Paullier, *El Ejecutivo Colegiado y la Reforma Constitucional* (Montevideo, 1914). Mateo A. Magariños, *Actualidad Política (Batlle, el Colegiado y Viera)* (Montevideo, 1914). Antonio Montenegro, Jr., *Batlle la Reforma y Viera* (Montevideo,

1914). Enrique de Bilbao, *Batlle y Su Obra (Del Fragor Político)* (Montevideo, 1915).

6. [Batlle], "La Carta del Dr. Viera," *El Día*, July 27, 1914. "El País Vencerá," *El Siglo*, July 26, 1914. "La Nota del Día," *Diario del Plata*, July 26, 1914. "El Estado, es Don Pepe Batlle," *La Democracia*, July 29, 1914.

7. "El Doctor Williman y la Candidatura Viera," *El Día*, July 25, 1914.

8. Juan C. Quinteros Delgado, *Vida y Obra de Pedro Cosio* (2nd edition, Montevideo, 1937), 47–55. Quinteros Delgado, Cosio's assistant, was with him at the conference with Batlle. See also "La Situación del Momento," *El Día*, August 3, 1914. "El Momento Político," *El Siglo*, August 2, 1914.

9. *Asamblea General*, XIII, 76–82. "La Situación Bancaria," *El Siglo*, August 4, 1914.

10. Within the 26 million top, the Bank of the Republic could rediscount up to 4 million pesos in private bank commercial paper. This privilege, designed to ease the pressure on private banks whose reserve ratios to deposits were low, would be limited to Uruguayan banks, since their solidity could be examined by Uruguayan authorities. "On the other hand it is very obvious that foreign branches can be affected by the condition of their central office, and we cannot now determine this condition at a moment when the whole world is undergoing profound turmoil."

11. Uruguay, Ministerio de Relaciones Exteriores, *Trabajos de la Delegación Uruguaya en la Pan American Conferencia Celebrada en Washington, D.C. del 24 al 30 de Mayo de 1915* (Montevideo, 1915), 35–41.

12. *Cámara*, CCXXXIV, 96–141. "En el Mundo Parlamentario," *El Siglo*, August 6, 1914. Pedro Cosio, *La Conversión y los Problemas del Crédito* (Montevideo, 1920), 83–84. Banco de la República Oriental del Uruguay, *1896–24 de Agosto–1917* (Montevideo, 1918), 124. *Senadores*, CVI, 285–301.

13. "Resistencias Injustas," *El Día*, August 8, 1914. H. W. Leslie, *"The Royal Mail" War Book: Being An Account of the Operations of the Ships of the Royal Mail Steam Packet Co., 1914–1919* (London, 1920), 11–17.

14. "El Régimen Colorado," *El Día*, August 3, 1914. "A Río Revuelto," *Diario del Plata*, August 18, 1914. "A Nuestros Cominos," *El Siglo*, August 20, 1914.

15. "El Gran Acto Partidario de Anoche," *El Día*, August 24, 1914. "La Convención Nacional Colorada," *El Día*, August 26, 1914. "Convención Nacional Colorada," *El Día*, September 2, 1914.

16. *Anuario Estadístico, 1913–1914*, 724. *Anuario Estadístico, 1911–1912*, 717–718.

17. Esteban F. Campal, *La Pradera* (Nuestra Tierra 28) (Montevideo, 1969), 20.

18. "Cámara Mercantil," *El Siglo*, September 1, 1914.

19. "El Mejor Billete," *Diario del Plata*, September 4, 1914. "Grave Rumor," *Diario del Plata*, September 10, 1914. "Congreso Rural," *El Siglo*, September 2, 1914.

20. [Batlle], "A Buena Hora," *El Día*, August 21, 1914.

21. The portion of the recently passed increase in inheritance taxes that was to pay public employees' life insurance benefits would now go toward paying off the Vales.

22. *Cámara*, CCXXXIV, 365–407, 411–463, 466–566, 568–606. *Cámara*, CCXXXV, 8–61, 64–109. During these debates no total budget figures were announced. Earlier Martín C. Martínez contended that the 1913–14 budget was 31,943,675 pesos. *Cámara*, CCXXX, 570–574. When the reduced budget returned from the Senate, Mora Magariños put it at 28,160,735 pesos. *Cámara*, CCXXXV, 304.

23. The *Vales* had already been revised. A higher interest rate, 8 percent, and sharply reduced amortization, down to 6 percent a year, would permit the new taxes to finance the larger amount of Vales in circulation and keep them from depreciating. Nine hundred thousand pesos would be used for road-building, one hundred thousand for completing the Boys' Educational Colony, and the rest to pay government bills.

24. The tax, now to be levied on livestock on the hoof, would yield the same amount or slightly more than the Executive's original .005 per kilo of meat.

25. *Senadores*, CVI, 462–473. *Cámara*, CCXXXV, 403–420. *Asamblea General*, XIII, 99–118.

23. TOWARD THE FUTURE

1. "La Imponente Asamblea de Florida," *La Democracia*, October 13, 1914. Partido Nacional Archivo, *Notas Recibidas por el H. Directorio, 1914*, Series II, XXII, 150, 161–167. Partido Nacional Archivo, *Actas del Directorio*, Series I, VII, 364–366.

2. V. V. Vives, Montevideo, to Batlle, October 31, 1914, Batlle Archive. "Propaganda Contubernal," *El Día*, November 9, 1914. "El Escándalo de la Aduana," *El Siglo*, November 14, 1914. "El Escándalo Aduanero," *La Democracia*, November 13, 1914. [Batlle], "Aclarando Ideas," *El Día*, November 13, 1914. *Cámara*, CCXXXVI, 230–265.

3. *Cámara*, CCXXXVI, 452–481, 485–510, 534–553. *Cámara*, CCXXXVII, 184–267. [Batlle], "El Asfaltado," *El Día*, December 23, 1914.

4. "Las Senadurías," *El Día*, November 30, 1914. "Las Elecciones en Florida y Durazno," *La Democracia*, December 1, 1914. "Las Elecciones Senaturiales," *El Siglo*, December 2, 3, 4, 9, 1914. "La Elección de Florida,"

El Día, December 9, 1914. *Asamblea General*, XIII, 3. The vote in Durazno was 1239 Colorado, 1147 Nationalist—a total of 2386. In 1913 the total Durazno vote had been 1528. The disputed Florida elections had either 2071 or 2085 Colorado votes and 2034 or 2110 Nationalist votes, 4105 or 4195 total votes compared with the 2028 total vote in 1913.

5. *Asamblea General*, XIII, 140. [Batlle], "La Jornada Comicial," *El Día*, December 1, 1914. "Ante el Dilema," *Diario del Plata*, December 1, 1914. Juan Andrés Ramírez, "Una Tregua," *El Siglo*, December 1, 1914.

6. "Perspectivas Económicas," *El Siglo*, November 5, 1914. "La Exportación de Frutos," *El Día*, November 6, 1914. "Los Frutos y la Valorización," *Diario del Plata*, November 13, 1914. "La Liquidación," *El Siglo*, November 20, 1914. *Senadores*, CVI, 572.

7. "Las Tierras Fiscales," *El Día*, December 8, 1914, prints the bill and accompanying message. "Tierras Públicas," *El Día*, July 10, 1914.

8. [Batlle], "Tierras Fiscales," *El Día*, January 19, 1915.

9. "En la Comisión N. Colorada," *El Día*, October 16, 1914. "Organización Partidaria," *El Día*, October 3, 1914.

10. "La Demonstración á Telémaco Braido," *El Día*, December 28, 1914. [Batlle], "El Gobernante y el Partido," *El Día*, January 21, 1915. *Comisión Permanente*, XII, 209. *Senadores*, CVII, 16–17. "En la Usina Eléctrica," *El Día*, January 15, 1915. "Demonstración á Telémaco Braido (hijo)," *El Día*, December 22, 1914.

11. [Batlle], "Los Empleados y el Colegiado," *El Día*, May 13, 1913.

12. José Arias Silva, Buenos Aires, to Batlle, February 19, 1915, and Juan Barbadora, Tacuarembó, to Minister de Guerra y Marina General de Brigada Juan Bernassa y Jérez, January 29, 1915, Batlle Archive. "Ruido de Latas," *Diario del Plata*, January 10, 1915. "Lo del Ejército," *La Democracia*, January 10, 1915.

13. *Cámara*, CCXXXVII, 308–339, 482–494. *Cámara*, CCXXXVIII, 3–12, 54–107. "La Pulverización del Ejército," *La Democracia*, December 17, 1914. Eduardo Acevedo, *Anales Históricos del Uruguay*, (6 vols., Montevideo, 1933–1936), IV, 143–144.

14. [Batlle], "Instrucción Para Todos," *El Día*, December 4, 1914.

15. *Anuario Estadístico, 1913*, 458, 193.

16. "El Ramo de Hermodio," *La Democracia*, January 26, 1915. Herrera did fall into the intellectual proletarian trap, and it was later used against him: "I believe this country, with two or three thousand Bachelors of Arts, would be a country of victims in the struggle for life . . .," beating on the government's door to become public employees. Technical, not intellectual, education was needed. Other Nationalist deputies quickly disavowed that view.

17. *Cámara*, CCXXXVIII, 257–308, 310–335, 345–400.

18. *Senadores*, CVII, 37–39. "La Presidencia del Senado," *El Día*, February 12, 1915. "Un Descanso Merecido," *El Día*, January 28, 1915.

19. *Cámara*, CCXXXVI, 299–302. *Anuario Estadístico, 1915*, 333.

20. The war provided an opportunity to reduce the long-term gold outflow by amortizing Uruguay's public debt on very favorable terms, but government revenues were too low to take advantage of the opportunity.

21. The maximum price for a steer had been 26.54 pesos in 1912. The price had more than doubled to 57.64 pesos in 1914 and was still rising. Wool prices were 4.55 pesos per 10 kilos in the first quarter of 1915, up from a 1908 low of 3.00 pesos and now rising even faster than the price of steers. *Anuario Estadístico, 1918*, 100, 279.

22. *Cámara*, CCXXXVIII, 285–293, 408–410. *Senadores*, CVI, 9–10. Banco de la República Oriental del Uruguay, *1896–24 de Agosto, 1917* (Montevideo, 1918) 335. *Anuario Estadístico*, 1920, 112–116.

23. *Anuario Estadístico*, 1918, 487.

24. *Anuario Estadístico*, 1916, 472. *Anuario Estadístico, 1913–1914*, 724. *Anuario Estadístico, 1915*, 21. The real post-1908 marriage rates per thousand were even higher than the official figures given here, because the official figures overestimated total population. In particular, the official figures, based on port entry and exit, grossly overstated the number of arriving immigrants. For 1910–14, 110,048 immigrants were supposed to have settled in Uruguay, a 10 percent increase in total population in only five years, considering that Uruguay's population was officially estimated at 1,094,688 in 1909. Relying on these immigration figures, some authors, notably Ricardo Martínez Ces, *El Uruguay Batllista* (Montevideo, 1962), 44, and Martin Weinstein, *Uruguay: The Politics of Failure* (Westport, 1975), 20, have argued for an immigrant-based Batlle. Since these figures represent a sharp reversal of the long-term decrease of foreign born in Uruguay, they would be extremely significant if true. But these figures have long been suspect. In the 1920's Julio Martínez Lamas warned that the number of immigrants arriving was exaggerated because of "defects in the passenger lists" given by ship captains to Uruguayan authorities, *Riqueza y Pobreza del Uruguay*, 2nd edition (Montevideo, 1946), 133. Juan José Pereira and Raúl Trajtenberg, *Evolución de la Población Total y Activa en el Uruguay 1908–1957* (Montevideo, 1966) did a computer study of the overseas passenger lists and concluded that 17,079 Europeans immigrated to Uruguay from 1910 to 1914 while slightly more Uruguayans migrated to Argentina and Brazil during the period than Argentines and Brazilians migrated to Uruguay, a net of 3,252. Pereira and Trajtenberg estimated Uruguay's 1914 total population at 1,223,131 instead of the official estimate of 1,315,714 (pp. 112, 116–117). The 92,580 difference in

total population mostly represents phantom immigrants. Pereira and Trajtenberg's conclusions, though they demolish the massive immigration myth,
probably need revision. If the passenger lists were defective, the lists may not
contain all the names of those who landed in Montevideo; conversely, some
European immigrants who stayed on ship and went to Buenos Aires may be
listed as debarking in Montevideo. Similarly, European immigrants who
bypassed Montevideo and then migrated to Uruguay from Argentina (the
untrustworthy official figures claim a very substantial migration of Europeans from Argentina to Uruguay) to the extent that their number exceeds
that of Europeans who migrated the other way, are not counted by Pereira
and Trajtenberg. *Anuario Estadístico, 1971,72–73.*

25. *Cámara*, CCXXXV, 424–438. *Cámara*, CCXXXVI, 302–378.

26. Batlle had already taken advantage of Italy's desire to buy Uruguayan
meat and had obtained Italian assent to a treaty the first clause of which
limited Italian companies to Uruguayan courts in the event of contract
disputes with the Uruguayan government. The treaty closed the areas of
diplomatic reclamation and international arbitration which had been used by
Lord Grimthorpe and England in the Rambla Sur controversy. And the
treaty was a precedent that could be used in future war negotiations when
other European powers wanted something from Uruguay. *Cámara*,
CCXXXV, 334–354, 375–391, 448–548.

27. Viera would have to decide who would build the state railroads.
Farquhar's Brazil Railway, in receivership, wanted its construction contract
held up in the legislature until "financial conditions warrant." Batlle, anxious
for quick construction, with Viera assenting, indicated to MacArthur
Brothers, which was going to build from Florida to the Brazilian border, that
they could get the Farquhar contract if they negotiated more favorable terms
on sale of the Pan American concession to the State (see note 29, Chapter 20,
pp. 411–412). The Senate was then able to convince MacArthur Brothers to
waive the 200,000-peso price for State repurchase of the concession, and the
State bought the 46 kilometers of railroad already built from Trinidad to
Durazno. W. Cameron Forbes Receiver, Brazil Railway Receivership Journal, I (October 13, 1914 to June 7, 1915), 197. [Batlle], "El Ferrocarril Pan
Americano," *El Día*, December 30, 1914. *Senadores*, CVI, 526–605. *Cámara*,
CCXXXVII, 350–387.

28. *Cámara*, CCXXXVIII, 284.

29. "Incidente Batlle-Ramírez," *Diario del Plata*, February 27, 1915. Juan
Andrés Ramírez, "Personal," *Diario del Plata*, February 28, 1915. "La Jefatura
P. de la Capital," *El Día*, February 26, 28, 1915. "Personal," *El Siglo*, July 9,
1911. "El doctor Ramírez Exasperado," *El Día*, July 8, 1911. "La Exaspera-

ción del Dr. Ramírez," *El Día*, July 10, 1911. If his press polemics were to be taken seriously, an Uruguayan newspaperman had to accept duel challenges. When, last June, José Pedro Ramírez' grandson challenged him, Batlle said that as President he could not accept, adding, "Dueling has never really seemed something very reasonable to him but in spite of that he submits to all the rules of honor." "Lance . . .," *El Día*, June 10, 1914.

30. Matilde wrote her note on the front page of a notebook titled "Impresiones Ana Amalia Batlle Pacheco," August 5, 1908, which is in the Batlle Archive. [Batlle], "Las Limitaciones Necesarias," *El Día*, February 26, 1915.

31. In Paris, Batlle had been a social disappointment to Uruguayan sophisticates. As President, he disappointed foreign diplomats. Count Ow-Wachendorf, the German Minister, reported to his Chancellor: "The President doesn't hide his democratic ideas; his manners and dress are absolutely contrary to elegance, and he is uncommunicative without being directly discourteous at official acts." When the German Crown Prince visited Montevideo, Batlle came to the embassy but "produced a poor impression, because of his lack of attention to his appearance." Hans-Hartman, Count Ow-Wachendorf, Montevideo, to Chancellor Dr. Von Bethmann-Hollweg, June 16, 1914, "Informes Diplomáticos de los Representantes del Imperio Alemán en el Uruguay," *Revista Histórica*, Vol. XLVI, Nos. 136–138, February, 1975, 174.

32. Partido Nacional, *Actas del Directorio* (I-7), 375–379. "La Minoría Independiente y la Candidatura Viera," *La Democracia*, January 3, 1915. "La Minoría Independiente y la Elección Presidential," *La Democracia*, February 19, 1915.

33. "De Interés Nacional," *El Día*, February 28, 1915.

APPRAISALS: III

1. It must be remembered that analysts have added together occupational groups from the 1908 census and called them middle class and working class. The specific percentages of total population assigned to each class depend on how the analyst apportions occupations. The most serious study so far published—Germán W. Rama, *El Ascenso de las Clases Medias. Enciclopedia Uruguaya* No. 36 (Montevideo, 1969), 116—was unable to disaggregate the middle class from the upper class. He did estimate the upper and middle classes in secondary and tertiary occupations (manufacturing, construction, commerce, and services) at 21.6 percent of the active population, and the lower class in these occupations at 50 percent. Assuming that some 5 percent of the members of these urban occupations were upper class and that the electorate resembled the active population, the urban middle and working classes, stipulated supporters of Batlle, would be some two thirds of the

electorate. Jaime Klaczko in an unpublished 1979 Montevideo monograph, "La Población Economicamente Activa del Uruguay en 1908 y Su Incidencia en el Proceso de Urbanización," argues convincingly that many day laborers and domestic servants in the interior who were listed in the census as urban workers were really rural. Klaczko's numerical transformations, basically that urban occupations were 11.5 percent less than Rama's estimates, point to a smaller urban working class. Although Klaczko argues otherwise, his transformations do not, of themselves, eliminate or even reduce the size of the middle class. Nor do they reduce a supposed urban middle class-working class coalition to below the majority of the electorate. Klaczko's conclusions should, however, alert researchers to the problems involved in trying to make the 1908 census answer questions on social structure it did not ask. Such problems are illustrated by a recent argument, based on this census, that Batlle failed to mobilize an additional potential (not actual) source of support, the "rural middle class." The "rural middle class" argument is discussed in note 8 below.

2. John J. Johnson, *Political Change in Latin America: The Emergence of the Middle Sectors* (Stanford, 1958), 45.

3. *Cámara,* CCXXXI, 192. Terra's reference came on June 6, 1914, during debate on life insurance for public employees.

4. *Cámara,* CCXXXVIII, 258. [Batlle] "Instrucción Para Todos," *El Día,* December 4, 1914.

5. Germán W. Rama, *El Ascenso de las Clases Medias,* 117. David Rock, "Radical Populism and the Conservative Elite, 1912–1930," in David Rock, editor, *Argentina in the Twentieth Century* (Pittsburgh, 1975), 67–68.

6. Peter Winn, "British Informal Empire in Uruguay in the Nineteenth Century," *Past and Present,* No. 73 (November, 1976) 125 and José P. Barrán and Benjamín Nahum, *Historia Rural del Uruguay Moderno,* V: *La Prosperidad Frágil (1905–1914)* (Montevideo, 1977), 31–32.

7. Part of the argument is that Uruguayan economic nationalism first appeared in the late 1880's among the sons of the *patriciado empobrecido* (impoverished patriciate). When a composite biography of the Uruguayan political elite during Batlle's second presidency is completed, we will know how many, like Batlle, came from old political families, how many, like Williman, were self-made, how many, like Viera, came from the old Colorado—or Nationalist—gaucho military, and how many, like Manini, were sons of immigrants. Of equal importance, the composite should indicate whether such differences in origin were important in grouping individuals around policies. Did, in fact, the descendants of old political families oppose foreign capital? Batlle did; Herrera did not. Were the sons of immigrants

pro-labor? Manini was not. The answers to such questions may well be surprising.

8. This description of Batlle-rancher political relations disagrees with the argument advanced by Barrán and Nahum, V, 137–156; VI, 251–266, that Batlle was reelected when large ranchers, "the rural upper class" who principally grazed cattle, were weakened by the *Tasajo* (jerked beef) crisis or stagnation but that their situation changed with the installation of the second refrigerated packing plant in 1912, which brought with it high prices for steers. Large ranchers, the argument holds, now recovered, and were able to resist Batlle. The argument also has an obverse side. The "rural middle class," Batlle's potential though not actual allies, made up principally of ranchers who relied on sheep, did well before 1912 but were weakened thereafter by the shift to cattle.

Neither half of the argument has a convincing economic base. Steer prices actually rose more than wool did before 1912, 23.5 percent to 20 percent for the years 1905–11, because steers sold for other uses besides jerked beef. Land values in the large ranch regions rose 80 percent during these years (Barrán and Nahum, VI, 429). These are solid indications of prosperity, not weakness, during Batlle's reelection period. And though steer prices zoomed in 1913 and through World War I, wool did very well too. Wool prices overtook steer prices, more than doubling from 1915 to 1919: *Anuario Estadístico* 1920, 197. Since *all* Uruguayan ranchers grazed both cattle and sheep, rather than large ranchers doing poorly and then well while smaller ranchers underwent the reverse experience, ranchers of all sizes were prosperous during Batlle's reelection period and more prosperous when his government ended.

The "rural middle class" postulated in this argument is an artificial construct obtained from the 1908 census by adding together all rural holdings from 101 to 2500 hectares, about 50 percent of Uruguay's land area. Barrán and Nahum acknowledge that some of these ranches were really large and some of those holdings small. For them, the "progressive middle class," who had a higher sheep/cattle ratio than larger ranchers, was centered in ranches of 500 to 1,000 hectares, about 14 percent of Uruguay's land area. Barrán and Nahum attribute this higher sheep/cattle ratio to superior range management and do not factor in soil fertility and distance from market. But even these "progressive middle class" ranchers grazed both sheep and cattle on unimproved natural pastures. Their operations were not fundamentally different from larger ranchers, and whether Batlle could have developed policies that would have split them away from larger ranchers is problematical. In fact, there were no discernible political differences among ranchers (as ranchers, not as Blancos and Colorados) during Batlle's government. In fact, it was around wool, which in the Barrán-Nahum model should have been divisive, that Batlle's opponents tried to unite all ranchers in the campaign for wool-based money.

Barrán and Nahum see revolutionary changes resulting from the installation of the second refrigerated packing plant, changes favoring large ranches, weakening moderate-sized ranches, making ranch rental more onerous. One would hypothesize that such changes would be reflected in a trend toward larger ranches and in a reduction in ranch renting. Yet censuses and estimates during this period claim a slight decrease in the number of large ranches and no appreciable change in ranch renting. Martín C. Martínez, *La Renta Territorial* (Montevideo, 1918).

9. Emilio Frugoni, *El Libro de los Elogios* (Montevideo, 1953), 88. Speech originally given October 22, 1936. Frugoni repeated this in an interview with me on September 24, 1952.

10. Even a sympathetic short biography, Luis Antonio Hierro, *Batlle, Democracia y Reforma del Estado* (Montevideo, 1977) concludes that had Batlle "not insisted so much on colegialist solutions, his party surely would have had more support," 74.

11. Carlos Real de Azúa, *El Impulso y Su Freno* (Montevideo, 1964), 9–11, 38.

12. José P. Barrán and Benjamín Nahum, *Historia Rural del Uruguay Moderno*, VII: *Agricultura, Crédito y Transporte Bajo Batlle 1905–1914* (Montevideo, 1978), 6, 78, 104. The use of the word "Batllismo" requires comment. Batllismo after 1919 was a distinct party within the Colorado Party. Before then it was frequently invoked, but it is vital to point out that it was to the wider Colorado Party, not Batllismo, that Batlle appealed before 1919.

13. By the time of Batlle's death, Uruguayan electoral democracy was strong enough to overcome, ultimately, Gabriel Terra's 1933 coup. Manini's role in these later events was very different from that in 1913.

14. W. Cameron Forbes, Receiver, Brazil Railway Company Receivership Journal, Baker Library, Harvard University, I (October 13, 1914, to June 7, 1915), 67.

15. During the first month of Viera's government, an Uruguayan government delegation to a Washington financial conference brought with them a kind of prospectus to interest United States banks and bond buyers in Uruguay. The prospectus, despite the adverse economic effects of the gold crisis and the outbreak of world war, was able to demonstrate the continuing profitability of the Bank of the Republic, the State Mortgage Bank, the State Insurance Bank, and the Electric Power System, together worth 77,580,000 pesos. The increase in the value of the State patrimony from 1910 to 1914, the prospectus proudly noted, was 34,991,000 pesos. [Uruguay Ministerio de

Relaciones Exteriores] *Trabajos de la Delegación Uruguaya en la PanAmerican Financial Conference Celebrada en Washington, D. C. del 24 al 30 de Marzo de 1915* (Montevideo, 1915), 52–55.

16. M. E. Tiscornia resigned from the board of the State Mortgage Bank over this issue, and the quotation is from Serrato's letter saying that "The President and I" accepted the resignation. This was preliminary to Serrato's enthusiastic support of Tiscornia in the famous Río Negro Senate election. "En el Banco Hipotecario," *El Día*, August 14, 1912. "La Renuncia del Dr. Tiscornia," *El Día*, August 15, 1912.

17. [Batlle], "El Gobierno de Tajes," *El Día*, March 25, 1912.

INDEX